CANADIAN SECRETARY'S HANDBOOK

Collier Macmillan Canada, Inc.

Collier Macmillan Canada, Inc.
1125B Leslie Street
Don Mills, Ontario M3C 2K2

Canadian Cataloguing in Publication Data
Main entry under title:
Canadian secretary's handbook

Bibliography: p.
Includes index.
ISBN 0-02-997850-5 (bound).–
ISBN 0-02-997810-6 (pbk)

1. Secretaries – Handbooks, manuals, etc. 2. Office practice – Handbooks, manuals, etc.

HF5547.5.C36 1983 651.3′741 C82-095318-0

2 3 4 5 87 86 85 84

Printed and bound in Canada

Contents

Preface

The Handbook attempts to answer questions secretaries are likely to encounter in their daily work. Where should *manifest* be divided when it occurs at the end of a typewritten line? What information should be included in the letter of transmittal that accompanies a business report? How should a government agency be indexed for filing? The Handbook functions as a reference for numerous topics like these.

A secretary's job, however, is no longer limited to relatively mechanical duties. Secretarial responsibilities now include many tasks once reserved for supervisory or professional personnel; in addition to typing the final report or letter, a secretary or administrative assistant may also be asked to take part in the planning and writing stages. Thus, the chapter on business reports offers detailed information on outline, footnote, and bibliography preparation. The chapter on grammar not only lists and explains the basic rules of good English usage, but serves as a guide to clear writing style as well.

The Handbook can help secretaries cope with many of the technological changes that affect the business world. Word processing methods, telecommunication, telephone, and postal services are highlighted in the text with emphasis given to the most efficient use of these services.

The Handbook is fully metric in its use of measures, adhering to Canada's adoption of SI. An entire chapter is devoted to measurement. Metric notation and rules of style are explained and exemplified. A comprehensive conversion table from customary to metric measures is also included.

The Handbook's scope is great. In it, topics range from word division to proration, and an important feature of the Handbook is the accessibility of information. As explained on the next page under "How To Use The Handbook," all topics are indexed and numbered to enable the reader to locate the desired information easily. Also, should the reader need to supplement the Handbook's text, the reference chapter, which lists and categorizes more than 90 titles, can be consulted.

The *Canadian Secretary's Handbook*, then, is useful to students, teachers, business executives, and librarians as well as secretaries. It is useful to everyone for whom good communication and organizational skills are essential.

How To Use The Handbook

The Handbook has been designed to provide quick and easy access to the information it contains. Each item of information is given a reference number that identifies the topic. These numbers are the keys to locating information.

How to read the numbers

Reference numbers are printed in gold in the left margin of each page. The inclusive reference numbers for each two-page spread are prominently displayed in the upper left corner. Each number is made up of two parts. The part to the left of the decimal point refers to the chapter number; the part to the right of the decimal point refers to the topic number within the chapter. All topics in a chapter are numbered consecutively.

Example: **10.25**

Chapter number — Topic number

How to use the index

When specific information is desired, refer to the index at the back of the Handbook. The index lists all topics in alphabetical order and gives a reference number for each topic. To look up a specific topic:

1. Locate the entry in the index and note the reference number that follows it.

2. Flip through the pages of the Handbook. Scan the top left corners of the pages and look for the page containing the reference number of the desired topic.

3. Open the book to the page that contains the desired reference number. Look down the left margins for the reference number that identifies the topic desired.

How to use the chapter contents

When you want to locate several items of related information, refer to the table of contents on page iii to find the page number of the chapter you want. Turn to the page indicated in the table of contents. The first page of each chapter contains an alphabetical listing of the topics contained in that chapter. From this list you can identify the topics you wish to look up and find them by using the reference numbers listed after each topic.

Grammar 1

Introduction: sentence structure and parts of speech

1.1 Grammar is the study of the structure of a language—the forms of words and their arrangement in sentences. Words are classified into eight categories—*noun, pronoun, verb, adverb, adjective, preposition, conjunction,* or *interjection*—according to their functions and relationships in a sentence. An understanding of the process by which words are organized into complete thoughts is essential for clear writing.

The analysis of sentence structure below is followed by a discussion of each part of speech, with a separate section on subject-predicate agreement (1.93–1.112).

Sentence structure

1.2 Sentence structure refers to the sequence of words in the sentence, the functions of words contained in the sentence (parts of speech), and the length of the sentence.

1.3 A sentence is a unit of speech: a word or group of words arranged to convey a thought. A sentence usually contains a subject and a predicate. Sentences are classified according to the type of statement or the arrangement of words, as follows:

1. A declarative sentence makes a statement.

   Mr. Roberson will be going to Saskatchewan this week.

2. An interrogative sentence asks a question.

   Is Mr. Roberson going to Saskatchewan this week?

3. An imperative sentence gives a command or makes a request.

   Mr. Roberson, you must go to Saskatchewan this week.

4. An exclamatory sentence expresses strong emotion.

   Oh, no! I can't go to Saskatchewan!

Clauses

1.4 A clause is a group of words containing a subject and predicate. Clauses may be independent or dependent (subordinate).

1.5 An independent clause can stand alone as a complete sentence.

Paul Mendez [subject] *is* [predicate] a capable supervisor.

The *meeting* [subject] *took place* [predicate] in Robbins Hall.

1.6 A dependent (subordinate) clause cannot stand alone as a complete sentence even if it contains a subject and predicate. This kind of clause depends on the independent clause for its meaning.

The president, *who lives in Halifax,* called the meeting for 2 p.m. in Sydney.

Please let us know immediately *when the order arrives.*

A representative will be selected *as soon as all applicants have been interviewed.*

The dispute, *if it is not satisfactorily settled,* must then be resolved in court.

Whether the factory is to be rebuilt is a question to be decided by the Board of Directors.

Correlative expressions

1.7 Certain expressions are written in pairs because they convey a related thought. Examples of such expressions are *both . . . and, either . . . or, neither . . . nor, not . . . but,* and *not only . . . but also.* Maintain consistency in the form and tense of the words used with these expressions.

Either Allan Fong *or* Glenda Baldwin would qualify for the teller's position.

Neither the employee *nor* the supervisor would admit any difficulty.

[In these examples, the words connected by the correlative expressions are singular; therefore, the verb forms used must also be singular.]

Neither the students *nor* the teachers expected such an entertaining speech.

[The words connected by the correlative expressions—*students* and *teachers*—are plural; therefore, the verb form must also be plural.]

She excels *not only* in her academic subjects *but also* in her extra-curricular activities.

Fragments

1.8 A sentence fragment, or incomplete sentence, occurs when words necessary to complete the thought are missing. A fragment also occurs when a punctuation mark is used incorrectly to chop the sentence into phrases. (It is acceptable to use a fragment in the subject line of a business letter. See 7.24.)

Fragment: Thank you for your letter. *Regarding your shipment of October 20.*

Sentence: Thank you for your letter *regarding your shipment of October 20.*

1.9 Dependent (subordinate) clauses that begin with such words as *although, as, because, if, since,* and *when* are often punctuated as complete sentences when in fact they are fragments.

Although we are leaving on Flight No. 415. [contains a subject and predicate but is only a subordinate clause]

The economy is facing the prospects of a depression. *Because of the inflationary period.* [The dependent clause should be in the same sentence as the independent clause, separated from it by a comma.]

1.10 Verbal clauses (those beginning with a verb form) are often incorrectly punctuated as complete sentences.

The Vancouver office, *trying to meet the June 15 deadline.* [The independent clause is incomplete.]

Supreme Court Judge Tierney dismissed the jurors. *Thanking them for their service.* [The subordinate clause should be in the same sentence and should be separated by a comma.]

1.11 Descriptive or explanatory expressions (appositives) are often incorrectly punctuated as complete sentences.

Honoured on her anniversary, Linda Yamauchi was credited for establishing many modern office procedures. *Methods that provided greater productivity at less cost.* [The appositive further describes the office procedures and should be set off with a comma.]

Modifiers

1.12 A modifier is a word or group of words that limits, restricts, or qualifies the meaning of another word. The relations between and among words in a sentence is developed by their sequence.

1.13 A modifier is ambiguous when the word modified is not obvious to the reader. Place words and groups of words close to their related thoughts, or rearrange the words to form a sentence that is logical in thought. Leave no doubt as to the meaning of the sentence.

Ambiguous: There was an important meeting he could not attend *at 10 a.m.*

Improved: He could not attend an important meeting *at 10 a.m.*

Ambiguous: We received your letter concerning the shipment of goods *on December 10*. [Was the *letter* or the *shipment* dated December 10?]

Improved: We received your letter *of December 10* concerning the shipment of goods.

1.14 Words used as connectives should be chosen carefully so their meanings are clear. Some common connectives are *and, or, as, when,* and *while*.

Confusing: Jones was elected a trustee *and* is employed as a systems analyst.

Improved: Jones, who was elected a trustee, is employed as a systems analyst.

Confusing: *While* our manager resigned, our sales have decreased dramatically. [*While* could mean *because, since, inasmuch as, seeing that,* or *during the time that*.]

Improved: *Because* our manager resigned, our sales have decreased dramatically.

Parallel construction

1.15 Related ideas should be stated in parallel grammatical style, whether in a series, in comparisons, within linking verbs, or with correlative expressions.

Nonparallel: John will go to the meeting, speak to the group, and is leaving at 3 p.m. [verb phrases not consistent]

Parallel: John will *go* to the meeting, *speak* to the group, and *leave* at 3 p.m.

Nonparallel: The dictionary shows us how to spell a word, its pronunciation, meaning, and where it originated. [words in the series not consistent]

Parallel: The dictionary shows us the *spelling, pronunciation, meaning,* and *origin* of a word.

Phrases

1.16 A phrase is a group of words without a predicate and therefore it cannot stand alone as a complete sentence.

McLaren Towers, the new office building, is *22 stories high*. [adjectival phrase]

The lecturers presented their topics in a *clear and concise manner*. [adverbial phrase]

A new representative *qualifying for the job* has been selected. [restrictive or essential phrase]

The stock, *which sold at $200 per share,* has just split 3 for 1. [non-restrictive or non-essential phrase]

On the job for only three weeks, the new file clerk was asked to resign. [prepositional phrase]

Subordination

1.17 See clauses, 1.4–1.6 and 1.9–1.10.

Sentence length

1.18 To avoid monotony of style, sentence length should be varied. Short sentences add spontaneity, while longer sentences help to achieve continuity. Too many short, simple sentences result in choppy thoughts and loss of continuity. The four principal types of sentence construction are identified by the complexity and organization involved.

1.19 A simple sentence contains one independent clause.

Mr. Johnson is our new supervisor.

1.20 A compound sentence contains more than one independent clause joined by a comma and conjunction or a semicolon. Omitting the comma and conjunction or the semicolon creates grammatically incorrect run-on sentences.

Mary received an appointment in the Personnel Department, but her sister did not.

or

Mary received an appointment in the Personnel Department; her sister did not.

1.21 A complex sentence contains one independent clause and one or more dependent clauses.

Don Redman will be the next supervisor, although he has been here only a year.

1.22 A compound-complex sentence contains two or more independent clauses and one or more dependent clauses.

Janice Redman will be the next supervisor, although she has been here only a year; Don Jackson was here for three years, but he never had the opportunity for the job.

1.23 A run-on sentence consists of two or more independent clauses (compound sentences) that are incorrectly separated by a comma. A run-on sentence is two complete sentences that should be made into two separate sentences, or separated by a comma and conjunction, or by a semicolon.

Run-on: A successful office worker is one who arrives at work on time, he or she gives a full day's work for a day's pay.

Sentence: A successful office worker is one who arrives at work on time; he or she gives a full day's work for a day's pay.

or

A successful office worker is one who arrives at work on time, *and* he or she gives a full day's work for a day's pay.

1.24 Regardless of sentence length and complexity, maintain one point of view per sentence and stay on the subject. Switching from one point of view or from one subject to another creates confusion.

Incorrect: When *you* purchase our product, *we* guarantee it for one year.

Correct: When *you* purchase our product, *you* have our one-year guarantee.

Nouns

1.25 A noun is the name of a person, place, or thing. Nouns may be common or proper.

1. A common noun is the name used to identify a class of things (such as dog, house, tree, pen, scissors), persons (boy, girl, teacher, minister, artist), or places (city, country, park, beach). A common noun that identifies a specific group—company, council, faculty, crowd, audience, committee—is called a collective noun.

2. A proper noun is the name used to identify a particular person, place, or thing (Alan Jones, Yukon, Niagara Falls, the Wheat Board).

Noun as subject

1.26 A noun as the subject of a sentence is the word about which the sentence is written. A singular subject refers to one person, object, or place. Singular subjects take singular predicates.

John is a student.

The *train* leaves at 12 noon.

1.27 The following collective nouns are considered singular subjects and take singular predicates.

audience	council	herd
board	crowd	jury
class	department	management
club	faculty	society
committee	family	staff
community	firm	team
company	flock	union
corporation	group	

The committee *has voted* unanimously in favour of the fund-raising project.

The jury *has returned* a guilty verdict.

That crowd *has remained* very orderly.

Our football team *deserves* a great deal of admiration.

1.28 The following collective nouns are considered plural subjects and take plural verbs.

goods	proceeds	savings	shears
pants	remains	scissors	thanks
pliers	riches		

These scissors *are* safe enough for small children.

His thanks *were conveyed* to the audience.

1.29 The following collective nouns may be used as either singular or plural subjects.

counsel	minority	series	species
deer	moose	sheep	swine
majority	number		

His counsel *are studying* the implications of the proposal.

My counsel *is drafting* a copy of the agreement.

The series of programs *is* very popular.

Which ticket series *are* still available at the Concert Hall?

1.30 A compound subject refers to two or more objects, persons, or places and takes a plural predicate.

English and math *are* my favourite subjects.

Tom and Mona *were* in charge of registration.

Noun as direct object

1.31 A direct object receives the action of a verb or a verb form directly. The direct object answers the question of who or what receives the action of the verb.

The bookkeeper mailed the *statements*.

Professor Muha delivered her *speech*.

Noun as indirect object

1.32 An indirect object receives the action of a verb indirectly. The indirect object is often preceded by a preposition (such as *to, of, by,* or *at*).

She gave the guest list *to Mr. McDowell*.

He aimed the attack *at Gibbs*.

Noun as complement

1.33 A complement is a word or phrase (predicate noun) that completes the meaning of the verb and explains or describes the subject. The subject is connected to the predicate noun by a linking verb, such as *am, appear, are, become, is, look, seem, was,* and *were*.

Brenton Wilks became the *East Coast representative*.

Don't those copies seem like the *originals?*

Noun as object of a preposition

1.34 When a noun follows a phrase beginning with a preposition, the noun becomes the object of the preposition. Some common prepositions are:

about	before	from	of	under
after	by	in	through	upon
at	for	into	to	with

Send a copy *of the book* today.

Mr. DeVries will stop *at the Simcoe Hotel*.

Pronouns

1.35 A pronoun takes the place of a noun and refers to the person, place, or thing named, asked for, or understood in the context. Pronouns are classified as *personal, relative, indefinite, demonstrative, interrogative, reflexive,* and *reciprocal*.

Personal pronouns

1.36 Personal pronouns are divided into three cases: *nominative, objective,* and *possessive*.

Table 1-1. Personal pronouns, nominative case

Person	*Singular*	*Plural*
First	I	we
Second	you	you
Third	he, she, it	they

1.37 Use the nominative case:

1. When the pronoun replaces the noun as the subject of the sentence.

   Dona and I study together, but *she* earns better grades on tests. [*She* refers to Dona.]

   He and Nancy will develop audio-visual materials for the lecture tour.

2. When the pronoun is the complement of a form of the verb *to be*.

   It was *I*.

   If I were *he*, I would have resigned.

3. When the verb form *to be* does not have a subject but is followed by a pronoun.

   The foreman was thought to be *he*.

   Is it going to be *she?*

Table 1-2. Personal pronouns, objective case

Person	*Singular*	*Plural*
First	me	us
Second	you	you
Third	him, her, it	them

1.38 Use the objective case:

1. When the pronoun is a direct object of a verb.

   The police officer called *us*.

   Ms. Tanaka hired *me* yesterday.

2. When the pronoun is an indirect object of a verb.

   The stock market gave *me* a scare.

   Mary read *them* their rights.

3. When the pronoun is the object of a preposition.

   Don and Joan are going with *him* now.

   Leave the job to *them*.

4. When the pronoun is the subject of an infinitive.

   Would you expect *us* to collect the debt?
   [*Us* is the subject of the infinitive *to collect*.]

It is up to *them* as buyers to provide insurance coverage. [*Them* is the subject of the infinitive *to provide*.]

5. When the pronoun is the second of two objects and the pronouns are connected by *and*.

Dr. Engel presented Sue and *me* with a plaque.

His parents are coming to visit Vic and *me*.

6. When the pronoun is the subject of the verb *to be*.

We expected *him* to be a better salesman.

It was like *her* to be waiting.

Table 1-3. Personal pronouns, possessive case

Person	*Singular*	*Plural*
First	my, mine	our, ours
Second	your, yours	your, yours
Third	his, hers, its	their, theirs

1.39 Use the possessive case:

1. When the pronoun precedes the noun it modifies, use *my, your, his, her, its, our,* or *their*.

It is *their* annual awards banquet.

The annual statement reflects *its* best year of sales to date.

2. When the pronoun immediately precedes a verb form ending in *ing* (gerund), use *my, your, his, her, its, our,* or *their*.

We appreciate *your* shipping the goods so promptly.

They planned on *our* completing construction by the 10th.

3. When the pronoun does not immediately precede the noun, use *mine, yours, his, hers, its, ours,* or *theirs*.

Dr. Herrera is a loyal customer of *ours*.

The selection is *hers* to make.

Relative pronouns

1.40 Relative pronouns (as with all pronouns) must agree with their antecedents in number, gender, and person.

Table 1-4. Relative pronouns

Nominative case	*Objective case*	*Possessive case*
that	that	that
who	whom	whose
whoever	whomever	
which	which	which, whose
what	what	

1.41 Relative pronouns are divided into the nominative, objective, and possessive cases, and each pronoun has its own function in sentences.

That refers to people, places, and things and is used in the nominative, objective, and possessive cases. *That* is used to introduce restrictive or essential clauses.

What refers to places and things and is used in the nominative and objective cases. *What* is often written in place of *that which* or *those which.*

Which refers to things and is used in the nominative, objective, and possessive cases. *Which* is always used to introduce non-restrictive or non-essential clauses.

Who and *whoever* refer to people and are used in the nominative case.

Whom and *whomever* refer to people and are used in the objective case.

Whose refers to people and is used in the possessive form.

1.42 Use the nominative form of the relative pronoun:

1. When the pronoun is the subject of the sentence. (Substitute a personal pronoun—*I, he, she,* or *it*—to test the correctness of the relative pronoun.)

> The situation *that* came up was exceptional.
>
> Could *that* have been it?
>
> *What* happened to the flow charts is not known.
>
> The method *that* we adapted for our use was the most up-to-date.
>
> The culprit, *whoever* committed the burglary, was extremely clever.

The girl *who* has maintained perfect attendance records is Mai-Ling.

2. When the pronoun *what* is used for *that which* or *those which*.

What seemed so simple was actually quite puzzling.

The homes, parks, and stables were *what* suffered most from the winds.

1.43 Use the objective form:

1. When the pronoun is the object of a verb. (Substitute such personal pronouns as *you, me, him, her,* or *them* to test the choice of the relative pronoun.)

The salesman disregarded *that*.

Hans Winneberger, *whom* we considered to be a clever scientist, declined the position.

Invite *whomever* you want.

2. When the pronoun is used as the object of the preposition.

This is the account in *which* you were overcharged.

The woman in *whom* you confided was my sister.

1.44 Use the possessive form to indicate ownership.

Among Hinckley, Benedetti, and Rice, *whose* territory is doing the best?

It was obvious *whose* error it was.

Indefinite pronouns

1.45 Indefinite pronouns do not refer specifically to any one person or thing. The words that relate to these indefinite pronouns must agree in number and tense. Most indefinite pronouns are singular, some are plural, and a few are either singular or plural.

The following singular indefinite pronouns must be written with singular verbs.

another	each one	everything	one
any one	either	much	some one
anybody	every	neither	somebody
anyone	every one	no one	someone
anything	everybody	nobody	something
each	everyone	nothing	

1.46 Use the singular form of the indefinite pronoun:

1. When the pronoun is the subject of a sentence and indicates a single person or thing. (Use a singular predicate with this form.)

Each has an undivided interest in the estate.

Something is to be presented to the speaker.

Nothing is to be accomplished or gained by his bitter attitude.

2. When two indefinite pronouns joined by the word *and* are used as the subject of a sentence.

Anything and *everything* is likely to happen at the auction Saturday.

3. When the pronoun is used as an adjective to modify a noun.

Every man is to report for roll call at 7 a.m.

It seemed that *no one* person was really liable for the damage.

1.47 To avoid confusion when indefinite pronouns are used to refer to either the feminine or masculine gender, or both, follow these rules.

1. When the pronoun is used to refer exclusively to the masculine gender, use the possessive personal pronoun *his:*

Has *everyone* put *his* wife's name on the list?

2. When the pronoun is used to refer exclusively to the feminine gender, use the possessive personal pronoun *her:*

Everyone on the girls' swim team selected *her* own endurance goal.

3. When the pronoun is used to refer to both feminine and masculine genders, *he or she* and *his or her* may be used. It is best to reword the sentence so that no pronoun is needed. (Often a simple substitution of a plural subject will solve the problem.)

Each applicant must pass *her or his* aptitude test to qualify.

Each applicant must pass the aptitude test to qualify.

When *someone* agrees to the contract terms, *he or she* accepts full responsibility for *his or her* part of the bargain.

When borrowers agree to the contract terms, they accept full responsibility for *their* part of the bargain.

1.48 The following indefinite pronouns are plural and must be written with plural verbs.

both few many others several

1.49 Use the plural form of an indefinite pronoun when the pronoun is the subject of a sentence and indicates more than one person, place, or thing. (Use a plural verb with this form.)

Many of the crew were ill during the cruise.

Several have already enrolled for the course.

1.50 The following indefinite pronouns are either singular or plural, depending on their use in the sentence as singular or plural subjects.

all more other such

any none some

1.51 Use the correct verb form with these indefinite pronouns.

We all are taking advantage of the current low tour prices.
All we need is evidence to substantiate our client's case.

None of the word processors have been installed as requested.
None of the four mechanics has been absent in the last six months.

There is a shortage of parks and recreation areas in the country; *more* are needed.
Much *more* is needed in the way of training in filing and records management.

Such are the circumstances of the boycott.
Such is the law of the land.

Interrogative pronouns

1.52 Interrogative pronouns are used in sentences that ask a question. Each of these pronouns has a different function.

1. *What:* nominative and objective cases

What is the agenda for the April 5 meeting?

From *what* country do the Maritimes import the most oil?

2. *Who:* nominative case

   Is she the girl *who* is most likely to succeed?

3. *Whom:* objective case

   For *whom* is this work to be done?

4. *Which:* nominative and objective cases

   Which will you be willing to supervise?

   In *which* department is the accident rate the highest?

   Which medium offers the largest storage capacity?

5. *Whose:* possessive case

   Whose desk is this?

Demonstrative pronouns

1.53 Demonstrative pronouns limit the number or kind of items being discussed. This class of pronouns is used in the nominative case as subjects. *This* and *these* are used to point out items nearest us in distance or time; *that* and *those* are used to point out items further away from us either in distance or time.

This is an interesting film.

That film we saw last week was fascinating.

These are our daily computer runs.

Those were recommended by Jon McGregor as being the best models.

1.54 Note that the demonstrative pronouns *this* and *that* are singular pronouns requiring singular verb forms; the pronouns *these* and *those* are plural, requiring plural verb forms.

Reflexive pronouns

1.55 Reflexive pronouns are formed by adding *-self* to the possessive personal pronouns (see 1.39). These words are used for emphasis following the subject of the sentence; they are also used as objects.

The building *itself* was nearly demolished.

She saw *herself* on video tape.

Reciprocal pronouns

1.56 Reciprocal pronouns relate specifically to another person discussed. *Each other* relates to two persons; *one another* relates to more than two persons.

Greg and Jan appear to work well with *each other*.

Linda, Anita, and Lori are in competition with *one another* for Campus Representative.

Pronoun usage problems

1.57 Possessive pronouns are often confused with contractions. Use the possessive pronouns to indicate ownership or other relationship between a pronoun and its antecedent. Use the contractions that sound like the possessive pronouns to indicate a subject-predicate relationship.

Possessive Pronouns	*Sound-Alike Contractions*
its	it's (it is, it has)
their	they're (they are)
theirs	there's (there is, there has)
whose	who's (who is)
your	you're (you are)

Our company offers *its* employees a comprehensive fringe benefit package. [possessive pronoun referring to *company*]

It's the policy of the agency to charge a 15 percent placement fee. [contraction of *It is*]

Their microfilm operations include several rotary and flatbed cameras and different models of readers for reels and fiche. [possessive pronoun]

They're performing the three-act play in fourteen cities across the state. [contraction of *They are*]

Theirs has been the highest-paying dividend since 1972. [possessive pronoun]

There's a solution to the problem if we can only meet to discuss it. [contraction of *There is*]

Whose application for district representative was filed first? [possessive pronoun]

Who's going to be responsible for auditing the safe-deposit contents? [contraction of *Who is*]

Your family should have the added protection offered by this new insurance policy. [possessive pronoun]

You're the best player on the team. [contraction of *You are*]

1.58 To avoid errors in using either nominative or objective pronouns, follow these rules.

1. When a pronoun is used with the comparison words *than* or *as,* use either the nominative or objective pronoun depending on how the sentence is constructed.

Roger is more effective as a supervisor than *I* [am]. [nominative as complement of verb *to be*]

The cashier would prefer to work with Mr. Saracho rather than [work with] *her*. [objective as object of a preposition]

2. When a pronoun identifies (is in apposition with) a noun, read the sentence without the noun to determine the construction.

We union officials must meet soon. [We . . . must meet soon; nominative as subject]

One of *us* executives will be promoted. [One of us . . . will be promoted; objective as object of preposition]

3. When a pronoun and a noun form a compound, read the sentence without the noun to determine the construction.

Danny wanted Jeff and *me* to work overtime tonight. [Danny wanted . . . me to work overtime tonight; objective as object of verb]

Lyn spoke to both Lillian and *me*. [Lyn spoke to . . . me; objective as object of preposition]

Verbs

1.59 A verb is a word used to express an action, state of being, or condition of the subject in a sentence. Like other parts of speech, verbs are classified according to their functions.

Active and passive verbs

1.60 The active voice places emphasis on the subject acting upon the verb. The active voice shows action. The passive voice places emphasis on the object or receiver of the action or de-emphasizes the action.

Active: Architect Ron Thom *drew up* a design for the new school.

Passive: A design for the new school *was drawn up* by the architect, Ron Thom.

Avoid the use of the passive voice. The active voice conveys a more direct and concise message.

Gerunds

1.61 A gerund, a verb form that ends in *-ing*, is used like a noun—as the subject of a sentence or as an object.

Interviewing possible award winners is a difficult task for the committee. [gerund used as noun and subject of sentence]

Did you get any results in *discussing* the problem with them? [gerund used as a noun and object of preposition]

Auxiliary (helping) verbs

1.62 An auxiliary verb is joined to another verb to help convey the action, state of being, or condition of the subject. Some helping verbs are *be, can, could, do, have, may, might, must, ought, shall, should, will,* and *would*. Each of these words can stand alone as a main verb; they can also be combined with one another as auxiliary and main verb. The auxiliary verb always precedes the main verb in the sentence.

I *must fly* to Ottawa this Friday.

If they had the time, they *could spend* a week with us.

Helping verbs are often grouped with each other as follows.

can be
can have
could be
could have
could have been
had been
has been
have been
may be
may have
may have been
might be
might have
might have been
must be
must have
must have been
ought to be
ought to have
ought to have been

shall be	will be
shall have	will have
shall have been	will have been
should be	would be
should have	would have
should have been	would have been

It *could have been* a total disaster.

She *has been* a loyal employee for fifteen years.

They *may have* to abandon the project because of insufficient public support.

I *would have been* a sales engineer for three years now, had I not become a banker.

Would it *have been* feasible ten years ago?

1.63 Some helping verbs used to convey a specific thought are often confused with other similar verbs.

Can indicates ability or capacity to do something in the present or future tenses.

Could indicates ability or capacity to do something in the past or future tense.

Can the mechanic fix the carburetor immediately?

That assignment *could* be accomplished in about three days.

The witnesses *could* have been mistaken about what they saw.

May can imply possibility or permission in the present tense. Use it with the first person.

Might can imply possibility or permission in the future or past tense. Use it with second and third persons.

May I introduce you to Ann Snyder from London? [permission]

Public relations *might* have been responsible for the successful ad campaign. [possibility]

There *might* be a reasonable explanation for his peculiar action. [possibility]

Shall has been replaced by the verb *will* in all but the most formal speech and writing. There was once a rule that the future tense required *shall* for the first person and *will* for the second and third. The reverse was true to express determination. However, today most people use *will* to express future tense as well as determination, intent, or threat. Usage should be guided by preferences of employer(s).

> I (we) *shall* come to your party next month. [formal expression of futurity]
>
> I (we) *will* come to your party next month. [common expression]
>
> He (they) *shall* attack if they do not surrender. [formal expression of intent or determination or threat]
>
> He (they) *will* attack if they do not surrender. [common expression]

Should and *would* generally follow the same rules as *shall* and *will* in expressions of future time, determination, willingness, and intent.

> I (we) *should* be honoured to be included in next year's program. [formal expression of futurity]
>
> I (we) *would* be honoured to be included in next year's program. [common expression]

Use *should* in all three persons to express ''ought to.''

> We *should* get to work on time.
>
> She *should* call her grandmother.

Should is also used in all three persons to express a condition in an *if* clause.

> If you *should* go now, you will get a ride.
>
> If he *should* admit guilt, he will not be punished.

Would is commonly used in all three persons to express habitual or repeated action.

> He *would* get up early and prepare his own breakfast.
>
> Once a year I *would* visit the old farm.

Would expresses willingness in all three persons.

> If you *would* agree to the nominations, we can proceed with the rest of the agenda.

Infinitives

1.64 An infinitive is a verb in the present tense (first person singular) preceded by *to*. An infinitive may be used as a noun, adjective, or adverb.

> It is our pleasure *to introduce* our newest associate, Cynthia S. Miller. [adverb modifying *pleasure*]

> *To do* Alicia a favour is a pleasure. [noun as subject of the sentence]

> Those films seem *to be* inadequate for the intended audience. [noun as object]

> There are six more manuscripts *to review*. [adjective modifying *manuscripts*]

> Please ask all parties *to read* the attached exhibits, *to initial* the changes, and *to return* all copies to me. [nouns]

See 1.74–1.75 for a discussion of split infinitives.

Intransitive verbs

1.65 An intransitive verb is a verb that does not need a direct object to complete the meaning of the sentence. (A direct object tells who or what receives the action of the verb.)

Verbs that are always intransitive include the various forms of *to be* and the following words: *appear, become, feel, grow, look, remain, seem, smell, sound, stay,* and *taste*.

> They *were* anxious to go on the African safari.

> Jackson *was* not *feeling* well.

Irregular verbs

1.66 An irregular verb does not conform to the ending patterns for past tenses described under Regular Verbs (1.73). Refer to Table 1-5 when you are uncertain about the spelling of a verb in one of the past or perfect tenses (see 1.81–1.86).

Irregular verbs are used as follows:

> To stay healthy, *drink* at least eight glasses of water each day.
>
> They *drank* a toast to the newly elected board officers.
>
> Manny *should* not *have drunk* as much as he did.
>
> Please *lay* those papers here on the desk.
>
> The builders *laid* the foundation yesterday.
>
> Our company *had laid* off several engineers last year because of insufficient contracts.

Note that auxiliary verbs are used with the past participle of irregular verbs but not with the past tense.

Table 1-5. Principal parts of common irregular verbs

Present	*Past*	*Past participle*
am, are, is*	was, were	been
become	became	become
begin	began	begun
bid (to tell)	bade	bidden
bid (to offer)	bid	bid
bite	bit	bitten
blow	blew	blown
break	broke	broken
bring	brought	brought
burst	burst	burst
buy	bought	bought
catch	caught	caught
choose	chose	chosen
come	came	come
do	did	done
drag	dragged	dragged
draw	drew	drawn
drink	drank	drunk
drive	drove	driven
eat	ate	eaten
fall	fell	fallen
fight	fought	fought
flee	fled	fled
fly	flew	flown
forget	forgot	forgotten
freeze	froze	frozen
get	got	got
give	gave	given
go	went	gone
grow	grew	grown
hang (to put to death)	hanged	hanged
hang	hung	hung
hide	hid	hidden
know	knew	known
lay	laid	laid
leave	left	left
lend	lent	lent
lie	lay	lain
pay	paid	paid
ride	rode	ridden
ring	rang	rung
rise	rose	risen
run	ran	run
see	saw	seen
set	set	set
shake	shook	shaken
shine	shone	shone

shine (to polish)	shined	shined	swear	swore	sworn
shrink	shrank	shrunk	swim	swam	swum
sing	sang	sung	take	took	taken
sit	sat	sat	tear	tore	torn
speak	spoke	spoken	throw	threw	thrown
spring	sprang	sprung	wake	woke	woken
steal	stole	stolen	wear	wore	worn
strike	struck	struck	write	wrote	written

*Forms of *to be*.

Linking verbs

1.67 Linking verbs are used to connect a subject with a predicate adjective or noun. The present and past tense forms of *to be* are commonly used as linking verbs: *am, are, is, was,* and *were*. *Appear, become, feel, grow, look, seem, smell, sound,* and *taste* are other linking verbs. These linking verbs do not convey any action between the subject and verb; the connecting words should be adjectives rather than adverbs.

Scott *looks* pale; *is* he *feeling* well?

The music over the loud speaker *sounds* too raucous for the office.

Participles

1.68 A participle is a verb that is combined with another verb to indicate differences in time. The participle is written in the present, past, and perfect forms.

- *Present participle:* ends in *-ing*.

The insurance company *is finishing* its work on the report.

- *Past participle:* ends in *-d* or *-ed* for regular verbs; irregular verbs end in their particular verb form. (The past participle is used to form the present perfect, past perfect, and future perfect tenses. See 1.66, 1.83–1.86.)

They *had leased* three office suites for a twenty-year period.

- *Perfect participle: having* plus the past participle.

Having leased the building to Dominion Stores Ltd., we can boast a 100 percent occupancy factor.

1.69 A participle standing alone functions as an adjective and modifies a noun or pronoun.

The *growing* number of inhabitants on the island is alarming.

Weakened by his recent illness, Mr. Farrell is not working long hours.

1.70 A participle can assume the characteristics of a verb and can take an object or be modified by an adverb.

Giving his support, Senator LaCroix lauded the candidates for their platform. [verb is *giving;* object is *support*]

Walking slowly to the podium, Dr. Agatha Guntermann impressed the audience with her dignity. [verb is *walking;* adverb is *slowly*]

Predicate

1.71 A predicate consists of a verb by itself, a verb and its complement, or two or more predicates in one sentence.

- *Simple predicate:* the verb itself.

The dog *ran*.

- *Verb and complement:* the verb and its object, predicate noun, or predicate adjective.

Mae Ling-Tsam *has rewritten* the office manual. [verb and its object]

Delmas Bugelli *is our department chairperson*. [verb and its predicate noun]

The secretarial program here *is comprehensive*. [verb and its predicate adjective]

- *Compound predicate:* two or more predicates in the sentence.

Their legal counsel *will determine the probable cause of action* and *will seek punitive damages*.

Principal verbs

1.72 The principal verb in a sentence is a single word that is the main verb. When used with an auxiliary verb, the principal verb follows the helping verb.

Stacey *writes* shorthand well. [principal verb]

Stacey *is learning* to type this semester. [auxiliary verb is *is*; principal verb is *learning*]

Regular verbs

1.73 A regular verb is a verb whose past tense and past participle are formed by adding *-d* or *-ed* to the present tense. In other words, the root of the verb is spelled the same in all tenses.

We usually *walk* to the engineering library every day. [present tense]

Jack Robbins *walked* to work this morning. [past tense]

Glenda and Dottie *have walked* ten blocks to find a telephone. [past tense]

Split infinitives

1.74 A split infinitive is an infinitive with a modifier between *to* and the verb. The modifier is an adverb that generally follows the object of the verb.

Infinitive: Dr. Bugelli wants *to review* our proposals carefully.

Split Infinitive: Dr. Bugelli wants *to* carefully *review* our proposals.

1.75 Whenever possible, word sentences to avoid split infinitives. Place the modifier (adverb) close to the word being modified so the meaning of the sentence is clear. Follow these guidelines:

1. Place the modifier after the object of the infinitive.

   Our choice at this time is *to make* an offer *immediately*.

2. Place the modifier either before or after the infinitive.

   Their idea was *apparently to propose* a stock split.

   It is difficult *to remember exactly* what he said.

3. Sometimes an infinitive must be split to form a clearer sentence. In the following example, the modifier is placed so it clearly refers to the word it modifies.

   To arbitrarily deny them a fair hearing by the Commission does not seem equitable in the circumstances.

Subjunctive mood

1.76 The subjunctive mood is used (1) to describe an impossible or uncertain condition or situation; (2) to express a wish or doubt; and (3) to indicate a request, command, or resolution. The subjunctive mood is introduced by such words as *if, that, though, unless,* or *whether*.

1.77 The verbs *be* and *were* are used for the subjunctive mood rather than *is* and *was* (*is* and *was* indicate definite conditions or assumed facts).

1. To indicate an impossible or uncertain condition or situation, use the verbs *be* and *were*.

> If I *were* only taller, I could easily reach that book on the top shelf.
>
> If this *be* the case, I shall be the first to apologize.

If a condition or situation is possible or could be true, use the verbs *was* and *are*.

> If Ron *was* promoted last week, he has not told us anything about it.

2. To express a wish or a doubt, use the verb *were* (rather than *was*).

> I wish I *were* coming to visit you next month.

3. To indicate a request, command, or resolution when preceded by the word *that,* do not use the verbs *shall* or *should* to complete the predicate:

> The company insists that all *customers obtain* credit approval before orders are shipped. [Not: . . . that all customers *should* obtain . . .]
>
> Their instruction was that *I be required* to remain in Moose Jaw for another two weeks. [not: . . . that I *should* be required . . .]

Transitive verbs

1.78 A transitive verb is a verb that needs a direct object to complete the meaning of a sentence. A direct object tells who or what receives the action of the verb.

> Messrs. Freeling and Myers *wrote* the first three chapters of the operations manual.

The vice-president, Carla J. Rapp, *acknowledged* the efforts of the entire staff.

Verb tenses

1.79 Verbs are written in different tenses to indicate various time relationships with their subjects. The three principal verb tenses are present, past, and future.

1.80 Use the present tense when an action is currently taking place, when a condition is stated, and when a state of being is expressed.

The board *is* meeting in the conference room now.

Accounting for Taxes *begins* at 9:30 a.m.

Our legal department *has* the subpoena.

1.81 Use the past tense to indicate an action that has already taken place or a condition that no longer exists. The past tense of regular verbs is formed by adding *-d* or *-ed*; the past tense of irregular verbs is formed as indicated in Table 1-5.

The *Albertan advertised* 153 jobs this week.

The cost-of-living index *rose* again last month.

1.82 Use the future tense for an action or condition that will take place in the future. The words *shall* or *will* precede the present tense form of the verb. There once was a rule that *shall* was used for the first person, singular or plural, and *will* was used for second and third persons (see 1.63). But this rule is rarely observed today, and *will* has generally replaced *shall*—except in very formal cases.

I *will work* on the manuscript next weekend. [common]

I *shall work* on the manuscript next weekend. [formal]

1.83 There are three additional tenses formed with the past participle: present perfect, past perfect, and future perfect.

1.84 Use the present perfect tense to indicate action that began in the past and has been completed in the present. The words *has* or *have* precede the past participle.

The auditors *have completed* the reports that were begun last month.

Gene Pinchuk *has assumed* the responsibilities of co-author.

1.85 Use the past perfect tense to indicate action that began and was completed in the past. The word *had* precedes the past participle.

Both witnesses *had testified* on behalf of the defendant.

1.86 Use the future perfect tense to indicate action that will be completed by some future date. The phrases *shall have* or *will have* precede the past participle. (See section 1.63 for use of *shall* and *will*.)

The incoming president, Angus Mothershead, *will have presented* his new board by the end of the meeting.

I *shall have rescheduled* our counselling patients by the end of the week.

1.87 The progressive tenses (present, past, future, and perfect) are used to indicate some immediate action or existing condition or action that is in progress or taking place over a period of time.

1.88 Use the present progressive tense to indicate an uncompleted action or condition.

Our programmers and analysts *are being defended* by their supervisors.

1.89 Use the past progressive tense to indicate an action or condition that has already taken place.

She *was preparing* the parcel when the buyer arrived.

1.90 Use the future progressive tense to indicate an action or a condition that will be taking place.

McMahan and Allister *will be thinking* seriously about a new office site.

1.91 Use the perfect progressive tenses as follows.

Present: The workmen *have been completing* the finishing touches to the hospital wing.

Past: Our representatives *had been dealing* with Jalisco Importers in Mexico.

Future: By Friday, we *will have been deciding* on a new design for three weeks.

1.92 The emphatic tenses are used to emphasize the action, condition, or state of being. The words *do, does* and *did* are used to form the present and past tenses.

Present: She *does read* all letters carefully before sorting them.

We *do give* special attention to all court-appointed guardians.

Past: They *did mention* the deadline to us, but we apparently forgot.

I *did* not *say* I would volunteer for that task.

Subject-predicate agreement

1.93 The subject and predicate of the sentence must agree with each other in number (singular or plural) and tense. The subject can be a noun, a pronoun, a clause, or a phrase.

A pronoun within the sentence must agree with its antecedent in number and gender. A modifier must agree with the noun or pronoun it describes.

Generally speaking, any verb ending in *s* is singular.

Books and magazines

1.94 Names of books or magazines, and the chapter or article titles from these works, are considered singular subjects and should be written with singular predicates and pronouns.

Consumer Reports is published to provide valuable information to all segments of the consuming public.

Economics has recently *been* published in *its* seventh edition.

Collective nouns

1.95 As noted under 1.27, collective nouns that are singular in form and represent one unit or group take a singular predicate; collective nouns that are plural in form and represent one or more units within the group take a plural predicate.

Companies and institutions

1.96 Names of companies and institutions (such as hospitals and schools) are usually written as singular subjects, which take singular predicates and the pronouns *it, its, which,* and *that.*

Lawrence & Tyson, Inc., one of the larger medical groups in this area, *is noted* for *its* research in endocrinology.

1.97 However, if a company or institution name is to be used as a plural subject, use a plural predicate and the pronouns *they, their,* and *who*.

> Willow and Dale, Chartered Accountants, *have prepared their* financial statements as of December 31.

When in doubt about subject-predicate agreement, rewrite the sentence so the company name is not the subject.

> The medical group of Lawrence & Tyson, Inc., one of the largest in this area, *is noted* for *its* research in endocrinology. [subject is *group*]

Compound subjects

1.98 A compound subject, consisting of two singular nouns (names of people, places, or things) joined by the conjunction *and,* should be written with a plural predicate. Be sure that plural modifiers and pronouns, as well as predicates, are used with compound subjects.

> Peter and Roger *were* sitting quietly at the opera when *they* noticed a small mouse in *their* box.

1.99 When a subject consists of two singular nouns joined by the conjunction *and,* but the subject refers to *one* person or thing, use a singular predicate:

> The vice-president and cashier *has approved* the new management policy. [compound subject refers to one person with a combined title]
>
> The vice-president and the cashier *have approved* the new management policy. [compound subject refers to two people]

1.100 When a compound subject is joined by either *or* or *nor,* the predicate should agree with the subject nearer it.

> Neither Helen nor the operators *have seen* the film on telephone techniques.
>
> Neither the operators nor Helen *has seen* the film on telephone techniques.

Foreign nouns

1.101 Many foreign words that have become part of the English language retain the foreign singular or plural endings. To identify a foreign word as singular or plural, refer to Table 1-6.

Table 1-6. Foreign singular/plural endings

Singular	*Plural*
addendum	addenda
alumna (feminine)	alumnae
alumnus (masculine)	alumni (masculine or both)
analysis	analyses
appendix	appendixes or appendices
basis	bases
crisis	crises
criterion	criteria
datum	data
formula	formulae or formulas
index	indexes or indices
medium	media
memorandum	memoranda or memorandums
parenthesis	parentheses

1.102 Use a singular predicate with a singular foreign noun.

Mary Ellen Reyes, an *alumna* of University College, *works* as an airline pilot travelling throughout the province.

The *basis* for the choice of plant site *was* its proximity to the railroad.

One *criterion* for filing a joint tax return *is* the advantage of a better tax rate.

1.103 Use a plural predicate with a plural foreign noun.

Their *analyses demonstrate* that the project is neither financially nor practically feasible.

The research *data reveal* a startling 40 percent retention rate.

Here or there

1.104 The words *here* and *there* at the beginning of sentences are *not* the subjects of those sentences. When a sentence begins with either of these words, the subject usually follows the predicate. If the subject is singular, use a singular predicate; if the subject is plural, use a plural predicate.

Here *are* 24 *copies* of the policy manual for your staff.

Here *is* our latest price *quotation*.

There *are* four *typewriters* in that office.

There *is* one *book* missing from the shelf.

Indefinite pronouns

1.105 Some indefinite pronouns are used as singular subjects, some are used as plural subjects, and some may be either singular or plural subjects. The predicates used with these indefinite pronouns must agree in number and tense, as described under 1.45–1.51.

Intervening words

1.106 Some sentences are constructed so that the normal subject-verb order is separated by one or more intervening words, but the predicate should agree with its subject in any case. Locate the subject, disregarding the noun or pronoun that may be the object of the verb or preposition.

The *reason* for his difficulties *was* his lack of enthusiasm.

Susan, as well as her friends, *was going* to lunch.

Number

1.107 The word *number* can be used as either a singular or plural subject, depending on its meaning in the sentence, its antecedent, and any modifiers. Intervening words between the subject and predicate do not affect the verb tense.

A number is used as a plural subject.

A number of senior citizens *are planning* a three-week cruise to the West Indies.

The number is used as a singular subject.

The number of accidents on the highways *has decreased* since the lower speed limit was enforced.

Phrases and clauses

1.108 A phrase is a group of words with no subject or predicate. When a phrase is used as the subject of a sentence, the predicate should be singular.

Establishing friendly relations with the community is the company's chief concern. [gerund phrase]

Whichever offers the most reasonable rate is the one we will purchase.

1.109 A subordinate clause is a group of words that includes a subject and verb but cannot stand by itself as a sentence because the verb is not a complete predicate. Subordinate clauses that begin with *what* may take either a singular or plural predicate to make them full sentences, depending on the words that complete the meaning.

What this world needs is compassion.

What this company strives for are higher ideals and goals.

Relative pronouns

1.110 The relative pronouns *who* and *whoever* belong to the nominative case; they are used as subjects in place of *he, she, it, they,* or *we*. These relative pronouns may be either singular or plural subjects, depending on their use in the sentence.

Who *is* responsible for the textbook exhibit? [*who* replaces *he, she,* or *it*]

Whoever *meets* the requirements *will* be elected. [*who* replaces *he, she,* or *it*]

Who *are* the new officers for the club? [*who* replaces *they* or *we*]

Subject and verb inverted

1.111 When the usual subject-predicate-complement form is not followed in constructing the sentence and the verb precedes the subject, the verb must still agree with the number and tense of the inverted subject.

Enclosed *is* a *copy* of our contract.

Attached *are* three *sets* of blueprints and specifications for your approval.

Time, amounts, quantities

1.112 Expressions of time, amounts, and quantities can be either singular or plural subjects, depending on whether they refer to a single unit or several individual units.

Four days is ample time to prepare the amendment.

The *$5595* is to be repaid over a two-year period.

The last *six months* of each year *have given* us many clues as to potential problem areas.

Adverbs

1.113 An adverb is a word, phrase, or clause that modifies, describes, limits, or qualifies an adjective, a verb, or another adverb. Adverbs are words that indicate some type of action and usually answer such questions as How? When? Where? Why? and To what extent?

How:	It was done *well*.
When:	It was done *yesterday*.
Where:	It was done *outside*.
Why:	It was done *because it rained*.
To what extent:	It was done *everywhere*.

Adverb functions

1.114 An adverb can be used to modify an adjective (adjectives modify the meaning of nouns or pronouns).

Fotiou and Sons will offer a *rather* reasonable rate.

Inflation dealt a *very* sharp blow to our purchasing power.

1.115 An adverb can be used to modify a verb (verbs express actions, states of being, and conditions).

Annie punched the cards *quickly,* but she did so *inaccurately*. [How? Quickly but inaccurately.]

The consignor delayed shipment *until April 10*. [How long? Until April 10.]

1.116 An adverb can modify another adverb either before or after the verb; but it should reflect the action of that verb.

Those contractors fulfilled their obligations quite carefully. [*quite* modifies *carefully*]

Phyllis Brzozowski almost always allowed them a week's leeway. [*almost* modifies *always*]

1.117 Some adverbs are written in two forms, and each has a somewhat different meaning and function. In many instances, one word may sound more correct than the other; however, in most cases, only one form is correct. (Note that the first word of each pair may also function as an adjective. When in doubt, consult the dictionary.)

clear, clearly	hard, hardly	quick, quickly
close, closely	heavy, heavily	quiet, quietly
deep, deeply	high, highly	sharp, sharply
direct, directly	late, lately	short, shortly
fair, fairly	light, lightly	slow, slowly
free, freely	loud, loudly	wide, widely

Our descriptive brochure will be sent *free* to anyone requesting it.

Recognition should be given *freely* to all who deserve it.

Merchandise on Invoice 14793-C will be shipped *direct* to Halifax.

Both assembly line workers were *directly* responsible for the faulty parts.

The order was shipped *clear* to British Columbia.

He spoke *clearly* into the microphone.

Adverbial clauses and phrases

1.118 An adverbial clause or phrase is used with an independent or main clause to indicate the time, place, manner, or extent. (A clause is a group of words containing a subject and predicate; some can stand alone as independent thoughts. A phrase is a group of words, lacking either a subject or a predicate, that cannot stand alone as a complete sentence.)

When you receive the invoice, please call our accounts receivable clerk. [adverbial clause at the beginning of the sentence that tells *when*]

His assignment was *near his home* on the west side of town. [adverbial phrase in the middle of the sentence that tells *where*]

Our factories will be temporarily closed *because of the flood damage*. [adverbial phrase at the end of a sentence tells *why*]

Forms of adverbs

1.119 A connective adverb is a word that joins a dependent (subordinate) clause to the main or independent clause. Connective adverbs are used in introductory clauses and phrases and in transitional expressions. (See 2.36 and 2.37 for placement of commas with connective adverbs.)

accordingly	consequently	so
after	furthermore	then
also	however	therefore
although	if	thus
as	nevertheless	when
because	otherwise	while
before	since	yet
besides	still	

After the examination, we must go for an interview with Sara Hawkins in the Personnel Department. [When?]

The police escort was a success *because* motorists were forced to drive slower. [Why?]

1.120 When a preposition follows an adverb, the *-ly* form of the adverb is usually preferred (see 1.117). In some instances, however, the other form is used.

agreeable to	independently of
agreeable with	irrespective of
consistent with	previous to
consistently with	regardless of
differently from	separately from
exclusively of	subsequently to

Students should attempt to learn and study *independently of* their teacher's direct guidance.

Irrespective of that fact, Burns Construction Company was still awarded the contract.

1.121 An adverb placed between *to* and the verb that follows usually produces an awkward sentence:

Awkward: It is not possible to *impartially* judge this contest.

Better: It is not possible to judge this contest *impartially*.

Sometimes, however, a split infinitive is not only acceptable but necessary (see section 1.75).

Note that *to be* followed by an adverbial clause is *not* an infinitive. Thus, an adverb may precede the clause.

Awkward: The new mayor is thought *essentially* to be moderate in her political views.

Better: The new mayor is thought to be *essentially* moderate in her political views.

1.122 Certain adverbs are used to convey a negative meaning. These negative adverbs should be used carefully to avoid forming a double negative, which consists of two negative expressions in the same sentence. Remember that *not* expresses a negation; *never* is an absolute term that means "at no time" or "in no way."

but	not
hardly	only
never	scarcely

The Johannsen Co. *never* considered opening a store within a block of its competitor.

He could *hardly* type the 45 words per minute required for passing the test.

1.123 The double negative may sometimes be used to express a thought more emphatically.

This is *not* an *unpleasant* task.

We *couldn't* care *less*.

When improperly used, the double negative cancels out the desired meaning instead of emphasizing it.

He *couldn't hardly* type the 45 words per minute required for passing the test.

Adjectives

1.124 An adjective is a word, clause, or phrase that modifies—describes, limits, or qualifies—a noun or pronoun. Adjectives answer such questions as What kind? How many? and Which one?

What kind: Our survey covered a *limited* market.

How many: Please order *twelve* reams of bond paper.

Which one: The *April 14* codicil is the most recent one.

Adjective functions

1.125 Adjectives are used to modify both nouns and pronouns as subjects. (An adverb should not be used for this purpose, as it indicates the action of a verb.)

1.126 The verb forms of *feel, look, smell, sound,* and *taste* are followed by adjectives. (Substitute the verbs *are, is, was,* or *were* for the other verbs to determine the correct use of an adjective to modify the subject.)

Mr. Rinaldi appears *healthy*. [Mr. Rinaldi *is* healthy.]

Mount Robson looked *distant*. [Mount Robson *was* distant.]

1.127 Within a sentence, an adjective is used to modify a noun.

Millions of readers were amused by the *clever* cartoons. [What kind of cartoons? Clever.]

1.128 An adjective clause is a dependent clause modifying a noun or pronoun in the independent clause. The relative pronouns *that, which, who, whom,* and *whose* are used to introduce the adjective clause. (A clause is a group of words containing a subject and predicate. Some clauses can stand alone as an independent thought while others cannot.)

The topic *that was being debated* did not draw much audience participation.

Hartmann Co., Ltd., *which distributed auto parts across the province,* recently became insolvent.

1.129 An adjective phrase is an infinitive phrase, a participial phrase, or a prepositional phrase that functions as an adjective to modify a noun or pronoun. (A phrase is a group of words without a subject or predicate that cannot stand alone as a complete sentence.)

Our salesmen have a lot more territory *to cover*. [infinitive phrase]

Alfred and Ida, *having driven across the country,* were glad to get home. [participial phrase]

The microfiche *on the counter* was returned today. [prepositional phrase]

1.130 A compound adjective includes two or more words that function as a unit to convey a single thought. A compound adjective may be used in place of an adjective clause or phrase.

1.131 Some forms of compound adjectives require a hyphen, some require a comma, and some require no punctuation.

1.132 When two or more independent adjectives are combined to modify a noun, neither a hyphen, conjunction, nor a comma is used if the first adjective is really acting as a modifier of the adjective-noun phrase.

Correct: an esteemed public servant

Incorrect: an esteemed and public servant
an esteemed, public servant

Public modifies servant, and *esteemed* modifies public servant.

Correct: blue denim shirt

Incorrect: blue, denim shirt
blue and denim shirt
blue-denim shirt

Denim modifies shirt. *Blue* modifies denim shirt.

1.133 When two independent adjectives modify the same noun, separate the adjectives with the conjunction *and.*

German and French ancestry
long and tedious task

1.134 When two independent adjectives modify the same noun and there is no conjunction between the adjectives, use a comma to indicate the omission of the word *and.* (Insert the word *and* between the two independent adjectives to test the correct use of the comma.)

old, decrepit building
tall, slender youngster

1.135 The following compound adjectives consist of an adjective and a verb ending in *-ed* (or an irregular form—see 1.66). These words are always hyphenated when they precede a noun.

air-conditioned	high-priced	old-fashioned
double-spaced	low-priced	small-sized
good-natured	lowest-priced	smaller-sized
heavy-handed	medium-sized	soft-spoken
high-flown	middle-aged	triple-spaced

1.136 An adjective and a noun are combined as a compound adjective to modify a noun. If the compound adjective immediately precedes the noun, hyphenate the compound adjective. If the compound adjective appears elsewhere in the sentence, it is not hyphenated.

fine-quality merchandise [merchandise of fine quality]

high-income property [property yielding a high income]

1.137 Certain adjective-and-noun combinations are spelled as one word without the hyphen. Consult the dictionary when you are in doubt.

cutout taxpayer
cutrate underrated

1.138 A participle is a word that ends in *-ed* or *-ing* or is the past tense form of an irregular verb. When used by itself, a participle functions as an adjective modifying a noun or pronoun. Hyphenate adjective–present participle modifiers before a noun.

high-ranking official *strange-sounding* noise

1.139 An adverb and adjective compound adjective is not hyphenated since the adverb is used to modify the adjective.

more complicated plot *very intelligent* person
most exciting experiences *very jealous* child

1.140 An adverb and a participle used as a compound adjective are hyphenated when they precede the noun. When the participle is written as part of the predicate, a hyphen is not used.

best-known reporter
[reporter who is best known]

faster-moving train
[train that is moving faster]

1.141 Certain adverb-participle compounds are hyphenated even when they follow a noun.

clear-cut responsibilities
[responsibilities are clear-cut]

far-reaching effects
[effects are far-reaching]

1.142 An *-ly* ending adverb and a past participle are not hyphenated.

highly respected administrator
newly decorated home
oddly shaped room
privately operated shop
poorly written letter
richly deserved award

1.143 An adverb and an *-ing* ending participle are often hyphenated.

highly-motivating lecture
exceptionally-pleasing meal

1.144 A series of hyphenated adjectives may be written with a suspended hyphen after each adjective. The noun is stated only after the last adjective. Leave one space after each suspended hyphen.

a *ten-* or *twenty-year* bond
short- or *long-term* loan
$40-, $50-, or *$60-a-day* suites
three- to *four-week* training

1.145 A compound noun consists of two nouns combined to modify another noun. A hyphen is not used with these compound nouns.

charge account customer
community college degree
income tax laws
life insurance coverage
real estate license
word processing centre

1.146 A phrase used as a compound adjective is hyphenated when it precedes the noun.

on-the-job training
on-the-scene reporter
$1200-a-month salary
out-of-pocket expenses
out-of-town address
question-and-answer period

1.147 When foreign words and phrases are used as adjectives, they should not be hyphenated.

ad hoc committee
au gratin potatoes
bon voyage party
bona fide complaint
de facto segregation
ex officio member

1.148 A number and noun combined as a compound adjective are hyphenated when the adjective precedes the noun. If the compound adjective appears elsewhere in the sentence, it is not hyphenated. The noun following the number is written in its singular form. Numbers below ten and numbers that can be written in one word are spelled out.

two-month leave
four-week vacation
thirty-year lease
136-page transcript

1.149 When a number (numeral or spelled out) is used with such nouns as *percent, million,* or *billion,* do not hyphenate the compound adjective.

a *nine percent* increase
$14 million project
120 percentage points

1.150 Ordinal numbers combined with nouns as compound adjectives are hyphenated. The words should be spelled in full if they can be written in one word.

first-rate campaign
first-run film
second-hand information

1.151 When proper names are used to modify other nouns, they are not hyphenated.

Canadian Pacific hotels
Air Canada jet
Supreme Court building
University Avenue address

1.152 When two or more proper names are combined as one modifying unit, a hyphen is used to connect the words. If the sentence is rewritten, the proper names are not hyphenated, except when the compound adjective is intended as a single unit.

The *North Bay-to-Toronto* flight takes about one hour. [The flight from North Bay to Toronto takes about one hour.]

Forms of adjectives

1.153 Adjectives are not easily identified by their form, since they may also be used as adverbs and as verb forms.

1.154 A descriptive adjective is a word that describes the quality of a noun or pronoun. This type of adjective answers the question, What kind?

James Smith decided to retire early because he was a *sick* man.

Please rearrange those *conference* chairs.

1.155 *This, that, these,* and *those* are demonstrative adjectives that limit the noun or pronoun.

This (singular form) and *these* (plural form) are used to point out people or objects nearest us in distance or time.

The data on *this* microfiche need to be updated.

These cities had the largest increase in air pollution since 1965.

That (singular) and *those* (plural) are used to point out people or objects further removed in distance or time.

I believe *that* date was November 30.

Those administrative secretaries are the most efficient people.

1.156 A limiting adjective is a word that limits the quantity of a noun or pronoun and specifies which one.

1.157 The articles *a* and *an* are indefinite adjectives used to refer to one person, place, or thing. Use *a* before a noun beginning with a consonant.

A mistake has been discovered in our recent statement.

Use *an* before a noun beginning with a vowel.

Lyn Clark and Don Busche were to submit *an* opinion in two weeks.

When the letter *h* at the beginning of a noun is pronounced, use the article *a*. If the letter *h* is not pronounced, use the article *an*.

A hangar on Field 13 is available for the light plane.

We will take a break for *an* hour.

When the letter *u* at the beginning of a word is pronounced *yoo*, use the article *a*. When the letter *u* is pronounced in other than the long *u* sound, use the article *an*.

He has developed *an* unusual formula.

A union strike would cripple all transportation services.

1.158 The article *the* is a definite adjective used to designate a specific person, place, or thing or a group or class.

Salaries are reviewed annually by *the* finance department.

The truth is quite obvious.

1.159 A proper adjective is an adjective derived from a proper noun and is capitalized.

The *Russian* cosmonauts and the *American* astronauts have made great strides in space.

Similar adjectives and adverbs

1.160 Many of the words classified as adjectives and adverbs are similar or identical, although their function in sentences and their meanings are different. For correct distinctions, check the dictionary.

The *wrong* man was accused. [adj]

Everything went *wrong* today. [adv]

Words ending in -ly

1.161 Words that end in *-ly* are usually adverbs; some, however, are adjectives; others can function as both adjectives and adverbs.

Adverbs	*Adjectives*	*Both*
badly	costly	daily
carefully	fatherly	early
clearly	friendly	likely
completely	motherly	monthly
immediately	neighbourly	only

It was the *only* way to keep our overhead expenses down. [adj]

It was *only* yesterday that we noticed the patient's change in blood pressure. [adv]

Jim Clark arrived *early* to prepare for the meeting with his editor. [adv]

The Winnipeg *Tribune* is a *daily* publication. [adj]

Comparisons

1.162 Adjectives and adverbs indicate degrees of comparisons between and among persons, places, and things. The three degrees of comparison are the simple, comparative, and superlative.

A simple adjective or adverb is used by itself or with another adjective or adverb to make a simple statement. No comparison is being made in the statement.

A comparative adjective or adverb compares a higher or lower degree between two persons, places, or things.

A superlative adjective or adverb compares the highest or lowest degree among three or more persons, places, or things.

Simple: The new street was made *wide* for the flow of traffic.

Comparative: The new street was made *wider* than the other streets.

Superlative: The new street was made the *widest* of all the streets in the area.

Simple: Ken is a *tall* boy.

Comparative: David is *taller* than Tracy.

Superlative: Ken is the *tallest* boy of the three.

1.163 The comparative form is written by adding *-er* to the simple form of one-syllable words. (Note the slight change in spelling of some words when *-er* is added.)

1.164 The superlative form is written by adding *-est* to the simple form of one-syllable words. (Note the slight change in spelling when *-est* is added.)

Simple	*Comparative*	*Superlative*
big (adj/adv)	bigger	biggest
cheap (adj/adv)	cheaper	cheapest
close (adj/adv)	closer	closest
deep (adj/adv)	deeper	deepest
fast (adj/adv)	faster	fastest
fine (adj/adv)	finer	finest
hard (adj/adv)	harder	hardest
loud (adj/adv)	louder	loudest

1.165 A few one-syllable words are written with the words *more* or *less* in the comparative form and *most* or *least* in the superlative form.

Simple	*Comparative*	*Superlative*
prompt	more/less prompt	most/least prompt
tired	more/less tired	most/least tired

Simple: The Dobbings are *prompt* people.

Comparative: The Dobbings are *more prompt* than the Healeys.

Superlative: The Dobbings are the *most prompt* people in the world!

1.166 The comparative form of two-syllable words is written by adding either *-er* to the simple form or *more* or *less* before the simple form.

1.167 The superlative form of two-syllable words is written by adding either *-est* to the simple form or *most* or *least* before the simple form.

Simple	*Comparative*	*Superlative*
active (adj)	more/less active	most/least active
careful (adj)	more/less careful	most/least careful
clever (adj)	more/less clever	most/least clever
costly (adj)	more/less costly	most/least costly
happy (adj)	happier	happiest
jolly (adj/adv)	jollier	jolliest
lonely (adv)	lonelier	loneliest
lovely (adj/adv)	lovelier	loveliest
mild (adj)	milder	mildest
often (adv)	more/less often	most/least often

Simple: Production recommended a *costly* proposal.

Comparative: Production recommended a *more costly* proposal than was expected.

Superlative: Production recommended the *most costly* proposal in the company's history.

Simple: I found the test *easy*.

Comparative: I found this test *easier* than the one I took in psychology.

Superlative: I found this test the *easiest* of the tests in psychology, biology, and English.

1.168 The comparative form of three- or more syllable words is written by adding *more* or *less* before the simple form.

1.169 The superlative form of three- or more syllable words is written by adding *most* or *least* before the simple form.

Simple	*Comparative*	*Superlative*
acceptable	more/less acceptable	most/least acceptable
beautiful	more/less beautiful	most/least beautiful
capable	more/less capable	most/least capable
enthusiastic	more/less enthusiastic	most/least enthusiastic

Simple: The company's work standards were *acceptable* to her.

Comparative: The company's work standards were *more acceptable* to her than to her co-workers.

Superlative: The company's work standards were the *most acceptable* of the five comparable organizations in the city.

1.170 Some adjectives and adverbs have irregular comparative and superlative degrees. Some of the more common irregular adjectives and adverbs are listed below.

Simple	*Comparative*	*Superlative*
bad (adj/adv)	worse	worst
far (adj/adv)	farther/further	farthest/furthest
good (adj)	better	best
ill (adj/adv)	worse	worst
late (adj/adv)	later, latter	latest, last
little (adj/adv)	littler, less, lesser	littlest, least
many (adj)	more	most
much (adj/adv)	more	most
well (adj/adv)	better	best

Simple: The company's credit position is *bad.*

Comparative: The company's credit position is getting *worse*.

Superlative: The company's credit position is at the *worst* point in its history.

Simple: Her associates were *many*.

Comparative: Her firm had *more* associates than the other medical groups.

Superlative: Her firm had the *most* associates of the groups in the association.

Comparisons within the same group

1.171 When a comparison is made between particular persons, places, or things in the same group, use the comparative form of the adjective or adverb and the word *other* or *else* to clarify the comparison.

> Their pharmacy is better stocked than any *other* in town.
>
> Our cheerleaders yelled louder than anyone *else* at the game.

1.172 When a comparison is made between one person, place, or thing and several others within the same class, use the superlative form and the phrase *of all* after the adjective or adverb.

> *Of all* diseases known to medical science, cancer is the most puzzling. [an inverted sentence with the dependent clause written first]

Troublesome adjectives and adverbs

1.173 Some words that can function as either an adjective or an adverb are often confused; the definitions below may help you avoid some of these problems.

1.174 *Fewer* is an adjective used to refer to *number* with plural nouns.

> There were *fewer* than five students at the tryouts.

Less is an adjective used to refer to *degree* or *amount* with singular nouns.

> *Less* interest on our savings is paid at the college foundation than at a savings and loan association.

1.175 *Good* is an adjective used to modify a noun.

> Many feel that Mrs. Willis is a *good* teacher.

Well is either an adjective or an adverb. As an adjective, it modifies a noun or another adjective. *Well* can refer to health.

> Dr. Norman Vincent Peale is a *well*-known lecturer on positive thinking.
>
> He is in fine health; his doctor says Mac is *well* enough to return to work.

As an adverb, *well* describes the action of the verb.

> For a drama student, she sings *well*.

1.176 *Most* is the superlative form of the adjectives *much* and *many*.

She is the *most* dedicated person I know.

Almost is an adverb.

Almost all the basketball players are at least two metres tall.

1.177 *Real* is an adjective used to modify a noun.

It wasn't a hairpiece; it was *real* hair.

Really is an adverb describing the action of a verb. Substitute the word *very* to test the correctness of *really* in a sentence.

He has been a *really* enthusiastic worker.

1.178 *Some* is an indefinite adjective used to modify a noun.

There is *some* rumour of financial difficulties.

Somewhat is an adverb that answers the question, What? Substitute the words *a little bit* to test the correctness of *somewhat.*

She was only *somewhat* positive in her description of the runaway car.

1.179 *Sure* is an adjective used to modify a noun. Substitute the word *certain* to test the correctness of *sure*.

He will be a *sure* winner in the next election.

Surely is an adverb used to describe the action of a verb. Substitute the word *certainly* to test the correctness of *surely*.

It was *surely* an unusual coincidence.

Prepositions

1.180 A preposition is a word that shows the relationship between a noun or pronoun and another word in the sentence. The noun or pronoun becomes the object of the preposition.

The following are commonly used prepositions:

about	at	but	of	under
above	before	by	off	until
after	below	except	on	up
against	beside	into	over	upon
among	between	like	to	with

Words that require prepositions

1.181 Certain prepositions are commonly used with certain words to convey a more precise meaning.

account *for* someone or something
account *to* someone

agree *on* something
agree *to* something
agree *with* a person or an idea

angry *at* or *about* something
angry *with* someone

argue *about* something
argue *with* someone

compare *to* something similar
compare *with* by analyzing for differences

couple *of* persons, places, or things

differ *from* something else
differ *with* someone
different *from* something else

discrepancy *in* one thing
discrepancy *between* two things
discrepancy *among* three or more things

identical *to* somebody
identical *with* something

part *from* someone
part *with* something

retroactive *to* a date

speak *to* someone (to tell)
speak *with* someone (to discuss)

similar *to* something

We finally *agreed on* a plan of action for the staff meeting. [We worked out a plan . . .]

All parties *agreed to* the stipulation that air travel be minimized to cut expenses. [All parties accepted . . .]

Eleanor requested a *couple of* brochures on Hawaii. [not a couple brochures]

Prepositional phrases

1.182 A prepositional phrase consists of a preposition followed by a noun or pronoun (the object of the preposition). It may be used either as an adjective or as an adverb.

1.183 When used as an adjective, the prepositional phrase is placed after the noun it modifies. (Note that the preposition and its object may be separated by one or more adjectives.)

> The automatic typewriter is a tool *with great timesaving potential*.

1.184 When used as an adverb, the prepositional phrase may follow either the verb or its object.

> He hit the ball *into the grandstand*.

A prepositional phrase used as an adverb may also be placed at the beginning of the sentence as an introductory, dependent element.

> *During that month,* sales increased by 10 percent.

Preposition usage problems

1.185 Difficulties may arise with prepositions in four contexts: when used improperly at the end of a sentence, used improperly in a series, inserted in a sentence when they should be omitted, and confused with similar prepositions.

1.186 It is generally preferable to avoid prepositions at the end of a sentence.

> It is her family's money and power that she wants to be independent *of.* [awkward]

In some cases, placement depends on whether a formal or an informal tone is desired.

> *Informal:* Whom did he give the report *to*?
>
> *Formal:* *To* whom did he give his report?

Short questions may end with a preposition.

> What is this needed *for*?
>
> How many people can we count *on*?

1.187 When a sentence includes a series of prepositional phrases or parallel clauses using words that require certain prepositions, be sure that each item in the series begins or ends with the appropriate preposition.

The settlers travelled *over* a mountain range, *across* a plain, and *through* dangerous territory to reach their destination.

He had a deep *devotion to,* and a sincere *interest in,* the work of the late composer.

1.188 Some colloquial speech patterns insert unnecessary prepositions after the verb; these are incorrect and should be omitted.

Does Jaime know where it is [*at*]?

Where are they going [*to*]?

We sent [*in*] for a free trial subscription.

1.189 Certain prepositions cause problems because their meanings may be confused with those of similar words or phrases.

1.190 *Beside* is a preposition meaning "next to."

She sat *beside* Jill at the luncheon.

Besides as a preposition means "except."

No one is going *besides* me.

Besides as an adverb means "in addition to."

Besides the fact that we are overloaded, we are already behind schedule in our work.

1.191 *Among* is a preposition used to refer to three or more persons, places, or things.

Among the three of us, I feel that I am the most fortunate.

Between is a preposition used to refer to two persons, places, or things.

The choice was *between* Dick and me.

1.192 Use the objective form of the personal pronoun after the preposition *except*.

Everyone had an opportunity to speak *except* Tom Rooney and *me*. [*not* . . . except Tom Rooney and I.]

1.193 Do not use the expression *help from* except when the word *help* is used to mean "assistance" or "aid."

She couldn't *help* offering all her ideas.

The Credit Bureau requested *help* [assistance] *from* our credit clerks.

1.194 *In* means something or someone located within or inside. *Into* implies some motion from the outside to the inside.

At the theatre, we ran *in* to see the manager. [*To* is part of the infinitive *to see*.]

The cattle were herded *into* the corral from the prairie.

1.195 *Of* is a preposition used to indicate a relationship. *Have* is a verb. These two words are misused because of poor pronunciation in speaking. The following verb forms are used with *have:*

could have	must have	should have
may have	ought to have	would have
might have		

She should *have* realized her skills earlier. [*not* She should *of* . . .]

1.196 *On to* implies physical movement or the physical action of placing a person or object. *Onto* refers to the direction of movement.

He went *on to* the presidency.

She manoeuvred her car *onto* the shoulder of the highway.

Conjunctions

1.197 A conjunction is a word used to connect two words, phrases, or clauses. The three types are co-ordinating, correlative, and subordinating conjunctions.

Co-ordinating conjunctions

1.198 A co-ordinating conjunction connects grammatical elements that are alike, such as two or more words, two or more phrases, or two or more clauses. The most common are:

and but for or nor yet

Other co-ordinating conjunctions, also known as conjunctive adverbs, are used to join independent clauses only. They include:

accordingly	however	notwithstanding
also	likewise	now
besides	moreover	so
consequently	neither	therefore
furthermore	nevertheless	thus
hence		

Co-ordinating conjunctions are used as follows:

Miss Reasons *and* Miss Lesley reserved a room in Brandon for the weekend. [conjunction *and* connecting two words]

Joe and Sam will fly to Lethbridge *and* to Medicine Hat. [conjunction *and* connecting two phrases]

Our sales have decreased, *but* we do not know the reasons. [conjunction *but* connecting two independent clauses]

Dick Carter ordered the new equipment *but* requested that it not be installed immediately. [conjunction *but* connecting two verb phrases]

1.199 A compound sentence consists of two or more independent clauses connected by a co-ordinating conjunction or conjunctive adverb. (A comma is generally used before the conjunction to separate the two clauses.)

Jake Mercado is handling the convention reservations, *and* Millicent Reese is planning the workshops.

Those books will be returned to the publishers; *therefore,* they should be packed carefully.

1.200 A series is a group of words, phrases, or clauses. The items in the series are usually separated by commas, and the conjunction precedes the last item in the series.

We placed our order for paper clips, rubber bands, *and* fasteners.

1.201 The items in the series, however, may be separated by co-ordinating conjunctions rather than commas if the items are short.

Is Billy *or* Ana *or* Diana going to the store?

Correlative conjunctions

1.202 A correlative conjunction is a pair of words that connects two elements of equal grammatical value—words, phrases, or clauses. These conjunctions include:

both . . . and	not . . . but
either . . . or	not only . . . but also
neither . . . nor	whether . . . or

They are used as follows.

Either Professor Tannenbaum *or* his assistant will perform the experiment.

Neither Ben *nor* I remembered that request.

She is *not only* an effective supervisor *but also* an expert in communication skills.

Both Florence *and* Milan were delightful cities to visit.

1.203 Care must be taken to use the correct verb form with these correlative conjunctions. Use a singular verb form with the singular noun and conjunction; use the plural verb form with the plural noun and conjunction.

Subordinate conjunctions

1.204 A subordinate conjunction is a noun, adverb, or adjective used to connect clauses of unequal grammatical value, such as dependent clauses and independent clauses. (The conjunction introduces the dependent clause.) The most common are:

after	if	that	whereas
although	in case that	then	wherever
as	in order that	though	whether
as if	inasmuch as	unless	which
as though	otherwise	until	while
because	provided	when	who
before	since	whenever	whom
for	so that	where	why

As we must move by the tenth, our rent should be prorated for that month.

Whether or not she receives a raise, she plans to quit her job soon.

Conjunction usage problems

1.205 The following pairs of conjunctions cause some difficulty in proper usage.

1.206 *And* means an addition. *But* indicates a contrasting view.

June *and* Lilly are both going.

She is going, *but* I am staying.

1.207 *As . . . as* is used to make a positive statement. *So . . . as* is used to make a negative statement.

He is *as* witty *as* he is clever.

Our fiscal policies are not *so* clear-cut *as* they ought to be.

1.208 *Like* is a preposition and should not be used as a conjunction. Use the words *as, as if,* or *as though* to mean "similar to" when a conjunction is needed.

Doesn't he look *as though* he were on top of the world?

Mamie's acting *as if* she didn't care.

1.209 *Whether* is used to express a question or to convey a doubt. *If* is used to state a condition.

We have wondered *whether* he would be the suitable man for the job.

If the company receives another government contract, everyone will be assured of a job for the next five years.

Interjections

1.210 An interjection is a word that expresses strong emotion. The word may stand by itself, or it may be used within a sentence. An exclamation mark is usually written at the end of the sentence or word.

The following are common interjections.

Ha!	Great!	Ouch!	Wow!
Hooray!	Oh!	Wonderful!	Boy!

Oh! What a beautiful parade!

Ouch! That bee stung me!

Punctuation 

Introduction

2.1 Punctuation marks are written signals that clarify the meaning of sentences and separate structural units of writing. To use punctuation marks correctly, keep these points in mind:

1. The chief purpose of punctuation is to help the reader understand the message.

2. Toward this end, punctuation marks can be as effective as a speaker's pauses and voice inflections.

3. Punctuation marks help to clarify the basic structure of the sentence; they cannot change a poorly written sentence into a well-written one.

4. Incorrect use of punctuation marks can drastically alter the meaning or emphasis of a sentence.

2.2 Punctuation marks are discussed in alphabetical order.

Apostrophe

2.3 Use an apostrophe:

1. To form a possessive to show ownership. (See 4.39-4.54, irregular possessive forms.)

To determine whether a word is possessive, change the expression to read "the bicycle *of* Joe." If the word *of* can be inserted, the apostrophe is correctly used. To form the possessive of a noun that ends in *s,* add only the apostrophe. To form the possessive of a noun that doesn't end in *s*, add the apostrophe and *s ('s).*

They only had a minute's notice before the tornado struck.

These will be the managers' decisions.

2. To indicate contractions.

it's [for *it is*]
I've [for *I have*]
don't [for *do not*]
she'll [for *she will* or *she shall*]
they're [for *they are* or *they were*]

3. In place of an omitted letter or letters.

class of '70 [for *1970*]

8 o'clock [for *of the* clock]

4. With a noun preceding a gerund. (A gerund is a verb form that ends in *-ing*.)

Paul's leaving upset the family.

5. To indicate a quotation within a quotation.

"Did you read that chapter entitled 'Improving Your Success Quotient'?" asked Betty.

6. To indicate plurals of lowercase letters, and letters followed by periods.

Cross those t's and dot those i's.

M.A.'s and M.D.'s

Do not use the apostrophe, however, to indicate plurals of words, numbers, or uppercase letters.

Omit the therefores and furthermores.

Learn your ABCs and the three Rs.

The decade of the 1960s will be remembered not only for the counter-culture protests among youth, but also for the changes in lifestyles for those in their 20s, 30s, and 40s.

Asterisk

2.4 **Use an asterisk:**

1. To indicate a footnote (where only one appears in the entire document) and its related reference or explanation.

Kisho Kurokawa* is one of the founders of Metabolism, an architectural movement and philosophy of change.

---

*Kisho Kurokawa, Metabolism in Architecture (London: Studio Vista, 1977), p. 28.

2. To indicate an omission of an entire paragraph.

* * *

Brace

2.5 **Use a brace to connect related information. A brace can be typed by using the right or left parenthesis key, or it may be drawn in pen.**

Alouisius Stevens,	)		}
Plaintiff,	)		
vs.	)	or	
MacGraw Farnham,	)		
et al.,	)		
Defendants,	)		

Brackets

2.6 Use brackets:

1. To make a correction or to insert a comment within quoted material. The brackets separate the information from the rest of the quoted material.

"These [industrial] statistics are crucial to understanding the events before the First World War."

2. To indicate a parenthetical expression within parentheses.

(See Exhibit D [Deed of Trust and Assignment of Rents] attached.)

2.7 If brackets are not on the typewriter, they are made as follows: To type the left bracket, type the diagonal, backspace, and type an underscore. Roll the paper back one line and type an underscore. To type the right bracket, type the underscore and the diagonal. Roll the paper back one line, backspace, and type an underscore. The brackets may also be written in pen.

Colon

2.8 Use a colon:

1. After the salutation in a business letter with mixed punctuation.

Gentlemen: Dear Madeline:

2. In typing reference initials, to separate the writer's initials from the typist's.

TG: wat

3. Between hours and minutes, parts of ratios, parts of biblical citations, or dates and page numbers in periodical citations.

9:30 a.m. Luke 3:1
20:1 Journal of Psychology 4 (1973): 24-26

4. To introduce a list of items following a complete sentence. The items listed may be words, phrases, clauses, or sentences. Key words used to introduce many listings are *the following, namely,* and *for example*.

Common business communications are:

announcements memoranda
letters reports

The following pronouns take a singular verb: anybody, anyone, each, either, everybody, everyone, neither, nobody, no one, somebody, and someone.

Do not use a colon in the following instances:

When the anticipatory expression (key words) appears near the beginning of a long sentence, use a period at the end of the sentence before the listing.

We must adhere to the following rules for our training program to be successful.

1. Eat three regular meals a day.
2. Get sufficient sleep and awake refreshed.

When there is an intervening sentence between the anticipatory expression and the listing, use a period at the end of both sentences.

The following items are to be included. Note the quantity needed.

one ream white paper
twelve sheets red construction paper
three pair scissors.

5. To emphasize a statement following a complete sentence.

Remember what John F. Kennedy said: "Ask not what your country can do for you . . . ."

6. To introduce quoted material or information placed in quotes following an explanatory or introductory sentence. (A quotation of one, two, or three lines is incorporated in the paragraph; however, a quotation of four or more lines is set off as a separate paragraph, indented from both margins and typed in single spacing.)

An English textbook may give the following rule concerning dangling modifiers:

> Gerunds, infinitives, and participial phrases should be placed in sentences so that their relationship to the words modified is instantly clear.

Comma

2.9 Commas help the reader slow down and pause before reading further. Commas are used to separate thoughts within a sentence and to help the reader properly interpret the meaning of the sentence.

Appositive

2.10 An appositive is a noun or pronoun phrase that identifies or explains the noun or pronoun that immediately precedes it. Use commas to set off an appositive.

Wilma Carrol, the business teacher, has become a new member of our organization.

This ancient Chinese vase, a priceless antique, is not for sale.

2.11 **Do not use commas to separate a noun from a closely related appositive. The noun and its appositive are considered one unit that is essential to the meaning of the sentence.**

Richard himself knew his potential was limited in that field.

The year 1967 was Canada's centennial year.

2.12 **Use commas to set off an identifying or explanatory word or phrase beginning with *or*.**

Set off an appositive, or an apposition, with commas.

Stenography, or writing in shorthand, will be taught this year.

2.13 **Use commas to set off a professional degree from the person's name. The degree may either be abbreviated or written out.**

"Judy Bradley, Doctor of Philosophy," was inscribed on her certificate.

Jasper Munro, CPS, works as a consultant to business.

2.14 **Use commas to set off personal titles written after a person's name to designate rank. Such abbreviations as *Esq., Jr.,* and *Sr.* are followed by a period.**

Francis Galloway, Jr., has been named representative for the shipping firm.

When Roman or Arabic numerals are used as personal titles to indicate rank, the commas may be omitted.

Francis Galloway III
Henry VIII
Alexander Van Wickle 2d

Dates

2.15 **Use commas to set off the year from the month and day when written in a sentence.**

The deadline for submitting the bid is May 10, 1984.

2.16 When only the month and year are written, the comma between them may be omitted.

That discovery took place in May 1974.

Geographic locations

2.17 Use commas to set off the names of a city and province; county, and city; city, county, and province; or province and country.

The Notary Public acknowledged the signatures in Toronto, County of York, Province of Ontario, at 2:30 p.m.

Our itinerary included Paris, France; Rome, Italy; and Munich, Germany. **[Semicolons instead of commas may be used to separate series with internal commas.]**

Names and addresses

2.18 Use commas to separate the name, street address, city, and province of an individual or a business.

Please send the magazines to Ms. Marcia Rose Trevino, 28 Highland Drive, Antigonish, Nova Scotia, B2G 1N8.

2.19 Use commas to set off a descriptive or explanatory statement that includes the name of a business within a city, province, or country.

The Reverend Sean Mallory, of the Boys' Academy in Port Alberni, is addressing the congregation this evening.

His mother and father, from the Fredericton, New Brunswick office, are assigned here for the next three months.

Business abbreviations

2.20 Use a comma to separate a business abbreviation from the company name, unless a comma is not written in the name. When the abbreviation appears within a sentence, use commas to set it off.

Collier Macmillan Canada, Inc.
Calgary Petroleum Co., Inc., is offering a new bonus plan.

But note:
Farrell Lines Inc. **[no comma in name]**

Business correspondence: salutation and closing

2.21 Use a comma after the salutation of an informal business letter or a personal letter. (A colon follows the salutation in business letters when mixed punctuation is used.)

Dear Jesse,

Use a comma after the complimentary closing when mixed punctuation is used.

Sincerely yours,
Very truly yours,

Clarification of thoughts

2.22 Use a comma to separate words or figures as necessary to avoid a misreading or misunderstanding.

What the problem is, is not known.

Rather than the expected 25, thirty people came to the party.

What the costs are, is for you to determine.

Compound sentences

2.23 Use a comma to separate the clauses of a compound sentence. (A compound sentence contains two or more independent clauses connected by *and, but, or,* or *nor*.)

We have ordered this style in several colours, but we have only received the shipment of green sweaters.

The comma may, however, be omitted between two short independent clauses.

He is the best and he knows it.

2.24 Do not use a comma to separate two independent clauses not joined by a co-ordinating conjunction. Use a semicolon or a dash, or begin a new sentence.

Refer this matter to Personnel; Bill Doud will contact them.

or

Refer this matter to Personnel. Bill Doud will contact them.

Contrasting expressions

2.25 Use commas to set off contrasting expressions that begin with such words as *but, not, yet, rather than,* and *instead of.*

> The business deal is due to close Tuesday, but only if all conditions have been met.
>
> Eddie, rather than Jimmy, delivered those drawings.
>
> Leave from Portage Avenue and Hargrave Street, not from Portage and Kennedy.

Descriptive words and explanations

2.26 Use commas to set off the following expressions when they further describe or explain the words immediately preceding: *as well as, accompanied by, attached to, in addition to,* and *besides*.

> The mother and father, as well as their children, are on vacation.
>
> Submit a written proposal, in addition to all supporting documents, to the Superintendent's Office by Tuesday.

Direct address

2.27 Use commas to set off a direct address. A direct address is a specific referral to the person's name, title, or other designation.

> You are correct, Mrs. Ruesge, in saying that your statement had been paid on June 10.
>
> Madam President, the motion has been made and seconded.

Interrupting expressions

2.28 Use commas to set off expressions that interrupt the flow of the sentence. These expressions may be afterthoughts or words inserted for special emphasis.

> He was, I suppose, entitled to the promotion.
>
> Interior Decor, I'll have to admit, did a beautiful job in the executive offices.

2.29 Use a single comma when the interrupting expression appears at the end of the sentence.

> Their anniversary date is February 14, if I recall correctly.

Introductory expressions

2.30 An introductory expression is a word, clause, or phrase used to introduce a subordinate clause.

2.31 An introductory clause begins with one of the following subordinating conjunctions:

after	in case	though
although	in order that	till
as	inasmuch as	unless
as soon as	otherwise	until
as though	provided	when
because	since	whenever
before	so that	wherever
even though	supposing	whether
if	then	while

2.32 Use a comma after an introductory clause at the beginning of the sentence.

> If you continue on Mount Royal Boulevard, you will reach Camillien Houde Drive.

2.33 An introductory phrase begins with a preposition, an infinitive, or a participle.

A comma can be used after an introductory prepositional phrase.

> In the meantime, darkness had fallen and the blackened forest aroused fears they would not be found until the next day.

If the introductory prepositional phrase is short (five or fewer words), or if the sentence flows smoothly after the phrase, the comma may be omitted.

> During the intermission we rushed to buy popcorn.

> In Act II Ismene confesses her love for Xiphanes.

Use a comma after an introductory prepositional phrase that contains a verb form, regardless of how short the phrase is.

> While reading the newspaper, I noticed an ad for a Steinway piano.

> At the moment you arrived, another customer had just walked into the store.

2.34 Use a comma after an introductory infinitive phrase.

To obtain ticket information, call 579-7356.

2.35 **Use a comma after an introductory participial phrase. A participle is a verb form that ends in *-ing, -ed,* or other past tense endings of irregular verbs. A participle may also consist of the verb *having* plus the past participle of a verb.**

Thinking out loud, she gave the secret away without realizing it.

Impressed by the responsibilities of the job, he was able to adjust quite rapidly.

2.36 **The following are introductory words:**

accordingly	however	obviously
actually	indeed	otherwise
also	meanwhile	perhaps
besides	moreover	so
consequently	namely	still
finally	naturally	then
first	nevertheless	therefore
fortunately	next	thus
further	now	yet
hence		

Introductory words are often used as transitional expressions connecting two independent thoughts. Use a comma after them.

The executive suite has been reserved by someone else; consequently, our meeting will be held in the conference chambers.

2.37 **Do not use a comma to set off one-syllable transitional expressions used as introductory words.**

Arrange these cards in the files; then prepare an index for them.

It can't be done that way. But I'm sure we can find another.

2.38 **Use commas to set off prepositional, infinitive, or participial phrases in the sentence (for usage at the start of a sentence, see 2.30–2.35). If the phrases are short, however, the comma is ordinarily omitted.**

He told me that, at the recommendation of Miss Lorenzo, we would look at the interior furnishings and designs.
[prepositional phrase]

Our teachers told us that, to type business correspondence easily, a secretary must be familiar with various types of letters and reports. **[infinitive phrase]**

Maria, having worked for the firm for five years, was hesitant to leave. **[participial phrase]**

The minutes disclosed that during the discussion several important decisions were made. **[short prepositional phrase—no comma needed]**

Inverted names

2.39 **When an individual's name is inverted, used a comma to separate the surname from the rest of the name.**

Coleridge, Samuel Taylor
Johnson, Raymond R.

When a title or degree designation follows the inverted name, use a comma to separate it from the name.

Clark, James L., Jr.
Clark, Sally N., Ms.
Doud, William R., Ph.D.

Non-restrictive (non-essential) clauses

2.40 **Non-essential or non-restrictive clauses offer additional information or an explanation but can be omitted from the sentence without changing the meaning of the statement. Use commas to set off non-essential clauses.**

Lee Whiting, who is the chairperson, conducted the meeting in a very efficient manner.

The grand opening must be held on March 21, because that is the most convenient day.

Non-restrictive (non-essential) phrases

2.41 **Use commas to set off non-essential prepositional, infinitive, and participial phrases that appear within the sentence.**

When, in your opinion, will the medical centre open?

Our advertising staff, to maintain its fine reputation, has produced some new publicity campaigns.

Omissions of words

2.42 Use a comma to indicate omission of a word or words from a sentence. Omitted words are usually verbs whose meanings are understood.

The $25 is due now; $15, in two weeks.

Clerical applicants must take the spelling test; secretarial applicants, the spelling and vocabulary tests.

Parenthetical expressions

2.43 A parenthetical expression is a word, phrase, or clause that may be omitted from the sentence without changing its meaning. Such expressions are used for emphasis or for transitional purposes.

accordingly	hence	obviously
actually	however	of course
after all	in addition	on the contrary
again	in fact	otherwise
also	in my opinion	perhaps
as a matter of fact	in other words	personally
	inclusive	respectively
as a result	indeed	still
as you know	meanwhile	that is
besides	moreover	then
certainly	namely	therefore
consequently	naturally	thus
finally	needless to say	too
first	nevertheless	well
for example	next	without a doubt
furthermore	no doubt	yes

2.44 Use a single comma:

1. To set off a parenthetical expression at the beginning or end of a sentence.

Nevertheless, the level of English usage is an important part of one's total personality.

Phyllis and Don were voted president and vice-president, respectively.

2. To set off a parenthetical expression at the beginning of the second independent clause in a compound sentence. A semicolon precedes the parenthetical expression in such a sentence.

Davis Adler has just been promoted; therefore, please request a change of status and change in office accommodations.

2.45 **Use two commas:**

1. To set off a parenthetical expression within a sentence. A comma must precede and follow such an expression.

It is our understanding, furthermore, that Abbott Industries must pay the penalty.

It is apparent, therefore, that he should not have acknowledged the letter received from the Beene Company.

Commas may be omitted with some parenthetical expressions depending on the emphasis given, the intended meaning of the statement, and whether the expression is essential or non-essential to the sentence.

Mr. Questa is indeed fortunate.

We are therefore cancelling our financial assistance.

2.46 **2. To set off the word *too* (meaning ''also'') used in the sentence other than at the end.**

You, too, can earn a higher rate of interest at our association.

Do not set off the word *too* (meaning ''also'') when it appears at the end of a phrase or sentence.

Please extend our invitation to your secretary too.

Restrictive (essential) clauses

2.47 A restrictive or essential clause is one that is necessary to the meaning of the sentence. Do not use commas to set off essential clauses.

Those councillors who favour increasing law enforcement personnel are in the minority.

Anything that is unanimously decided will be publicized in the morning papers.

Telephone service will be discontinued unless your 60-day overdue bill is paid.

Restrictive (essential) phrases

2.48 Do not use commas to set off essential prepositional, infinitive, or participial phrases within the sentence:

> The memorandum addressed to Holly Peterson contained the justification that we were expecting. **[participial phrase]**

> Their decision to lay off the workers was reached after a great deal of discussion. **[infinitive phrase]**

> The proposal at the end of the report seems impractical. **[prepositional phrase]**

Separating a statement and question

2.49 Use a comma between a statement and a question in the same sentence.

> I think the annual corporate report is comprehensive, don't you?

Separating pieces of information

2.50 Use commas to separate pieces of information written within the sentence.

> Send the subscription to Anne Montgomery, 56 Glovers Shore, Summerside, Prince Edward Island, C1N 1B4.

Series

2.51 A series is a group of related words, phrases, or clauses separated by commas. Use commas to set off items within the series. A comma is generally placed before the conjunction and the last item; it may be omitted if the practice is followed consistently.

Use a comma:

1. To set off words, clauses, or phrases in the series.

   > A dictionary shows the spelling, pronunciation, meaning, and origins of a word.

   > John boarded the plane at 10:30, landed in Bedeque at 11:45, and arrived at the hotel at 1:15. **[series of clauses]**

   > They saw Mae at the bookstore, Dona at the market, and Alicia at the library. **[series of phrases]**

2. After the last item of the series when there is no conjunction.

   > Orange, yellow, black, are the colours in our drapery fabric.

3. Before and after *etc.* as the last item in the series. (*Etc.* means "and so forth," so the conjunction *and* is not written before it.)

Paper, pencils, pens, paper clips, etc., are important supplies to be kept in a desk.

When *etc.* appears at the end of a sentence, a comma is written before the abbreviation only.

Our Spring Clearance will feature office supplies, equipment, furniture, etc.

2.52 Do not use a comma in a series:

1. When co-ordinating conjunctions are written between the items.

We have openings for machinists and draftsmen and chemists.

2. When the ampersand symbol (&) in a company name stands for the word *and*.

Our counsel is Feeney, Bolger & Reickert.

3. After the last item unless the structure of the sentence requires a comma.

January 1, December 25, and July 1, all such national holidays, should be noted on our calendars.

Comma usage problems

2.53 Do not use a comma:

1. Between a subject and its verb.

Our minister is Reverend Jefferson.

2. Between a verb and its complement.

They were heroes in the last war.

3. Between a compound adjective and the noun it modifies.

Those truckers had to drive that long, lonely stretch of highway at night.

4. Before or after a short prepositional phrase (see 2.33 and 2.38).

The technician in the laboratory had taken the specimens and had analyzed them by morning.

5. After the co-ordinating conjunctions *and, but, or,* or *nor* except when the structure of the sentence requires it.

They are a bit disappointed, but they will get over it soon.

6. To group large numbers. Use a space (see 6.7). (Four-digit numbers may be written with or without a space.)

    2224 ***or*** 2 224 ***not*** 2,224
    10 386 ***not*** 10,386
    1 982 684 ***not*** 1,982,684

See also 2.11, 2.20, 2.23, 2.37, 2.47, 2.48, and 2.52.

Dash

2.54 The major function of a dash is to emphasize a point. On a typewriter the dash is typed as two hyphens with no space before, between, or after them. On a word processor the dash is made by one hyphen with a space on either side. (It appears as one long dash in printed matter.) Use a dash:

1. In place of commas to set off a parenthetical expression more clearly.

    The mechanical aspects of modern writing--punctuation and capitalization--were absent from, or inconsistently used in, ancient writing.

2. In place of a semicolon for emphasis before the second independent clause.

    I campaigned the hardest--but she won the presidency!

3. In place of a comma for emphasis in a compound sentence before the conjunction.

    He was very upset by that confrontation--and I don't blame him at all.

4. In place of parentheses for emphasis or clarity.

    Refer to the April 10 letter from Corsican Limited--the one written by the manager--for the details.

5. In place of commas to set off a parenthetical expression when commas appear within the parenthetical expression.

    Representatives from all western provinces--British Columbia, Alberta, Saskatchewan, and Manitoba--are required to attend the annual sales conference.

6. After an introductory statement that needs explanation.

    Writing began as pictographs--symbols that resembled definite objects such as a man or a fish.

7. Before or after a single word used for emphasis.

    Read--that is the key to knowledge.
    His goals focus on one thing--promotion!

8. **To repeat, emphasize, or summarize a statement.**

   Test drive our newest model today--Monday--for the smoothest ride you'll ever experience.

   Meet us on the second floor--not the mezzanine--in a half hour.

9. **Before a significant final statement or one that summarizes several ideas.**

   Gladys arrives at work on time, gives a full day's work for a day's pay, and treats fellow employees with respect--she is a successful office worker.

Diagonal

2.55 **Use the diagonal (or slash):**

1. **When fractions are typed.**

   The sum of 6 1/3 and 2 2/3 is 9.

Note: All fractions should be typed using the diagonal, even when there are $^1/_4$ and $^1/_2$ keys on the typewriter, unless $^1/_4$ and $^1/_2$ are used alone.

2. **To type or write the expression *and/or*.**

   Joan and/or John will go to the store.

3. **When certain business terms are indicated.**

   2/10, n/30

4. **With certain abbreviations.**

B/F	brought forward	C/O	carried over
B/L	bill of lading	c/o	in care of
C/D	certificate of deposit	L/C	letter of credit

5. **In typing reference initials or writer's surname in business correspondence to separate the writer's initials or surname from the typist's initial(s).**

   CJS/pm   Morrise/I

Ellipsis points

2.56 Ellipsis points are used to indicate the omission of one or more words in quoted material. For instructions on the correct use of ellipses, see 8.74–8.76.

Exclamation point

2.57 **An exclamation point is used to indicate a strong emotion such as excitement, surprise, anger, or fear.**

Wonderful! These are the results I was hoping to achieve.

He shouted at the top of his voice, "Help!"

Several times he said, "I am going to the movies"!

[Note that the exclamation point is typed after the quotation mark because the complete sentence is an exclamation.]

Use the exclamation point to punctuate a one-word expression or a short exclamatory statement.

Stop! There is a terrible accident ahead.

Hyphen

2.58 **Use a hyphen:**

1. To divide a word at the end of a line.

One should not guess in dividing words, and the dictionary should be consulted frequently.

2. To write out numbers consisting of two or more words read as a single unit.

thirty-five
one hundred fifty-four
ten thousand three hundred seventy-nine

3. Between a compound adjective that functions as a single unit to modify a noun (see 1.135–1.152).

first-class mail
well-known physician
up-to-date invoice

4. In place of the words *to* or *through* (these appear as medium-long dashes in printed matter).

1985-1986
pp. 56-75
4:30-6:15 p.m.

5. With certain prefixes.

ex-president
quasi-judicial
self-made

6. To separate a prefix from a proper noun.

mid-Atlantic
post-World War I era

7. With improvised words, combining a letter and a word or two different words.

L-shaped desks
X-ray picture

8. When a fraction is written in words and used as an adjective.

He was elected by a two-thirds vote.

9. With compound adjectives modifying the same noun (suspended hyphens).

The theatre features first- and second-run movies.

10. In writing out amounts on cheques and legal documents.

One Thousand Two Hundred Seventy-Five and 36/100 Dollars

11. When amounts are used as a compound adjective.

75-cent fare
16-cylinder engine

Parentheses

2.59 Use parentheses:

1. To indicate a period of time.

Philologists generally divide the story of the English Language into three periods: namely, Old English (499-1100), Middle English (1100-1500), and Modern English (1500-present day).

2. To express an amount of money when more than one dollar is indicated.

The bill from the attorney was for five hundred dollars ($500).

3. To set off parenthetical expressions when commas would be confusing.

Our new management trainee was transferred from the Sherbrooke (Quebec) office.

4. To set off special references, instructions, or other explanatory statements.

The Nova Scotia Agricultural College (well-known for its two-year course in Animal Science) prepares students for careers as animal specialists or technicians.

5. To include expressions that help clarify the meaning of a sentence.

A list of some acronyms include radar (radio detecting and ranging), sonar (sound navigation ranging), and laser (light amplification by stimulated emission of radiation).

6. To enumerate items in a sentence.

General requirements include (1) the ability to see relationships, (2) mature judgement, (3) the ability to analyze problems before solving them, and (4) efficient work habits and methods.

Period

2.60 Use a period:

1. After each declarative and imperative sentence.

The mechanics of English aid the reader in understanding the meaning of the sentence and the intention of the writer.

Please stop playing the piano.

2. After abbreviations such as titles, degrees, calendar months, and geographic names. Only one space follows the period at the end of the abbreviation; however, do not space after a period *within* the abbreviation as in degrees or geographic names.

Mr. Arthur Jameson
Cmdre.
Ph.D.
U.S.A. (or USA)
Alta.
Dec. 12
Thurs.
U.S.S.R. (or USSR)

When a sentence ends with an abbreviation followed by a period, do not use another period.

Your order will be sent C.O.D.

3. After initials, except for radio and television broadcasting call letters.

Arthur R. Jameson CBC

4. After a sentence containing a request that is phrased in the form of a question. (If a *yes* or *no* response choice is not intended, use a period; otherwise, use a question mark.)

Will you please send us your cheque for $105 today.

5. **As a decimal point.**

   $37.95   44.9%   1.25

Do not use a decimal point after even dollar amounts. Dollar amounts within tabulations should be written with decimal points and zeros, however.

Please submit a requisition for $50 to the controller's office today.

$57.00	$135.95	$17.90
49.85	17.00	4.08
3.92	26.30	15.00

Note that the decimal points are aligned.

6. **In outlines and lists, after all complete sentences.**

I. Purposes of Typewriting
   A. Language Arts Skill
   B. Vocational Competence

I. Purposes of Typewriting
   A. You will acquire a language arts skill.
   B. Vocational competency will enable you to obtain a job.

The following must still be done:

1. Paint the reception area.
2. Carpet the reception area.
3. Order drapery for conference rooms.

2.61 **Do not use a period when numbers or letters are enclosed in parentheses.**

Carol has taken the following courses: (1) typewriting, (2) shorthand, and (3) business law.

Question mark

2.62 **Use a question mark:**

1. **At the end of a sentence that asks a question.**

   What time is it?

2. **To express doubt. The question mark is written in parentheses.**

   The captain of the team is two (?) metres tall.

   His uncle was born in 1921 (?).

3. **To raise several questions within one sentence. Leave only one**

space after the internal question marks; the items within the series of questions are not capitalized unless proper names are included.

Is he a writer? editor? printer? publisher?

Quotation marks

2.63 **Use quotation marks:**

1. To enclose a direct quotation.

"I shall be home in an hour," John said.

Dr. Philip B. Gove, editor of Webster's New International Dictionary, says: "The proper function of the dictionary maker is to record the language as it is used by the majority of its users, not create it or legislate concerning it."

[Note that the period is placed inside the final quotation mark.]

2. To emphasize a word or phrase.

The word television was invented during the twentieth century by combining the Greek tele, meaning "far," with vision, the Latin root "to see."

What are the correct uses of "to," "too," and "two"?

[Note that the question mark is placed *outside* the last quotation mark because the entire sentence is the question.]

3. To indicate titles of magazine articles and complete but unpublished works (eg. reports), chapters of books, and speeches.

The title of his article in the Canadian Business Education Forum is "Business Classroom and Laboratory Equipment."

"Canadian Business" is the title of the first chapter in the book he co-authored.

The title of his speech was listed as "You--The Consumer in the Market Place."

4. To set off a quotation consisting of a sentence or paragraph. In manuscripts and reports, a quotation of four or more lines is typed in single spacing as a separate paragraph; quotation marks are not necessary, since the quoted material is set apart from the text (see 8.73).

Synonyms may be used in a message to add variety, to adapt the level of vocabulary to the reader, and to be more definitive. While synonyms have the same basic meanings as their counterparts, it should be emphasized that different shades of meaning are involved.

5. To indicate titles of songs and other short musical compositions, and titles of radio and television programs.

One of the best shows on TV is "Man Alive."

6. With other punctuation marks.

John stated, "Now is the time to make a decision."

"I don't like to go to the dentist," Pete said.

[Note that periods and commas are placed inside the quotation marks.]

I sent you the article, "The Future of Young Canadians"; therefore, you shouldn't have trouble with your presentation.

The following food items were in the box marked "Perishable": bread, butter, and eggs.

[Note that semicolons and colons are placed outside the quotation mark because they relate to the entire sentence.]

He shouted, "Stop!"

She asked, "What time can I go home?"

[Note that the exclamation point and question mark are placed inside the quotation mark because they are an integral part of quoted matter.]

He exclaimed, "What a piercing shout"!

Did she ask the question, "What time can I go home"?

[Note that the exclamation point and question mark are placed outside the quotation mark because they relate to the entire statement, not just to the expression within quotes.]

2.64 Semicolon

The semicolon holds the reader at a particular point in the sentence before reading on. Use the semicolon:

1. To indicate that a conjunction has been omitted between the independent clauses of a compound sentence.

His first payment was due in March; the second payment was due in April.

2. In a compound sentence connected by a co-ordinating conjunction to provide a longer pause or more emphasis between the clauses.

Someone must have realized the error; but apparently he or she did not think it important enough to question it.

3. **When the second clause of a compound sentence begins with an introductory or transitional expression.**

   Spelling is not always logical or consistent; nevertheless, an educated person is expected to know how to spell.

4. **In a series that consists of long items or complete sentences.**

   Dick is preparing the draft of the report; Joanne is typing the tables, charts, and graphs; and Erik is proofreading the completed pages.

5. **To separate clauses that have internal commas.**

   Many common English surnames were derived from personal characteristics, such as Little, Small, and Young; from locations, such as Hill, Brooks, and Wood; and from occupations, such as Baker, Miller, Shepherd, and Weaver.

Underscore

2.65 **An underscore is a solid line used to underline words. In typed material, underscore information that would appear in italics in a printed book, as follows:**

1. **To indicate the titles of books, magazines, and newspapers.**

   Gone With the Wind is a book that John thoroughly enjoyed.

2. **To identify distinctive names of ships, trains, and planes.**

   He sailed from Halifax on the Bluenose the Third.

3. **To place emphasis on a task or command.**

   Please hand-carry this material to the printer.

4. **To emphasize a word or expression being defined.**

   Knowing the meaning of prefixes helps to define the words. The prefix re means again, con means with, pre means before, and pro means for.

5. **To identify unfamiliar or foreign terms. Note that foreign words that have become part of the language are *not* underscored. Refer to a dictionary to determine whether an underscore is needed.**

   The hors d'oeuvres were delicious.

6. **To refer to a word, letter, or figure.**

   The h in Lindbergh is silent.

Capitalization 3

Introduction

3.1 Proper capitalization helps clarify the meaning of what has been written. In general, capitalize proper nouns—those that specifically identify persons, places, or things. Other parts of speech are not usually capitalized unless they appear at the beginning of a sentence.

Academic subjects

3.2 Academic subjects are not capitalized unless reference is made to a specific course title. Names of languages, however, are always capitalized.

During his senior year in high school, John took algebra, chemistry, English, German, and typewriting.

While in college, Mary found Algebra I, English III, chemistry, German I, and Typewriting I to be the most interesting.

Addresses

3.3 Important words in an address are capitalized. (See also 7.15–7.20.)

Mr. Walter Bilitz
Valley Park Apt.
One East Waterloo Cresc.
Saskatoon, Saskatchewan
S7K 1X3

Mr. Jacques Bouvier
President, Educational
Management Systems
Mata Corporation
2952 Camillien Houde Drive
Montreal, Quebec
H3J 1W7

Armed forces

3.4 Each word of a title of a specific formation, unit, or appointment is capitalized.

Canadian Armed Forces
Canadian Forces College
5 Air Movements Unit

Since integration of the armed forces in Canada in 1968, there is no capitalization in the following expressions.

Canadian army	the army
Canadian navy	the navy
Canadian air force	the air force

Note that all general references or expressions used for the Canadian Armed Forces are also not capitalized.

the brigade	naval officer
the corps	commanding officer

Astronomical bodies

3.5 Names of specific planets (except *earth*), stars (except *sun*), and constellations are capitalized. However, if *earth, moon,* and *sun* are in a list of astronomical bodies, capitalize these words to maintain consistency.

the Big Dipper   Jupiter   the Milky Way   Saturn

The four planets nearest the sun are Mercury, Venus, Earth, and Mars.

Businesses

3.6 Important words in business names are capitalized. Such words as *and, of,* and *the*, when written within a name, are not capitalized. *The* is capitalized when it is the first word of a company's name.

Community Education Centre	Jeff Brown Fine Fabrics
The Cut and Curl Place	Leonard's Restaurant by the Sea

Calendar periods

3.7 Calendar periods include days of the week, months of the year, seasons of the year, historical events, holidays, and periods of time.

Days/months

3.8 Days of the week and months of the year are always capitalized.

Wednesday, February 24		in nineteen sixty-nine
the second Monday in July	*but*	the mid-seventies
the tenth of November		third-quarter earnings

Historical events/time periods

3.9 Important words in historical events and periods of time are capitalized.

Rebellion of 1837	the Ice Age
Louis Riel Rebellion	the Roaring Twenties
War of 1812	the Middle Ages

Holidays

3.10 Names of holidays are capitalized, including the word *day* written with the event.

Remembrance Day Labour Day

Seasons

3.11 Seasons of the year are not capitalized unless they refer to a specific time period or event.

Fall Quarterly Report, 1983	spring cleaning chores
Spring Clearance Sale at Sears	their winter wardrobe

Common nouns

3.12 Common nouns—those that refer to people, places, or things in general—should not be capitalized. Note, however, that the following words may be used as common or proper nouns.

act	college	department
avenue	committee	division
board	company	president
board of directors	corporation	province
city	county	supervisor

3.13 When these and similar words are written as part of a name, they are capitalized. However, when they are used alone to stand for the entire name or for the general category to which the name belongs, do not capitalize them. (See also 3.37, Proper Nouns.)

the Royal Trust Company

Their company was conducting an involved title search.

Canada Department of Agriculture

That department publishes several booklets on proper health care and diet for everyone.

He goes to Centennial College.

Her hopes for admission to a college in London were soon diminished.

the Board of Directors of Manufacturers Life Insurance Company

Members of the board of directors accepted the proposed increase in premium rates.

Compass terms

3.14 The points of the compass are not capitalized unless they refer specifically to a particular region or are used as part of a proper name. (See also 3.19–3.21, Geographic Names.)

north side of the street		North Dakota
southwest corner		East Third Street
drive west	*but*	the West'
just south of Temiskaming		Central Canada

3.15 The adjectives *northern, eastern, southern,* and *western* are not capitalized unless they are written as part of a proper name.

northern coastal area	*but*	Northern Ireland
eastern shores		Southern Section Conference
midwestern drought		Middle Eastern
eastern standard time (EST)		Western world

Derivatives of proper names

3.16 Words derived from proper names are capitalized.

New Yorker	Vancouverite
Elizabethan	Turkish tobacco

3.17 Certain derivatives have acquired a common meaning so that capitalization is not needed. Consult the dictionary for correct capitalization.

french cuff	plaster of paris
manila envelope	roman candle

Family titles

3.18 Family titles are capitalized when they are followed by a personal name and when the title itself is used as a name.

Uncle Joe was kind to everyone.
His uncle had interesting hobbies.

Grandfather Timpkin was a stamp collector.
It seems Grandpa was still able to drive his car.

Geographic names

3.19 Geographic names—of continents, nations, provinces, cities, towns, mountains, bodies of water—are capitalized. (See also 3.14–3.15, Compass Terms.)

North America	Brownsville	Fraser River
Mexico	Atlantic Ocean	Peggy's Cove
Alberta	Mount St. Anne	Montreal Harbour

3.20 Regions, localities, and nicknames of cities are also capitalized.

Hogtown	the Ward
Elgin County	the South Pole

3.21 Sections of countries or other geographic subdivisions should be capitalized; compass points indicating general directions should not be capitalized.

the Middle East	John travels south to go home.
northern Manitoba	The sun sets in the west.

Government officials and titles

3.22 The following titles of high-ranking government officials at the international, national, and provincial levels are capitalized when written before, or in place of, a specific individual's name. They are not capitalized, however, when used to refer to an entire class of officials.

Ambassador
Attorney General
cabinet ministers (e.g., Minister of Labour)
Chief Justice
Governor General
Lieutenant-Governor

Premier
President
Prime Minister
Queen
Vice-President

Prime Minister John A. Macdonald was re-elected in 1878.

The Prime Minister approved of the War Measures Act.

Government bodies

3.23 The following words are capitalized because they refer to specific government units.

the House of Commons
the Senate
the Legislature (preceded by province's name)
the Privy Council

3.24 The names of government agencies, authorities, boards, commissions, and departments are capitalized.

Newfoundland's Department of Labour
Liquor Control Board
Statistics Canada
National Film Board
Nova Scotia Human Rights Commission
Agricultural Relief Adjustment Board (Alberta)

Hyphenated words

3.25 Capitalize only those parts of hyphenated words that are normally capitalized. (See also 3.35 and 3.36, Prefixes.)

English-Canadian explorer
Trustee-elect Sarver
Merriam-Webster dictionaries
mid-August workshops

Institutions

3.26 The names of such institutions as churches, libraries, schools, hospitals, synagogues, colleges, and universities are capitalized.

First Presbyterian Church
Central Hills Public Library
Vaughan Road High School
Lansdowne Public School
University of Alberta
Beth Adam Temple
Hospital for Sick Children

3.27 School, college, or division names within a university or college are also capitalized.

School of Agriculture
Faculty of Journalism
Department of English
Social Sciences Division

Legal terminology

3.28 Important words in legal citations are capitalized.

Smith v. Johnson Securities Corp., 403, D.L.R. (3D) 206 (B.C.C.A.)

Furlong v. Burns & Co. Ltd., 1964 2 O.R.3

3.29 In legal documents, certain introductory words are typed in solid capitals.

SECOND: I hereby give, devise, and bequeath. . . .

IN WITNESS WHEREOF, the parties. . . .

WHEREAS, the co-operation of both organizations. . . .

THEREFORE, BE IT RESOLVED, that the establishment and maintenance. . . .

between the PLAINTIFF and DEFENDANT. . . .

Letter elements

3.30 The first letter of the salutation, attention line, subject line, complimentary closing, and company name are capitalized; sometimes an entire element may be capitalized.

Dear John:
My dear Mr. Hendricks
Attention: Ms. Irene Messina
SUBJECT: Policy No. IR39050

Sincerely yours
Very truly yours
MANAGEMENT CONSULTANTS, INC.

Names and nicknames

3.31 Words used as nicknames designating particular people, places, or things, are capitalized.

the Great Gretzky
the Windy City
the Van-Doos
Dief the Chief

Nationalities and races

3.32 All nationalities and races are capitalized, but the terms *black* and *white* are not.

Caucasian	German	Mexican	Puerto Rican
Chinese	Italian	Nigerian	Swedish

Noun preceding a letter or number

3.33 The descriptive word before a number or letter should be capitalized to clarify and place proper emphasis on the term as a single unit. When the noun and the number or letter are separated in the sentence, the descriptive word is not capitalized.

Appendix A	Room 40
Enclosure 3	Conference Room G
Table 15	Public School 39
Form Y	Catalogue No. 421

The number of the room where we will meet is 40.
The course number is given as 421 in the catalogue.

Organizations

3.34 Organizations include associations, clubs, foundations, political parties, societies, etc. Important words in these names are capitalized.

Boy Scouts of Canada	New Democratic Party
Jewish Family and Child Service	Progressive Conservative Party

Prefixes

3.35 Hyphenated prefixes are capitalized only when the sentence begins with the hyphenated word. Even if the prefix precedes a proper noun, only the first letter of the proper noun is capitalized.

ex-President	pre-Trudeau years
mid-July wedding	post-war era

Post-war Germany was characterized by economic instability.

Germany's economy suffered during the post-war period.

3.36 Foreign surname prefixes do not follow a specific rule for capitalization. Certain surnames with prefixes begin with a capital letter; others are written with a space between the name and the prefix. In general, follow the individual's preference in spelling his or her last name.

de Catur (*or* Decatur)	Di Iorio	O'Brien
De La Cruz	MacRae	Van Laanen
de la Torre	McCray	Van Osdel
Del Prado	M'Creery	von Kalinowski
DeMille	McEvily	Von Posch

Proper nouns

3.37 The first letter of each significant word in proper names of people, places, and things is capitalized (see also 3.12 and 3.13, Common Nouns).

Balfour Building	CN Tower
Fort Henry	the Fort Gary Hotel
Confederation Park Plaza	the Canadian National Railways
Stanley Park	
Victoria Day	Queen Mary

Publications

3.38 Important words in titles of books, magazines, newspapers, articles, and historical documents are capitalized. Except for articles and some documents, such titles are also underscored (in print they are in italics) or, less commonly, typed in solid capital letters. Article titles are placed within quotation marks.

New Standard Reference for Secretaries and Administrative Assistants

"Care and Feeding of Persian Cats"

The Operas of Mozart

Declaration of Independence

Encyclopaedia Britannica or ENCYCLOPAEDIA BRITANNICA

Quotations

3.39 If a statement within quotation marks is a complete sentence or a one-word exclamation, the first word should be capitalized. However, a sentence fragment in quotations should not begin with a capital letter.

> In opening his speech, Mr. Roberts said, "Today is the tomorrow all of us worried about yesterday."
>
> Referring to the "severe problems facing our modern cities," the speaker expanded in some detail.
>
> After the home team won the game, everyone shouted, "Hooray!"

Religious terms

3.40 Specific religious terms, including names of saints and deities, titles of sacred works, and names of holy days, are capitalized; such general terms as *biblical* and *godlike*, however, are not.

Apostles' Creed	Genesis	the Lord
the Bible	God	Mohammed
Buddha	the Holy Ghost	St. Mark
Catholicism	Judaism	Saviour
Easter Sunday	the Koran	Ten Commandments

Sentences

3.41 The first word of all sentences begins with a capital letter.

> Having a dictionary within easy reach may bring the secretary closer to the revered "dictionary habit."

Within parentheses

3.42 The first word of a complete sentence written within parentheses is capitalized only if the sentence is not part of another sentence. Words in sentence fragments in parentheses are capitalized only if they would normally be capitalized.

> Because of the late hour, they decided to skip supper. (Their plane had been delayed before taking off.)
>
> Because of the late hour (their plane had been delayed before taking off), they decided to skip supper.
>
> Our next door neighbours (the Eisners) will be travelling to Europe this summer.

In outlines

3.43 The first word of each item in a main or secondary heading is capitalized whether or not the item is a complete sentence. (See also 8.14-8.18, Outline Styles.)

I. Company Fringe Benefits

A. Paid vacations
B. Accumulated sick leave
C. Medical insurance

Lists within sentences

3.44 The first word of an enumerated item written within a sentence is not capitalized, even if the item is a complete sentence, unless the first word would normally be capitalized.

The following items must still be taken care of: (1) the Pictou office must make hotel reservations; (2) Artie Maxwell must organize the committee on convention programming; and (3) our Saint John office must submit a tentative budget.

Titles

3.45 Titles preceding a name are capitalized. Titles that follow a name are capitalized only with positions that indicate special distinction. (See also 7.83-7.90, Forms of Address.)

General de Witte	the Mayor of Etobicoke
Vice-President Harris	the Reverend David Sork

Heather Tunnah, assistant director of purchasing, will be the speaker.

Sales Manager Bernard Van Goal resigned his position.

Trade names

3.46 Names of common business products or services are capitalized.

Bayer Aspirin Pyrex Coca Cola

3.47 Certain trade names have become accepted as everyday words and may not require capitalization. (Check the dictionary to determine whether or not a trade name should be capitalized.)

mimeograph nylon

Spelling and Word Division 

Word endings and letter combinations

4.1 In using the general guidelines provided below, remember that there are always exceptions to most spelling rules. Remember also that many words in the English language are not spelled the way they are pronounced. One rule you can depend on is this: when in doubt, refer to a dictionary.

4.2 The only guideline offered for the use of words ending in *-able* and *-ible* is to become familiar with the more common words and the correct spelling of the suffix.

-able endings	*-ible* endings
acceptable	admissible
likable	eligible
noticeable	flexible
probable	intelligible
valuable	irresponsible
washable	susceptible

4.3 Eight words end in *-cede*.

accede	intercede
antecede	precede
cede	recede
concede	secede

Only three words end in *-ceed*.

exceed   proceed   succeed

Only one word ends in *-sede*.

supersede

4.4 Derivatives of these words are often spelled differently from the root word.

accede	accession
exceed	excess
proceed	procedure, procession
recede	recession
secede,	secession
succeed	succession, successive

4.5 Write the *i* before *e* except after *c* and when the sound is pronounced like *a*. (Note the exceptions carefully!)

e before *i* (after *c*)	*i* before *e*
ceiling	achieve
conceit	belief, believe
conceive	field
receipt	piece
receive	relieve
	reprieve

ei sounded like *a*	exceptions
eight	height
heir	leisure
neighbour	neither
vein	seize
weigh	weird

4.6 There are no rules regarding the suffixes *-ize, -ise,* and *-yze*. Familiarize yourself with the more common words and the correct spelling of their endings.

-ize	*-ise*	*-yze*
apologize	advertise	analyze
authorize	compromise	paralyze
characterize	enterprise	
criticize	exercise	
liberalize	merchandise	
realize	supervise	
summarize	surprise	

4.7 Words ending in *-ll* retain the double letters before a suffix.

full	fuller
install	installment, installed
skill	skillful, skilled

If the suffix is *-ly*, drop one of the consonants.

full + *-ly*	fully
dull + *-ly*	dully

If the suffix is *-like,* hyphenate the words.

shell	shell-like

Combining words

4.8 When a prefix or suffix is added to a word or when words are combined that create a double letter, retain both letters.

bookkeeper	irrespective	skiing
dissatisfaction	irresponsible	underrated
dissimilar	meanness	withholding
dissolve	misspelled	

Consonant before *y*

4.9 Change the final *y* to *i* when preceded by a consonant before adding a suffix (except for one beginning with *i*).

beauty	beautiful	beautifying
biography	biographical	
carry	carries, carrier	carrying
clumsy	clumsiness	

4.10 One-syllable words retain the *y* before *-ly* and *-ness* suffixes, with some exceptions.

dry	dryly	dryness
sly	slyly	slyness

Exceptions:

day	daily	gay	gaiety
fly	flier	lay	laid

Final consonant doubled

4.11 There are several guidelines to follow when the final consonant is doubled. Double the final consonant:

1. After a word that ends in a consonant preceded by a vowel, when the suffix begins with a vowel or *y*.

bag	baggage	baggy
drop	dropped	dropping
fit	fitted	fitting
skin	skinny	skinnier

2. After a word that ends in a consonant preceded by a vowel with the accent on the last syllable, when the suffix begins with a vowel.

begin	beginning	handicap	handicapped
confer	conferring	recur	recurrence

Do not double the final consonant:

1. After a word that ends in a consonant preceded by a vowel, when the accent is not on the last syllable.

credit	credited	crediting
profit	profited	profiting

Exceptions:

cancel	cancelled	cancelling
travel	travelled	travelling
total	totalled	totalling
program	programmed	programming

2. When a suffix beginning with a consonant is added to a word that ends in a consonant and is preceded by a single vowel.

authorship
development
shipment

3. When a suffix is added to a word that ends in a consonant preceded by more than one vowel.

brief	briefly	briefing
cheer	cheerful	cheering
cloud	cloudy	

4. When a word ends in more than one consonant before the suffix.

attach	attachment
condemn	condemned
length	lengthen

Silent *e*

4.12 Here as above, several guidelines apply.

Drop the silent *e* when a word ending in silent *e* is followed by a suffix that begins with a vowel.

advise	advisable
desire	desirous
hope	hoping

Exceptions:

agree	agreeing
hoe	hoeing
mile	mileage

Do not drop the silent *e*:

1. When a word ending in silent *e* is followed by a suffix that begins with a consonant.

enforce	enforcement
hope	hopeful
manage	management

Exceptions:

argue	argument
idle	idly
nine	ninth
subtle	subtly

Note in some cases, the silent *e* may or may not be kept.

acknowledgement	acknowledgment
judgement	judgment

2. When a word could be mispronounced or confused if the silent *e* were dropped.

die	died	dying
dye	dyed	dyeing
eye	eyeing	
hoe	hoeing	

3. When a word ends in *ce* or *ge* and is followed by a suffix beginning with a vowel.

courage	courageous
manage	manageable
notice	noticeable

Vowel before *y*

4.13 Do not change *y* to *i* before adding a suffix when a final *y* is preceded by a vowel.

convey	conveyed	conveyance
employ	employer	employing

Exceptions:

day	daily
lay	laid
pay	paid
say	said

Forming plurals

4.14 The general rule for forming plurals of words is to add an *s* to the singular form of words that do not end in *s* (or an "s" sound). The plural of words ending in *s* is formed by adding *es*. Exceptions are discussed below.

4.15 Few nouns end in *f* or *fe*. The *f* or *fe* is sometimes changed to *ves* to form the plural. In other cases, however, the plural is formed by adding *s* to the singular form.

brief	briefs	knife	knives
chief	chiefs	leaf	leaves
dwarf	dwarfs	life	lives
half	halves	proof	proofs

4.16 The plural of words ending in *s, x, ch, sh,* and *z* is formed by adding *es* to the singular form.

bus	buses	rush	rushes
business	businesses	stretch	stretches
church	churches	waltz	waltzes
mix	mixes	wish	wishes
quartz	quartzes		

Abbreviations

4.17 The plural of most abbreviations is formed by adding *s*.

mo.	mos.
no.	nos.

4.18 The plural of abbreviations written in capital letters is formed by adding *s* with no apostrophe unless a misreading would otherwise occur.

ABCs	YWCAs
CPAs	three Rs
CPS's	XYZs

4.19 Other abbreviations are pluralized by doubling the consonants in the singular form.

p. 482
pp. 482-485 (page 482 to or through page 485)
pp. 114 f. (page 114 and the following page)
pp. 114 ff. (page 114 and the following pages)
v. or vv. (verses)

Compound words

4.20 A compound word consists of two or more words combined as a single unit. Some compound words are hyphenated; others are not. Follow the general rules for forming plurals of words and these specific guidelines as well.

1. The most significant word takes the plural form.

adjutant general	adjutants general
court-martial	courts-martial
deputy chief of protocol	deputy chiefs of protocol
father-in-law	fathers-in-law
Judge Advocate General	Judge Advocate Generals
lieutenant-colonel	lieutenant-colonels
notary public	notaries public or notary publics
passer-by	passers-by

2. If both words are of equal significance, both should be written in the plural form.

coat of arms	coats of arms
secretary-treasurer	secretaries-treasurers

3. If there is no one significant word and neither word is a noun, the last word takes the plural form.

go-between	go-betweens
higher-up	higher-ups

Consonant before *o*

4.21 The plural of most words ending in *o* preceded by a consonant is formed by adding *s*. However, some plurals are formed by adding *es*; others may be formed with either ending (first spelling is preferable).

domino	dominoes	dominos
hero	heroes	
piano	pianos	
steno	stenos	
tango	tangos	
tomato	tomatoes	
veto	vetoes	

Consonant before *y*

4.22 The plural of a word ending in *y* preceded by a consonant is formed by changing the *y* to *ies*. (See also 4.31 and 4.32, Proper Names.)

authority	authorities
company	companies
county	counties

Foreign origin words

4.23 The plural forms of foreign origin words deviate from the guidelines for English words. Learning the following singular and plural word endings of these words will make spelling easier.

Singular ending	*Plural ending*
a	ae or as
is	es
ix	ices
on	a
um	ums or a
us	i
addendum	addenda
alumna	alumnae
alumnus	alumni
appendix	appendices or appendixes
basis	bases
crisis	crises
criterion	criteria
curriculum	curriculums or curricula
datum	data
executrix	executrices
formula	formulae or formulas
matrix	matrices or matrixes
medium	mediums or media
memorandum	memorandums or memoranda
parenthesis	parentheses
stimulus	stimuli
thesis	theses

Geographic names

4.24 The plural of geographic names is formed by adding *s* to the name, regardless of the last letter in the name.

Waterloo (in Iowa, Ontario, Belgium)	the Waterloos

North Carolina and South Carolina	the Carolinas

The following geographic words are already plural.

Niagara Falls, Ontario
Twin Rivers, Ontario
United States
West Indies

Irregular plurals

4.25 Certain singular words are spelled differently in their plural form.

child	children	man	men
foot	feet	mouse	mice
goose	geese	tooth	teeth
louse	lice	woman	women

4.26 When these words are used as suffixes in other words, the irregular plural form is used.

dormouse	dormice
eyetooth	eyeteeth
forefoot	forefeet

Numbers

4.27 The plural of numbers written in figures is formed by adding *s*, without an apostrophe.

in the 1980s   in the high 20s   the middle 200s

4.28 The plural of numbers spelled out is formed by adding *s* or *es*, depending on the word ending.

fifty-two	fifty-twos
forty	forties
six	sixes
sixth	sixths

4.29 When a fraction is spelled out, place the plural at the end of the fraction.

three-fourths of a piece
thirty one-hundredths

Personal titles

4.30 The following are the plural forms of personal titles.

Dr. or Doctor	Doctors
Miss	Misses
Mr.	Messrs.
Mrs.	Mmes.
Professor	Professors
Rev. or Reverend	Reverends

When two or more surnames are written with the same personal title, the plural form precedes the surnames. The singular form may also be written before each surname—as with *Ms.*, which has no plural.

Messrs. Dvorak and Constant served as hosts for the annual Rotary Club dinner.

Mr. Dvorak and Mr. Constant served as hosts for the annual Rotary Club dinner.

Mmes. Busche and Pinchok were elected to serve on the city council for three years.

Mrs. Busche and Mrs. Pinchok were elected to serve on the city council for three years.

Misses Wills and Fong received their law degrees last June.

Miss Wills and Miss Fong received their law degrees last June.

Ms. Jane Blank and Ms. Jane Doe have been promoted to executive positions by the Bank of Montreal's Board of Directors.

Proper names

4.31 The plural of surnames is formed by adding either *s* or *es* to the name, depending on the last letter in the name. The spelling of the name is not changed in any way except for the addition of the *s* or *es*.

Judy and Allen Bradley	the Bradleys
Marcie and Rich Trevino	the Trevinos
the Cox family	the Coxes
the Wolf family	the Wolfs
the Chiu family	the Chius
the Dobbings family	the Dobbingses
the Guterrez family	the Guterrezes

4.32 The plural of first names is formed by adding either *s* or *es* to the name without changing the spelling of the name.

Marys	Mitches	Tracys
Joes	Charleses	Margoes
Chucks	Kenneths	Jessies
Alexes		

Silent *s*

4.33 Words that end in silent *s* in their singular form retain the same spelling for the plural form.

corps
chassis
faux pas

Vowel before *o*

4.34 The plural of words ending in *o* preceded by a vowel is formed by adding *s*.

duo	duos
radio	radios

Vowel before *y*

4.35 The plural of a word ending in *y* preceded by a vowel is generally formed by adding *s*. For some words, however, the *y* is changed to *ies*.

attorney	attorneys
bay	bays
display	displays
money	moneys (or monies)

Other words

4.36 The plural of words is formed by adding either *s* or *es* depending on their last letters.

dos and don'ts	ins and outs
the ayes have it	buts
pros and cons	

4.37 Several words are written in the same way for both the singular and plural forms.

counsel	moose	sheep
deer	number	species
majority	series	swine
minority		

4.38 The following words are always in the plural form.

cattle	pants	remains	scissors
data	pliers	riches	shears
goods	proceeds	savings	thanks
grounds			

Possessives

4.39 The possessive form of a word indicates that something is owned or is part of an item or a place. Possession is indicated by adding an apostrophe and *s* (*'s*) or by adding only an apostrophe to the word.

Abbreviations

4.40 To show possession of abbreviated words, add an apostrophe and *s*.

RCMP's investigation CPS's examination

Compound nouns

4.41 The possessive of a singular compound noun is formed by adding apostrophe and *s* to the last word of the compound.

adjutant general's orders
court-martial's decision
president-elect's speech

4.42 The possessive of a plural compound word is formed by adding an apostrophe to the last word of the compound.

administrative secretaries' classifications
editors-in-chiefs' remarks

Compound possessives

4.43 To indicate the possessive of two or more nouns, add the appropriate possessive form to each word.

the Pinchuk's and the Oakes' boats
the Davises' home and the Nanko's home

4.44 To indicate joint possession, add the appropriate possessive form to the last word only.

Bullock & Yagami's consulting firm
Loui, O'Connor & Stevens' mortuary

Plural nouns

4.45 The possessive of regular plural nouns is formed by adding an apostrophe.

directors' decisions	secretaries' typewriters
doctors' offices	students' records

4.46 The possessive of irregular plural nouns is formed by adding an apostrophe and *s*.

children's daytime programs
women's rights

Possessives understood

4.47 When the item possessed is understood, the word in its possessive form may stand by itself.

David's [grades] are higher than Jaime's.

John's skills in shorthand and typing are more polished than Chris's [skills].

Pronouns

4.48 Indefinite pronouns ending in *one* are written as one word except for the pronoun *no one* and when the preposition *of* follows the word ("any one of distinction"). The possessive is indicated by adding an apostrophe and *s*.

another's responsibilities	everyone's ideals
anybody's interest	no one's blame

4.49 The possessive of personal pronouns is formed irregularly.

Personal pronoun	*Possessive*
I	my, mine
you	your, yours
he	his
she	her, hers

it	its
we	our, ours
they	their, theirs

4.50 The possessive of relative pronouns is formed irregularly.

Relative pronoun	*Possessive*
who	whose

Proper nouns

4.51 The possessive of a singular proper noun is written with an apostrophe and *s* even though the word ends in *s*.

Clark's desert home
Jan Prentiss's promotion
Los Angeles's debating team
Arien and Ross's tax seminar
Fox's Studios
Dawson City's population
Bruce & Glencoe's publications
General Hospital's Intensive Care Unit

4.52 The possessive of a plural proper noun is written with an apostrophe only.

The Clarkses' desert home
Bay Cities' transit system
Twin Falls' river systems

Singular nouns

4.53 The possessive of singular nouns not ending in *s* is formed by adding apostrophe and *s*.

student's record
secretary's typewriter
Poe's "The Raven"
salesman's territory

Troublesome possessives

4.54 The possessive forms of pronouns are often confused with contractions because they are sounded alike.

Possessives	*Contractions*
its	it's (for *it is* or *it has*)
their	they're (for *they are* or *they were*)
theirs	there's (for *there is* or *there has*)
whose	who's (for *who is* or *who was*)
your	you're (for *you are* or *you were*)

Prefixes

4.55 Learning the meanings of prefixes makes it easier to spell and define prefixed words.

ante before or in front of

antedate, anteroom, antecedent

anti against

antibiotic, antifreeze, anti-European

bi two or occurring twice per time period

biannual, bicycle

co with or together

co-ordinate, co-partnership

com, con with or together

company, companion; confer, connect

counter against

counterbalance, countercheck (v)

dis apart

disburse, disassemble, discard

ex out of or from

exchange, exemption, exit

inter between or among

interoffice, interprovincial

mis badly or wrongly

misdeed, mismanage, misspell

multi much or many

multimillionaire, multiplicity

non not or absence of

non-support, non-government, nonconformist

post after or subsequent

postdate, postpaid

pre before or prior

prepay, presell, preclude

pro in favour of or prior to

probate, proceed, pro-German

super over and above, exceeding

superabundance, superhighway

trans across or beyond

transatlantic, transcontinental, trans-Mexico, trans-Canada

un not or none

unanswered, uncared for, unpopular

Word division rules

4.56 At the end of a line, divide a word between syllables. A dictionary or other reference source should be consulted when in doubt about syllabication. Type a hyphen at the end of the line to indicate the division and type the remainder of the word on the succeeding line.

Rules to follow

4.57 The rules below must be observed in deciding how, or whether, to divide a word.

1. A word that has five or fewer letters or that is pronounced as one syllable should not be divided.

allot	could	fuel	rotor
change	echo	length	though

2. A one-letter syllable at the beginning of a word should not be separated from the other letters.

achieve	eclipse
again	oblige

3. A two-letter syllable at the end of a word should not be separated from the other letters.

hanger	lively
heaven	mother

4. Root words ending in double letters are divided between the double letters.

bag-gage	ship-per
get-ting	swim-ming

5. Compound words should be divided at the hyphens.

mother-in-law self-confidence
hand-me-down Massey-Ferguson

6. Contractions should not be divided.

can't (for *cannot*)
don't (for *do not*)

7. Abbreviations should not be divided.

a.m. Dr. p.m.
B.C. CJRT S & K

8. Proper names should not be divided. However, compound names may be separated between the words.

Annie Jean-Guy Thomas / William
Kennedy Mary / Louise

9. Amounts and numbers should not be divided.

$15 750.36 4 673 550
25 cents $23 million

10. Information that is read as one unit should not be divided.

Article IV page 13
chapter 6 Section 1A

11. A word with two single-letter accented vowels written together should be divided between the vowels.

abbrevi-ate medi-ocre
continu-ally recre-ation

Rules to follow whenever possible

4.58 1. Retain the prefixes by dividing after the prefix.

circum-stances post-pone
con-venience pur-chase

2. Retain the suffixes by dividing before the suffix.

atten-tion offi-cial
glad-ness promis-ing

3. Do not divide more than two lines in succession.

4. Do not divide a word at the end of the first line of a paragraph.

5. Do not divide the last word on the page.

6. Words that might be misread by the reader or otherwise confused should not be divided.

demonstration superfluous

7. Avoid making a division before a single vowel that alone forms a syllable. However, this does not apply to the suffixes *able* and *ible* (con-si-der-able) and words in which the vowel is the first syllable of a root (dis-united).

Consult the Word List, beginning on page 365, for spelling and word division help. The hyphen indicates a preferred place for a word break. The dash indicates a compound word that has retained the hyphen.

Glossary of words that sound alike

4.59 The sound of words does not necessarily conform to their spelling. Some words with the same or almost the same pronunciation are spelled and/or used differently; those most commonly confused are paired and defined below.

4.60 **accept** (v) to receive
The store was willing to *accept* a small down payment.

except (v) to leave out
(prep) with the exclusion of
Jane *excepted,* no one in the class really enjoys studying.

Everyone went to the movies *except* John.

4.61 **access** (n) admittance or approach
In his position as vice-president, he had *access* to all the files.

excess (n) more than necessary
There was an *excess* of onions in the sauce.

4.62 **ad** (n) advertisement
The McCords put an *ad* in the local paper when they decided to sell their second car.

add (v) to total
Although Mr. Roberts was a successful businessman, he could not *add* a long column of figures.

4.63 **adapt** (v) to make suitable
Ramos Industries will *adapt* the machine to suit the customer's specific needs.

adept (adj) skilled or proficient
John Luciero is an *adept* keypunch operator.

4.64 **addition** (n) increase
We expect an *addition* of three assistants to our paramedical staff.

edition (n) a copy or version
The *Bramalea Operations Manual* is in its third *edition*.

4.65 **advice** (n) recommendation(s)
The *advice* that Mr. Brajak gave his son was excellent.

advise (v) to counsel
Her uncle will *advise* her to attend college.

4.66 **affect** (v) to influence
The quality of the food might *affect* his stomach.

effect (v) to bring about
(n) a result
As hard as the new manager tried, he could not *effect* any changes.

One *effect* of inflation is higher prices for most goods and services.

4.67 **all ready** (adv) prepared
The corporation's executive secretary was *all ready* to leave on a week's vacation when he received a call to return for a conference.

already (adv) previously
James was *already* gone when Zuber reached the hotel.

4.68 **all right** (adv) yes, certainly
(adj) in good health, satisfactory
All right, I will come.

He looks *all right*.

alright Same meanings as above but generally considered slang. It is not considered acceptable.

4.69 **allude** (v) to make indirect reference
One should not *allude* to an event that might be misunderstood by others.

elude (v) to avoid skillfully; to evade
The burglars were able to *elude* their pursuers for only a few minutes.

4.70 **allusion** (n) an indirect reference
The mayor's *allusion* to the cost of mass transit was not ignored by reporters.

illusion (n) a misleading image or idea
The heavy fog strengthened his *illusion* that the house was shrouded in mystery.

Before the guests arrived, Theresa had been under the *illusion* that only two were coming.

4.71 **all ways** (n) every respect
He is in *all ways* an understanding and a fair executive.

always (adv) at all times, without exception
Fred has many interests and is *always* going somewhere.

4.72 **allowed** (v) permitted
The company *allowed* him to take two weeks' vacation.

aloud (adv) a manner of speaking
Since Frank enjoys talking, he presented the entire report *aloud*.

4.73 **all together** (adj) collectively, everyone in a group
The crew boarded the ship *all together*.

altogether (adv) entirely, absolutely
He *altogether* rejected the advice.

4.74 **altar** (n) a raised structure as a centre of religious worship
The couple took their vows before the *altar*.

alter (v) to change
It is against the law to *alter* the reading on an automobile odometer.

4.75 **annual** (adj) yearly
The *annual* cocktail party has been a tradition for fifty years.

annul (v) to cancel
She tried to *annul* the agreement after the argument.

4.76 **any way** (n) any manner or fashion
Local industries were forbidden to pollute the river in *any way*.

anyway (adv) nevertheless, in any case
Anyway, she made every effort to win the contest.

4.77 **appraise** (v) to estimate the value of
He requested the assessor to *appraise* the property.

apprise (v) to inform
Be sure to *apprise* the buyers of the exact closing fees.

4.78 **are** (v) plural present tense of verb *to be*
The Hafners *are* leaving the province and will settle in Manitoba.

hour (n) time of day
The party broke up at a late *hour*.

our (pron) possessive pronoun; first person plural
Our home was not destroyed by the flood.

4.79 **assistance** (n) help or support
Please call us whenever you need *assistance* in making your household purchases.

assistants (n) helpers
My *assistants,* Joan de la Cruz and George Retana, are experienced interior designers.

4.80 **attendance** (n) the fact of, or number, attending
The seminar had 350 professors in *attendance*.

attendants (n) persons who wait on others
Ambassadors usually travel with a large group of *attendants*.

4.81 **biannual** (adj) twice a year
The *biannual* report is published on March 15 and September 15.

biennial (adj) every other year
Since the statistical material is not published annually, the *biennial* report is important.

4.82 **bibliography** (n) list of writings pertaining to a given subject or author.
The *bibliography* is always at the back of the book.

biography (n) written history of a person's life
Historian Donald Creighton has probably written the best-known *biography* of John A. Macdonald, Canada's first prime minister.

4.83 **canvas** (n) closely woven cloth
Covering the boat with *canvas* will protect it from the elements.

canvass (v) to examine or solicit
Volunteers will *canvass* their neighbourhoods for charitable contributions.

4.84 **capital** (adj) important; punishable by death; excellent
(n) wealth; seat of government (city)
The *capital* point of his paper was the need for energy conservation.

In some American states, premeditated murder is still a *capital* crime.

Moby Dick is a *capital* novel.

Adrian Bradshaw had $50 000 in *capital* to expand his business.

St. John's is the *capital* of Newfoundland.

capitol (n) buildings in which the U.S. state governments function
The state legislature meets on the second floor of the *capitol*.

Capitol (n) building in which the federal American government meets
As a U.S. senator, Mr. Schweiker spends much time at the *Capitol*.

4.85 **casual** (adj) incidental, happening by chance, not planned
Unlike the other office trips, this sudden visit by the manager was most *casual*.

causal (adj) pertaining to a cause
There was a direct *causal* relationship between the discovery of a polio vaccine and the rapid decline of the polio disease.

4.86 **cease** (v) to discontinue
Because of increasing costs, we will have to *cease* publishing a weekly newsletter.

seize (v) to confiscate or capture
The police *seized* the suspect's gun collection after his arrest.

4.87 **censor** (n) official who removes objectionable material
In an unfree society, the *censor's* job is important.

censure (n) a judgement involving condemnation
(v) to criticize adversely; to disapprove of or dispraise
Several academy members used their power of *censure* during the demonstration.

Members of the reviewing committee have the authority to *censure* textbooks not suitable for use in schools.

4.88 **cite** (v) to quote
You may *cite* the encyclopaedia as your source of reference.

sight (n) vision
Although he was over ninety years old, his *sight* was excellent.

site (n) location
The *site* chosen for the summer cottage was perfect in every respect.

4.89 **complement** (n) that which completes
Now that a new vice-president has been named, the executive staff has a full *complement* of personnel.

compliment (n) praise
(v) to praise
His immediate superior gave John a well-deserved *compliment* on his presentation.

Robin was *complimented* several times after she won the steeplechase.

4.90 **conscience** (n) one's awareness of moral implications
The jurors, with clear *consciences,* found the defendants not guilty on all counts.

conscious (adj) aware
McGee's supervisors had been *conscious* of his absenteeism for the past two months.

4.91 **consul** (n) representative for a nation's commercial interests
The French *consul* was asked to discuss several Common Market problems with the prime minister.

council (n) group of elected or appointed advisers
The city *council,* which meets every two weeks, gave the mayor some good suggestions.

counsel (n) advice
(v) advise
After receiving the letter, he went to his attorney for *counsel.*

The personnel director's job was to *counsel* new employees.

4.92 **correspondence** (n) letters or other communications
Please return these documents to the *correspondence* files.

correspondents (n) letter writers; distant news reporters
Our foreign *correspondents* are scattered throughout the world.

4.93 **credible** (adj) believable
The plaintiff's defence was *credible* to the jury.

creditable (adj) deserving of praise
His hard work achieved the most *creditable* sales record in the office.

credulous (adj) too ready to believe, easily deceived
His lack of experience perhaps accounts for his *credulous* personality.

4.94 **decent** (adj) adequate
Without a high school education, no one can expect to earn a *decent* living.

descent (n) a downward step; one's derivation from an ancestor
The politician's *descent* into corruption was slow but steady.

Pierre Gant is an Englishman of French *descent.*

dissent (v) to differ in opinion
(n) difference of opinion
Their intention was to *dissent* from the majority opinion.

There was much *dissent* among the three candidates

4.95 **depositary** (n) person entrusted with something
The executor of the estate was named *depositary* of the funds.

depository (n) place of safekeeping
Use the bank's night *depository* for your cash and cheques.

4.96 **desert** (n) dry area
(v) to abandon
A number of camels were seen on the *desert*.

He was the type of man who would not *desert* a friend.

dessert (n) final course in a meal
They served ice cream and cake for *dessert*.

4.97 **device** (n) instrument; plan
That tool is a good *device* to use in fixing the kitchen table.

The animated toys in the window served as an effective *device* to draw people into the store.

devise (v) to contrive
The car is so old that the mechanic will have to *devise* a new part to repair it.

4.98 **disapprove** (v) to pass unfavourable judgment upon
That committee, led by its chairperson, was the first to *disapprove* our newest proposal.

disprove (v) to prove something false
The attorney successfully *disproved* the allegations submitted in the complaint.

4.99 **disburse** (v) to pay out
The company had to *disburse* $350 for reprographic supplies.

disperse (v) to spread or scatter
The advertising department will *disperse* fliers to the appropriate markets.

4.100 **dual** (adj) double
The actor played a *dual* role—both father and son.

duel (n) a conflict or combat
Some would rather fight a *duel* of wits than a *duel* with pistols or swords.

4.101 **elicit** (v) to draw forth
Let the mediators try to *elicit* the facts from the union officials.

illicit (adj) unlawful
There was speculation that the merger was *illicit*.

4.102 **emigrate** (v) to leave a country
Will more French citizens *emigrate* to other countries?

immigrate (v) to enter a country
In the past several decades, relatively few people have been allowed to *immigrate* to the U.S.

4.103 **eminent** (adj) conspicuous; famous
Stone walls are an *eminent* feature of the New England landscape.

His mother was an *eminent* surgeon who had saved many lives.

imminent (adj) threatening or impending
Gasoline and oil price increases are *imminent.*

4.104 **envelop** (v) to enclose
The fire had begun to *envelop* the firefighters on top of the hill.

envelope (n) container for letters
The quality of the *envelope* should match that of the stationery.

4.105 **every day** (n) each day
Every day made a difference in her recovery from the operation.

everyday (adj) daily
He did fifty push-ups as an *everyday* routine.

4.106 **exceed** (v) to extend outside of or enlarge beyond; to surpass
Automobile drivers should not *exceed* the posted 60 km/h limits.

accede (v) to express approval or give consent
The minority group had to *accede* to the wishes of the majority in budget allocations for the fiscal year.

4.107 **expand** (v) to spread out, open wide; to unfold; to increase
We should *expand* the width of the freeway to allow more lanes of through traffic.

expend (v) to spend, pay out, or distribute; to consume by use
Efficient office workers should not have to *expend* much physical energy in performing their work.

4.108 **farther** (adj) at a greater distance
The planet Neptune is *farther* from the sun than Jupiter.

further (adv) in addition, moreover
(adj) additional, extending beyond
(v) to promote or advance

It is *further* understood that a $1 000 deposit will be paid by the tenth.

If our competitors expand their market *further* west, they will soon have the entire district.

Successful executives are those who continue their educations to *further* their careers.

4.109 **foreword** (n) preface

The *foreword* to the book was well written.

forward (adj) situated in advance
(adv) toward what is before or in front
(v) to advance or transmit

He chose a *forward* seat on the plane.

The troops moved *forward* at the command of General Smith.

Please *forward* three copies of the book.

4.110 **formally** (adv) in a formal manner

The new senator *formally* assumes office on January 20.

formerly (adv) before

She was *formerly* the mayor of a large city.

4.111 **forth** (adv) forward

The troops showed their bravery when they went *forth* in battle.

fourth (adj) number

Fred was the *fourth* member of his family to attend Dalhousie University.

4.112 **incidence** (n) rate of occurrence

The *incidence* of drug use among young people is alarming.

incidents (n) events

Several unfortunate *incidents* involving alcohol preceded his dismissal from the job.

4.113 **indigenous** (adj) native

The Iroquois were *indigenous* to North America particularly around Ontario, Quebec, and New York State.

indigent (adj) needy

The *indigent* citizens in the city's east end were without adequate housing facilities.

4.114 **ingenious** (adj) clever
The self-correcting typewriter is an *ingenious* device.

ingenuous (adj) natural, naive
He was remarkably *ingenuous* in his assumption that car salespeople were always truthful.

4.115 **interprovincial** (adj) between provinces
Regulation of *interprovincial* commerce is one of that ministry's major functions.

intraprovincial (adj) within a province
The premier's main responsibility is to concentrate on *intraprovincial* affairs.

4.116 **its** (pron) possessive pronoun
The car's old battery is *its* main problem.

it's (contraction) it is
It's a great day to go swimming.

4.117 **knew** (v) past tense of the verb to know
He *knew* Paul Smythe for many years.

new (adj) recent
They buy a *new* car every fall.

4.118 **later** (adv) after a particular time; at another time
John Chow-Kim was seen *later* in the Information Systems Centre.

Enroll in the accounting course now or *later*.

latter (adj) relating to the second of two items
The Cambridge and Kitchener representatives will plan the conference; the *latter* group will host the dinner meeting.

4.119 **lay** (v) to set or put down
Please *lay* the report on my desk.

lie (v) to recline
Lie with your feet above your head for improved circulation.

4.120 **leased** (v) granted or held for a term
The Al Turnbull family *leased* the condominium for a three-month period.

least (adj) lowest, smallest
The orchestra seats were the most expensive in the theatre; the balcony seats were the *least* expensive.

We were *least* impressed with the manner in which the lecturer presented her ideas.

4.121 **lessen** (v) to minimize or decrease
Receipt of a new government contract would *lessen* the chances of worker layoffs next year.

lesson (n) a unit of instruction
The *lesson* for the day was on caring for indoor plants.

4.122 **liable** (adj) responsible or susceptible
The company was held *liable* for the accident because of its negligence in providing safety precautions.

libel (n) a defamatory statement in writing
The employer's negative report was presented as evidence of *libel*.

4.123 **local** (adj) nearby, neighbourhood
Brogan's Drugs has been in the *local* area for many years.

locale (n) location, site, situation
The *locale* for next year's convention is Montreal.

4.124 **loose** (adj) not tightly bound
The front porch has a *loose* board, and Angus tripped over it.

lose (v) to suffer loss or deprivation
Though Herbert always tries to be careful, he managed to *lose* his watch.

If Peter is not more alert, the team will *lose* another game.

4.125 **maybe** (adv) perhaps
Maybe he'll make a trip to Thunder Bay.

may be (v) [auxiliary verb plus verb]
Alfredo *may be* able to make the trip to St. John's.

4.126 **overdo** (v) to do something to excess
Some actors have a tendency to *overdo* their gestures.

overdue (adj) past due
John's *overdue* phone bill caused him much embarrassment.

4.127 **passed** (v) moved or transferred
He *passed* the book along to his best friend.

past (adj) former; recently elapsed
(prep) beyond
(n) time gone by
(adv) so as to reach and go beyond a point
Dorothy is the *past* president of the faculty club.

Carla could see *past* the pier to the boats moored in the bay.

Each nation celebrates great events from its *past*.

Do not drive *past* the detour sign ahead.

4.128 **personal** (adj) private
He had a *personal* problem that he refused to discuss with anyone.

personnel (n) employees
The bank *personnel* were delighted with the increase in salary.

4.129 **principal** (adj) most important
(n) school administrator; capital placed at interest
The double indemnity clause was the *principal* article they quoted.

Mr. Jones, formerly an English teacher, is the high school *principal*.

John borrowed money from the bank, and he pays a high interest on the *principal*.

principle (n) rule
In making a decision of this type, one should consider the *principle* of probability.

4.130 **residence** (n) structure that serves as a home
The Bertrams have a beautiful *residence* in the country.

residents (n) individuals living in a particular place
The apartment house was large enough to accommodate several hundred *residents*.

4.131 **respectfully** (adv) with a reverence or respect
I *respectfully* request a one-month leave of absence.

respectively (adv) each in the order given
Reggie and Kalman are from Sarnia and Waterloo, *respectively*.

4.132 **role** (n) part in a play
Michael is a natural actor; therefore, he had a leading *role* in the play.

roll (n) list
The *roll* names outstanding graduates from the local college.

4.133 **set** (v) to place
She *set* the briefcase on the desk.

sit (v) to rest in a seated position
He was so tired that he decided to *sit* on the floor.

4.134 **some time** (n) a period of time
To do the job properly I will need some time.

sometime (adv) at some unspecified point of time
I'll finish the job sometime next week.

4.135 **spacious** (adj) having ample room
The living room was *spacious* enough to accommodate two large sofas.

specious (adj) apparently good or right but without real merit
The judge told the lawyer his argument was *specious* and unacceptable.

4.136 **stationary** (adj) still, not moving
The beagle remained *stationary* until the hunters flushed their quarry.

stationery (n) writing paper
Company policy requires the use of white *stationery* only.

4.137 **suit** (n) a court action
(v) to adapt or to agree
The lawyer filed a *suit* on behalf of his client.

Our present plant facilities should *suit* our needs in the future.

4.138 **than** (conj) used with the second member of a comparison
(prep) in comparison with
Developing a new set of blueprints is more expensive today *than* it was several years ago.

An electric typewriter is faster *than* a manual.

then (adv) at that time; as a necessary consequence
(n) that time
I would prefer to attend at 8 a.m. if a seat is available *then*.

Check these figures; *then* you can vouch for their accuracy.

The authors decided to submit the manuscript on May 1; publication would be scheduled a year from *then*.

4.139 **their** (pron) [possessive, third person plural]
Their blazers certainly are well-tailored.

there (adv) in or at that place
(n) that point
John was sitting over *there*.

"You take it from *there,* Dan," suggested the coach.

they're (contraction) they are
They're going to face some stiff competition.

4.140 **therefor** (adv) for or in return for that
The sum of $450 will be paid to the contractor by the owner; in consideration *therefor* the contractor will begin construction by January 10.

therefore (adv) consequently
The trucking company went on a three-week strike; *therefore,* all shipments are on backlog.

4.141 **through** (prep) from end to end of, from beginning to end
The soldiers marched *through* the town.

thorough (adj) complete, all that is needed
The doctor made a *thorough* examination of his patient.

threw (v) did throw
She *threw* a fast ball to the catcher.

4.142 **to** (prep) direction
(adv) indicates direction toward
Invite students from nearby schools *to* the bank for field trips.

The children ran *to* and fro in the field.

too (adv) excessively; also
Some employees use their coffee-break time *too* freely.

I, *too,* believe that a certified public accounting firm should be called in immediately.

two (adj) a given number
Two men were looking at the accident.

4.143 **waive** (v) to give up, refrain from claiming or pressing
The lawyer *waived* his privileges of cross-examinations.

wave (n) a swell of water
The last *wave* tipped the canoe.

wave (v) to gesture
She *waved* him away with an imperious gesture.

4.144 **weak** (adj) lack of skill or strength
John was in the hospital for two months, and he was indeed *weak* when he came home.

week (n) period of seven days
Fran spent one *week* of her vacation in Cape Breton.

4.145 **weather** (n) atmosphere or climate
The *weather* was so beautiful that the family went swimming.

whether (conj) if
Because of a recent illness, Arnold couldn't decide *whether* or not to make the trip.

4.146 **whose** (pron) [possessive]
Whose pencil are you using?

who's (contraction) who is
Who's going to the bank to make the deposit?

4.147 **your** (pron) [possessive, second person singular and plural]
Your desk always looks so neat.

you're (contraction) you are
You're going to the store, aren't you?

Abbreviations 5

Introduction

5.1 Basic guidelines for the use of abbreviations are:

1. Use the generally accepted forms of abbreviations, as listed in the dictionary or other reference.

2. Be consistent in using an abbreviation. Some abbreviations may be written in different ways, but the same form should be used throughout a typewritten document.

Acronyms

5.2 An acronym is a word formed from the first letters or syllables of other words, such as UNESCO (United Nations Educational, Scientific, and Cultural Organization). Unlike abbreviations, which are pronounced letter by letter, acronyms are pronounced like words and can be used any time. Most acronyms are written in capital letters and without periods.

SALT	Strategic Arms Limitation Talks
ZIP	Zone Improvement Plan (U.S. mail code)
NATO	North Atlantic Treaty Organization

Broadcasting stations

5.3 Radio and television broadcasting stations are known by their call letters. These call letters are written in capital letters with no periods or spaces between them.

BBC (British Broadcasting Corporation)	CHTN
CKEY	CFQR-FM
CBC	CFRN-TV

Calendar dates

5.4 Months of the year and days of the week should not be abbreviated except within tables, financial documents, or where space is limited. If abbreviations must be used, follow the guidelines below.

5.5 Days may be abbreviated as follows:

Sun.	Thu. or Thurs.
Mon.	Fri.
Tue. or Tues.	Sat.
Wed.	

Note that when space is very tight, the days may be abbreviated without periods.

5.6 With the exception of the months of May, June, and July, the months can be abbreviated as follows:

Jan.	Apr.	(July)	Oct.
Feb.	(May)	Aug.	Nov.
Mar.	(June)	Sept.	Dec.

Compass points

5.7 Compass points written within sentences as adjectives and nouns should be spelled in full.

The aircraft made an emergency landing somewhere in the *northwest*.

Our new site will be the *southeast* corner of Dorchester and Peel.

5.8 Compass points preceding a street name in an address are spelled in full.

1570 East Colorado Boulevard

5.9 When compass points follow the street name in addresses, use the abbreviated forms. Capitalize each letter and use periods after each letter.

1263 Queen St. E.
1401 Sixteenth Street N.W.

Business Terms

5.10 The following abbreviations are frequently used in business communications.

ad. val., A/V	ad valorem (according to value)
B/E	bill of exchange
b.l., B/L	bill of lading
B/S	bill of sale
c.i.f., CIF	cost, insurance, freight
c.l., CL	carload
c.o., c/o	in care of
c.o.d., C.O.D.	cash on delivery
dr.	debit

E. and O.E.	errors and omissions excepted
e.o.m., EOM	end of month
f.o.b., FOB	free on board
L.C.L.	less than carload
mfg.	manufacturing
N.B.	nota bene (note well)
n/c, NC	no charge
NSF	not sufficient funds
n/30	net in 30 days
w.b., W.B.	way bill

Data processing terminology

5.11 Specialized data processing terms and their abbreviations include the following.

ADP	automatic data processing
ALGOL	algorithmic oriented language
ALU	arithmetic logical unit
ARU	audio-response unit
COBOL	common business oriented language
CRT	cathode ray tube
EAM	electrical accounting machine
EDP	electronic data processing
EDST	elastic diaphragm switch technology
EMD	Environmental Monitoring Device
EOF	end of file
FORTRAN	formula translation system
IDP	integrated data processing
I/O	input-output
MICR	magnetic ink character recognition
OCR	optical character reader

Degrees

5.12 Abbreviations of degrees have a period after each element in the abbreviation, but no internal spacing. Where academic degrees follow a person's name, do not use titles such as *Dr.*, *Mr.*, or *Ms.* before the name; but note that other titles may precede the name if they do not have the same meaning as the degree that follows. For example:

Dean Margaret Knittl, Ph.D.
Professor Gary Stern, M.B.A.
the Reverend Dr. Fader

Some common degrees are abbreviated as follows:

A.C.C.A.	Association of Certified and Corporate Accountants
B.A. or A.B.	Bachelor of Arts (Artium Baccalaureus)
B. Arch.	Bachelor of Architecture
B.Ed.	Bachelor of Education
B.S. or B.Sc.	Bachelor of Science
C.A.	Chartered Accountant
C.L.U.	Chartered Life Underwriter
D.D.S.	Doctor of Dental Surgery
D.Eng.	Doctor of Engineering
P.Eng.	Professional Engineer
D.P.Ec.	Doctor of Political Economy
F.I.I.C.	Fellow of the Insurance Institute of Canada
F.R.C.M.	Fellow of the Royal College of Music
L.L.B.	Bachelor of Laws (Legum Baccalaureus)
L.L.D.	Doctor of Laws (Legum Doctor)
M.A.	Master of Arts
M.Com.	Master of Commerce
M.D.	Doctor of Medicine
M.L.S.	Master of Library Science
Mus. Doc. or Mus.D.	Doctor of Music
Ph.D.	Doctor of Philosophy
Phm.B.	Bachelor of Pharmacy
R.N.	Registered Nurse
Th.D.	Doctor of Theology
V.S.	Veterinary Surgeon

Foreign expressions

5.13 The following are abbreviations for some foreign expressions used in business. Because these expressions are common enough to appear in the dictionary, they are not underscored.

ad hoc	''for a particular purpose''
a.m.	ante meridian; ''before noon''
cf.	confer, meaning compare
e.g.	exempli gratia; ''for example''
et al.	et alii; ''and other people''
et seq.	et sequens; ''and the following'' et sequentes; ''those that follow''
etc.	et cetera; ''and so forth''
ibid.	ibidem; ''in the same place''

idem	"the same"
i.e.	id est; "that is"
loc. cit.	loco citato; "in the place cited"
op. cit.	opere citato; "in the work cited"
P.S.	postscriptum; "postscript"
quid pro quo	one thing in return for another; compensation
R.S.V.P.	réspondez s'il vous plait; "please reply"
re	"regarding" or "in the matter of"
viz.	videlicet; "namely"
vs., v.	versus

Geographic names

5.14 Geographic names are usually abbreviated only for use in tables, business forms, and occasionally in correspondence when necessary. *Exception:* U.S.S.R. is most often used in place of the full name, Union of Soviet Socialist Republics.

5.15 Note also that two-letter abbreviations (for example, IN for Indiana) were created by the U.S. and Canadian postal services and can only be used (for either states or provinces) when accompanied by the postal or zip code.

Note that the two-letter abbreviations have no periods and are written in capitals (see 5.17 and 5.18).

5.16 Geographic names are generally abbreviated by capitalizing the first letter of each word in the name.

If the abbreviation has more than just single initials, space once after each internal period.

S. Dak.   W. Va.

If there are only single initials, a period is put after each initial but there are no spaces between the initials.

U.S.S.R.   U.S.A.   U.K.

5.17 Names of Canadian provinces and territories are abbreviated as follows.

Provinces and Territories	Abbreviations Standard (Preferred)	Two-letter
Alberta	Alta.	AB
British Columbia	B.C.	BC
Labrador (part of Newfoundland)	Lab.	LB
Manitoba	Man.	MB
New Brunswick	N.B.	NB
Newfoundland	Nfld.	NF
Northwest Territories	N.W.T.	NT
Nova Scotia	N.S.	NS
Ontario	Ont.	ON
Prince Edward Island	P.E.I.	PE
Quebec	P.Q. or Que.	PQ
Saskatchewan	Sask.	SK
Yukon Territory	Yuk.	YT

5.18 Names of states, districts, and territories of the United States are abbreviated as follows. (The two-letter U.S. Postal Service abbreviations must appear on all envelope addresses.)

States, Districts, and Territories	Abbreviations Standard	Two-letter
Alabama	Ala.	AL
Alaska	Alaska	AK
Arizona	Ariz.	AZ
Arkansas	Ark.	AR
California	Calif.	CA
Canal Zone	C.Z.	CZ
Colorado	Colo.	CO
Connecticut	Conn.	CT
Delaware	Del.	DE
District of Columbia	D.C.	DC
Florida	Fla.	FL
Georgia	Ga.	GA
Guam	Guam	GU
Hawaii	Hawaii	HI
Idaho	Idaho	ID
Illinois	Ill.	IL
Indiana	Ind.	IN
Iowa	Iowa	IA
Kansas	Kans.	KS

States, Districts, and Territories	Abbreviations Standard	Two-letter
Kentucky	Ky.	KY
Louisiana	La.	LA
Maine	Maine	ME
Maryland	Md.	MD
Massachusetts	Mass.	MA
Michigan	Mich.	MI
Minnesota	Minn.	MN
Mississippi	Miss.	MS
Missouri	Mo.	MO
Montana	Mont.	MT
Nebraska	Neb.	NE
Nevada	Nev.	NV
New Hampshire	N.H.	NH
New Jersey	N.J.	NJ
New Mexico	N. Mex.	NM
New York	N.Y.	NY
North Carolina	N.C.	NC
North Dakota	N. Dak.	ND
Ohio	Ohio	OH
Oklahoma	Okla.	OK
Oregon	Oreg.	OR
Pennsylvania	Pa.	PA
Puerto Rico	P.R.	PR
Rhode Island	R.I.	RI
South Carolina	S.C.	SC
South Dakota	S. Dak.	SD
Tennessee	Tenn.	TN
Texas	Tex.	TX
Utah	Utah	UT
Vermont	Vt.	VT
Virgin Islands	V.I.	VI
Virginia	Va.	VA
Washington	Wash.	WA
West Virginia	W. Va.	WV
Wisconsin	Wis.	WI
Wyoming	Wyo.	WY

Government agencies

5.19 Abbreviations for some government agencies are listed below. These abbreviations are usually written in capital letters with no periods or spaces after the letters.

AEC	Atomic Energy of Canada
CBC	Canadian Broadcasting Corporation
CBDC	Cape Breton Development Corporation
CCC	Canadian Commercial Corporations
CEIC	Canada Employment and Immigration Commission
CFDC	Canadian Film Development Corporation
CIDA	Canadian International Development Agency
CJC	Canadian Judicial Council
CNR	Canadian National Railways
CMHC	Canada Mortgage and Housing Corporation
CRTC	Canadian Radio-Television and Telecommunications Commission
CWB	Canadian Wheat Board
ECC	Economic Council of Canada
IJC	International Joint Commission
MRC	Medical Research Council of Canada
NFB	National Film Board
NMC	National Museums of Canada
RCM	Royal Canadian Mint
SCC	Science Council of Canada
Stat Can	Statistics Canada
Air Canada	)
Canada Council	) No abbreviation
Parks Canada	)

Organized groups

5.20 Many business, professional organizations, associations, and other organized groups are known by their abbreviated names. In such cases, all letters in the abbreviated name are capitalized. Generally, no periods or spaces are used within the abbreviation.

ACBC	Associated Credit Bureaus of Canada
ACTRA	Association of Canadian Television and Radio Artists
CAA	Canadian Automobile Association
CBA	Canadian Bankers' Association
CCLA	Canadian Civil Liberties Association
CIIA	Canadian Institute for International Affairs
CJC	Canadian Jewish Congress
CLC	Canadian Labour Congress
CMA	Canadian Manufacturers' Association

CMA	Canadian Medical Association
CMHA	Canadian Mental Health Association
CNIB	Canadian National Institute for the Blind
CRFSA	Canadian Restaurant and Food Services Association
CSAE	Canadian Society of Agricultural Engineering
CUPE	Canadian Union of Public Employees
HUDAC	Housing and Urban Development Association of Canada
IIC	Insurance Institute of Canada
IODE	Imperial Order of Daughters of the Empire
IOF	Independent Order of Foresters
IOOF	Independent Order of Odd Fellows
SCM	Student Christian Movement
SPCA	Society for the Prevention of Cruelty to Animals
SSRC	Social Science Research Council of Canada
UN	United Nations
YMCA	Young Men's Christian Association

Personal names

5.21 Some people prefer to use the abbreviated forms of their given names in correspondence and in their signatures. Space once after the period before typing the last name.

Chas.	Charles	Jas.	James	Thos.	Thomas
Edw.	Edward or Edwin	Jos.	Joseph	Wm.	William
Geo.	George	Robt.	Robert		

5.22 Some people use initials in place of their first and/or middle names. Space once after each period after an initial.

J. G. Muha   Nancy P. Lee   J. Donald Curry

Personal titles

5.23 A personal title written before a complete name is written in its abbreviated form. One space follows the period after the abbreviation.

Mr. Norman Rittgers	Ms. Kathy Tyner
Mrs. Rosalba Salinas	Dr. Kenneth Zimmer

5.24 Except for the titles *Mr.*, *Mrs.*, *Ms.*, *Messrs.*, and *Mmes.*, personal titles written alone before a surname are spelled out.

Reverend Bingham	*but*	Rev. Jimmy Bingham
Doctor Bray	*but*	Dr. Alice Bray

Numbers and Symbols 

Introduction

6.1 Guidelines are provided in this section for typing numbers (as words and as numerals) as well as various symbols commonly used by office workers.

Numbers

Figures under 10

6.2 In general, numbers between one and ten are spelled out in full.

Figures over 10

6.3 Numbers above ten are written in figures.

28 students 2278 replies
10 000 glasses 128 634 voters

One-word numbers

6.4 Note that numbers which can be written as one word are often spelled out.

eight cows twenty corn
five students forty tires

6.5 The plurals of figures are formed by adding *s* alone.

the 1980s

The plurals of spelled-out numbers are formed like the plurals of other nouns.

His parents are in their forties.

Related numbers

6.6 It is important to write related numbers consistently. In a sentence, if numbers first appear in word form, express all numbers in word-style. If figures are used first, use figure-style. Note that numbers above ten are usually expressed in figures. For example:

Only 185 of the 1000 seats in that theatre were occupied.

Sue bought three oranges and ten apples.

I sent out 46 invitations but only 32 returned.

Use spaces not commas

6.7 It is still common to see large numbers written with commas. However, use of metric number style, which groups large numbers by means of a space, is becoming increasingly popular.

Reading from right to left, spaces group digits by threes in whole numbers of five or more digits.

682 745 10 926 367

Note that the space is optional in 4-digit numbers—except when they are aligned in a column.

4965 [acceptable by itself]

But note in the following column:

4 965 [space required for alignment]
611 638
29 262

Numbers with abbreviations or symbols

6.8 Numbers written with abbreviations or symbols are indicated in figures.

5 doz. $14 @ $1.02 1 kg #2 6 p.m.

Numbers with time

6.9 Use figures with abbreviations of time. Otherwise, the time can be spelled out.

8:30 a.m. 9 p.m. nine in the morning

Street addresses

6.10 Use figures for house and building numbers in street addresses except the number one, which should be spelled out. Use figures for numbered streets beginning with 13. A hyphen should be placed between a house or building number and a numbered street. Do not use *th* and *st* after numerals.

One East Twelfth Street 2 East 13 Street
2 West Twelfth Street 751 - 34 Street

Postal codes

6.11 The postal code (see 14.3 and Figure 14-1 for fuller explanation of how to use postal code) is inserted two spaces after the name of the province—or preferably typed on a line by itself.

Regina, Saskatchewan S4T 1B8

or

Regina, Saskatchewan
S4T 1B8

To begin sentences

6.12 When a sentence starts with a number, spell the number out—regardless of the number of words it takes. If possible, however, avoid beginning a sentence with a number.

Thirty-eight people were invited to the party at the Joneses, and everyone attended.

The Joneses invited 38 people to their party, and everyone attended.

Dates

6.13 When the day follows the month, use numerals only. When the day precedes the month, use numerals and the *-st, -nd, -rd,* or *-th* endings.

February 22   22nd of February

6.14 When a date consists of a month and year, do not use a comma after the month. When the day is included, use a comma.

The December 1975 issue of that magazine featured an excellent article about sun spots.

John mailed his income tax cheque on April 16, 1979.

Numeric dating

6.15 Numeric dating is a simple means of reporting a date entirely in numbers. The year, month, and day are expressed by eight digits—four for the year, two for the month, and two for the day.

August 2, 1978	February 27, 1980
becomes	**becomes**
1978 08 02	1980 02 27

Decimals

6.16 Decimal amounts should be written in figures with the decimal marker (i.e. a period) positioned on the line. The metric system is decimal in nature. Therefore, use decimals rather than mixed fractions to express metric measures.

3.75 305.085 5396.174

Note that, unlike Canada, many countries use a comma as a decimal marker.

6.17 Always place a zero to the left of the decimal point in numbers less than one.

0.75 kL 0.6241

6.18 Do not add extra zeros to the right of any decimal figures except when the numbers are aligned in columns or exact measures are required.

12.040
1.000
3.875

6.19 Use a space to group digits to the right of the decimal point. Group by threes from left to right.

1.976 05
62 349.205 49

Note that a space is optional in a decimal number of four digits except when it must be aligned in a column.

4.9762 [acceptable by itself]

But: 2.670 89
4.976 20 [space required for alignment]
6.700 33

Fractions

6.20 Fractions written with whole numbers are expressed in figures. Fractions used without whole numbers are spelled out except in a series. When whole numbers are typed with fractions made on the typewriter, a space separates the whole number from the fraction so the number is read correctly. A hyphen may also be used to separate the whole number from the fraction. (See also 9.27.)

8 4/5 or 8-4/5 three-fourths of the stock 1/4 = 3/12

6.21 Most typewriters have the fractions $\frac{1}{4}$ and $\frac{1}{2}$ on the keyboard. When only these two fractions occur within business communications and reports, the typewriter fractions may be used. However, when $\frac{1}{4}$ and $\frac{1}{2}$ are used with other fractions, all fractions should be made with the figures and diagonal for consistency of form.

Incorrect: 7/8 + 2/3 + 5$\frac{1}{2}$ = ?
Correct: 7/8 + 2/3 + 5 1/2 = ?

Hyphenated numbers

6.22 Numbers from 21 to 99 are hyphenated when written out, as is any number that is part of an adjective compound.

twenty-one   forty-two thousand
one hundred eighty-three   thirty-cent stamp

6.23 Use hyphens to connect figures representing a continuous sequence, as in calendar dates and page numbers. Do not space before or after the hyphen. The hyphen takes the place of the word *to* in the sequence.

the years 1975-1980   pages 11-18

6.24 The second number of a hyphenated number may be abbreviated if the main number of the second item is the same as the first.

1970-78	instead of	1970-1978
pages 204-11	instead of	pages 204-211

6.25 Do not, however, abbreviate the second number of the sequence if the first number contains two zeros or if the second number begins with a new series of digits.

1970-2001   pages 200-264

Dollars

6.26 Type the dollar sign immediately before the amount. Do not use a decimal point or zeros after an even dollar amount unless a high degree of exactness is required.

$15 $278

John has a balance of $2836 in his savings account.

. . . monthly payments of three hundred ninety-five dollars ($395.00) each.

6.27 When dollar amounts are written in a series, repeat the dollar sign before each amount.

> The quarterly dividends for the past year have been \$1.05, \$1.15, \$1.04, and \$1.02.

6.28 When typing tables or columns of amounts, use the decimal point and zeros after even dollar amounts if there are mixed amounts within the columns. The dollar sign is written next to the first amount, positioned in front of the largest amount in the column. The dollar sign would also be written in the total.

\$ 15.00	\$128.95	\$390
207.06	40.00	30
\$222.06	15.30	198

6.29 The dollar sign should not be used with an amount less than one dollar unless the amount is in a series or a table with amounts greater than one dollar. Instead of the cent symbol, the dollar sign is used with a zero preceding the decimal point.

> John's earnings for shovelling snow were \$0.95, \$1.50, \$0.75, \$2.25, and \$1.85.

6.30 Whenever amounts are written out, the word dollars is written after the amount. Money in round amounts of a million or more may be expressed partially in words.

> \$12 million thirty-five dollars

Cents

6.31 Write out the word *cents* for amounts under a dollar. Spell out numbers between one and ten (see 6.2–6.4) as well as those that can be written in one word. Otherwise, use figures with the word cents.

> three cents 98 cents

6.32 Use the cents symbol (¢) and numerals on invoices, purchase orders, and other business forms.

> 39¢ 14¢

Ordinal

6.33 Ordinal numbers that can be written in one or two words should be spelled out; otherwise, the figures are used with the ordinal endings.

first	tenth	350th
hundredth	twenty-fifth	three thousandth

Percentages

6.34 Percentages are written in figures (unless they begin a sentence), and the word *percent* is spelled out.

The credit manager approved a 5 percent discount for us.

Ten percent of the students had never taken typewriting in high school.

6.35 Percentages of less than one percent should be written out or converted into decimal equivalents.

three-fourths of a percent	0.75 percent
one-half of 1 percent	0.5 percent

6.36 Fractional percentages of more than one percent are expressed in figures, either with the whole number and the fraction or as the decimal equivalent.

9 1/2 percent	9.5 percent
10 3/4 percent	10.75 percent

6.37 When hyphens are used to connect percentages representing a continuous sequence or a range, the word *percent* is written after the last percentage. If, however, the percent symbol (%) is used with the percentages, it must be used with each percentage figure.

15-20 percent
15% to 20%
returns of up to 15, 20, and 25 percent
returns of up to 15%, 20%, and 25%

Ratios and proportions

6.38 Numbers indicating ratios and proportions are written in figures.

5 to 1 ratio or 5:1 ratio
odds of 1000 to 1

Roman numerals

6.39 Roman numerals are formed as follows:

1	I	50	L
2	II	60	LX
4	IV	90	XC
5	V	100	C
6	VI	400	CD
9	IX	500	D

10	X	600	DC
11	XI	800	DCCC
14	XIV	900	CM
30	XXX	1000	M
40	XL	1975	MCMLXXV
41	XLI	2000	MM

6.40 Roman numerals used to indicate major divisions in outlines are written with a period and two spaces after them. Roman numerals in outlines and in columns of information are aligned at the right.

I.
II.
III.

6.41 Roman numerals are also sometimes used to indicate chapter numbers, volumes of books, years, and family heritage of names.

I. Philosophy [first major division in an outline]
Chapter III
Volume VI
ii [small numerals for prefatory pages]
MCMLXXI [1971]
Charles L. Steel, III

Round numbers

6.42 Use words rather than figures to indicate round numbers.

Never in a million years will this happen again.
Approximately five hundred men work in this plant.

Successive numbers

6.43 When two numbers are used successively in a sentence, write out the smaller number and use figures for the larger number, if possible. Otherwise, try to write the sentence so a comma may be inserted between the numbers.

John bought 8 two-cent stamps at the post office.

Of the eight, three men were experienced in telephone technician work.

Time

6.44 Time periods are usually expressed in words.

ten seconds five days
three minutes six months

6.45 **When precise units of time must be expressed, use figures.**

30-day overdue obligation
2 years, 6 months, 5 days

6.46 **The words *noon* or *midnight* and abbreviations *a.m.* or *p.m.* are used to express 12-hour clock times.**

7:55 a.m. 12 noon
10:45 p.m. 12 midnight

6.47 **When *o'clock* is used to report 12-hour clock time, the time may be expressed either in figures or words.**

8 o'clock in the evening	eight o'clock
12 o'clock	twelve o'clock noon
12 o'clock	twelve o'clock midnight

Note that the quickest way to write and read time is with the forms *a.m.* or *p.m.*

He will be arriving at 10 a.m.
He will be arriving at ten o'clock in the morning.

6.48 **When time on the hour is expressed with either *a.m., p.m.,* or *o'clock,* do not add zeros for minutes.**

6 a.m. 6 o'clock
11 p.m. 11 o'clock

This rule is followed when time on the hour is included in a series of times, even though it may appear inconsistent.

The departure times are 6:15 a.m., 10 a.m., and 1:10 p.m.

6.49 **The 24-hour clock is commonly used to report time in computer prepared documents and in schedules of most railways, airlines, and travel agents.**

12-Hour Clock	*24-Hour Clock*
6:30 a.m.	06:30
9:45 a.m.	09:45
12:00 a.m. (noon)	12:00
3:07 p.m.	15:07
8:59 p.m.	20:59
12:00 p.m.	00:00 or 24:00

Units of measure

6.50 See Chapter 11, Units of Measure

Symbols

6.51 Like abbreviations, symbols reduce the time and effort needed to write or type out a given word. This section presents guidelines for using business symbols, mathematical symbols, and proofreader's marks; and instructions for typing some of these symbols.

Business symbols

6.52 Common business symbols include the following.

Symbol	*Definition*	*Example*
'	accent	Busché
&	ampersand (*and* sign)	Merrick & Poore
*	asterisk	1980*
@	at, each	@ 12 cents
( ) ( ) ( )	braces	January) February) $395.00 March)
[ ]	brackets	[Exhibit B]
¢	cent, cents	75¢
©	Copyright	© Collier Macmillan Canada, Inc., 1983
°	degree, degrees	69°
/	diagonal	and/or, either/or 3/4, 15/16, 3 1/4
$	dollar, dollars	$15.00
"	ditto	Grand & Toy 15 desks " 100 chairs
:	is to, ratio	5:1
#	number	#402
%	percent	100%
§	section	UBC §1104

Mathematical symbols

6.53 Common mathematical symbols include the following.

Symbol	*Definition*	*Example*
+	plus	5 + 5
−	minus	10 − 7
±	plus or minus	±6
∓	minus or plus	∓8
×	times	10 × 10
÷	divided by	10 ÷ 4 = 2.5
=	is equal to	10 × 10 = 100
≠	is not equal to	8 ÷ 2 ≠ 3 + 2
≐	is approximately equal to	1 inch ≐ 2.5 cm
>	is greater than	12 > 11
≯	is not greater than	11 ≯ 12
<	is less than	10 < 11
≮	is not less than	11 ≮ 10
∥	is parallel to	Line AB ∥ line CD.
⊥	is perpendicular to	Line BD ⊥ line MN.
∠	angle	∠ABC
∟	right angle	∟ABC measures 90°
△	triangle	△ABC is isosceles
□	square	Line QR intersects □ ABCD.
▭	rectangle	In ▭ HIJK, HI = 10 cm.
○	circle	○A
√	radical, root, square root	$\sqrt{4} = 2$
∛	cube root	$\sqrt[3]{8} = 2$
π	pi	The area of a circle is πr^2.
⬡	hexagon	⬡ ABCDEF

6.54 For metric symbols, see Chapter 11, Units of Measure.

6.55 Proofreaders' marks

Proofreaders' marks are symbols used to indicate any changes in rough draft copy—handwritten or typewritten—before final typing is done.

Symbol	*Definition*	*Example*
cl or ⁀‿	close up the space	no s pace here
tr or ∿	transpose	out of odrer
⊐	move to right	⊐ indent one space
5⊐	indent 5 spaces	5⊐ Make a paragraph
⊏	move to left	⊏ uneven margin
cap or ≡	capitalize	proper noun
═	all caps	report title
∨ or ∧	insert	make corection here
ℓ	delete, take out	exxtra letter
#	add space	make aspace here
l.c. or /	lower case; small letters	not Capitalized
— or ital	underline (or italics)	book title
( )	insert parentheses	(by the way)
⊙	insert period	end of sentence⊙
¶	paragraph	¶ Make a paragraph here
no ¶	no paragraph	no ¶ Do not make a paragraph here
word	delete the word	extra extra word
word	delete the letter	extra lettter
stet	let it stand; leave it as it was	stet this correction is a mistake—ignore it
	Dots under the crossed out material indicate what is to be left.	

Instructions for typing symbols

6.56 If the typewriter contains the appropriate combination of keys to type symbols that are not included on the keyboard, use these keys to make the symbols. To save time when symbols cannot be made quickly on the typewriter, leave extra spaces so symbols can be handwritten when the typing has been completed.

6.57 For style guide to metric symbols, see 11.4–11.14.

6.58 Subscripts are numbers or letters typed slightly below the line of typing. Subscripts are used in mathematical and scientific formulas and equations.

In chemical equations:

H_2O $NaClO_3$ $C_{12}H_{22}O_{11}$ CH_4

In mathematical equations:

$\sin^{\theta}_{12}$

6.59 Subscripts are placed immediately after a letter, word, or figure and are typed as follows:

1. Engage the ratchet release lever of the typewriter.
2. Roll the cylinder knob slightly, turning the cylinder away from you.
3. Type the subscript.
4. Disengage the ratchet release lever.
5. Return the cylinder to the original line of typing.

6.60 Superscripts are numbers or lowercase letters typed slightly above the line of typing. Superscripts are used for footnote numbers in the body of the text or table, for mathematical formulas, and for equations.

Footnotes in text:	Ralph S. Spanswick states:[4] $14 million deficit[10]
Footnotes in tables:	14.2 3.5[a] 11.0[b]
Mathematical formula:	The area of a square is equal to s^2.
Mathematical equation:	$14 (x^2 - y^2) 56 =$

6.61 A superscript is placed immediately after the word, letter, or figure and is typed as follows:

1. Engage the ratchet release lever of the typewriter.
2. Roll the cylinder knob slightly toward you.
3. Type the superscript.
4. Disengage the ratchet release lever.
5. Return the cylinder to the original line of typing.

Business Correspondence 

Letters

Business letters

7.1 Most business letters fall into one of three categories: the individual (or personalized) letter, the guide letter, or the form letter. Each style is defined below.

7.2 An individual letter is required for all correspondence that cannot suitably be answered by using a form or guide letter.

7.3 A carefully written personalized letter builds goodwill and creates a favourable impression of the writer and the company. To determine whether you have written an effective letter, ask yourself the following questions.

1. *Purpose*. Have you determined the purpose of the letter? Is it to sell, to inform, to persuade, to entertain? Defining the purpose helps organize your thoughts.

2. *Conciseness*. Are only the essential facts included? Information that is irrelevant or wordy reduces comprehension.

3. *Clarity*. Has your purpose been set forth clearly? Are ideas presented in logical sequence?

4. *Completeness*. Did you include all the facts, figures, dates, names, and addresses? Are all possible questions answered that might be raised?

5. *Tone*. Does the tone of your letter indicate friendliness and co-operation? The manner in which ideas are conveyed will influence the reader's response.

6. *Correctness*. Are the dates, facts and figures correct?

7.4 A guide letter (see Figure 7-1) makes use of paragraphs prepared in advance to meet situations encountered in daily correspondence.

7.5 The prepared material usually includes standard opening and closing paragraphs phrased in general terms. Several more specific paragraphs, designed to suit a variety of common queries or problems, are also supplied—with blank spaces left for the insertion of dates, names, addresses, and other variable information (see Figure 7-1). These paragraphs are used individually or in different combinations for the body of each routine letter.

Each guide paragraph is coded with a number. To prepare a letter, the writer selects the paragraphs that are most appropriate to the situation and lists their numbers in the desired sequence. The secretary or typist can then refer to the paragraphs identified by these numbers and type the letter quickly and easily.

7.6 A form letter (see Figures 7–2 and 7–3) is a standard communication printed for large volumes of routine correspondence. Such letters contain specific information carefully tailored to fit circumstances anticipated in daily correspondence.

As in guide letter paragraphs, blank spaces are usually provided for variable information.

7.7 Offices that handle a large volume of routine correspondence often use word processing equipment to expedite form letters. All the form letter paragraphs are recorded on these special machines by means of such media as punched paper tape, magnetic tape, magnetic discs, or magnetic cards. When a letter is to be typed, the typist refers to the specific reference code, the machine selects the desired paragraphs, and the letter is typed automatically. (For more information on information processing, see 13.2–13.24.)

Letter styles

7.8 The arrangement of a business letter usually follows one of five major styles.

1. Full block style is one of the most popular letter styles because it is easy to set up. Every line of the letter begins at the left margin and nothing is indented except tables, lists, and similar material. Open or closed punctuation can be used with full block style. (See Figures 7–4 and 7–5.)

2. Block style is also very popular because it is easy to set up and gives a balanced appearance. The date line, complimentary closing, and writer's name usually begin at the centre of the page. All other lines begin at the left margin. This style is combined with mixed punctuation. (See Figures 7–6, 7–10, and 7–11.)

3. In semiblock style, the first line of each paragraph is indented five spaces. All other material is set up as in block style. This style is also used with mixed punctuation. (See Figure 7–7.)

4. In simplified style, as in the full block style, all lines begin at the left margin. There is no salutation or complimentary closing. A subject line, which takes the place of the salutation, is typed all in capitals. The writer's name and official title are typed in capitals as well. Open punctuation is always used. (See Figure 7–8.)

Figure 7-1. Sample guide letter paragraph

1 (opening)

I am concerned to learn of the disappointment you experienced in connection with your recent trip to _____. Thank you for bringing the matter to our attention.

2 (opening)

Thank you for taking the time and trouble to write us in detail about your recent experience with us. You are due our apology, of course; and I want to be prompt in extending it.

3

Your comments are disturbing, for you certainly did not receive the kind of service we want to extend to our passengers. Please accept our apologies. Your experience has, of course, been brought to the attention of our Flight Service Manager, who will review the matter in very serious terms with the flight crew concerned and will take other measures to ensure better performance in the future.

4

We strive for on-time performance of all our flights. However, in view of the fact that no transportation company can guarantee its schedules, we must decline reimbursement for any extra expenses incurred as a consequence of the late arrival.

5

I am very sorry about the problem you had with your excess baggage, and I can well understand your disappointment. Although it is difficult to account for the difference in weight you mentioned, unfortunately there is little we can do in an after-the-fact investigation. As you know, we are a highly regulated industry and have to follow certain rules from which we cannot deviate. Under these rules, the excess baggage receipt accepted by the traveller at check-in must be considered as the correct record of the weight of the baggage presented at the time, and an adjustment of an excess charge is possible only when a computation error has been made.

6

Under the circumstances, there appears to be no way that the charge you paid can be adjusted. I realize that this will be disappointing to you, but we hope that you will understand our position.

7

While we have done little on this occasion to merit your goodwill, I hope that we may have another opportunity to demonstrate that we can provide a fine service.

8

Thank you for taking the time to commend ____. It is always reassuring to learn that our people have done an especially good job. ____, I am sure, was only too pleased to be of assistance and will join us in looking forward to serving you again soon.

9

This is to certify that ____ is an employee in good standing with Trans Mountain Air Services Ltd. and is eligible to participate in the Universal Airlines Interline Tour program.

10 (closing)

Thank you for writing, ____. It is our policy to offer the finest service in every respect, and we hope that this policy will be more evident when you travel with us again.

Figure 7-2. Sample rejection letter

Thank you for submitting your manuscript entitled ________ to Coles. It has been read with interest.

However, because of previous commitments in the same subject area, we are returning the manuscript to you for publication elsewhere.

Please do not hesitate to submit other manuscripts you have authored, as we would like to see more of your work.

Thank you again for thinking of publishing with Coles.

Sincerely,

Jane Brown
Editor

COLES PUBLISHING COMPANY LIMITED
90 RONSON DRIVE, REXDALE, ONTARIO, CANADA • 249-9121

Figure 7-3. Sample acceptance letter

COLES

Thank you for submitting your manuscript entitled ____________.

The manuscript is now receiving our careful consideration and we are looking forward to being in touch with you in a few weeks' time.

Sincerely,

Jane Brown
Editor

COLES PUBLISHING COMPANY LIMITED
90 RONSON DRIVE, REXDALE, ONTARIO, CANADA • 249-9121

5. Because hanging indented style is an attention getter, it is frequently used in advertising letters. However, because it involves extra time in setting up, it is rarely used in ordinary business correspondence. (See Figure 7–9.)

Punctuation patterns

7.9 Normal punctuation is used throughout the body of the business letter. However, there are two patterns for the other parts of the letter.

1. Mixed punctuation is still the most common style. A colon is used after the salutation and a comma after the complimentary closing. (See Figures 7–5, 7–6, and 7–7.)

2. With open punctuation, no punctuation mark follows either salutation or closing. (See Figures 7–4 and 7–8.)

Standard parts of letters

7.10 The standard parts of a business letter (discussed in 7.11–7.47) are the letterhead, date, inside address, salutation, body, complimentary closing, typed name, official title, and reference initials. Figures 7–4 through 7-11 illustrate several acceptable arrangements for these parts. Special letter parts, such as enclosure, copy, and blind copy notations, postscript and post-postscript, mailing and addressee notations, and page headings, are discussed in sections 7.48 through 7.65.

Letterhead

7.11 Letterhead refers both to the high-grade paper used for business letters and to the company insignia, trade name, or product name printed at the top of each sheet. The printed information also includes the company name, address, and telephone number. More detailed letterheads may list the name and title of an executive officer, the name of a department, or the company's cable address. Several examples are illustrated in Figures 7–4 through 7-11.

Typed return address

7.12 When business letters are written on plain paper (Figure 7–11), the writer's address must be typed in place of the printed letterhead. The return address includes the writer's street address, city, province, and postal code. If an address includes an apartment, suite, or room number, place that number after the street address using the appropriate abbreviation: *Apt.*, *Ste.*, or *Rm.* (see 7.16) or on a separate line above the street address. This information is typed immediately above the date of the letter in block style, single space.

Figure 7-4. Full block style (open punctuation)

Letterhead	UNION CARBIDE UNION CARBIDE CANADA LIMITED 123 EGLINTON AVENUE EAST, TORONTO, CANADA. M4P 1J3 CABLE UNICARB TWX: 610 491-2314 TELEX 06-217703 PHONE 416-487-1311
Date	February 7, 1984
nside address	Ms. Jane Doe Executive Secretary Communications Business Box 252 Vancouver, B.C. V5K 4A4
Salutation	Dear Ms. Doe
Body	This is an illustration of a letter prepared in the full block style. Every line of the letter begins at the left margin. The full block style is frequently used by office employees because it is easy to set up and letters can be typed more quickly. Stenographers and typists often prefer it for these reasons. Because of its simplicity and distinctiveness, the full block style has become one of the more popular letter styles in business. To increase efficiency, open punctuation is usually used with the full block style letter. There is no punctuation after the salutation nor after the complimentary closing.
mplimentary closing	Yours sincerely
Typed name	John Doe
Official title	Office Manager
Reference initials	pg

apartment number	Apartment 20
street address	5512 Macleod Trail
city, province, postal code	Calgary, Alberta T2P 0V5
date	October 10, 1985

The placement of the return address depends on the letter style used. If the full block style is used, these lines are typed at the left margin. If the block style, semiblock style, or hanging indented style is used, these lines are typed beginning at the centre of the page.

Figure 7-5. Full block style (mixed punctuation)

Letterhead	DRG Stationery Company 71 Todd Road Georgetown Ontario Canada L7G 4T4 telephone 416 864 1460 telex 06 97624 Division
Date	February 3, 1983
Inside address	Mrs. Jane Doe 277 Elizabeth Drive Gander, Newfoundland A1V 1J7
Salutation	Dear Mrs. Doe:
Subject line	SUBJECT: Account No. 14701-K
Body	This letter illustrates the use of a subject line in full block style. The subject line is typed a double space below the salutation and a double space before the body of the letter. Since all lines in the full block style of letter begin at the left margin, the subject line must also be typed in that position. However, the subject line in block style is usually centred on the page to call attention to the content of the letter. The use of a subject line in business correspondence helps the reader focus on the main topic of the letter, and it is also an aid for the person filing correspondence.
Complimentary closing	Yours very truly,
Typed name Official title Reference initials	John Smith General Manager mlm
	Division of DRG Limited A Dickinson Robinson Group Company

Date

7.13 The date the letter is written may be typed (1) at the left margin (in the full block style letter), (2) beginning at the centre point of the page (in the block, semiblock, and hanging indented styles), or (3) centred on the page (block style, semiblock, and hanging indented styles) to match the arrangement and design of the company letterhead.

The date is typed three to five lines below the last line of the letterhead. The month is always spelled out, with the day of the month and the year written in full.

Figure 7-6. Block style (mixed punctuation)

Letterhead

SPEEDY MUFFLER KING
2323 Yonge Street, Toronto, Ontario, M4P 2C9, Tel: (416) 484-1166
At Speedy you're a Somebody

Date

1984 08 11

Inside address

Mr. John Doe
355 Burrard St.
Marine Building
Vancouver, B.C.
V6G 2G6

Salutation

Dear Mr. Doe:

Body

This letter is typed in block style with mixed punctuation. When mixed punctuation is used, a colon is typed after the salutation, and a comma is typed after the complimentary closing.

The date and the closing lines begin at the centre of the page. The closing lines may also be typed beginning five spaces to the left of the centre and blocked in that position.

Most typists like to place the date to begin at the same point as the closing lines because only one tabulator stop has to be set. Some letter writers, however, prefer to type the date to end even with the right margin. The date should be positioned where it looks best in conjunction with the design of the letterhead.

Block style is one of the most popular because it is easy to set up and gives a balanced appearance.

Complimentary closing

Sincerely,

Typed name

Jane Smith

Reference initials

df

7.14 The preferred style for typing dates in business letters is February 10, 1980.

However, the numeric dating system (see 6.15) can be used in a business letter to express a date entirely in figures.

Using the numeric dating system, February 10, 1980 becomes 1980 02 10. State the year, month, and day—always in that order.

Inside address

7.15 The complete name and address of the person to whom you are writing is called the inside address. It is typed at the left margin

Figure 7-7. Semiblock style with attention line (mixed punctuation)

Letterhead

Date

Inside address

Attention line
Salutation

Body

Complimentary closing

Typed name
Official title
Reference initials

COLDSTREAM
PRODUCTS OF CANADA LTD. 1855 SARGENT AVENUE, WINNIPEG, MANITOBA R3H 0E3 Area Code 204 775-8274
Telex 07-57152

1985 08 11

Taylor's Industry Digest
Box 40
Irricana, Alberta
TOM 1B0

Attention: Mr. Jon Jones

Dear Sir or Madam:

Please note the arrangement of information in the inside address of this letter typed in the semiblock style with five-space paragraph indentions. The letter is addressed to the company but is to be directed to the attention of the individual named.

The attention line is always typed at the left margin a double space below the inside address and a double space before the salutation. It is considered part of the inside address. Notice that although the letter is addressed to the attention of a known individual, the salutation is "Dear Sir or Madam."

The attention line may contain the name of an individual or the name of a particular department or section of the business.

Including an attention line in a letter helps expedite delivery of correspondence to the person or department concerned.

Yours truly,

James Smith
Registered Representative

lh

approximately four to eight lines below the date. When a window envelope is used (see Figure 7-18), the inside address also serves as the envelope address.

7.16 A complete inside address for letters, written to individuals or a company, will include a title or department.

name of individual	Mr. James C. Garven
title or department	Vice-President
name of company	Acme Paper Co.
street address	2221 Yonge Street
city, province, postal code	Toronto, Ontario M4B 2B4

Figure 7-8. Simplified style (open punctuation)

Letterhead

GLENDON COLLEGE
2275 BAYVIEW AVENUE
TORONTO, ONTARIO, M4N 3M6, CANADA
COLLÈGE UNIVERSITAIRE GLENDON

OFFICE OF THE REGISTRAR
BUREAU DU REGISTRAIRE

Date

March 17, 1983

Inside address

Miss Jane Smith
729 Wolfe Avenue
Moose Jaw, Sask.
S6H 1J6

Subject line

SIMPLIFIED LETTER STYLE

Body

This letter is an example, Miss Smith, of the simplified letter style. It incorporates the following features:

1. Full block style

2. No salutation or complimentary closing

3. A subject line typed in all capitals

4. Frequent use of enumerated items, always typed at the left margin

5. The writer's name and official title typed in capital letters

This letter style is designed for maximum efficiency, saving time for both the typist and the recipient. To maintain a business-like yet personalized tone, the addressee's name is usually included in the opening sentence of the letter.

Typed name and official title

JOHN DOE, REGISTRAR

Reference initials

fg

name of company	Canadian Biscuits Corp.
department name	Advertising Department
street address	3875 Canada Way, Ste. 200
city, province	Burnaby, B.C.
postal code	V5G 1G6

7.17 Use a title, such as *Miss, Mr., Mrs.,* or *Ms.,* only when you are sure it is accurate. If you are not sure, use the person's first name or initials.

Pat Green   L.P. Brown

Follow this procedure for the salutation, too. (See 7.22.)

Dear Pat Green

Figure 7-9. Hanging indented style (mixed punctuation)

Letterhead

Armstrong the Mover

ARMSTRONG-MARTIN MOVING AND STORAGE, P.O. BOX 938, PRINCE ALBERT, SASKATCHEWAN Phone 763-6428

Date

March 15, 1983

Inside address

Mr. Tom Brown
Box 5111
Bedford Tower
Bedford, N.S.
B0N 1B0

Salutation

Dear Mr. Brown:

Body

This letter illustrates the format of the hanging-indented style letter with mixed punctuation.

The hanging-indented style is a variation on the semiblock style. You will agree that it has an attention-getting format. That is why this style is used in advertising letters.

The paragraphs begin with the first line blocked at the left margin, and the second and succeeding lines are indented five spaces. The date and the complimentary closing are typed beginning at the centre of the page. The hanging-indented style is not used for most business correspondence because of the additional time involved in setting up and typing correspondence.

Please note the use of mixed punctuation in this particular letter - a colon after the salutation and a comma after the complimentary closing.

Complimentary closing

Yours very truly,

Typed name

Jon Jones

Reference initials

krg

Member
Allied Van Lines

THE PUR-R-FECT MOVER

7.18 An inside address should not consist of more than six lines nor less than three lines.

7.19 The province should be written using the abbreviation adopted by the post office (see section 5.17 for complete list).

Jones, Katz & Bloom
Attorneys at Law
Box 328
Stephenville, Nfld. A2N 2Z5

7.20 The six-figure postal code, used on all correspondence, is typed

Figure 7-10. Block style, executive stationery

Letterhead

MacMillan Bloedel Limited

1075 West Georgia Street, Vancouver, Canada V6E 3R9

Executive's name/title

C. CALVERT KNUDSEN
President and
Chief Executive Officer

Telephone: 683-6711
Area Code: 604

Date

June 21, 1985

Inside address

Mr. John Doe
Northern Forest Research Centre
Box 5320
Edmonton, Alberta
T6X 3S6

Salutation

Dear John:

Body

Please note the use of executive-size stationery by a high-ranking officer in an organization. The name and position of the executive officer is usually imprinted on executive-size stationery.

Executive stationery (also known as monarch stationery) measures 18.4 cm x 26.8 cm; its matching envelope measures 18.4 cm x 9.8 cm.

This size stationery is used most often for informal business and social correspondence. Letters are usually brief so that a second page is not necessary, and 2.5 cm side margins are usually sufficient for an attractively placed letter. The date should be typed so that it balances the information in the letterhead. In this example, it is placed slightly to the right of centre across from the executive's title.

Correspondence typed on executive or monarch stationery should reflect the prestige and integrity of the office held by the writer.

Complimentary closing

Yours sincerely,

Calvert Knudsen

Reference initials

bs

two spaces after the province; or the postal code can also be typed on a separate line by itself, particularly with short inside addresses.

Jones, Katz & Bloom
Attorneys at Law
Box 328
Stephenville, Nfld.
A2N 2Z5

Attention line

7.21 An attention line (see Figure 7.7) is used when a letter is addressed to a company but directed to a specific individual or department for

Figure 7-11. Block style, plain paper

Return address	Place Ville Marie Montreal, P.Q. H3B 3B7
Date	July 18, 1984
Inside address	Mr. Jack Smith 18 Hunter Street E. Hamilton, Ont. L8N 1M1
Salutation	Dear Mr. Smith:
Body	This is an illustration of the letter style used for personal and business correspondence typed on plain paper. Because letterhead stationery is not used, the return address of the writer must be typewritten at the top of the page for identification. The return address is typed in single spacing above the date approximately 6.5 cm from the top edge of the page. It consists of the writer's street address, city, province, and postal code. The province may be spelled out or the abbreviation may be used. The return address and date lines begin at the centre point of the page in this block style letter. They would be typed at the left margin if the full block style were used. In personal letters, the writer's typed name and/or official title may be omitted, as may reference initials.
Complimentary closing	Yours sincerely,
Typed name	Jon Jones

processing. The attention line, part of the inside address, is typed at the left margin a double space below the inside address and a double space before the salutation. If typed in capital and lowercase letters, the word *Attention* is followed by a colon; if it is typed all in capitals, no colon is used.

Grand River Railway
101 King St. W.
Cambridge, Ontario N3H 1B5

Attention: Mrs. Aretha Baska

Greater Winnipeg & Water District Railway
598 Plinquet St.
St. Boniface, Manitoba R2J 2W7

ATTENTION Accounting Department

Salutation

7.22 The salutation, or greeting, is typed at the left margin a double space below the inside address or attention line, if one is used. If mixed punctuation is used in the letter, a colon follows the salutation. If open punctuation is used, no punctuation follows the salutation.

Mr. Al Bertason 130 Granville St. Vancouver, B.C. V6C 2K1	C. Chu 3004 Balfour Rd. Toronto, Ont., M4C 1T8
Dear Mr. Bertason:	Dear C. Chu

7.23 The following salutations meet the majority of letter-writing needs (see 7.90 for other forms of address).

Dear Sir or Madam	**To a company, group, or individual when names are unknown**
Dear Miss Dear Mr. Dear Mrs. Dear Ms.	**To an individual**
Dear Mr. and Mrs. **or** Dear Dr. and Mrs. **or** Dear Mr. and Dr.	**To a husband and wife**
Dear Chadwick Dear Virginia	**To an individual; informal business and social form**
Dear Mr. Jackson and Mr. Ruiz **or** Dear Messrs. Jackson and Ruiz	**To two men with different names**
Dear Mrs. Busche and Mrs. Fargo **or**	**To two married women with different surnames**

Salutation	Use
Dear Mmes. Busche and Fargo	
Dear Miss Rozowski and Miss Fung **or** Dear Misses Rozowski and Fung	To two single women with different surnames
Dear Ms. Irvine and Ms. Iwahashi	To two women whose marital status is unknown and/or who prefer the title
Dear Messrs. Freeman	To two or more men with the same surname
Dear Mmes. Johnson	To two or more married women with the same surname
Dear Misses Dionisio	To two or more single women with the same surname
Dear Professor Clark and Professor Casey **or** Dear Professors Clark and Casey	To two persons with different surnames
Dear (Customer, Educator, Householder, etc.)	Use whatever designation applicable

Subject line

7.24 The subject line refers to the topic of the letter and is considered part of the body. It is typed a double space below the salutation (see Figure 7-5) and a double space before the body. (See Figure 7-8 when there is no salutation.) It may be centred on the page in the block, semiblock, and hanging indented styles, but it must be typed at the left margin in the full block style. Including an account number or case title within the subject line helps the reader focus on the main subject. SUBJECT or RE may be typed before the subject and followed by a colon.

Dear Mrs. LaCroix:

SUBJECT: Account No. 14701-K

Dear Mrs. LaCroix:

Re: Account No. 14701-K

SUBJECT or RE is not essential in the subject line, however, since the placement of information below the salutation indicates that it is the subject.

> Dear Mrs. LaCroix:
>
> Account No. 14701-K

Body

7.25 The body of the letter, which contains the message, is typed single spaced with double spacing between paragraphs. The style of the letter determines whether paragraphs are blocked, indented, or hanging (see Figures 7-4 through 7-11). One-paragraph letters may be typed double spaced.

Numbered lists

7.26 A list is used to set off specific items the writer wishes to call to the reader's attention. Each item is introduced either by Arabic numbers (1, 2, 3, etc.) or by letters (A, B, C, or a, b, c, etc.). The sentence immediately preceding—or introducing—the list must be a complete thought. No punctuation is used after each item unless each is stated as a complete sentence.

7.27 Short lists may be typed within a sentence as a series, with the items separated by commas (if there are commas within items, separate items with semicolons). Arabic numerals or lowercase letters, written in parentheses, identify each item. Items may consist of either phrases or complete sentences, but they always begin with a lowercase letter.

> The guidelines for typing lists within sentences are: (1) use Arabic numbers or lowercase letters within parentheses to introduce each item, (2) use commas to separate the items from each other, (3) maintain parallel construction in writing each item, and (4) word each item as concisely as possible.
>
> A list may be used to (a) draw the reader's eye to important information, (b) present key ideas in condensed form, or (c) indicate the correct order of steps in a procedure.

7.28 A short list may also be placed outside the paragraph to which it refers, and long lists must be typed this way. Very short items may be written as phrases, but longer items should be written in sentence form.

Lists in a block style letter are typed as follows:

1. Each item begins at the left margin.

2. The second and succeeding lines may also be typed beginning at the left margin.

3. Individual items are single-spaced with a double space between each item and the next.

Complimentary closing

7.29 The complimentary, or formal closing of a letter is typed a double space below the last line of the body. It is typed at the left margin in a full block letter or beginning at the centre of the page in block, semiblock, and hanging indented letters. (See also Figures 7–4 through 7–11.)

7.30 The following closings are customarily used in business correspondence.

Cordially	Yours sincerely
Respectfully	Yours truly
Sincerely	Yours very truly

7.31 More personal closings such as the following may take the place of formal closings at the writer's discretion.

Best wishes	Regards
Kindest regards	Warmest regards

7.32 The punctuation after the complimentary closing depends on whether mixed or open punctuation is used in the letter. If mixed punctuation is used, a comma follows the closing; if open punctuation is used, no punctuation mark follows the closing.

Typed company name

7.33 Although the company name appears in the letterhead, some companies like to highlight the name by including it in the closing as well. The name should be typed as it appears in the letterhead, a double space below the complimentary closing in solid capital letters.

Yours very truly,

BARRY, LORD & DYKES, INC.

Signature line

7.34 Sufficient space should be left after the complimentary closing or typed company name to allow for the writer's signature. Three or four blank lines is usually ample space, but more space can be left if the writer has large handwriting.

Yours very truly

Raymond L. Lewis

Yours very truly,

BARRY, LORD & DYKES, INC.

Raymond L. Lewis

7.35 The formal signature includes a combination of the writer's given names and initials. Titles such as *Miss, Mrs.,* and *Ms.* may be written in parentheses before the signature or the typewritten name below. Professional titles or degrees may be included with the typewritten name but should not be written as part of the signature.

Randal B. Parks, Jr.

(Ms.) D. Claire Almeida

Randal B. Parks, Jr.

7.36 When business or social correspondence is signed in an informal manner, the writer's first name alone may be used, but the typed signature includes the full name.

Randal B. Parks, Jr.

Signing for another

7.37 When a secretary signs correspondence in the absence of or on behalf of the employer, the employer's name is written with the secretary's initials just below (see Figure 7–10).

Jackson P. Collins
C/N

Jackson P. Collins
General Manager

7.38 When the secretary writes a letter, the secretary's name is typed as the writer. His or her capacity is indicated on the next line as an official title.

Jean Harris

Jean Harris
Secretary to Mr. Starkey

Jean Harris

Jean Harris
For Mr. Starkey

Jean Harris

For Peter L. Starkey
Advertising Department

Writer's typed name

7.39 The writer's name should be typed in full as it appears on all business correspondence, regardless of how the letter is signed. A typed name helps the reader identify the writer easily, especially when the writer's signature is difficult to read. The name is typed three or four lines below the complimentary closing or typed company's name.

Yours sincerely,

EXECUTIVES'
CONSULTANTS, INC.

Jackson P. Collins

Jackson P. Collins

Yours truly,

M. Clifford Kajiwara

M. Clifford Kajiwara

7.40 A divorced woman may use her first name and birth name with her former husband's surname unless she reverts to her birth name. She may also use her first name and her former husband's surname.

Mrs. Isabella Garcia Lopez   Mrs. Isabella Lopez

7.41 A professional woman who is married may wish to use her birth name for business purposes. The title preceding her typewritten name in business correspondence is *Miss* or *Ms.*; or her typewritten name is followed by her professional title or degree.

Maiden name for business purposes: Ms. Janice Engel or Janice Engel, M.D.

Title, degree, and department name

7.42 The writer's official title or capacity should follow the typewritten name, either on the same line or the next, depending on the length of name and the title. When both name and title are typed on one line, a comma separates them.

Peter L. Starkey
Office Manager

David X. Gonzales, Cashier

Also, when both name and title are typed on one line, the line should not extend beyond the right margin of the letter. A long title may be divided as follows:

(Miss) Marcella Avakian
Assistant Vice-President
and Cashier

7.43 When both a professional degree and an official title are included as part of the typewritten name, only the degree is typed on the same line as the name. When a degree is included, no other designation, such as *Dr.* or *Ms.,* is used.

Janice Engel, M.D.
Chief Resident

7.44 When a department or section name is to be included in the closing lines, it is typed on a separate line below the typewritten name or official title.

James D. Curry
Assistant Professor
Department of Business

Eugene Pinchuk, CPA
Accounting Department

Reference initials

7.45 Reference initials are used to identify the typist and/or dictator of a letter. These initials are typed at the left margin a double space below the last line of the signature block. Lowercase letters are used, with no periods or spaces separating them.

Yours sincerely,

Norman Rittgers
Operations Manager

csm

7.46 When the initials of the dictator are used, they always precede those of the typist. Any of the following styles are permissible.

LCH:csm	LCHenning:csm
LCH/csm	LCHenning/csm

7.47 When the letter is dictated by someone other than the person who signs it, it is then necessary to include the dictator's initials.

Enclosure notation

7.48 When documents or other papers are to be enclosed with or attached to correspondence, an enclosure notation should be typed a single or double space below the reference initials at the left margin.

Single Enclosure	*Multiple Enclosures*
Enc.	Encs.
Encl.	Encls.
Enclosure	Enclosures

Enclosures may be itemized for the reader's convenience, also, when there is more than one enclosure, the number may be indicated.

Enclosures: Release Form Contract

Enclosures: 2 **or** Enclosures (2)

Copy notation

7.49 When an extra copy of correspondence is prepared—either by making a carbon copy or by photocopying—and distributed to another person, this fact should be noted on all copies for the addressee's information, when appropriate. The copy notation is typed at the left margin a double space below the last reference line.

cc: William McDaniels
CC: William McDaniels
Copy to William McDaniels

7.50 The expressions *cc* and *Carbon copy* are still used even though copies are commonly made by various photocopying methods.

7.51 The complete name and address of the copy recipient may also be indicated on the letter, again if appropriate.

cc: John Doe
Library Services
Whitehorse, Yuk.
Y1A 2C6

Copy to: Bob Sarkisian,
Controller's Dept.

7.52 When several copies of one letter are to be made and distributed, all names should be indicated in the notation.

cc: John Fitzhugh
William Hartford
Elena C. Castagna

Copies to: John Fitzhugh
William Hartford
Elena C. Castagna

Blind copy notation

7.53 When an extra copy of a letter is prepared for another person—by making a carbon copy or by photocopying—but the addressee is not to be informed, a blind copy notation is indicated on all but the original letter (hence ''blind''). The original and first carbon sheet are removed from the typewriter so the notation can be typed on all copies. This notation is typed a double space below the last reference line at the left margin.

Bcc: Gloria Fielding

bcc: Gloria Fielding

BCC: Gloria Fielding

BC: Gloria Fielding

Bc: Michael Ramirez
John C. Carroll

Postscript

7.54 A postscript is an afterthought, sometimes used for emphasis at the very end of the letter. The postscript is typed a double space below the last reference or notation line. It should be typed in the same style as the body of the letter—with blocked, indented, or hanging indented paragraphs.

7.55 The position at the end of the letter identifies the addition as a postscript; therefore, the letters *P.S.* are omitted.

Post-postscript

7.56 When a writer wishes to add still another afterthought, a separate paragraph or post-postscript is typed a double space below the postscript and follows the same paragraph style as the letter. The letters *P.P.S.* are typed to separate it from the postscript.

P.P.S. Dave Williams is planning to show his movies of the Annual Sales Conference in Ottawa, so the June meeting should be an interesting one for all.

P.P.S. Dave Williams is planning to show his movies of the Annual Sales Conference in Ottawa, so the June meeting should be an interesting one for all.

P.P.S. Dave Williams is planning to show his movies of the Annual Sales Conference in Ottawa, so the June meeting should be an interesting one for all.

A post-postscript eliminates the need to retype the letter in order to insert additional information.

Mailing notations

7.57 Mailing notations such as AIRMAIL, SPECIAL DELIVERY, REGISTERED MAIL, and CERTIFIED MAIL tell the post office that special processing is desired. Such notations are typed in solid capital letters at the left margin a double or triple space above the inside address.

REGISTERED MAIL	AIR MAIL
Miss Rita Legion Executive Secretary National Museum of Man Communications Division Ottawa, Ontario K1A 0M8	Mr. Robert C. Wolfinger Building 810, Pleasantville St. John's, Nfld. A1A 1P9

7.58 Note that on the envelope, the mailing notation is typed in solid capital letters in the upper left corner below the return address.

Addressee notation

7.59 Addressee notations indicate how mail is to be handled when received. These special notations include PERSONAL, CONFIDENTIAL, PLEASE HOLD FOR ARRIVAL, PLEASE FORWARD, and PERSONAL AND CONFIDENTIAL. Addressee notations are typed above the inside address of the letter at the left margin. On the envelope, they appear in the upper left corner below the return address.

CONFIDENTIAL	PERSONAL
Fresh Water Fish Marketing Corp. 1199 Plessis Road Winnipeg, Manitoba R3X 3L4	Ms. Elizabeth Chang Personnel Services Dept. of Finance Box 2000 Charlottetown, P.E.I. C1A 7N8

Second and subsequent pages

7.60 The second and subsequent pages of business letters are typed on plain paper of the same quality as the letterhead applying the same side margins used on the first page.

7.61 The last word on the first page is never divided.

7.62 To identify subsequent pages, a heading is typed at the top of each page, which includes the following information:

individual's name	Mr. Allen Robair
page number	Page 2
date	January 5, 1983
company's name	Jurgenson Brothers
attention line, if used	Attention: Mr. Jason Myers
page number	Page 2
date	January 17, 1983

7.63 The block style of heading is typed in single spacing 2.5 cm from the top of the page at the left margin. This style must be used with full block letters and may be used with block and hanging indented letters.

Mr. Allen Robair	Jurgenson Brothers
Page 2	Attention Mr. Jason Myers
January 5, 1983	Page 3
	January 17, 1983

7.64 The horizontal style heading is typed across the top of the page 2.5 cm from the top. This style is used with either block, semi-block, or hanging indented letters. The name of the individual or company is typed beginning at the left margin. The page number is typed at the centre of the page by itself, and the date is typed so it ends close to the right margin.

Mr. Allen Robair	2	January 5, 1983
Jurgenson Brothers	2	January 17, 1983
Attention: Mr. Jason Myers		

7.65 On the second and subsequent pages the body of the letter is continued three to four lines below the heading and is typed in the same form as the first page.

Mr. Allen Robair	2	January 5, 1983

Continue the body of the letter approximately three to four lines below the heading. More space may be left if the letter is not going to fill the entire page.

Stationery sizes

7.66 Paper sizes for letterhead, memoranda, notepads, figuring pads, copy and duplication paper have been standardized by the Canadian Government Specifications Board (see Table 7–1).

Table 7-1. Standard sheet sizes

Size designation	*Standard sheet size* (cm)	*Size replaced* (in)
P1	56 × 86	22 × 34
P2	43 × 56	17 × 22
P3	28 × 43	11 × 17
P4	21.5 × 28	$8\frac{1}{2}$ × 11
P5	14 × 21.5	$5\frac{1}{2}$ × $8\frac{1}{2}$
P6	10.7 × 14	$4\frac{1}{4}$ × $5\frac{1}{2}$

Letter placement

7.67 Regardless of format or punctuation style, a letter must be attractively centred on the page. Table 7–2 illustrates both pica and elite type faces. Table 7–3 illustrates guidelines for line length and spacing of business letters typed on P4 stationery. Figure 7–12 sets up a sample guide page.

Table 7-2. Standard type faces

	Pica	*Elite*
To determine your type size, compare it with these samples.	Pica Type 10 spaces per 2.5 cm (one inch)	Elite Type 12 spaces per 2.5 cm (one inch)

Figure 7-12. Guide page

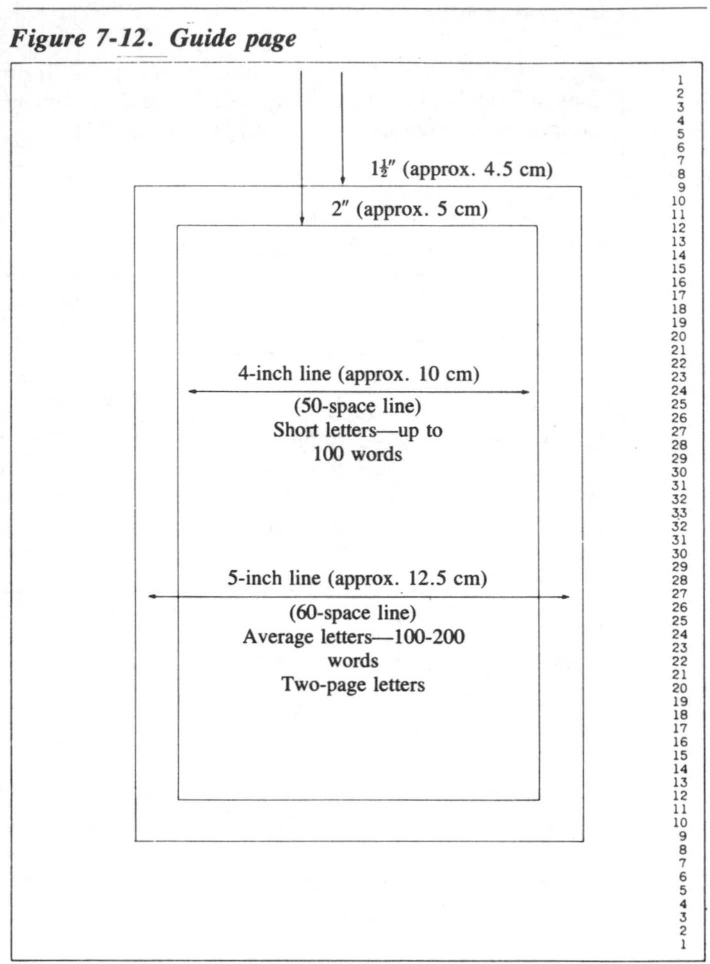

Guide page

7.68 A guide page is a specially ruled and/or numbered page containing guide lines or numbers to indicate the various margin settings for letters and reports. The guide page is placed behind the original page so lines and numbers are visible; the typist can see how much space is left on the page for side and bottom margins. (See Figure 7-12.)

Margin settings

7.69 Use a standard margin setting for all letters. Adapt margins for shorter letters by allowing more space between the letterhead and date, and date and inside address. Adapt for longer letters by leaving less space between these parts. (See 7.73 and 7.74.)

Top margin

7.70 For printed letterheads, the date line is always the first line to be typed about three to five lines below the last line of the letterhead depending on the length of the letter.

For stationery without letterheads, the top margin will depend on whether you type a letterhead address or a return address. A letterhead address will be double-spaced beginning on the sixth line from the top of the page as below:

name of company	International Computers Inc.
street address	1371 Mountain Street
city, province, postal code	Victoria, B.C. V8W 2E7
telephone area code and number	604-489-2756

The date line can fall on line 12 or 15 depending on the length of the letter.

Side margin

7.71 The side margins will be determined by size of stationery and size of typewriter type. See Table 7–3 for a guide to side margin settings on P4 stationery.

Table 7-3. Spacing length guide for standard size P4 stationery

Letter length	*Number of words*	*Pica strokes**	*Elite strokes**	*Lines from top of page to date*
Short	Under 100	40	50	15-20
Average	101-200	50	60	15
Long	201-300	60	70	10-15
Two-page	Over 301	60	70	15

*Does not include allowance for bell at right margin.

Bottom margin

7.72 In a one-page letter, the bottom margin must be at least six lines. If the letter continues on to a second page, the bottom margin on the first page may be increased up to twelve lines. (See 7.60–7.65.)

Lengthening a short letter

7.73 A short letter of under 100 words may be spaced over one page by incorporating any one or more of the techniques listed below.

1. If the letter is very short, the inside address and body can all be double-spaced, but indent the first line of each paragraph.

2. Lower the date line up to five lines from line 15, and increase the space between the date and inside address by five lines.

3. Allow $1\frac{1}{2}$ blank lines before and after the salutation, between the paragraphs, between the message and the complimentary closing, and between the complimentary closing and the company name.

4. Allow four to six blank lines for the signature, and type the signer's name and title on separate lines.

5. Lower the reference initials one or two lines.

Shortening a long letter

7.74 A long letter (over 200 words) can be tightened to fit one page by incorporating any one or more of the techniques listed below.

1. Raise the date line and allow only two or three blank lines between the date and the inside address.

2. Allow only two blank lines for the signature.

3. Raise the reference initials one or two lines.

Addressing envelopes

7.75 There are proper procedures to follow in addressing envelopes. (See 14.2–14.26 on postal services for more complete information.)

7.76 **Envelope sizes**

The Canadian postal authorities have designated the minimum envelope size as 9 cm × 14 cm, and the maximum as 15.2 cm × 25.5 cm. Anything in between is permissible. Note that postal authorities will accept only closed cellophane window envelopes.

The following envelope sizes are suggested by the post office.

Table 7-4. Standard envelopes with corresponding stationery

Size of stationery (see Table 7-1)	*Standard envelope size* (cm)	*Size replaced* (in)
P4	No. 9 (10.2 × 22.9)	4 × 9
P4	No. 10 (10.5 × 24.1)	$4\frac{1}{8} \times 9\frac{1}{2}$
P5	Special (11.4 × 14.6)	$4\frac{1}{2} \times 5\frac{3}{4}$

7.77 Most companies have their return addresses preprinted on all company envelopes to match the design of the letterhead stationery (see Figure 7-13).

Figure 7-13. Envelope with preprinted return address

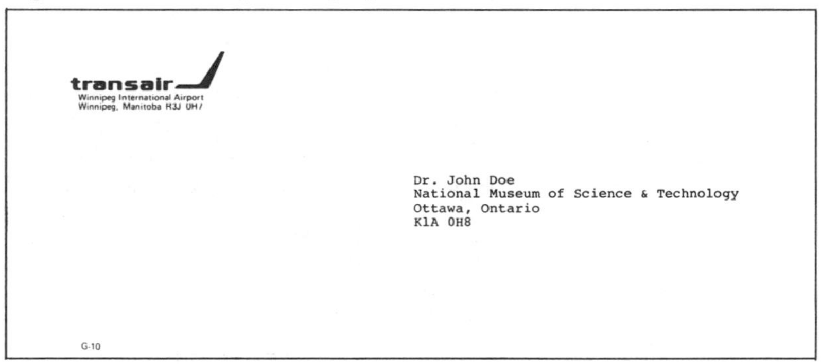

7.78 If plain envelopes are used, the complete return address should be typed in the upper left corner of the envelope, approximately two lines from the top edge and two or three spaces from the left edge. The single-spaced address is typed in block style.

Some large international or nation-wide organizations preprint only the company name on envelopes. In that case, type above and below company name (see Figure 7-14).

The typed return address should always include the province and the postal code.

Figure 7-14. Envelope with typed return address and preprinted company name

Mr. Thwackum
1 Place Ville Marie
Montreal, P.Q. H3P 3P7

Mr. Tom Jones
Atmospheric Environment Service
4905 Dufferin Street
Downsview, Ontario
M3H 5T4

Envelope address

7.79 1. The envelope address should always be identical to the inside address (see Figure 7.15).

2. Always use single spacing and blocked style.

3. An envelope address must always contain at least three typed lines. When a street address is not necessary (when mail is sent to large organizations or to individuals in small communities) the town or city may be put on a separate line from the province.

Mrs. Jean N. Harris	Lockwood Trust Company
Pointe-au-Chêne	Selkirk
Quebec J0V 1T0	Manitoba
	R1A 1B9

4. Type the postal code either two spaces after the name of the province, or preferably alone on the last line. The postal code is always the last item in the mailing envelope address.

5. The name of the province can be spelled out in full or abbreviated according to proper post office abbreviations.

Mitzi Rearden, President	Mr. Joel Grayson
Top-of-the-Line Company	182 Dufferin Avenue
2685 Angus Street	Selkirk, Manitoba
Regina, Sask. S4T 2A3	R1A 1B9

Figure 7-15. Inside address and envelope address

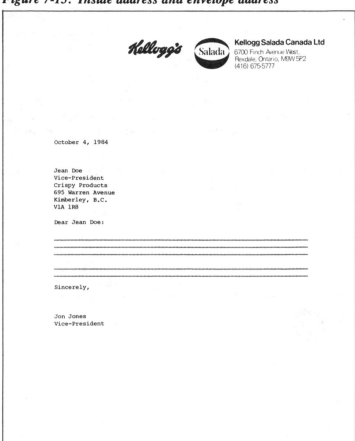

Kellogg's Salada
Kellogg Salada Canada Ltd
6700 Finch Avenue West,
Rexdale, Ontario, M9W 5P2
(416) 675-5777

October 4, 1984

Jean Doe
Vice-President
Crispy Products
695 Warren Avenue
Kimberley, B.C.
V1A 1R8

Dear Jean Doe:

____

Sincerely,

Jon Jones
Vice-President

Kellogg Salada Canada Ltd
6700 Finch Avenue West,
Rexdale, Ontario, M9W 5P2

Jean Doe
Vice-President
Crispy Products
695 Warren Avenue
Kimberley, B.C.
V1A 1R8

6. A 19 mm (3/4 inch) blank space must always be left across the base of the envelope for electronic handling.

7. In addressing of large envelopes such as No. 9 (10.2 cm × 22.9 cm) and No. 10 (10.5 cm × 24.1 cm), begin about 46 to 48 spaces from the left edge, and approximately 14 lines from the top edge of the envelope.

In addressing a small envelope such as the Special envelope for P5 stationery, begin the address about 24 spaces from the left edge, and about 12 lines from the top edge of the envelope.

8. In addressing U.S. mail, the city, state, and ZIP (postal) code are placed together on the last line. The state name may be spelled out or abbreviated (see 5.18).

Mr. Calvin M. Gregory
Western Milling Company
819 Central Avenue
Denver, CO   80203

Figure 7-16. Envelope with postal notation

ONTARIO FILM LABORATORIES LTD.
191 Lakeshore Drive, North Bay, Box 840, Ontario P1B 8K1

AIRMAIL

Canadian Broadcasting Corporation
French Services Division
Box 6000
Montreal, P.Q.
H3C A3S

Postal notations

7.80 Postal notations such as AIRMAIL, SPECIAL DELIVERY, CERTIFIED MAIL, REGISTERED MAIL, and RETURN RECEIPT REQUESTED are typed in solid capital letters in the upper left corner of the envelope below the return address (see Figure 7–16).

Addressee notations

7.81 Addressee notations are typed in solid capital letters in the upper left part of the envelope below the return address (see Figure 7–17). They request special handling by the recipient. Examples include:

ATTENTION	When correspondence is to be directed to the attention of a specific person or department of an organization.
CONFIDENTIAL	When correspondence contains information that is privileged and is to be seen only by those persons authorized to receive and handle such matters.
HOLD FOR ARRIVAL	When correspondence is mailed to arrive before the individual addressee; arrival date is included in the notation.
PERSONAL	When correspondence is intended only for the addressee's eyes and/or is of a personal nature.
PLEASE FORWARD	When correspondence is sent to an individual whose address may since have changed.

Figure 7-17. Envelope with addressee notation

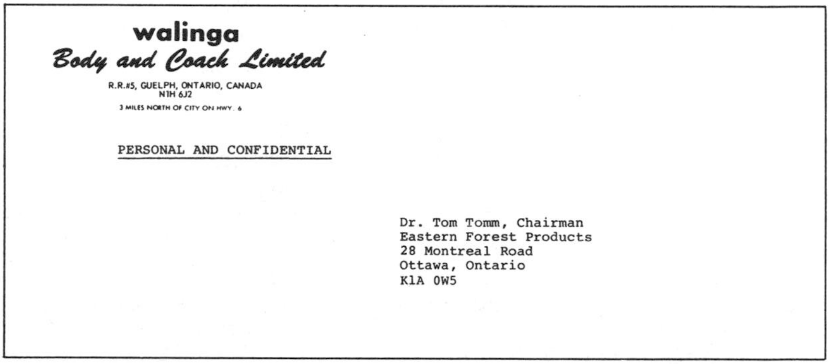

walinga
Body and Coach Limited
R.R.#5, GUELPH, ONTARIO, CANADA
N1H 6J2
3 MILES NORTH OF CITY ON HWY. 6

PERSONAL AND CONFIDENTIAL

Dr. Tom Tomm, Chairman
Eastern Forest Products
28 Montreal Road
Ottawa, Ontario
K1A 0W5

Folding and inserting letters

7.82 Folding and inserting letters properly into their envelopes is important. Always ensure that all enclosures mentioned in the letter are inserted into the envelope with the letter. If the enclosure is smaller than the letter, such as a receipt or cheque, it should be placed inside the folds of the letter or clipped to the face of the letter before folding. If an enclosure is the same size as the letter, it should be placed behind the letter and folded with it. Before sealing the envelope, a secretary should decide whether or not a copy of the enclosure is needed to file with the carbon copy of the letter.

Figure 7-18. Window envelopes for P5 and P4 stationery

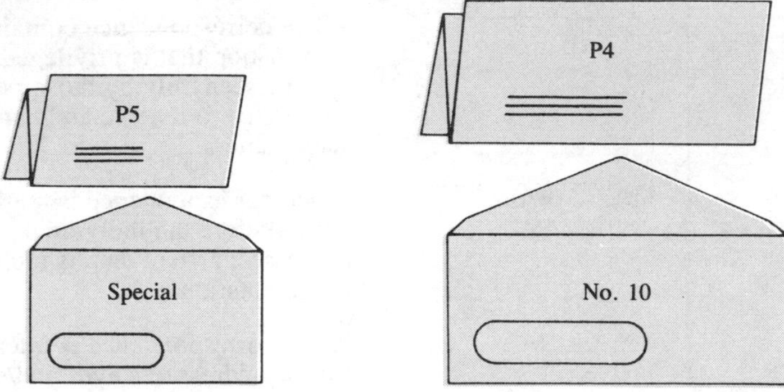

The inside address on correspondence for window envelopes must be typed so it can be properly aligned with the window. Fold bottom of letter up approximately one third of the page; fold top edge backwards and down to about 1 cm from bottom fold.

Figure 7-19. Folding P5 stationery for Special envelope

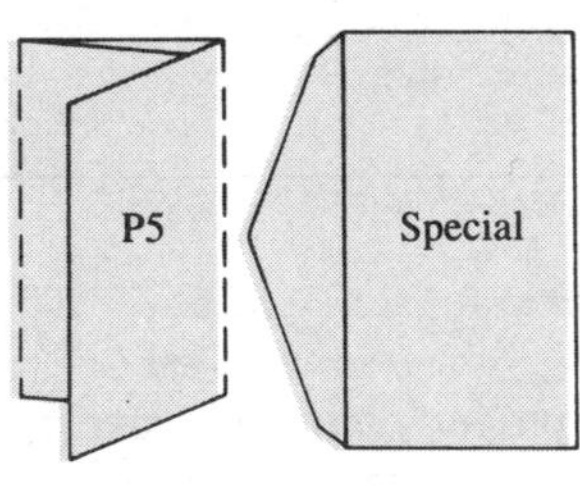

Fold left side of letter approximately one-third of the page to the right; fold right side over to left about 1 cm from the left crease.

Figure 7-20. Folding P4 stationery for Special envelope

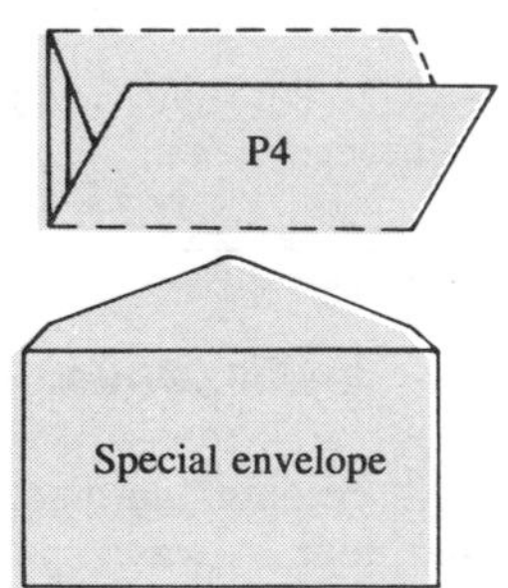

Fold bottom edge up to within 1 cm of top of page; fold right side of letter about one third to the left; fold left side over to right about 1 cm from the right crease. (Or start with the left side, if you are left-handed.)

Figure 7-21. Folding P4 stationery for No. 9 and No. 10 envelopes (most common)

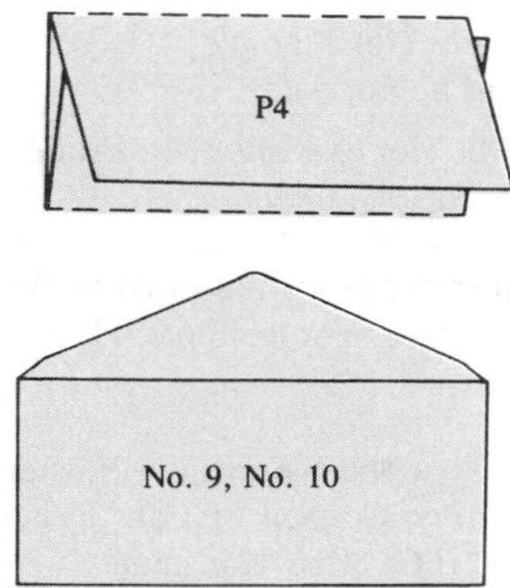

Fold bottom edge up about one third of the page; fold top of letter down to about 1 cm from bottom fold.

Figure 7-22. Envelope for Executive or Official stationery

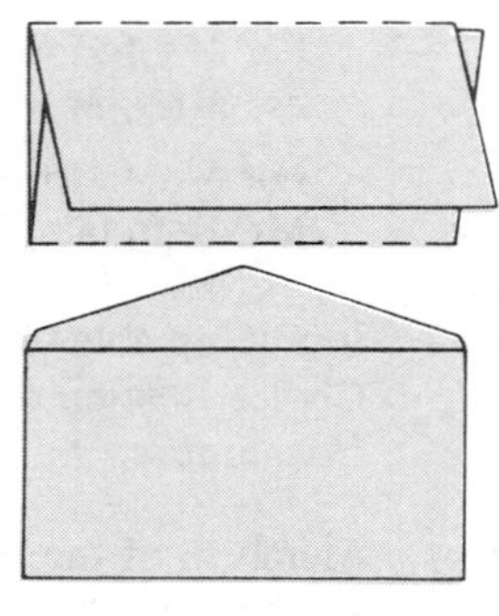

Fold bottom edge of letter up approximately one third of the page; fold top of letter down to about 1 cm from bottom fold.

Forms of address

7.83 The following list indicates proper ways to write titles and salutations for various government, judicial, religious, military, and education officials.

7.84 In the salutations that follow the forms of address, the most formal one is listed first.

7.85 The most common complimentary closings are:

Formal: Yours very truly; Yours truly; Respectfully yours
Less formal: Sincerely; Yours sincerely; Cordially
Personal: Kindest regards; Best wishes

7.86 When the address is too long for one line, carry over on to a second line.

The Rt. Hon.
James Brown, P.C., M.P.
Prime Minister of Canada
Ottawa, Ontario
Postal Code

7.87 For the sake of simplicity, the masculine forms of address are used throughout. When an office is held by a woman, make the following substitutions:

For *Sir,* use *Madam*.

For *Mr.* followed by a name (for example, Mr. Turner), use *Miss, Mrs.*, or *Ms.* as appropriate.

For *Mr.* followed by a title (for example, Mr. Prime Minister, Mr. Secretary, Mr. Mayor), use *Madam*.

7.88 It is acceptable to abbreviate titles as well as to write them in full. Choice is often dictated by space. For example: *Hon.* instead of *Honourable*.

7.89 Members of the federal cabinet and the Prime Minister are considered members of the Privy Council (P.C.). It is therefore customary to add the letters *P.C.* after their names.

Government and judicial officials

7.90

Title	*Salutation*
Alderman	
Alderman James Brown	Dear Alderman Brown:
or	
James Brown, Alderman of _______	Dear Mr. Brown:
Ambassador	
James Brown Canadian Ambassador to _______	Dear Sir: Dear Ambassador: Dear Mr. Brown:
Cabinet Minister	
The Hon. James Brown, P.C., M.P. Minister of _______	Dear Sir: Dear Mr. Brown:
Chief Justice of Canada	
The Rt. Hon. The Chief Justice of Canada Supreme Court of Canada	Sir:
or	
The Rt. Hon. James Brown, P.C. Chief Justice of Canada	Dear Sir: Dear Mr. Chief Justice:

Title	*Salutation*
Chief Justice of a Province or Territory of Canada	
The Hon. James Brown Chief Justice of ______	Sir: Dear Sir: Dear Mr. Chief Justice:
Commissioner: Government Commission, Board, or Bureau	
The head or member commissioner of a government board, bureau, or commission in Canada has no title and is addressed in the terms of ordinary correspondence. (See 7.23.)	
Controller	
A controller is addressed in the terms of ordinary correspondence. (See 7.23.) The name *controller* can be included in the address.	
James Brown	Dear Mr. Brown:
or	
James Brown, Controller	Dear Controller:
or	
Controller James Brown (City, Borough, or Region)	Dear Controller Brown:
Governor General	
The Governor General of Canada has the title Rt. Hon. for life, and is a Canadian Privy Councillor (P.C.) as well as Chancellor of the Order of Canada (C.C.).	
His Excellency the Rt. Hon. James Brown, P.C., C.C.	Sir: Dear Governor General:
Judge (federal and provincial courts)	
The Hon. Mr. Justice James Brown	Sir: Dear Justice Brown:
Judge (county or district court)	
His Honour Judge James Brown	Sir: Dear Judge Brown:

Title	Salutation
Lieutenant-Governor	
His Honour The Lieutenant-Governor of (province)	Dear Sir: Dear Lieutenant-Governor:
or	
His Honour The Hon. James Brown Lieutenant-Governor of (province)	Dear Mr. Brown:
Mayor	
His Worship the Mayor of ________	Dear Sir:
or	
His Worship Mayor James Brown	Dear Mr. Mayor:
Member of a Legislative Assembly of a Province	
James Brown, M.L.A. (M.P.P. in Ontario, M.N.A. in Quebec) Parliament Buildings	Dear Sir: Dear Mr. Brown:
Member of Parliament	
James Brown, M.P. House of Commons	Dear Sir: Dear Mr. Brown:
Premier	
The Hon. James Brown, M.L.A. (M.P.P. in Ontario, M.N.A. in Quebec) Premier of ________	Dear Sir: Dear Mr. Brown:
Prime Minister of Canada	
The Rt. Hon. James Brown, P.C., M.P. Prime Minister of Canada	Dear Sir: Dear Mr. Prime Minister: Dear Prime Minister:
Senator	
The Hon. James Brown The Senate	Dear Sir: Dear Senator Brown:

Title	*Salutation*
Religious officials	
Archbishop, Anglican	
The Most Rev. James Brown, D.D. Archbishop of ________	Most Reverend Sir: Dear Archbishop:
Archbishop, Roman Catholic	
The Most Rev. James Brown Archbishop of ________	Most Reverend Sir: Dear Archbishop:
Bishop, Anglican	
The Rt. Rev. James Brown Bishop of ________	Right Reverend Sir: Dear Bishop Brown:
Bishop, Roman Catholic	
The Rt. Rev. James Brown Bishop of ________	Right Reverend Sir: Dear Bishop Brown:
Cardinal	
His Eminence, James Cardinal Brown Archbishop of ________	Your Eminence: Dear Cardinal Brown:
Commissioner, Salvation Army	
Commissioner James Brown Salvation Army Headquarters	Sir: Dear Commissioner Brown:
Minister	
The Rev. James Brown	Sir: Reverend Sir: Dear Mr. Brown:
or The Rev. James Brown, D.D. (or LL.D. or Ph.D. if minister has a doctor's degree)	Sir: Reverend Sir: Dear Dr. Brown:
Moderator	
The Right Rev. James Brown, D.D. Moderator of ________ Church	Right Reverend Sir: Dear Dr. Brown:
Monsignor	
The Right Reverend James Brown	Right Reverend Monsignor: Dear Monsignor Brown:

Title	Salutation
Mother Superior	
The Rev. Mother Superior The Congregation of ________	Dear Madam: Reverend Mother Superior: Dear Mother Superior:
Priest	
The Rev. James Brown	Reverend Sir: Dear Father Brown:
Rabbi	
The Rev. Rabbi James Brown or	Dear Sir:
Rabbi James Brown or	Dear Rabbi Brown:
Dr. James Brown (if rabbi has doctor's degree)	Dear Dr. Brown:
Sister	
The Reverend Sister Saint Mary	Dear Madam: Dear Sister Saint Mary:

Military

The following lists show the approved formal and informal rank titles for officers of the army, air force, and navy of the Canadian Armed Forces as authorized by the Canadian Forces Reorganization Act, 1967 and reaffirmed in the revised National Defence Act of 1970.

Rank Titles for Army and Air Force Officers

Formal	*Informal*
General	General
Lieutenant-General	General
Major-General	General
Brigadier-General	General
Colonel	Colonel
Lieutenant-Colonel	Colonel
Major	Major
Captain	Captain
Lieutenant	Mister, or Lieutenant
Second Lieutenant	Mister, or Lieutenant

Rank Titles for Naval Officers

Formal	*Informal*
Admiral	Admiral
Vice-Admiral	Admiral
Rear-Admiral	Admiral
Commodore	Commodore
Captain	Captain
Commander	Commander
Lieutenant-Commander	Commander
Lieutenant	Mister
Sub-Lieutenant, Commissioned Officer	Mister

Note that in an inside address, the rank and name are always used. In the salutation, use of rank is optional.

Lieutenant-General James Brown	Sir: Dear General Brown:
Admiral James Brown	Sir: Dear Admiral Brown:

Education officials

Dean of a College or Faculty

James Brown, Ph.D. (or other doctorate) Dean of ________	Dear Sir: Dear Dr. Brown: Dear Dean Brown:

Member of Board of Education

Mr. James Brown Member of (name of city) Board of Education	Dear Sir: Dear Mr. Brown:

President of a University

James Brown, LL.D. (or other doctorate) President University of ________	Dear Sir: Dear Dr. Brown: Dear Mr. President:

Principal

Mr. James Brown (use Dr. if applicable) Principal, ________ School	Dear Sir: Dear Mr. (or Dr.) Brown: Dear Principal Brown:

Title	*Salutation*
Professor	
James Brown, Ph.D., (or other doctorate) University of ________	Dear Sir: Dear Professor Brown: Dear Dr. Brown:
Superintendent of Schools	
Mr. James Brown (use Dr. if applicable) Superintendent of ________ Schools	Dear Sir: Dear Mr. (or Dr.) Brown:

Interoffice correspondence (memoranda)

7.91 Interoffice correspondence—called an interoffice memorandum or memo—conveys information among company employees and is seldom seen by outsiders. Memos communicate the ideas, suggestions, facts, and requests for data that are the basis of company decisions; these decisions, in turn, generate correspondence to people outside the company.

7.92 Formal memoranda are generally typed on printed memorandum or interoffice communication forms (see Figures 7-23 and 7-24). These forms come in two sizes — 21.5 cm × 28 cm (standard size) and 21.5 cm × 14 cm (half sheet). The standard size forms are preferable to ensure that all correspondence placed in the files will be of uniform size.

7.93 Less formal memos may consist simply of a handwritten note on regular memo form or on a sheet of note paper. When an inquiry requires a quick response and the exchange of information need not be filed, the handwritten note (or a telephone call) provides an efficient means of soliciting and obtaining information.

Writing effective memos

7.94 Just as effective letters project a positive impression to people outside the company, carefully prepared memos will build goodwill and create a favourable impression within the company. To determine the effectiveness of your memos, ask the same questions pertaining to letters (see 7.3).

Memorandum styles

7.95 Figures 7–23 and 7–24 illustrate two forms of printed memoranda. Note the use of a subject line in Figure 7–23.

Memorandum parts

7.96 Note that the procedures for setting up a memo do not always correspond to those for typing a letter.

7.97 The letterhead of a memorandum usually consists of the company's name. Large organizations with several branch offices or departments may have the branch or department name imprinted below the company name for identification purposes. Since interoffice communications do not go outside the company, a company address is not necessary.

7.98 The memorandum heading is usually printed with the words TO, FROM, SUBJECT, and DATE, to save typing time. Headings may be arranged in different ways.

7.99 The addressee's name, title (if space allows), and department name or number are typed after TO. The same information for the writer is typed after FROM. Such words as *Department, Section, Building,* and *Number* may be abbreviated. The designations *Dr., Miss, Mr., Mrs.,* and *Ms.* are not used. The identifying information may be arranged in various ways depending on the printed memorandum form.

Addressee

TO: Patsy P. Mark, Interviewer
Personnel Department (**or:** Personnel Dept.)

TO: Patsy P. Mark, Interviewer
Department 102 (**or:** Dept. 102)

Writer

FROM: Ellen C. Fong, Attorney
Legal Department (**or:** Legal Dept.)

FROM: Ellen C. Fong, Attorney
Department 107 (**or:** Dept. 107)

7.100 SUBJECT (often the caption under which related correspondence is filed) may be typed with initial or solid capital letters. When SUBJECT is printed below FROM, the subject should be typed across the page; a long subject can be typed on two lines.

Figure 7-23. Block style memorandum with subject line

collier macmillan canada inc

To: Nick Slade, Consultant
School Department
From: Janice Jackson, Assistant
Marketing Department
Date: December 21, 1984
Subject: HISTORY SERIES

This memorandum form illustrates the block style of typing both the heading and the body. All information is typed at the same point. Although the words To, From, Date, and Subject in the printed heading are staggered, the block heading gives a more balanced appearance.

The subject line aids the reader to focus attention on the topic of the communication and is a valuable aid for the typist or secretary in filing and retrieving correspondence. The subject line may be typed in solid capital letters, or the first letter of important words may be capitalized.

An important factor in creating an attractive communication is that of properly aligning each item of information with the printed words in the heading. The variable line spacer on the typewriter will help in proper alignment.

ml

FROM: Glenda Baldwin

SUBJECT: Bradbury Wills v. Atlantic Insurance Co.

When SUBJECT is printed below DATE near the right margin, two lines are used:

DATE: September 13, 1983

SUBJECT: Bradbury Wills v.
Atlantic Insurance Co.

Figure 7-24. Block style, heading only

```
  TO:  Menaka Gopal                       DATE:  August 19, 1985
       Advertising Department
FROM:  Alicia Gonzales
       Personnel Department


This memorandum illustrates the block style of typing the head-
ing.  All information except the date is typed at the same point--
two or three spaces after the colon.  This facilitates the typing
of information and is easier to read because all information with-
in the heading begins at the same place.

The body of the memorandum begins three or four lines after the
last line of the heading.  The left margin in this illustration
is set even with the longest line in the heading.  Memoranda are
usually typed in single spacing with double spacing between para-
graphs and are typed in the block style with no paragraph inden-
tions.  A short memorandum may be typed with double spacing.

Because memoranda are internal correspondence, the salutation and
complimentary closing are omitted.  The writer may simply write
his or her initials next to the typed name or at the end of the
memorandum.

rmn
```

The subject line should be as brief as possible yet include sufficient information for the reader to focus on the topic of the communication.

7.101 The date of the communication is typed with the month spelled out, unless space is limited:

DATE: November 10, 1983

DATE: Nov. 30, 1983

7.102 **The body of the memorandum, which contains the typed message, begins three to four lines below the last line of the heading. It is usually typed in single spaced block style paragraphs with double spacing between them.**

SUBJECT: Bradbury Wills v. Atlantic Insurance Co.

Begin the message three to four lines below the last line of the heading. This is generally sufficient space between the heading and the body of the memo.

7.103 **The margin settings for interoffice correspondence depend on the format of the printed heading.**

TO: Arthur B. Segal
Operations and Planning
FROM: Cynthia Wong
Personnel Services
DATE: May 5, 1983
SUBJECT: MARGINS FOR INTEROFFICE MEMOS

When the words in the printed heading of the memorandum end at the same point, set the left margin two or three spaces after each line in the heading. This format is easy for the reader to follow because all information begins at the same place on the page.

This form is especially attractive when there is a narrow margin at the left because of the placement of the lines in the heading.

ehs

TO: Arthur B. Segal
Operations and Planning
FROM: Cynthia Wong
Personnel Services
DATE: May 5, 1983
SUBJECT: MARGINS FOR INTEROFFICE MEMOS

When the words in the printed heading of the memorandum end at the same point, the left margin may be set even with the longest word of the heading. This format is pleasing to the eye because it provides a balanced appearance of information on the page.

This format should be used when there is a wide enough left margin before the printed heading.

ehs

TO: Arthur B. Segal
Operations and Planning
FROM: Cynthia Wong
Personnel Services
DATE: May 5, 1983
SUBJECT: MARGINS FOR INTEROFFICE MEMOS

When the words in the heading of the memorandum begin at the same point and are staggered, the left margin for the message may be set either where the printed words begin or it may be set beginning with the typewritten words.

ehs

7.104 Reference initials, which identify the typist, are typed in lowercase letters at the left margin a double space below the last line of the memorandum. No periods or spaces appear between the letters, as shown under 7.103.

7.105 Memoranda are not generally signed by the writer, but the memo may be initialled next to the typed name in the heading or at the end of the memorandum.

TO: Legal Department

FROM: Ellen C. Fong ECF

SUBJECT: Bradbury Wills v. Atlantic Insurance Co.

7.106 When one or more papers will be enclosed with or attached to the memorandum, this fact should be noted a double space below the reference initials at the left margin.

Enc.	or	Encs.
Encl.	or	Encls.
Enclosure	or	Enclosures
Attachment	or	Attachments

The enclosure(s) or attachment(s) may also be itemized, or the number of enclosures may be indicated.

Enclosures: ACV Letter, Dec. 10, 1983
Escrow Instructions
Deposit Slip

Enclosures: 3 **or** Enclosures (3)

7.107 The second and subsequent pages of a memorandum are typed on plain white paper of the same quality as the first page. A blocked or horizontal heading is typed 2.5 cm from the top of each additional page, starting at the left margin, that lists the addressee's name and department, the page number, and the date.

Gerald Manning
Real Estate Dept.
Page 2
February 4, 1984

Gerald Manning	2	February 4, 1984
Real Estate Dept.		

7.108 The body of the memorandum is continued three to four lines below the heading and is typed in the same form as the first page.

Business Reports 8

Report writing guidelines

8.1 A business report is prepared to present factual information to persons within or outside the company, based on a study or investigation of a given subject. Information is conveyed to those concerned with the business operations of the company—stockholders, employees, customers, prospective customers, and the public. Reports provide the bases for determining progress and shaping decisions within the organization.

Writing effective reports

8.2 Report writing may be divided into three tasks: defining the objective(s) of the report, gathering information and constructing an outline (see 8.6 through 8.18), and writing the actual report. The list below includes questions you should ask as the report is being prepared.

Business Report Checklist

1. *Purpose*. Has the purpose of the report been determined? Is there a problem to be solved? Is certain information needed to keep a department running smoothly or to serve as the basis for a decision? Ideally, to simplify the writer's task, the report purpose should be stated as a series of specific objectives.

2. *Scope*. Has the scope of the report been defined? What limitations, if any, will determine the writer's approach to the subject? Is an in-depth analysis called for, or will a brief factual summary do?

3. *Conciseness*. Is all pertinent information presented as briefly, yet completely, as possible? Business reports should contain the minimum number of words needed to accomplish the intended goals.

4. *Completeness*. Does the report include all facts, figures, and supporting information that relate to the topic?

5. *Tone*. Does the tone of the report reflect a consistent, businesslike point of view? It is the writer's responsibility to present various aspects of the topic to the reader based on the data gathered; it is up to the reader to interpret the facts and decide on subsequent courses of action.

6. *Accuracy*. Are all facts cited in the report accurate? Do the data substantiate the conclusions? Incorrect information is worse than no information at all because it may lead to misunderstandings and can involve additional time in obtaining the correct data.

A note on style

8.3 The way a report is written determines its effectiveness. Unless facts and ideas are communicated in the proper order and in direct, simple language, the report will fail to meet its objectives. Avoid such awkward, redundant expressions as those indicated below.

Avoid	*Use*
absolutely complete	complete
actual experience	experience
along these lines	similar to, like this
arrived at the conclusion	concluded
articulate	explain
as per	as, according
assemble together	assemble
at a cost of	at
at a later date	later
at all times	always
at the present time	now
attached please find	attached is
basic fundamentals	fundamentals
by means of	by
circumstances surrounding	circumstances
close proximity	close
consensus of opinion	consensus
continue on	continue
disseminate	distribute
due to the fact that	because, since
during the course of the day	during the day
during the time that	while
each and every one of us	each of us
enclosed please find	enclosed is
entirely completed	completed
for the purpose of	for, to
for the reason that	because, since
held a meeting	met
if it is possible	if possible
in accordance with your request	as you requested
in connection with	about
in order that	so
in regard to	regarding, about
in the event that	if
in the neighbourhood of	about
in the normal course of our procedures	normally
in the very near future	soon
in this day and age	today
in view of the fact that	because, since

Avoid	*Use*
inasmuch as	since
inside of the	inside the
later on	later
might possibly	might
my personal opinion	my opinion
necessary requisite	requisite
party	person
past experience	experience
reason is because	the reason is
remembering the fact that	remembering that
repeat again	repeat
revert back	revert to
same identical	same, identical
significant	important
small in size	small
square in shape	square
still persists	persists
subsequent to	after
the reason is due to	because
thrust	direction, emphasis
under date of	on
under separate cover	separately
uniformly consistent	consistent
unique	somewhat different
until such time	until
up until	until
utilize	use
whether or not	whether
will you be kind enough	please
with a view to	to
with regard to	about
with respect to	about
with the result that	so that
without further delay	now, immediately

8.4 Avoid using two words that mean the same thing. In the list below, either word would be adequate by itself.

agreeable and satisfactory
anxious and eager
courteous and polite
first and foremost
full and complete
hope and trust
if and when

8.5 Eliminate such trite expressions as the following; they have been used so often that they are meaningless.

along these lines	for your information
as a matter of fact	I have your letter
beg to acknowledge	permit me to say
beg to inform	replying to yours
contents duly noted	this letter is for the purpose of

Outlines

8.6 The outline, or organization plan for the report, enables the writer to structure the report before starting to write. An outline indicates the major points, the secondary topics, and substantiating information. The number of divisions in an outline varies, but there should be no more than five divisions.

8.7 The most common standard outline employs a combination of Roman numerals, Arabic numerals, and alphabet letters to identify various heading levels.

Figure 8-1. Structure of a standard outline

I. PURPOSE OF STUDY (First Major Division)

A. Scope

B. Limitations
1. Time
2. Money
3. Personnel
a. Existing employees
(1) Full-time
(2) Part-time
b. Outside consultants

II. DEFINITION OF STUDY (Second Major Division)

A new heading level is introduced only if it will be used more than once. In a standard outline, for example, an *A* must be followed by a *B*, a 1 by a 2, and so on.

Typing a standard outline (Figure 8-1)

8.8 Roman numeral I, which identifies the first major division heading, is typed at the left margin, followed by a period and two spaces. Subsequent Roman numerals are aligned at the right, as follows:

1. Return the carriage or the carrier to the left margin.

2. Depress the margin release key.

3. Backspace the desired number of spaces outside the left margin setting. (For example, to type Roman numeral II, backspace once; to type III, backspace twice.)

```
Left margin              ↓
                         I. MAJOR DIVISION

                            A.  Secondary Division (First Item)

                            B.  Secondary Division (Second Item)

Backspace once          II. MAJOR DIVISION (SECOND ITEM)

Backspace twice        III. MAJOR DIVISION (THIRD ITEM)
```

8.9 The capital letters that identify secondary headings are typed at the first tabulator stop, set four spaces from the left margin, followed by a period and two spaces. Each secondary heading begins a double space below the major division heading. If the secondary heading is followed by an Arabic numeral sub-division, single-space before the next item. If it is followed by another secondary heading, single-space or double-space, depending on the length of the outline.

8.10 The Arabic numerals that identify the third division are typed at the second tabulator stop, set four spaces from the first stop, followed by a period and two spaces. These items are single-spaced, except in very short outlines.

8.11 The lowercase letters that identify the fourth division are typed at the third tabulator stop, set four spaces from the second stop, followed by a period and two spaces. These items are always single-spaced.

8.12 Use of Arabic numerals in parentheses (identifying the fifth division) should be kept to a minimum. A fourth tabulator stop is set four spaces from the third stop. One or two spaces follow the right parenthesis before the item is typed.

8.13 To continue an outline on a second or subsequent page, follow these guidelines.

1. Maintain a minimum 2.5 cm bottom margin. A slightly wider margin is better than a narrow one.

2. Begin the second or subsequent page with a secondary subdivision (identified by a capital letter).

3. Start a new page with items beginning with Arabic numerals if:

a. at least two Arabic numeral items are carried over to the page, and

b. the outline does not end with these items.

4. Do not start a new page with items beginning with lowercase letters and Arabic numerals in parentheses.

5. Complete an entire section at the bottom of a page, if possible.

6. Do not type only one line of any division at the bottom of the page.

7. Do not type only one line of any division at the top of the next page.

8. Follow the margin settings, spacing, and tabulator stops used on the first page; begin second and subsequent pages at the appropriate tabulator stop to continue the outline.

Outline styles

8.14 The headings and subdivisions in an outline may follow one of three styles: topic, descriptive, or full caption.

Topic outline

8.15 In a topic outline, the items consist of one-, two-, or three-word phrases. The first letter of each important word is capitalized.

noun	I. Purpose
verb phrase	A. Solve Problem
verb phrase	B. Seek Information
noun	II. Definition
verb phrase	A. Determine Scope
verb phrase	B. Determine Limitation
noun	1. Time
noun	2. Money

Descriptive outline

8.16 In a descriptive outline, the major headings and subdivisions are written in phrases or clauses (known also as "talking captions") to provide more details about the information in each section. In major and secondary headings, the first letter of each important word is capitalized; in lesser headings, only the first letter of the first word and the first letters of proper names are capitalized.

noun phrases used throughout	I. Description of the Study
	A. Attempt to Solve a Problem
	B. Attempt to Seek Information
	II. Definition of the Extent of the Study
	A. Scope or Range of the Study
	B. Limitations of the Study
	1. Time not of the essence
	2. Money critical factor

Full caption and sentence outline

8.17 A full outline may be written in complete sentences (see Figure 8-2), it may combine sentences and noun phrases, or it may combine sentences and verb phrases. Capitalize the first letter of each sentence, proper names, and each important word in the phrases.

noun phrase	I. Purpose of the Study
sentence (question)	A. Is it to solve a problem?
sentence (question)	B. Is it to obtain information?
noun phrase	II. Definition of the Study
sentence (question)	A. What is the scope or range of the study?
sentence (question)	B. What limitations are there?
noun	1. Time?
noun	2. Money?

8.18 If a full outline is not written entirely in complete sentences, care must be taken to construct all divisions of equal importance in parallel form. If heading I is written in sentence form, for example, all other Roman numeral headings must be in the same form. Similarly, if one secondary division (identified by capital letters) is written as a noun phrase, all secondary divisions must be written the same way. Parallelism can be achieved by consistently following one pattern throughout: complete sentences, noun clauses or phrases, or verb clauses or phrases.

Informal reports

8.19 There are two kinds of informal reports: the letter report and the memorandum report. Briefer than the formal reports, the letter and memorandum reports are appropriate when information is necessary on a routine or periodic basis, or when a special situation demands a quick, concise response.

Figure 8-2. Sentence outline

```
                    TYPING A SENTENCE OUTLINE

   I.   Placement

        A.  Centre the outline attractively on the page.
        B.  Set margins.
            1.  Use a 60-space line for most outlines.
            2.  Begin outline 4 cm to 5 cm from the top of the
                first page.
            3.  Continue outline 2.5 cm to 6.5 cm from the top
                on succeeding pages.
            4.  Allow approximately 2.5 cm for bottom margin on
                all pages.

  II.   Capitalization

        A.  Centre the main heading (outline title) in all
            capitals.
        B.  Capitalize the first letter of each important word
            in all Roman numeral headings.
        C.  Capitalize only the first letter of the first word
            in the secondary headings (those beginning with A.
            B. C. etc.) and any proper names in the sentence.
        D.  Capitalize only the first letter of the first word
            in the following subheadings.
            1.  The second subdivision (which begins with Arabic
                numerals).
            2.  The third subdivision (which begins with lower-
                case letters).
            3.  The fourth subdivision items (which begin with
                Arabic numerals in parentheses).

 III.   Spacing

        A.  Follow these rules for line spacing.
            1.  Triple-space after the main heading.
            2.  Double-space before and after main divisions.
            3.  Single-space all subdivision items.
            4.  Double-space very short outlines.

        B.  Follow these rules for indentions.
            1.  Align Roman numerals at the left margin.
            2.  Set tabulator stops for four-space indentions
                for each division in the outline.
            3.  Begin the second line of an item directly under
                the first letter of the first line.

        C.  Follow these rules for punctuation.
            1.  Use a period after numerals and letters.
            2.  Space twice after the period.
            3.  Use a period after an item if a complete
                thought is expressed.
            4.  Do not use a period after single words or phrases.
```

Letter report

8.20 When an informal report is to be distributed outside the company, it is prepared in the form of a business letter on company letterhead stationery (see Figure 8-3). Letter reports are usually three to four pages long. While the elements of a letter report are similar to those in business letters (see 7.10–7.65), there are a few minor distinctions, as explained below.

8.21 The letter report may be prepared either in the semi-block, block or full block style (see Figures 7-4–7-7).

Figure 8-3. Sample letter report with side headings

CONTROLLED ENVIRONMENTS LIMITED. 1461 St. James St., Winnipeg, Manitoba, Canada R3H 0W9 Phone (204) 786-6451 Telex 07-57777

September 19, 1984

Peter Brown
Suite 2900
630 Dorchester Blvd. W.
Montreal, P.Q.
H3B 1S6

Dear Mr. Brown:

This is an illustration of a letter report prepared and distributed to persons outside the company. Letter reports generally follow the same format used for other business correspondence. This letter is typed in the block style with mixed punctuation.

Use of Side Headings

The use of side headings, especially in lengthy letter reports, helps divide information into smaller pieces for the reader's comprehension. Side headings are typed at the left margin and are underscored. A double space precedes and follows each side heading.

Body of the Report

The body of the report is the report itself, the facts, analyses, recommendations, or conclusions. The report should be written briefly, yet completely.

Recommendation or Conclusion

The closing paragraph(s) should contain some recommendation or conclusion based on the facts presented within the report. Information must therefore be correct and logically presented.

Yours very truly,

Joe Smith

ftv

8.22 Because the date indicates when the report data were presented, it should be written in full on each page of the letter report.

8.23 The report is addressed to the person or organization that requested or authorized it; it may also be addressed to the person responsible for taking action based on the report findings. The elements of the inside address for an individual or a company correspond to those in a business letter.

8.24 When a subject is used in a letter report, it is typed a double space below the salutation, preceded by SUBJECT or RE.

8.25 The body of the letter contains the text of the report: introductory paragraph, description and analysis of the facts, and recommendations or conclusions. It is typed single-spaced with double spacing between paragraphs.

8.26 The introductory paragraph identifies the request or authorization for the report (the purpose) and summarizes the method of investigation and the conclusions or recommendations.

8.27 If the report is lengthy or detailed, use side headings to divide it into sections (see Figure 8-3). Type each side heading at the left margin, underscored; side headings should not be more than a few words long. Double-space before and after each heading. Capitalize the first letter of each important word. No punctuation follows a heading.

8.28 If side headings are used, at least two must be included within the report; one should be used to set off the recommendation or conclusion paragraph(s).

8.29 The complimentary closing for a letter report is more formal than that used in other business correspondence. Type the complimentary closing a double space below the last line of the body of the letter report.

Respectfully	Yours truly
Respectfully submitted	Yours very truly
Respectfully yours	Very truly yours

8.30 If the company name is typed as part of the closing lines in other business correspondence, it should be included in letter reports. As in business letters, it is typed a double space below the closing in solid capital letters above the writer's signature (see 7.33 and 7.34).

8.31 The writer's signature, typed name, and full title, as well as the reference initials, are included in letter reports as in business correspondence (see 7.34–7.47).

8.32 When documents such as charts, illustrations, or other information are to be sent with the letter report, this fact is indicated by typing an enclosure notation at the left margin a double space below the reference initials. The word *Enclosure* or *Enclosures* is sufficient, but if there are numerous enclosures it may be desirable to list them (see 7.48).

Memorandum report

8.33 When an informal report is distributed within the company, it may be organized as an interoffice memorandum and typed on a company memorandum form. The elements in memorandum reports correspond to those in standard memoranda (see 7.96–7.108). A few differences are explained below.

8.34 The report is addressed to the person(s) within the organization who requested or authorized the report; it may also be addressed to those who will take action based on the report findings. The addressee's official title and/or department name or number are typed after TO on the memorandum form.

8.35 The FROM heading usually consists of the name, title, and/or department name or number of the person preparing the report. When the report will be transmitted by someone other than the writer, however, that person's name is typed after FROM.

8.36 The SUBJECT heading consists of the full title of the report or study, typed in solid capital letters or with the first letter of each important word capitalized.

8.37 The body of the memorandum contains the same kinds of information and is typed the same way as the body of a letter report (see 8.25–8.27 and Figure 8-3). If side headings are used, they are typed as in a letter report.

Formal reports

8.38 When a brief, informal report is not sufficient to provide the necessary data, a more comprehensive, formal report is prepared. This longer report is the result of a study or investigation of all aspects of a particular topic.

Elements of a formal report

8.39 Formal reports usually contain the following elements, assembled in the sequence shown below.

Introductory Pages (8.52–8.63)
- Cover
- Title Page
- Letter or Memorandum of Transmittal
- Preface or Foreword
- Acknowledgements
- Table of Contents
- List of Illustrations
- Synopsis

Body of the Report (8.64–8.80)
- Introduction
- Discussion
- Concluding Pages
- Quoted Material
- Ellipses
- Lists
- Statistical Data

Supplementary Pages (8.81–8.85)
- Appendix
- Bibliography
- Index

Setting up a formal report

8.40 Margin settings depend on the binding style selected for the report: left-bound, top-bound, or unbound (see Table 8-1, Placement of report margins). If the report is to be unbound, the pages should be held together with a paper clip and the report placed in a folder.

Table 8-1. Placement of report margins

		Type of report	
	Unbound	*Leftbound*	*Topbound*
Top Margin, First Page	5 cm	5 cm	6.5 cm
Top Margin Succeeding pages	2.5 cm	2.5 cm	3.5 cm
Left Margin	2.5 cm	3.5 cm	2.5 cm
Right Margin	2.5 cm	2.5 cm	2.5 cm
Bottom Margin	2.5 cm	2.5 cm	2.5 cm
Page Numbers	Bottom or right corner	Right corner	Bottom

8.41 The text of the report is typed double-spaced, although lengthy quotations and lists are typed single-spaced to make them stand out. Five-space paragraph indentions are used.

8.42 The headings within the report usually correspond to the major and secondary headings in the preliminary outline. They are useful to the reader in both locating and understanding information. Each level of heading is typed and arranged somewhat differently than other levels (see Figure 8-4) so the importance of a particular topic will be evident to the reader at a glance.

8.43 The title or main heading of the report may be stated in topic form or may describe the nature of the report. It is centred and typed in solid capitals 5 cm to 6.5 cm from the top of the first page. Depending on its length, the title may be typed in one, two, or possibly three lines, with each line centred on the page.

MICROFILM—AN EFFECTIVE
RECORDS MANAGEMENT TOOL

RECOMMENDATIONS FOR THE ACQUISITION
AND IMPLEMENTATION OF A WORD PROCESSING CENTRE

Triple-space after the main heading before beginning the report, unless a secondary heading follows the main heading. In that case, double-space after the main heading.

8.44 A subtitle may accompany a one- or two-line title to identify the report topic more specifically. The subtitle is centred and typed a double space below the main heading. Only the first letters of important words are capitalized.

MICROFILM—AN EFFECTIVE
RECORDS MANAGEMENT TOOL

A Study of Its Applications and Uses
in the Banking Industry

Since the subtitle is part of the main heading, a triple space follows it.

8.45 Centred headings, used to introduce major divisions or topics, correspond to Roman numeral headings in the outline and may be preceded by Roman numerals.

Figure 8-4. Heading arrangement

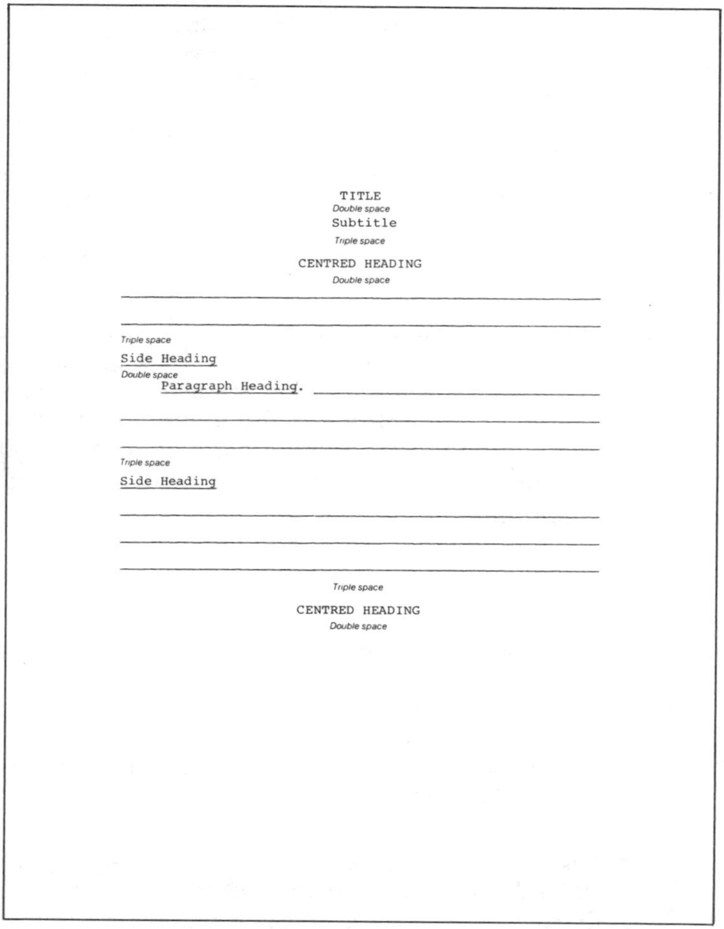

TITLE
Double space
Subtitle
Triple space
CENTRED HEADING
Double space

Triple space
Side Heading
Double space
Paragraph Heading.

Triple space
Side Heading

Triple space
CENTRED HEADING
Double space

A centred heading is typed a triple space below the line above. It may be typed in solid capital letters, or it may be underlined with only the first letter of each important word capitalized.

PURPOSE OF THE REPORT

or

Purpose of the Report

Also, double-space after the centred heading before typing the information under it.

8.46 Side or marginal headings, which correspond to capital letter heads in the outline (those preceded by *A*, *B*, and so on), are typed beginning at the left margin to introduce subdivisions within the report. A triple space precedes each side or marginal heading, and a double space follows it. Capitalize only the first letters of important words, and underline the entire heading. No punctuation is used after the heading.

Side Heading

Side headings are typed at the left margin to introduce subdivisions within the report.

8.47 Paragraph or run-in headings correspond to items preceded by Arabic numerals in the report outline. These headings, typed at the paragraph indention, introduce the information within the paragraph. Only the first letter of the first word is capitalized unless a proper name appears within the heading. Underline the heading and type a period after it. Leave two spaces after the period before beginning the paragraph.

Paragraph heading. A paragraph heading introduces the information typed within the paragraph. This heading begins at the paragraph indention and is underscored.

8.48 Every page of the report except the cover and title page is numbered consecutively. The introductory pages are numbered in small Roman numerals; the body of the report and the supplementary pages are numbered in Arabic numerals.

8.49 Begin numbering introductory pages with Roman numeral ii centred and typed at the bottom of the page following the title page. Continue to type small Roman numerals. The page number on all introductory pages is centred and typed approximately 1 cm from the bottom edge (see 8.52–8.63).

8.50 Arabic numerals are used for all pages within the body of the report, beginning with page 1. The number of the first page of each new division, section, or chapter is centred and typed approximately 1 cm from the bottom edge. With the exception of topbound reports, other report pages are numbered in the upper right corner at the margin approximately 1 cm from the top edge. In topbound reports, page numbers appear at the bottom of each page, centred approximately 1 cm from the edge (see 8.64–8.80).

8.51 Supplementary pages are numbered consecutively, starting with the number following that on the last body page (see 8.81–8.85).

Figure 8-5. Introductory pages

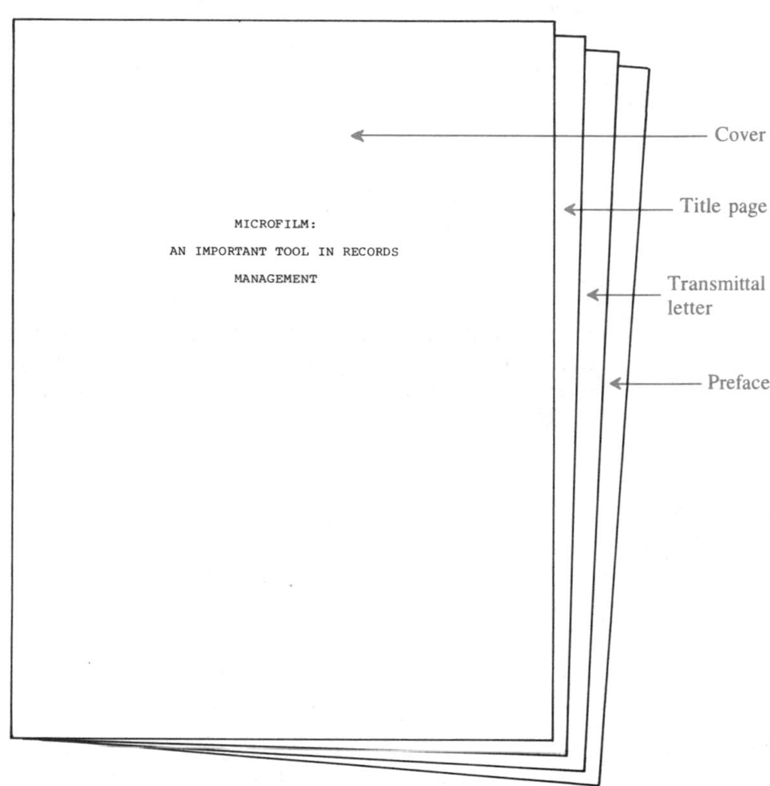

Introductory pages

8.52 Introductory pages (see Figure 8.5) include the cover, title page, letter or memorandum of transmittal, preface, acknowledgements, table of contents, list of illustrations, and summary. These pages are prepared after the report has been typed and page numbers assigned.

8.53 The report cover is a typewritten or printed sheet, on paper of the same quality as the report. It contains only the report title, centred and typed in solid capitals. A title of two or more lines is double- or triple-spaced.

Figure 8-6. Sample title page

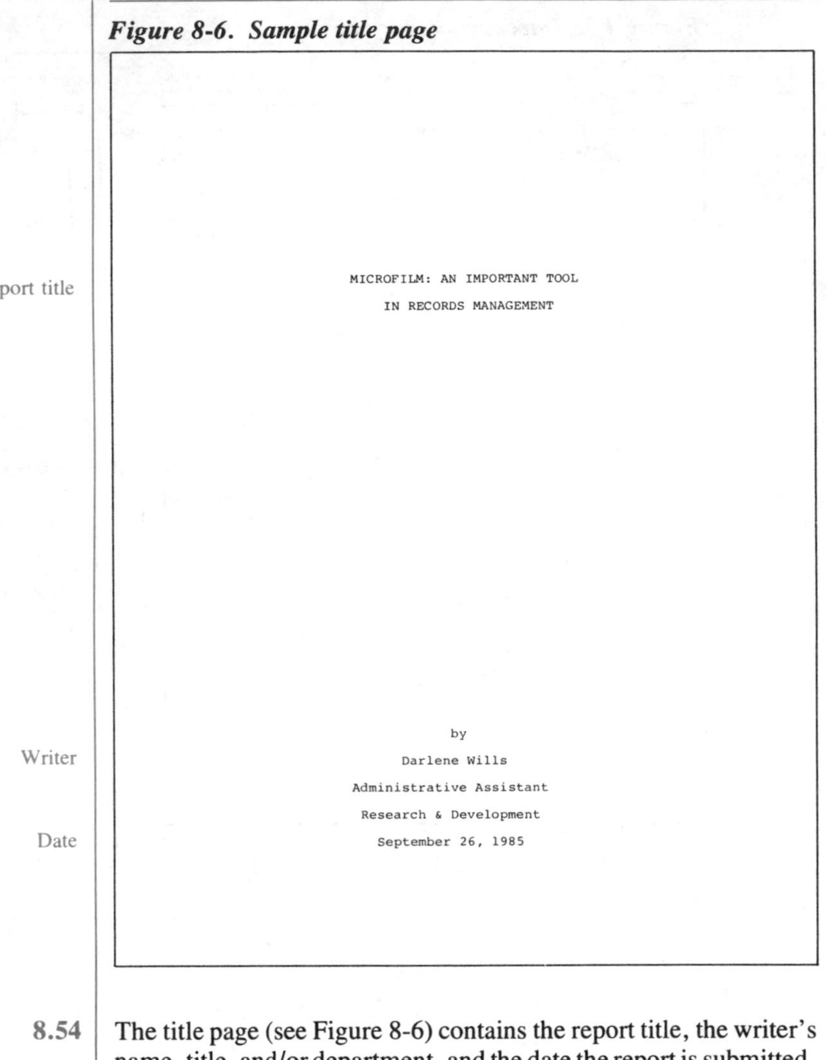

Report title

MICROFILM: AN IMPORTANT TOOL
IN RECORDS MANAGEMENT

by

Writer

Darlene Wills

Administrative Assistant

Research & Development

Date

September 26, 1985

8.54 The title page (see Figure 8-6) contains the report title, the writer's name, title, and/or department, and the date the report is submitted. Each piece of information is centred horizontally across the page, and all information is spread over the page to provide a balanced appearance.

8.55 The name of the person who prepared—or is transmitting—the report is centred and typed about midway between the report title and the bottom of the page. If the writer has a title, such as Doctor or Professor, it should precede the name. An official title and department or company name may be typed below the writer's name.

Figure 8-7. Sample letter of transmittal

ADRESSE TELEGRAPHIQUE BEVERAGE MONTREAL

CORBY DEPUIS 1859

1201 OUEST, RUE SHERBROOKE, MONTREAL, QUEBEC, CANADA H3A 1J1 **LES DISTILLERIES CORBY LIMITEE**
(514) 288-4181

May 5, 1984

Mr. John Blank
Data Processing Inc.
4908 Dewdney Ave.
Regina, Saskatchewan
S4T 1B8

Dear Mr. Blank:

SUBJECT: Word Processing Centre Study

Attached is the report on the Recommendations for the Acquisition and Implementation of a Word Processing Centre. The board of directors approved this study at its regular meeting on April 18.

I am particularly pleased with the outcome of this study. According to the R & D staff, our company can definitely benefit by a word processing installation to eliminate much of the downtime expenses. As mentioned on page 58 of the report, a single factor against such a centre would be the attitudes of our present clerical staff. This, however, I believe we can overcome through some well-planned in-service training sessions with personnel and equipment manufacturers.

This report seems to have accomplished all of our objectives--and more! Please do not hesitate to call me if you have any questions or if you need additional information.

Yours sincerely,

Mrs. Jane Doe
Vice President, Operations

Dorothy Linton
Managing Editor

If the report is prepared by an outside consultant, the name and address of the consulting firm is typed on the title page.

MANAGEMENT CONSULTANTS, LTD.
Box 34
Toronto Dominion Centre
Toronto, Ontario
M5K 1B7

The date—month, day, and year—is centred and typed near the bottom of the page by itself.

Figure 8-8. Sample contents page

ii

CONTENTS

8.56 A letter of transmittal, also called a covering letter, accompanies the report. It mentions the request or authorization and—if the report has no preface—also covers the purpose or scope of the report, the method of study, and a summary of the conclusions or recommendations (see Figure 8-7).

Written in business letter style on company letterhead stationery, it consists of the date of transmittal, inside address, salutation, subject line, body, complimentary closing, and signature line.

8.57 When a preface is included in addition to the transmittal letter, the letter is very brief; it simply describes the recipient's original request, and all detailed information on the report itself is then included in the preface.

Figure 8-9. Sample illustration list

TABLES AND CHARTS

8.58 When a report is prepared for submission to an individual within the organization, a transmittal memorandum is prepared on inter-office correspondence stationery. It serves the same purpose as the letter of transmittal and contains the same information.

8.59 The preface, or foreword, is the introduction to the report. As noted in 8.56 and 8.57, when a preface and letter of transmittal are both included, all explanatory details (purpose of report, method of study, and so on) are contained in the preface; the letter is used only to transmit the report to the recipient. When a letter or memorandum of transmittal is not included, the preface would also mention the original request or authorization for the report.

8.60 The acknowledgements on a separate page give credit to individuals or organizations who assisted in the preparation of the report. The acknowledgements may be a listing of credits, or they may be written in narrative form.

8.61 A table of contents (headed simply *Contents*) lists each major heading in the report with the corresponding page number. The contents usually parallel the Roman numeral and secondary (capital letter) headings in the report outline. While a table of contents is not essential, it should be included when a report is lengthy or is divided into several sections.

8.62 When tables, charts, or other illustrations are contained in the report, an illustration list is included either with the table of contents or on a separate page. Each table, chart, or illustration is labelled in sequence by number as *Figure 5* or *Figure 4-2* (i.e., chapter or section 4, second illustration).

The list is typed in the same form as the table of contents. Each illustration is given a title. If illustrations other than charts and tables are included in the report, the list may be headed *Illustrations*.

8.63 A synopsis concisely summarizes the report and includes the major facts, results, recommendations, and conclusions.

Body of report

8.64 The body of the report, the text itself, includes the introduction, discussion, summary, conclusions, and recommendations. The presentation of information follows the sequence indicated in the report outline.

8.65 The introduction provides the reader with background information to help focus attention on the topic. This section includes the following information.

1. *Authorization:* Who authorized the report and when?

2. *Purpose:* What are the objectives or aims?

3. *Scope:* What are the boundaries of the study?

4. *Limitation:* What conditions or problems existed prior to or during the investigation?

5. *Organization of Data:* How is information presented?

6. *History or Background:* What events generated the report?

7. *Method of Investigation:* How was the research conducted? By whom?

8. *Sources of Information:* What authorities were consulted?

9. *Definition of Terms:* How are certain words used in the report?

8.66 The discussion is the report itself—the facts, the analyses, and the findings. Written in formal language (third person), the report must be presented in an objective manner. The discussion may contain the following:

1. Strengths and weaknesses of existing situation
2. Details of the methods or functions of existing situation
3. Proposals or recommendations
4. Facts and their substantiating data
5. Narrative or chronology
6. Proposed procedure(s) to improve situation
7. Comparison of procedures and data
8. Alternative methods or routes
9. Advantages and disadvantages of alternatives

8.67 The closing parts of the report include the summary, conclusions, and recommendations. In formal, lengthy reports, all three parts are included for the convenience of the reader in interpreting and summarizing information. Each of these words is typed as a side heading at the left margin to introduce the information in that particular section of the report.

8.68 A summary is a compilation of all the facts and findings contained in the report. It summarizes or brings together the purpose of the report, the main points discussed, and the results of the study or investigation.

8.69 The conclusions are statements or inferences based on the writer's interpretation of the facts derived from the study. Conclusions, therefore, should be logical extensions of these facts. Conclusions may be presented in narrative form or listed according to their importance.

8.70 Recommendations are suggested methods to be followed or action to be taken as a result of the data presented in the report. Recommendations must be directly related to the original purpose of the study and be fully substantiated by the facts. Alternative methods or actions may also be included.

8.71 When information is quoted verbatim from another source or when a portion of a direct quotation is cited, the source of the material must be stated.

8.72 Short quotations (three or fewer typewritten lines) are typed within the body of the report with quotation marks before and after.

> The authors note that "Quotations of three or four typewritten lines are typed within the body of the report with quotation marks before and after."

8.73 A long quotation (four or more typewritten lines) is typed as a separate paragraph, single-spaced and indented five spaces from the right and left margins.

> The authors suggest that longer quotations be typed in the following manner:
>
> > Quotations of four or more lines should be typed in single spacing and indented five spaces from the right and left margins. Quotation marks should not be used. If the first line of the quotation begins a paragraph, it is indented five spaces from the new margin. Otherwise the quotation is typed in block form.

8.74 Ellipsis points are used to indicate the omission of a word, phrase, sentence, or paragraph from a quotation. An ellipsis is made by typing either three or four periods with spaces between them.

8.75 Use three spaced periods to indicate omission of part of a sentence, in the middle of that sentence.

> Quotations are easier for a reader to understand if they include only information that is crucial to the writer's point.

becomes

> Quotations are easier . . . to understand if they include only information that is crucial to the writer's point.

8.76 Use four spaced periods (a period followed by three spaced periods) to indicate omission of the last part of a sentence, the first part of the next sentence or paragraph, a sentence or more, or a paragraph or more.

End of Sentence:

> Quotations are easier for a reader to understand if they include only information that is crucial. . . . The idea is that ellipses help writers tailor quoted information to their needs.

Beginning of Next Sentence:

> Quotations are easier for a reader to understand if they include only information that is crucial to the writer's point. . . . ellipses help writers tailor quoted information to their needs.

Note that the second sentence does not begin with a capital letter. In this way, the reader knows that the beginning of the sentence has been omitted.

Beginning of Paragraph:

> Quotations are easier for a reader to understand if they include information that is crucial to the writer's point.
>
> . . . . writers must use ellipses with restraint.

Note that when the beginning of a paragraph is omitted, the ellipsis follows the paragraph indention.

A Sentence or More:

> Quotations are easier for a reader to understand if they include only information that is crucial to the writer's point. . . . Of course, writers must use ellipses with restraint.

Note that the second sentence begins with a capital letter. This indicates that information between the two sentences has been omitted.

A Paragraph or More:

> Quotations are easier for a reader to understand if they include only information that is crucial to the writer's point. . . .
>
> Of course, writers must use ellipses with restraint.

Note that a new paragraph is begun after the omission of one or more paragraphs.

8.77 Itemized lists, preceded by Arabic numbers or lowercase letters, present detailed information in a form that is easy to read.

8.78 Arabic numerals or lowercase letters typed within parentheses are used to introduce lists within a sentence or paragraph of a letter or report. The items are treated as a series and separated by commas.

Each of the following items contributes to an attractive report: (1) arrangement of the headings to indicate divisions of information, (2) correct spacing throughout, and (3) correct display of quoted information.

8.79 Arabic numerals, followed by a period and two spaces, are used to introduce items when each is listed by itself. No punctuation follows the items unless they are stated as complete sentences.

Here is the suggested method for typing a list of short items (no more than one line each):

1. Use double spacing in reports.

2. Use single spacing in letters.

3. Indent items five spaces.

1. Lists of long items may be typed as separate paragraphs within the body of the report or letter; they are double-spaced, and the first line of each item is indented five spaces before the number is typed.

1. Long items may also be typed in single spacing, indented from both right and left margins.

2. Leave a double space before the list and between the items in the list.

8.80 Statistical data consist of tables, graphs, and charts. Such illustrations can save words by presenting complex information in visual form. (See chapter 9 for detailed information on typing tables.)

Supplementary pages

8.81 Supplementary pages consist of notes or bibliography, appendix, and index. The decision to include these pages depends on the length and detail of the report. These pages are prepared after the report has been typed and page numbers have been assigned.

8.82 The sources of all material quoted or paraphrased in the report should be cited in the footnote references and in the bibliography that accompanies the report. See 8.86–8.127 for information on constructing notes and bibliographies. In scientific reports the procedure is somewhat different; see 8.128–8.131.

8.83 An appendix consists of additional written or illustrative material that substantiates or expands on a fact or idea presented in the report. These supporting documents, questionnaires or surveys, summary tables, and reference materials are usually more technical or detailed than information in the report.

8.84 Materials in the appendix may be combined into one section and labelled *APPENDIX*, or each item can be given a title and labelled individually such as *Appendix 1, 2,* or *3, Appendix A, B,* or *C.* When documents are labelled separately, the table of contents should list each item.

APPENDIX 1. Sample Questionnaire 87

APPENDIX 2. Summary Tabulations 89

8.85 An index is an alphabetical list of all topics and subtopics in the report. Each entry in the index is followed by the page number(s) on which the topic is mentioned or discussed. Placed at the end of the report, an index is valuable in helping locate specific information. But it can take a long time to prepare an index, and for most reports a table of contents is sufficient.

Footnotes[1]

8.86 Footnotes in business reports serve two purposes: (1) they cite the source of a direct or indirect quotation or a specific fact or group of facts; and (2) they provide additional details or information that is useful but not essential to the text of the report itself. The first type is called a reference or source footnote, and the second type is called an explanatory or descriptive footnote.

Reference footnote:

1. Brian A. Brown, <u>The New Confederation</u> (Saanichton, B.C.: Hancock House, 1977), p. 16.

---

1. The instructions regarding footnotes, bibliographies, and scientific references presented here are based on the University of Chicago Press *Manual of Style,* 12th ed. rev. (Chicago: University of Chicago Press, 1969). Other style books (some of which are listed under Secretarial Handbooks and Textbooks, 15.14) may differ from the *Manual* in certain details of form. The *Manual,* however, does offer the most consistent and common-sense approach to the documentation problems likely to arise in business situations.

Explanatory footnote:

2. The circumstances are similar to those in Massey v. FitzSimmons, cited earlier.

Numbering footnotes

8.87 Footnotes are generally numbered consecutively throughout a report. If the report is divided into separate chapters and the overall number of notes is great enough, they may be numbered consecutively within each chapter.

(A writer may sometimes need to insert a new footnote at the last minute. If notations are numbered consecutively throughout a long report, some hasty renumbering may be necessary, and errors—notes and text references that don't correspond—can result.)

Typing footnote numbers

8.88 The Arabic numerals used for footnotes are typed above the line (superscript) in the text. Type the numbers above the line at the point of reference in the text, which may be at the end of the last quoted word, sentence, or paragraph or at the end of any factual information that requires a source note.

Type the number reference in the text as follows.

1. Use the ratchet release level on the typewriter and turn the cylinder slightly toward you. Type the footnote number and return the ratchet release to its position. Return the cylinder knob to the line of typing.

2. Spacing after the footnote number follows the normal spacing after words or marks of punctuation. For example, since two spaces follow a period, two spaces would be left after the footnote number before the next sentence is begun.

. . . same records on paper.[6] Microfilming processes provide reductions . . .

8.89 Symbols other than Arabic numerals, such as asterisks and daggers, should not be used for footnotes in business reports.

Typing footnotes

8.90 Footnotes (references or explanations) are often typed at the bottom of the page on which the footnote number appears in the text. While typing the report, observe the number and length of the footnotes that will appear at the bottom of each page. Allow enough space at the bottom of the page for them to be typed. Follow this procedure for typing the footnotes:

1. Allow approximately 1 cm for each footnote at the bottom of the page, using this method:

a. Place a light pencil mark approximately 2.5 cm from the bottom of the page for the bottom margin.
b. After typing each footnote number within the text, place another pencil mark approximately 1 cm above the first marking(s) to indicate the point where the footnote will be typed.

2. Continue to type the body of the report on the page until a pencil mark is visible. Type a 3.5 cm footnote separating line (using the underscore key) a single space below the last line of the text. Double-space after the line.

3. Indent the first line of each footnote five spaces.

4. Precede each footnote with the reference number typed on the line and followed by a period and two spaces (or typed as a superscript with no space following it).

> 1. Marvin Zuckerman, Words Words Words (Beverly Hills, Calif.: Glencoe Press, 1974), p. 27.

5. Type all source and explanatory footnotes in single spacing with double spacing between entries.

6. Type the footnotes within the margin settings used for the report.

8.91 Source and explanatory notes may also be grouped together and typed on a separate page at the end of the report. If this arrangement is used, the word *Notes*—not *Footnotes*—is centred and typed as the heading at the top of the first page of notes. The numbers of the notes are typed on the line, followed by a period and two spaces.

Footnote elements

8.92 The information contained in a footnote varies depending on whether a book, periodical, or public document is being cited; but all footnotes should be as complete and as consistent as possible. All footnotes referring to the same type of source should follow the same pattern. For example, all footnotes for books should follow one pattern; all footnotes for periodicals another pattern, and so on. When a particular work is cited more than once in a report, however, only the first reference must be complete (see Shortened References, 8.117–8.119).

Books

8.93 The first time a book is cited, the notation must include the name(s) of the author(s) and/or editor(s), the full title of the book, the place of publication, the publisher's name, the copyright date, and the page number(s).

1. Richard Swanson and Charles Marquardt, On Communication: Listening, Reading, Speaking and Writing (Beverly Hills, Calif.: Glencoe Press, 1974), pp. 10-11.

8.94 The author's name, as it appears on the title page of the book, is typed first. The name typed in normal order—first name, middle name or initial, and surname, followed by a comma.

2. Robertson B. Davies, Fifth Business (Toronto: Macmillan Co. of Canada Ltd., 1970), pp. 27-48.

8.95 If a book has more than one author, the names are listed in the order in which they appear on the title page, even though they may not be in alphabetical order.

3. Douglas Steubing, John Marshall and Gary Oakes, Trudeau: A Man for Tomorrow (Toronto: Clarke, Irwin & Co. Ltd., 1969), p. 54.

4. Celia Halas and Roberta Matteson, I've done so well - Why do I feel so bad? (London: Collier Macmillan Publishers, 1978), pp. 98-100.

8.96 If a book has more than three authors, you need list only the name of the author listed first on the title page, followed by the Latin abbreviation *et al*. (''and others''). There is no comma separating the author's name and the abbreviation, and the abbreviation is not underscored. Type a period after the abbreviation. (Note: the abbreviation et al. should not be used in bibliographies.)

5. David Skwire et al., Student's Book of College English (Beverly Hills, Calif.: Glencoe Press, 1975), p. 303.

8.97 Three kinds of books include an editor's name on the title page, which means it must be included in a footnote: anthologies (writings drawn from various sources), collected works (all the works by an important author, usually with comments and introductions by the editor), and compilations (information on one subject from different sources, organized into a coherent book by the editor).

8.98 When citing anthologies, the footnote begins with the author and title of the article, story, or essay quoted in the report and continues with the title of the book and the name of the editor. The book title is underscored; the title of the article is typed within quotation marks.

6. Herbert J. Muller, "Education for the Future," in The Conscious Reader, eds. Caroline Shrodes, Harry Finestone, and Michael Shugrue (New York: Macmillan Publishing Co., Inc., 1974), p. 634.

8.99 When citing collected works, note that the author's name usually appears in the title. Thus, if the full name of the author is mentioned in the report, the footnote begins with the title of the work.

7. The Poems of Irving Layton, ed. Eli Mandel (Toronto: McClelland & Stewart Ltd., 1977), p. 48.

When only the last name of the author is mentioned in the report, the footnote should begin with the author's name.

8. Irving Layton, "Misunderstanding" in The Poems of Irving Layton, ed. Eli Mandel (Toronto: McClelland & Stewart Ltd., 1977), p. 48.

If the name of the editor is mentioned in the report, the footnote begins with the name(s) of the editor(s).

9. Eli Mandel, ed., The Poems of Irving Layton (Toronto: McClelland & Stewart Ltd., 1977), p. 48.

8.100 Compilations are cited in the same manner as collected works.

10. Robert E. Spiller et al., eds., Literary History of the United States (New York: Macmillan Publishing Co., Inc., 1974), p. 72.

8.101 When a book is cited in a footnote for the first time, the complete title should be supplied, including the subtitle, if any.

Book titles are underscored, while chapter or article titles appear within quotation marks.

11. Robert Harney and Harold Troper, Immigrants: A Portrait of the Urban Experience, 1890-1930 (Toronto: Van Nostrand Reinhold Ltd., 1975), p. 58.

12. Kenneth McNaught, "Violence in Canadian History," in Studies in Canadian Social History, eds. Michael Horn and Ronald Sabourin (Toronto: McClelland & Stewart Ltd., 1974), p. 376.

Note that chapter titles (see 8.108) are treated differently from article titles (see footnote 12) and selections from collected works (see 8.99), magazines and journals (see 8.111) or newspapers (see 8.112).

In all the above mentioned cases, article titles and selections are inserted immediately after the author's name. Chapter titles, however, follow publication data.

8.102 If a book is part of a series, the series title and number are written immediately after the book title. Only the title of the book is underscored.

> 13. Julian H. Steward, ed., Handbook of South American Indians, Smithsonian Institution, Bureau of American Ethnology Bulletin No. 143 (Washington, D.C., 1949), p. 14.

Because the publisher (the Smithsonian) is part of the series title, no publisher's name is included with the place and date of publication.

8.103 The first edition of a book does not need to be numbered. However, if a book has been published in more than one edition, the edition number will be stated on the copyright page. This number is typed after the book title (or series title) in abbreviated form.

> 14. W. D. Kenneth Kernaghan, ed., Bureaucracy in Canadian Government, 2d ed. (Toronto: Methuen Publications, 1973), p. 80.

Note that the abbreviated form for *second,* is 2d instead of 2nd. Note also that no period follows the abbreviated edition number.

If the copyright page includes dates of revisions, this information is included after the edition number.

> 15. Ernest R. Kamm, Derald D. Hunt, and Jack A. Fleming, Juvenile Law and Procedure in California, 2d ed. rev. (Beverly Hills, Calif.: Glencoe Press, 1971), p. 34.

8.104 If a work has more than one volume, the footnote for any particular volume usually would cite the total number of volumes in the series, using Arabic numerals. The number of the individual volume is also given in Arabic numerals, even though it may appear on the title page in Roman numerals.

If the volume does not have a specific title, its number is typed after the publication data followed by a colon and the page number for the reference.

16. James A. Gould and H. C. Kiefer, eds., The Western Humanities, 2d ed., 2 vols. (New York: Holt, Rinehart & Winston, Inc., 1971), 2:8.

If the volume does have a specific title, the title is typed after the publication data, and the volume number is preceded by the abbreviation *vol.*

17. Ernest A. Baker, A History of the English Novel, 11 vols. (New York: Barnes & Noble, Inc., 1960), vol. 7, "The Age of Dickens and Thackeray," p. 95.

When a work is still in progress (as with the collected works of a particular author, when the volumes may be published one at a time over a long period), the number of volumes may be omitted.

8.105 Publication data includes place of publication, publisher's name, and copyright date. It is typed in parentheses following the book title, series title, or volume title.

If the publisher is located in a major city, the city name alone is sufficient.

(Toronto: University of Toronto Press, 1976)

If the name of the city will not necessarily reveal the publisher's location to the reader, the province should follow in abbreviated form.

(Don Mills, Ont.: Musson Book Company, 1977)

8.106 The publisher's name is separated from the place of publication by a colon.

In citing an older book, check to determine the publisher's current name; the name on the copyright page may have changed.

Copyright Page of 1950 Book:

Harcourt, Brace & World, 1950

Footnote for the Same Book:

Harcourt Brace Jovanovich, 1950

(The correct wording for the names of all Canadian publishers may be found in *Canadian Books in Print* published annually by the University of Toronto Press.)

8.107 Type the copyright date after the publisher's name, separated by a comma. This information is located on both the title and copyright pages in most books. When more than one copyright date is listed, cite the most recent one.

8.108 Sometimes a particular chapter is considered significant enough to be mentioned in a footnote. When referring to a chapter title, insert reference right after publication date. *Chapter* is abbreviated to *chap*. and the title is typed within quotation marks.

18. Kenneth L. Melmon, M.D. and Howard F. Morellie, M.D., Clinical Pharmacology, 2d ed. (Toronto: Collier Macmillan Canada, Inc., 1978), chap. 1, "Basic Principles of Drug Administration," pp. 110-17.

8.109 Page numbers must be included not only in footnotes that refer to direct quotations but also in notes for a particular fact or group of facts that the report writer has drawn from another author. Page numbers may be omitted, however, when a footnote refers either to an entire book or to a general body of information that has been paraphrased over a few paragraphs in the report. In that case, the footnote should begin "Adapted from" or "Summarized from."

Page numbers are abbreviated *p.* if only one page is cited or *pp.* if several pages are cited. Give specific page numbers whenever possible.

Periodicals

8.110 The major elements of a periodical footnote are the author's name, title of the article (in quotation marks), name of the periodical (underscored), volume number (if any), month and year of publication (or the year, for annuals), and the inclusive page numbers of the article—not just the page number from which information was taken.

8.111 When a volume number is included for magazines and journals, use parentheses around the date and a colon after the date to separate it from the page numbers. Eliminate use of *p*. or *pp.* after the colon and just use page numbers.

19. Margaret Atwood, "Night Visits, Torture, Elegies, Bread, Beginnings," The Canadian Forum, Vol. 58, No. 681 (June-July 1978): 20-52.

But note the absence of parentheses around the date when a volume number is not included.

20. Bertha McHaffie-Gaw, "Vancouver Island," Camera Canada, March 1978, p. 46.

In some magazines, articles are written by teams of writers, and no byline is included with the stories. In that case, the citation is written without an author's name.

21. "New Ideas for Clean Elections," U.S. News and World Report, June 4, 1973, p. 79.

8.112 When citing a newspaper article with a byline, insert the author's name. The name of the newspaper and the city of publication are underscored.

22. Peter Foster, "Husky: Winners, Losers--But No Answers," The Financial Post, Toronto, July 18, 1978, p. 1.

Such newspapers as the *New York Times*, however, do not need a city name for identification.

23. "High-Energy Studies Indicate the Existence of New Particle," New York Times, February 3, 1975, p. 48.

Public documents

8.113 The information included in footnotes for public documents varies considerably depending on the kind of document cited. Notes for some basic documents are illustrated here.

8.114 Accuracy in the use of citation is essential. The abbreviation itself and all other descriptive details must be correct. Numerous legal reference works (see 15.18) provide lists of abbreviations for citations and, if possible, these lists should be consulted.

When citing statutes (new laws and amendments to previously published acts) of either the federal or provincial governments, note that for general purposes, a footnote or bibliographic reference would be written out.

24. Statutes of Ontario 1974

For any legal work or legal report, however, use the formal abbreviated method of reference.

25. S.O. 1974 **(Statutes of Ontario 1974)**

26. S.M. 1976 **(Statutes of Manitoba 1976)**

At intervals of approximately ten years, consolidations of statutes in force appear. These are called revised statutes. Both annual and revised statutes are identified by year.

27. Revised Statutes of Ontario 1970 **or** R.S.O. 1970

8.115 In citing a specific act, the name of the act, the statutes or their revision where the act may be located, as well as its chapter number, are shown. If specific sections or subsections of an act are required, reference to them follows immediately. Commas separate each part of the inference in a citation of this kind.

28. The British North America Act, 1867, 30 & 31 Vict., c.3 (U.K.)

29. St. Lawrence Ports Operations Act, S.C. 1972, c. 22

30. The Public Health Amendment Act, S.O. 1975, c.61, s.6 (e)

Government publications

8.116 Most government publications do not include an author's name, so the following information would be sufficient to locate an original document: name of the government agency; title of the publication (underscored); the publication, bulletin, or volume number (if any); place and date of publication (in parentheses); and the page reference.

31. Statistics Canada: Education, Sciences and Culture Division, Educational Staff in Community Colleges, 1974-75 (Ottawa, 1977), pp. 9-23.

32. National Energy Board: Ministry of Energy, Mines and Resources, Energy: Supply and Demand in Canada (Ottawa, 1969), pp. 42-8.

Note that if the name of the author is included, it is listed first with the department name written as the publisher.

33. David Lindley Clark, Labor Laws That Have Been Declared Unconstitutional, U.S. Department of Labor, Bureau of Labor Statistics Bulletin no. 321 (Washington, D.C., 1922), p. 14.

Shortened references

8.117 After a book or article has been cited in full the first time in a footnote, subsequent references may be shortened somewhat by the use of certain Latin abbreviations or abbreviated titles.

8.118 Ibid. (*ibidem*) is used to cite consecutive references to the same work, whether it is the same page or a different page. If the page number is different from that originally stated, the new page number is written in the subsequent reference.

34. John A. B. McLeish, A Canadian for All Seasons: A Biography of John E. Robbins (Toronto: Lester & Orpen Ltd., 1978), pp. 169-172.

35. Ibid. **[meaning exact work and same page number]**

36. Ibid., p. 175 **[meaning exact work but different page]**

8.119 For non-consecutive references to a work, op. cit. and loc. cit were once widely used. But now, op. cit. (*opere citato,* "in the work cited") and loc. cit. (*loco citato,* "in the place cited") have been discarded by the *Chicago Manual of Style.* For greater simplicity and ease of reference, the short-title is now used. For example:

The title for footnote 34, *A Canadian for All Seasons: A Biography of John E. Robbins,* would be shortened to *Canadian for All Seasons* when referred to again in footnotes. See the treatment of this title in the following list of footnotes:

37. William E. Strunk and E. B. White, The Elements of Style (New York: Macmillan Publishing Co., Inc., 1972), pp. 57-59.

38. Hartwell Bosfield, Louis Riel (Toronto: Copp Clark Co., 1969), pp. 59-75.

39. McLeish, Canadian for All Seasons, p. 88-92.

40. James K. Bell and Adrian A. Cohn, Handbook of Grammar, Style, and Usage (Beverly Hills, Calif.: Glencoe Press, 1972), p. 84.

41. McLeish, Canadian for All Seasons, p. 167.

Bibliographies

8.120 For business report purposes, a bibliography is a list of all sources cited in the report and all other works consulted by the writer in preparing the report. The bibliography is typed on a separate page (or pages) and is placed at the end of the report. The author's name is inverted so the surname appears first. Separate the surname from the rest of the name with a comma.

8.121 An annotated bibliography includes a brief comment for each book and article in the bibliography, explaining why it was useful in preparing the report and why it might be of interest to readers. (For an example, see 8.123.)

8.122 A very lengthy bibliography may be divided into sections, as follows:

By type of work:	books periodicals government publications unpublished works
By an author's works:	subjects (all the works on a given subject grouped together) dates (all the works published in a given year or period grouped together)
By importance:	primary sources secondary sources

Leave a triple space before and after the division heading, which is centred on the page:

BOOKS

Thomson, Dale. Louis St. Laurent: Canadian. Toronto: Macmillan Company of Canada Ltd., 1977.

Typing a bibliography

8.123 The heading BIBLIOGRAPHY or ANNOTATED BIBLIOGRAPHY (if appropriate) is centred and typed on a separate page to be added to the end of the report. Follow these guidelines:

1. Use the same margin setting that was used for the report.

2. Type the first line of each entry beginning at the left margin. Succeeding lines are typed beginning at a five-space indention.

Watkins, Mel. Dene nation--the colony within. Toronto: University of Toronto Press, 1977.

3. Type each entry in single spacing; double-space between entries.

4. For an annotated bibliography, type the annotation on a new line a double space below the bibliographic entry. Each line of the annotation begins at the indention.

Bell, James K., and Adrian A. Cohn. Handbook of Grammar, Style, and Usage. Beverly Hills, Calif: Glencoe Press, 1972.

Presents standard guidelines for grammar, word usage, punctuation, and writing style in alphabetical order so a reader can use it like a dictionary.

Note that this annotation is not written in sentence form. Consistency should be maintained, however, in the wording of each annotation so all annotations are written in the same form—either complete sentences or phrases.

Elements of a bibliographic entry

8.124 Bibliographic entries contain the same information as that in footnotes but are arranged somewhat differently. Entries are listed in alphabetic sequence by authors' surnames, so that each name is inverted—surname, first name, and middle name or initial.

The elements of each entry include the name(s) of the author(s) or editor(s), title, edition number (if any), and publication data. Note that the parts of an entry are separated by periods rather than commas or parentheses.

Wojciechowska, Maia. Shadow of a Bull. Toronto: McClelland & Stewart Ltd., 1969.

8.125 When a work has several authors or editors, only the first author's name is inverted, but all names that appear on the title page or a byline must be listed. The abbreviation et al. should not be used in bibliographies, even if a work has more than three authors or editors.

Maedka, Wilmer O., Mary F. Robek, and Gerald F. Brown. Information and Records Management. Beverly Hills, Calif: Glencoe Press, 1974.

Lexchin, Joe (ed.) and Peter Warrian (intro.). Occupational Health. Toronto: New Hogtown Press, 1977.

If more than one work by the same author is listed, do not repeat the name in succeeding entries. Type eight hyphens at the beginning of the line, followed by a period and two spaces before the entry. A series of eight underscores may be typed instead of the hyphens.

Solzhenitsyn, Aleksandr I. The Gulag Archipelago 1918-1956: An Experiment in Literary Investigation. Translated by Thomas P. Whitney. New York: Harper & Row, 1974.

________. The Cancer Ward. Translated by Rebecca Frank. New York: Dial Press, 1968.

8.126 Titles of books and magazines are underscored, as in footnotes.

Findley, Timothy. The Wars. Toronto: Clarke, Irwin, 1977.

Do not underscore the word *magazine* unless it is part of the actual title.

Chapters or articles from books and magazines are typed within quotation marks before the name of the book or magazine.

Smith, Allan. "Quiet Revolution in the West." In The Canadian Forum, June-July 1978.

When a work does not have an author, or the author is unknown, the work is listed in alphabetic order by the first word in the title, except for the words *A*, *An*, and *The*.

8.127 Volume numbers are included for periodicals that are published less than once a month. For books published in more than one volume, the total number in the series is cited in the bibliography, even though only one volume was referred to in preparing the report. (The specific number and title of that volume is included in the footnote reference, but the work as a whole is cited in the bibliography.)

Scientific references and bibliographies

8.128 When a report deals with a scientific or technical subject, the references are cited in abbreviated form within the text rather than as footnotes. The bibliography appearing at the end of the report contains the full citation for each work mentioned in the text.

Elements of a citation

8.129 The citation includes two or three elements written in parentheses: the author's last name, the date of the work being cited, and the page number (if reference is to a direct quotation). An alternative method involves numbering each bibliographic reference beforehand and inserting the reference number in the text wherever it is cited. This method makes it difficult for the reader to identify the source, however, and increases the chance of errors in citations.

Typing citations

8.130 Type the author's name, the date of the work, and the page number (if any) in parentheses, and place the citation at the end of the sentence to which it refers, before the period.

Rutherford's atomic model sharply undermined a traditional premise of scientific investigation: the assumption that scientists should only accept the evidence of their own eyes (Hameka 1967).

If a citation refers to part of a sentence, place the citation at a logical break in the sentence, ideally before a comma or other mark of punctuation.

> The rate of erosion is usually highest "in semiarid and arid regions where vegetation is sparse or absent" (Kolendow 1974, p. 352), because in humid areas the moisture stimulates growth of sufficient vegetation to retard erosion.

If the author's name is already mentioned in the sentence, only the date and page number (if necessary) are typed in the citation.

> This conclusion is based on the success of the process modules for investigating environmental science that were devised by Litherland and Hungerford (1975).

Scientific bibliographies

8.131 **Entries for the references cited in scientific reports contain the same elements as other bibliographies (see 8.120–8.127), but the elements are arranged differently. The following illustrate the bibliographic entries for the works mentioned above.**

Type the date following the author's name. Capitalize only the first letter of the title of the work.

> Hameka, Hendrik F. 1967. Introduction to quantum theory. New York: Harper & Row.

When reference is to a journal article, the title of the article is typed with only the first letter capitalized. The journal title is underscored, with the first letter of important words capitalized. Volume number follows journal title with no punctuation between; volume and page numbers are separated by a colon.

> Litherland, Ralph A., and Harold R. Hungerford. 1975. Process modules for investigating environmental science. The Science Teacher 42: 40-47.

Tables 9

Tables

9.1 A table presents figures and/or words in column form. Thus, it is useful for presenting comparisons involving numbers, dates, or amounts.

Placement of tables

9.2 Short tables generally are typed within the text of the document—letter, memorandum, or report—to which they refer. Longer tables are typed on separate pages and inserted close to the related discussion. In either case, tables should be constructed so they are self-explanatory and can be understood without reading the related discussion.

9.3 Use the following guidelines when typing a table within the text (Figure 9-1).

1. Type the table within the margin settings for the letter, memorandum, or report.

2. Precede the table with a double or triple space; follow it with a double space before continuing the text.

3. Single-space the information within the table unless it includes long columns of figures, which should be double-spaced.

4. Type the entire table on one page.

5. Introduce the table with a brief statement preceding it in the text; any discussion or explanation should be placed after the table.

9.4 Use the following guidelines when typing a table outside the text (Figure 9-2).

1. Use plain bond paper of the same quality as that used for other pages of the letter, memorandum, or report.

2. Change the type style, if necessary, to accommodate the information in the table (e.g., pica type for a table with many figures) or the size of the table (e.g., elite type for a long table with few or no figures).

3. Type the table so it is attractively displayed both horizontally and vertically (see 9.15-9.20 for centring methods). If the table is part of a bound report, allow an extra 1 cm for the binding.

4. Use either single or double spacing depending on the length and detail of the table.

Figure 9-1. Table within business letter

ADDRESSOGRAPH MULTIGRAPH OF CANADA LIMITED

June 25, 1984

Ms. Jane Jones
1016 Rossland Street
Vancouver, B.C.
V5K 4A4

Dear Ms. Jones:

SUBJECT: Typing a Table Within the Letter

Below is an illustration of a table typed within the body of a letter. This letter is typed in the block style with mixed punctuation, and it follows the guidelines for typing business correspondence.

Only a short table should be typed within the body of business correspondence; lengthy tables should be typed on separate pages. Lengthy tables should be identified by number and/or title and should be placed close to its discussion or explanation in the letter, memorandum, or report.

The table must be typed within the margin settings of the letter and should be preceded and followed by either a double or triple space. The following illustrates the form and spacing suggested for typing short tables:

TERM INSURANCE PREMIUM FOR FIVE-YEAR PERIODS

(Face Value at $25 000)

Age	Annual Premium
25	$104
30	106
35	119
40	155

Sincerely yours,

Jon V. Smith
Supervisor

ADDRESSOGRAPH MULTIGRAPH OF CANADA LIMITED, 42 HOLLINGER RD., TORONTO, ONTARIO, CANADA M4B 3G6
SUBSIDIARY OF ADDRESSOGRAPH MULTIGRAPH CORPORATION TEL. (416) 751-8700 TWX. (610) 491-1476

5. Rule or box the table if it does not occupy the full page.

6. Identify each table by number and/or title so that a specific reference can be made in the text.

7. Place the table close to its related discussion, with any explanation or discussion following the table.

Elements of a table

9.5 The main heading, the title of the entire table, is centred and typed in solid capital letters. It may consist of one, two, or possibly three lines. Double space two- or three-line headings. The title should be specific in identifying the information presented. A triple space follows the main heading except when a secondary heading is used.

9.6 A secondary heading further identifies the contents of the table. This heading is typed a double space below the main heading. Only the first letter of important words is capitalized. The secondary heading may be enclosed in parentheses. Triple-space after the entire heading before beginning the table.

9.7 A spanner heading ''spans'' or extends over two or more columns of information to group different categories or classifications of data. It is centred and typed a single or double space above the column headings to which it refers. Spanner headings are helpful in lengthy or detailed tables.

9.8 Column headings are titles or captions centred and typed above each column of information. The number of columns and the length of the entries within each column determine the length of the column headings. Tables with few columns across the page may have longer headings; tables with many columns would need either short headings or headings centred and typed in two or three lines.

Column headings are typed a single or double space below the spanner heading and a double space above the first column entries.

9.9 Other headings may be necessary in the left-hand column of the table to identify important categories of information within that column. If so, information under these heads can be indented for greater clarity.

9.10 Footnotes are used to explain or expand on the data in the table (explanatory footnote) or to cite the source of a specific piece of data (source footnote).

9.11 Footnote references are typed within the table in consecutive sequence. The words or figures to which the footnotes apply can be indicated by asterisks (when there is only one or two footnote references), or by lowercase letters or numbers—all typed as superscripts to the right of the words or figures in question.

Production[1]   50%[c]   99*

To place the footnote reference within the table, move from left to right, and from top to bottom within the table. (See location of superscripts in Figure 9-2.)

Figure 9-2. Table on separate page

Main heading → CINEMA ATTENDANCE IN CANADA IN 1975

Double space

Secondary heading → Based on Occupation of Population[1]

Triple space

Spanner heading → Regular Cinema Attenders in Each Occupation

Single or double space

Column headings →

Occupation	Percentage of all Cinema Attenders Occupation Group Comprised	Average Times per Month Total Group went To the Cinema	Regular Cinema Attenders in Each Occupation: Percentage of Group who were Cinema Attenders	Regular Cinema Attenders in Each Occupation: Average Times per Month Cinema Attenders Went to the Cinema[2]
White Collar & Service	22	0.81	58.3	1.39
Student	20	1.32	76.5	1.72
Homemaker	17	0.38	34.1	1.10
Blue Collar & Craftsmen	14	0.73	50.2	1.45
Professional, Artistic, Paraprofessional, Technical	10	0.85	64.4	1.32
Resource Industry Workers	6	0.59	43.1	1.37
Unemployed	4	0.98	60.6	1.61
Managerial & Administrative	4	0.76	62.5	1.22
Retired & Other	2	0.18	14.7	1.25
Total	99[3]	0.70	50.1	1.40

Footnotes

1 Geography, age, sex and mother tongue are other variables influencing cinema attendance habits. 2 Note that as a group, regular attenders in any occupation never went less than once a month, but never attained a frequency of twice a month. 3 Due to rounding.

Credit line

Source: Statistics Canada, Catalogue No. 11-003E, Canadian Statistical Review.

9.12 Type a footnote-separating line of 15 to 18 underscores a single space below the data. Double-space after the footnote-separating line before typing the notes. If the table is boxed or ruled, the separating line is not necessary.

9.13 Footnotes are typed as run-on text, one footnote after another (see Figure 9-2).

9.14 The source from which the table was obtained is cited at the end of the table below the last footnote, if any. It is usually preceded by the word *Source*, followed by a colon (see Figure 9-2).

Centring table columns

9.15 Tables must be centred on the page both vertically and horizontally, to ensure even margins at top, bottom, and sides and even spaces between the columns. Table 9-1, Standard paper dimensions, is a useful aid in centring tables.

Table 9-1. Standard paper dimensions

Width of paper	21.5 cm	28 cm
Elite type		
Spaces per 2.5 cm (1 inch)	12	12
Spaces on page	102	132
Centre point	51	66
Vertical lines	51	66
(Paper on side)		
Pica type		
Spaces per 2.5 cm (1 inch)	10	10
Spaces on page	85	110
Centre point	42	55
Vertical lines	51	66
(Paper on side)		

9.16 Effective methods of centring horizontally include the backspace-from-centre method, the mathematical method, and the eye judgement method.

9.17 The backspace-from-centre tabulation method (used to type tables that are separate from the related text) involves backspacing from the centre point of the paper to determine the left margin setting.

There are three major tasks: determining the left margin setting; setting tabulator stops for the columns; and centring column headings. In each case, you must work with the longest item in each column. The procedure is as follows:

1. Clear all tab stops; move margin stops to the ends.

2. To find left margin for table:

a. Find the longest item in each column of the table.
b. Determine how many spaces are to be left between columns. (It should be an even number, such as 4, 6, 8, 10, or 12, depending on the number and widths of the columns.)
c. From the centre of the paper, backspace once for every two letters in the longest item in each column. Begin with the longest item in column 1, then to the longest item in column 2, etc. As you go from one column to the next, if there is an extra letter in one column, carry it over into the longest item in the next column. Continue backspacing once for every two letters in the longest item in each column across the page.
d. Backspace once for every two spaces to be left between columns. (For instance, if you are to leave 10 spaces between columns, backspace 5 for the space between the first and second columns, 5 for the space between the second and third columns, etc.)
e. After you have backspaced for every two letters in the longest item of each column and backspaced once for every two spaces to be left between columns, where you stop is the left margin. Set your left margin here.

3. To find tab stops before typing the table:

a. From the left margin, space forward once for every letter in the longest item in the first column. Space forward once for each space to be left between columns 1 and 2. Set your first tab stop here.
b. From the beginning of column 2, space forward once for each letter in the longest item of the second column, plus once for each space to be left between columns 2 and 3. Set a second tab stop here.
c. Continue spacing forward in this manner until tab stops have been set for all columns to be typed across the page.

Note: You must space forward to set your tab stops because each letter to be typed must occupy one space across the page; each space between the columns must also be accounted for. Thus you are allowing for each letter and each space.

4. To type column headings:

a. Once the tab stops have been set across the page, column headings can be centred and typed before typing the table.

b. Column headings must be centred above each column of information. In some cases, column headings may be the longest item in the columns so that the information within the column will be centred below the heading.

c. You must find the exact centre of each column before the column heading can be typed. Find the longest item in each column. Space forward once for every two letters in the longest item in the first column (if there is an extra letter, disregard it). This is the centre of the column.

d. To centre the heading from the centre of the column: backspace once for every two letters in the heading.

e. Begin typing the heading at this point. The heading should be centred above the longest item in the column. (When the heading is the longest item within the column, find the centre point of the column based on the heading; find the longest item below the heading and backspace-centre it. This will now be the new tab stop for this column, and other items within this column will not seem centred. In other words, the second longest item in the column will be centred below the column heading.)

f. Continue to find the centre of each column. Tab over to the next column, spacing forward once for every two letters in the longest item within the column. Then backspace-centre the heading and type.

9.18 The mathematical method of horizontal centring is used when information must be typed to accommodate specific dimensions of the page. Like the preceding method, it is used when the table is typed on a separate page. The procedure is as follows:

1. Use the boxes illustrated below and count the letters and spaces of the longest entry in each column of data across the page.

Yukon	230	500	80	2050
Alberta	185	75	45	965
Newfoundland	1025	135	115	1440
Nova Scotia	290	210	100	850
12	4	3	3	4

2. Add all of these figures to determine the total number of spaces to be used for the table.

12 4 3 3 4 = 26

3. Determine the number of spaces remaining and specify the number of spaces to leave between columns. Leave a minimum of four spaces and a maximum of ten spaces between columns for easier reading.

4. Add the remaining spaces to the right and left margins.

5. Insert the paper so the left edge is even with the zero or its equivalent on the paper scale.

6. Clear all tabulator stops. Position the carriage or the carrier to correspond with the centre point of the page (42 for pica and 50 or 51 for elite on 21.5 cm wide paper; 55 for pica and 65 for elite on 28 cm wide paper.)

7. Set the left margin as indicated by the rough sketch in item 2 above. The right margin does not need to be set.

8. Set tabulator stops before beginning to type the data.

a. From the left margin, space forward once for every letter in the longest entry in the first column plus once for every space between the first and second columns. Set the first tab stop here.

b. From the beginning of column 2, space forward once for each letter in the longest entry of the second column, plus once for each space between the second and third columns. Set a second tab stop here.

c. Continue spacing forward in this manner until tabulator stops have been set for all columns in the table.

9. Type column headings, following the procedure outlined in item 4 under the backspace-from-centre method (9.17).

9.19 A two-, three-, or four-column table included within the text of a letter, memorandum, or report may be centred by using eye judgement rather than a more precise and involved method. The table must be typed within the margins set for the correspondence.

If the table is to be indented from the right and left margins, follow these steps. (This style cannot be used if the letter is typed in the full block style.)

1. Decide on the number of spaces for the indention from both margins.

2. Space forward from the left margin and reset the margin; backspace from the right margin and reset the margin.

3. Begin the first column at the indention; type the last column so it ends even with or near the reset right margin.

4. Using eye judgement, centre and type the middle column or columns so the number of spaces between the columns is approximately the same.

If the table is not to be indented, follow these steps:

1. Begin the first column at the left margin; type the last column so it ends even with or near the right margin.

2. Using eye judgement, centre and type the middle column or columns so the number of spaces between the columns is approximately the same.

To type column headings, follow the procedure outlined in item 4 under the backspace-from-centre method (9.17).

9.20 Tables are usually centred vertically so that top and bottom margins are even, but they may also be typed a little higher on the page than vertical centre for a more pleasing appearance. Follow these steps to plan the vertical centring of a table.

1. Determine the vertical spacing for the different parts of the table: main heading, spanner heading, column headings, column entries.

2. Count the total number of lines the table will take; include the blank lines between the typewritten ones. (A double space equals one blank line; a triple space equals two blank lines.)

3. Subtract this figure from the total number of lines on the page vertically (21.5 cm length equals 51 lines; 28 cm length equals 66 lines).

4. Divide this figure by two to arrive at the number of lines to leave for the top and bottom margins. (If there is an odd number, round it to the next lower number.)

5. Type the table a little higher than vertical centre, if desired, beginning two or three lines higher than the figure obtained in step 4.

Typing figures in columns

9.21 Type whole numbers so they are aligned at the right. Use a space to group digits by threes (see 6.7).

```
   905
 2 378
    25
56 257
```

9.22 Type numbers with decimal points so the decimal points are aligned. Use a space to separate digits by threes to the right of the decimal point (see 6.19). Extra zeros are added to the right of decimal figures when numbers are aligned in columns.

```
11.500 54
 0.900 60
 2.155 00
 5.637 05
```

9.23 Type mathematical symbols so they are aligned in a column in front of the figures. Thus, the figures should be aligned at the right.

```
+ 59
+100
-  7
```

9.24 Type the percent symbols so they are aligned in a column after the figures. When the entire column consists of percents, type the percent symbol only after the first entry and after subtotals and totals within the column.

```
100%       12.500%
 12       137.875
 96         1.500
 14         0.500
  2       ________
____      152.375%
224%
```

9.25 Type dollar signs so they are aligned in a column in front of the amounts. When the entire column consists of dollar amounts, type the dollar sign before the first entry only and before subtotals and the total within the column.

```
$1535.07     $ 5 000.00
  200.00         150.50
 3216.45          35.75
    2.50       8 750.25
________          14.85
$4954.02     __________
   24.95     $13 951.35
  100.00     ==========
________
$5078.97
========
```

9.26 Type the dollar sign before both amounts in the first entry only when a range of amounts is shown.

```
$1500-$2500     $ 125.00-$ 550.00
 7000- 8500        25.75-   28.50
  400-  750      1100.00- 1300.00
```

Align the dollar sign with the longest dollar amount.

9.27 Type fractions consistently by using the ¼ and ½ keys on the typewriter or by using the number keys for all fractions. Align the fractions in a column after the figures. When a whole number precedes the fraction, a hyphen may be typed to separate the whole number from the fraction.

10-1/2 13-1/4 5-3/4

9.28 Type various kinds of figures either aligned at the left or centred above one another.

$190.00	$190.00
10 mL	10 mL
#1225-A	#1225-A
39-1/2%	39-1/2%
$3500.86	$3500.86

Typing ruled or boxed tables

9.29 Ruled tables consist of horizontal lines, typed across the table to separate various headings, and vertical lines, which separate the columns of data. These ruled lines aid the reader in following information from column to column and down the page.

9.30 Boxed tables are ruled horizontally at the top, below the column headings, and at the end of the table. This table is ruled vertically between the columns in addition to being ruled at the sides (see Figure 9-3). Thus, the entire table is enclosed.

9.31 A double horizontal line is typed at the top of the table below the main or secondary heading. Triple-space after the heading and type an underscore the width of the table. Return the carriage or carrier. Engage the ratchet release lever and roll the cylinder slightly away from you. Type the second underscore below the first one and make sure to end the line at the same point as the first line. Return the ratchet release lever to its position to continue the table.

MAIN HEADING

Secondary Heading

9.32 Separate the column headings by a single horizontal underscore. Begin this line at the left margin a single space below the column

Figure 9-3. Boxed table

Main heading — PERCENT OF EMPLOYEE TURNOVER

Double space

AT PROSPECTS CORPORATION*

Double space

Secondary heading — (Period from December, 1980, to June, 1981)

Triple space

Branch/Office	Dec.	Jan.	Feb.	Mar.	Apr.	May	June
Alberta							
Calgary	--	--	2.0%	--	--	--	--
Edmonton	0.4%	1.0%	--	--	2.0%	0.4%	0.5%
Red Deer	--	0.8	--	--	--	1.2	--
New Brunswick							
Moncton	1.0	0.9	--	--	--	1.0	2.0
Shediac	--	--	**	0.5	--	--	--
Nova Scotia							
Dartmouth	0.5	0.9	1.0	3.5	--	1.0	2.0
Halifax	0.4	0.5	1.0	2.0	**	--	3.5
Sydney	--	--	--	--	1.5	--	**

* Survey based on 350 employees during the six-month period.

** Data not available.

headings. This line should end at the same point as the double horizontal lines above.

Branch/Office December January February March April

9.33 Leave a single space after the last item in the table and type a single horizontal line across the width of the table. This line should end at the same point as the other horizontal lines.

9.34 Vertical lines are used to separate the data within the columns, especially if the columns are close together.

9.35 Make typewritten vertical lines when all information has been typed in the table. Remove the page from the typewriter and insert it on its side. The paper must be inserted straight so that the lines are straight and the columns appear evenly spaced.

Use the underscore key to type the lines between the columns. Type each line in the middle of the spaces between columns. The line should not extend beyond the double horizontal lines at the top of the table nor the single line at the bottom of the table.

9.36 To make hand-drawn vertical lines, remove the page from the typewriter when all information has been typed in the table. Use a fine-point black-ink pen and a ruler or other straightedge to draw the vertical lines. Draw each line in the middle of the space between columns. The line should not extend beyond the double horizontal lines at the top of the table nor the single line at the bottom of the table.

Numbering tables

9.37 Tables typed on separate pages should be placed within the letter, memorandum, or report immediately after the related discussion or explanation. Each table within the communication should be given a number and title so it can be referred to easily within the text.

The tables are numbered consecutively within the communication, preferably in Arabic numerals. The number is typed a double space above the title of the table.

TABLE 4

PERCENT OF LEGAL SECRETARIES IN THE REGINA AREA

PURSUING PARALEGAL OR LEGAL ASSISTANT JOBS

Numbering pages

9.38 Each table within the letter, memorandum, or report is assigned a page number. A 21.5 cm wide page with a table is numbered in the upper right corner at the right margin, except for topbound report pages, which are numbered at the bottom of the page and centred.

When a table is typed on a 28 cm wide page, the page is numbered like the other pages in the report, usually in the upper right corner. The top of the table becomes the left-hand side of the page.

Business Mathematics 10

Calculating discounts

10.1 A discount is a percentage figure by which a dollar amount is reduced from an original price.

Example: \$44.95 less 3% discount

To calculate the discount:

1. Convert the percentage rate of discount to its decimal equivalent.

3% = 0.03

2. Multiply the gross amount by the discount. Be sure to insert the decimal point in the appropriate position.

```
 $44.95
 × 0.03
$1.3485
```

3. Round the answer to the nearest cent.

\$1.3485 = \$1.35 discount

Net amounts

10.2 The net amount is the gross amount less the amount of the discount.

Example: \$150 less 15% discount = \$127.50

1. Convert the rate of discount to its decimal equivalent.

15% = 0.15

2. Subtract the discount rate from 100%. The gross amount is equal to 100%, and the discount is a reduction from 100%. (The difference is known as the complement.)

```
 100%        1.00
-  15%      -0.15
   85%       0.85
```

3. Multiply the gross amount by the complement.

```
   $150
 × 0.85
$127.50 = net amount
```

10.3 Discount and net amounts

The discount-and-net amounts method of computation provides both the amount of the discount and the net amount (the gross amount less the discount).

Example: $285 less 12% discount = $250.80

To use this method:

1. Determine the amount of the discount as explained in 10.1.

```
  $285    gross amount
× 0.12    rate of discount
-------
$34.20 = amount of discount
```

2. Subtract the amount of the discount from the gross amount.

```
 $285.00
−$ 34.20
--------
 $250.80 =  net amount
```

Cash discounts

10.4 A cash discount is an amount deducted from an invoice amount to encourage customers to make payment promptly upon receipt of the invoice. The following terms are commonly used to describe various methods of cash discounting:

2/10, n/30	2 percent discount if invoice paid within 10 days of invoice date; otherwise, net amount must be paid within 30 days
2/10 EOM	2 percent discount if invoice paid within 10 days after the end of the month
2/10 ROG	2 percent discount if invoice paid within 10 days of receipt of goods

To calculate discounts:

1. Determine in all instances whether payment was made within the discount period allowed.

2. Convert the percent of the discount to its decimal equivalent.

3. Multiply the invoice amount by the rate of discount to obtain the amount of the discount.

4. Subtract the amount of the discount from the invoice amount to determine the net amount.

10.5 **Chain discounts**

A chain discount is a series of two or more discounts allowed in a sales transaction. (Note: Never add up chain discounts and multiply by their total!)

Example: $175.50 less 10% – 5%

To calculate the discount:

1. Convert the percentages to their decimal equivalents.
2. Determine the complement of each discount rate.

```
  100%     1.00        100%    1.00
 - 10%     0.10       -  5%    0.05
 -----     ----       -----    ----
   90%     0.90         95%    0.95
```

3. Multiply the gross amount by the complement of the first discount.

```
   $175.50
  ×   0.90
  --------
$157.9500= $157.95
```

4. This net amount becomes the gross amount, which is now multiplied by the second discount.

5. Multiply the new gross amount by the complement of the second discount.

```
   $157.95
  ×   0.95
  --------
$150.0525 = $150.05 = net amount
```

6. The amount of the discount is determined by subtracting the final net amount from the original gross amount.

```
  $175.50
 -$150.05
 --------
   $25.45
```

Computing interest

10.6 Interest is the amount of money charged for borrowing money.

Simple interest

10.7 Simple interest is calculated by using the following formula:

$$\frac{\text{Principal} \times \text{Rate} \times \text{Time}}{365 \text{ Days}} = \text{Interest}$$

Example: Principal = $7450

Rate = 16%

Time (365-day basis) = 2 years

To calculate the amount of interest:

1. Convert the percentage rate into its decimal equivalent.

   16% = 0.16

2. Convert the time in years to days.

   2 years = 730 days

3. Multiply the principal amount by the rate.

   $7450 × 0.16 = $1292.00

4. Multiply the result by time.

   $1292.00 × 730 = $942 260.00

5. Divide this result by 365 days.

   365)$942 260.00 = $2 581.53 = amount of interest

Computing percentages

10.8 Percentage figures are used to express the relation that one number has to another. A percentage is a fraction of a total amount expressed in hundredths (see Table 10-1).

Amount and percent of decrease/increase

10.9 Computing the percentage of decrease or increase provides a comparison of figures on which management decisions may be based. Such comparisons may be expressed in dollar amounts as well as percentage figures.

To calculate percent and amount of increase or decrease:

1. Obtain the amounts of the figures to be compared, such as the previous year's sales and the current year's sales, the previous year's expenses and the current year's expenses, etc.

Department	Sales Previous Year	Sales Current Year	Amt. of Increase/ Decrease	% of Increase/ Decrease
A	$10 205	$12 368	$2 163	21.20%
B	3 562	2 117	(1 445)	(40.57)

2. Determine the amount of increase or decrease between the previous year and the current year, using the figure for the previous year as the base for the comparison.

(A) $12 368 = current
− 10 205 = previous
$ 2 163 = difference

(B) $3 562 = previous
− 2 117 = current
$1 445 = difference

3. Divide the difference by the previous year's or month's figure to determine the percent of increase or decrease.

(A) 10 205) 2163.000 000 = 0.211 954

(B) 3562) 1445.000 00 = 0.405 67

Table 10-1. Decimal equivalents of common fractions

1/3 = 0.333 33	1/6 = 0.166 67	1/12 = 0.083 33
2/3 = 0.666 67	2/6 = 0.333 33	2/12 = 0.166 67
	3/6 = 0.50	3/12 = 0.25
1/4 = 0.25	4/6 = 0.666 67	4/12 = 0.333 33
2/4 = 0.50	5/6 = 0.833 33	5/12 = 0.416 65
3/4 = 0.75		6/12 = 0.50
	1/8 = 0.125	7/12 = 0.583 33
1/5 = 0.20	2/8 = 0.25	8/12 = 0.666 67
2/5 = 0.40	3/8 = 0.375	9/12 = 0.75
3/5 = 0.60	4/8 = 0.50	10/12 = 0.833 33
4/5 = 0.80	5/8 = 0.625	11/12 = 0.916 66
	6/8 = 0.75	
	7/8 = 0.875	

The decimal equivalent of a common fraction is calculated by dividing the numerator (top number of the fraction) by the denominator (bottom number of the fraction). If necessary, carry the quotient (the number resulting from this division) at least five decimal places to the right.

4. Convert the quotient to a percentage figure by moving the decimal point two places to the right.

(A) 0.211 954 = 21.20% increase (B) 0.405 67 = 40.57% decrease

5. Indicate a percentage decrease by enclosing the figure in parentheses.

(A) 21.20% increase (B) (40.57%)

6. Indicate an amount decrease by enclosing the figure in parentheses.

(A) $2 163 increase (B) (1 445)

Base amounts

10.10 In determining the base amount, the percentage amount and the percentage rate are known.

Example: $560 is 12½% of what amount?

To calculate the base amount:

1. The percentage rate is the divisor and the amount is the dividend.

2. Convert the percentage rate into its decimal equivalent.

12½% = 0.125

3. Divide the amount by the percentage rate.

$$\begin{array}{r} 4.480 = \$4480 \\ 0.125\overline{)560.000} \end{array}$$

4. To check the calculation, multiply the percentage rate by the quotient, rounding off to the next higher number where necessary.

$4480 × 12.5 = $560

$560 is 12½% of $4480

Rate percentages

10.11 In calculating rate percentages, the dollar amounts are known.

Example: $3000 is what % of $4500?

To calculate the rate percentage:

1. Determine the base number to which the other number is being compared. The base number follows the word *of*.

2. Convert the numbers into a fraction. The base number becomes the denominator.

$$\frac{3000 \text{ numerator}}{4500 \text{ denominator}}$$

3. Divide the numerator by the denominator, carrying the quotient to at least four decimal places.

$$4500\overline{)3000.000\ 00}\quad = 0.666\ 66$$

4. Convert the quotient into a percentage by moving the decimal point two places to the right, rounding off where necessary.

0.666 66 = 66.67%

5. To check the calculation, multiply the base amount by the quotient, rounding off to the next higher number where necessary.

$4500 × 0.666 66 = $2999.700 00 = $3000

Estimating answers in multiplication

10.12 When an approximation is sufficient to obtain an estimated answer to a problem, round each of the factors before multiplying. Round to retain one non-zero digit. In the following example, 578 rounds to 600; 321 rounds to 300.

Problem: 578 × 321

```
   578
 × 321
   578
  1156
 1734
185538 = product
```

Estimate: 600 × 300

```
    600
  × 300
180 000 = estimated product
```

With factors like 4500 and 5500, round so that the non-zero digit is even. 4500 rounds to 4000, 5500 rounds to 6000.

Problem: 4500 × 5500

```
    4500
  × 5500
 2250000
 22500
24750000
```

Estimate: 4000 × 6000

```
      4000
    × 6000
24 000 000
```

Proration

10.13 Prorating means proportionately distributing an amount among several individual amounts.

Example:	Department	Gross Revenue	% of Department
	A	$15 650	27.82%
	B	10 073	17.90
	C	12 245	21.77
	D	9 830	17.47
	E	8 462	15.04
		$56 260	100.00%

To prorate the revenue:

1. Determine the total amount of sales, revenue, expenses, etc., involved. It is this total—100 percent of the revenue—that will be prorated among the other departments, sections, divisions, branches, etc.

2. Divide this total into the individual revenue figures indicated on the chart above.

$$56\,260\overline{)15\,650.000\,00}\quad = 0.278\,17$$

3. Convert the quotient to a percentage figure by moving the decimal point two places to the right.

0.27817 = 27.82%

4. Continue in the same manner until all percentages have been calculated. When all percentages are determined, they will total 100 percent or slightly more or less, depending on rounding.

Units of Measure 11

The metric system[1]

11.1 The metric system or SI (Le Système International d'Unités) is an international decimal system of measures. The relations among units are based on a scale of ten, which simplifies calculation and conversions from one unit to another. (See Tables 11-2 and 11-3.)

Table 11-1. Common metric units and symbols

Unit	*Symbol*	*Quantity*
metre	m	length and distance
litre	L	liquid volume/capacity
gram	g	mass
second	s	time
degree Celsius	°C	temperature

Metric prefixes

11.2 Metric prefixes, when attached to a unit, change the magnitude of that unit. For example, when the prefix *kilo* is attached to *metre*, the unit *kilometre* is formed; *kilo* means 1000, so one kilometre is 1000 m. Similarly, when the prefix *milli* is attached to *litre*, the unit *millilitre* is formed; *milli* means thousandth, so one millilitre is 0.001 L.

Table 11-2. Common prefixes

Name	*Symbol*	*Meaning*	*Multiplier*
mega	M	one million	1 000 000
kilo	k	one thousand	1 000
hecto	h	one hundred	100
deca	da	ten	10
deci	d	one tenth	0.1
centi	c	one hundredth	0.01
milli	m	one thousandth	0.001
micro	μ	one millionth	0.000 001

1. The following tables and rules of style are based on *The Metric Guide*, Second Edition, published by the Council of Ministers of Education, Canada, March 1976, and *How to Write SI*, Fifth Edition, published by the Metric Commission, Canada. *The Metric Guide* may be obtained from the Canadian Standards Association, 1978 Rexdale Boulevard, Rexdale, Ontario M9W 1R3. *How to Write SI* may be obtained from Metric Commission Canada, Box 4000, Ottawa, Ontario K1S 5G8.

11.3 Table 11-3 presents a list of the most commonly used units of length/distance, liquid volume/capacity, mass, and temperature as well as corresponding symbols and relationships.

Table 11-3. Metric units, symbols, and relationship

Quantity	*Unit*	*Symbol*	*Relationship*
length/distance	kilometre	km	1 km = 1000 m
	metre	m	1 m = 10 dm = 100 cm = 1000 mm
	decimetre	dm	1 dm = 0.1 m = 10 cm
	centimetre	cm	1 cm = 0.01 m = 10 mm
	millimetre	mm	1 mm = 0.001 m
liquid volume/capacity*	kilolitre	kL	1 kL = 1000 L
	litre	L	1 L = 1000 mL
	millilitre	mL	1 mL = 0.001 L
mass	tonne (or megagram)	t (or Mg)	1 t = 1000 kg
	kilogram	kg	1 kg = 1000 g
	gram	g	1 g = 0.001 kg
	milligram	mg	1 mg = 0.001 g
temperature	degree Celsius	°C	The freezing point of water is 0°C. The boiling point of water is 100°C.

*Note: Capacity of container with volume: 1 cm^3 is 1 mL
1 dm^3 is 1 L
1 m^3 is 1 kL

Metric style

11.4 Since SI is a universal system of measure, basic rules of style must be followed when typing metric symbols.

Basic rules

11.5 **Metric symbols are not abbreviations. Therefore, a period is never used after a symbol unless it appears at the end of a sentence.**

The tomatoes have a mass of 5 kg and the cabbages have a mass of 9 kg.

11.6 **In printed matter, metric symbols are shown in upright roman type regardless of the type in the rest of the text. This avoids confusion between the symbols m for metre and *m* for the quantity mass. Other common quantity symbols that appear italicized are:**

l for length
w for width
h for height
A for area
V for volume
c for circumference
r for radius
d for distance and diameter
t for time and temperature

11.7 **Use symbols only in conjunction with numerals. Otherwise, spell out the unit.**

The standard sheet size is 21.5 cm × 28 cm.

We walked three kilometres today.

11.8 **Leave a full space between a numeral and a symbol.**

45 mL

Exception: 45°C

11.9 **Symbols are never pluralized.**

60 km   1 km   328 km

11.10 **Symbols appear in lowercase type unless they are derived from a person's name.**

cm for centimetre
W for Watt
kW for kilowatt
Pa for Pascal
N for Newton

Exception: Capital L is used as the symbol for litre to avoid confusion with the numeral 1.

11.11 Symbols for prefixes appear in lowercase type, except those greater than *kilo*.

kg for kilogram
Mg for megagram

11.12 Exponents ^{2} and ^{3} are used with symbols for units that are squared or cubed.

3 m^2 **(three square metres)**
5 m^3 **(five cubic metres)**

11.13 Use a solidus (/) to indicate *per* between two SI symbols.

200 km/h

11.14 Do not leave a space between a prefix symbol and the unit symbol.

mL for millilitre
km for kilometre

Conversions from Imperial to metric measures

Length/distance

11.15 1 inch = 25.4 mm
1 inch = 2.54 cm
1 foot = 30.48 cm
1 yard = 0.9144 m
1 mile ≐ 1.609 km

Area

11.16 1 square inch = 6.4516 cm^2
1 square foot ≐ 9.2903 dm^2
1 square yard ≐ 0.8361 m^2
1 acre ≐ 0.4047 ha (hectare)
1 square mile ≐ 2.59 km^2
1 square mile ≐ 259 ha

Volume

11.17 1 cubic inch = 16.387 064 cm^3
1 cubic foot = 28.316 846 dm^3
1 cubic yard ≐ 0.764 555 m^3

Liquid capacity

11.18 1 teaspoon ≐ 5 mL
1 tablespoon ≐ 15 mL
1 fluid ounce (Imperial) ≐ 28.4 mL
1 cup ≐ 227 mL
1 quart (Imperial) ≐ 1.1365 L
1 quart (Imperial) ≐ 1136.5 mL
1 gallon (Imperial) ≐ 4.5461 L

Mass

11.19 1 ounce (avoirdupois) ≐ 28.3 g
1 pound (avoirdupois) ≐ 0.4536 g
1 ton (short, 2000 lb) ≐ 907.1847 kg

Temperature

11.20 5/9 × (number of degrees Fahrenheit − 32)
= number of degrees Celsius

Speed

11.21 1 mile per hour ≐ 0.447 m/s
≐ 1.609 km/h

Other measures

Circular and angular measure

11.22 1 second (″)
60″ = 1 minute (′)
60′ = 1 degree (°)
90° = 1 right angle
360° = 1 complete rotation

Counting measure

11.23

	1 dozen =	12 units
12 dozen =	1 gross =	144 units

Measure of time

11.24

60 seconds (s)	= 1 minute (min)
60 min	= 1 hour (h)
24 h	= 1 day (d)
7 d	= 1 week
365 d	= 1 year (a)
366 d	= 1 leap year
10 a	= 1 decade
100 a	= 1 century
1000 a	= 1 millenium

Paper measure

11.25

24-25 sheets	= 1 quire (qr)
500 sheets	= 1 ream (rm)
2 rm	= 1 bundle (bdl)
5 bdl	= 1 bale

Filing Systems 12

Introduction

12.1 These are the commonly used business filing systems: *alphabetic, numeric, subject,* and *geographic*.

Filing procedures vary according to the functions of each office: the ways records are used determine the choice of filing system. All systems, however, share certain specific procedures, some of which occur simultaneously:

Figure 12-1. Flow chart: filing procedures

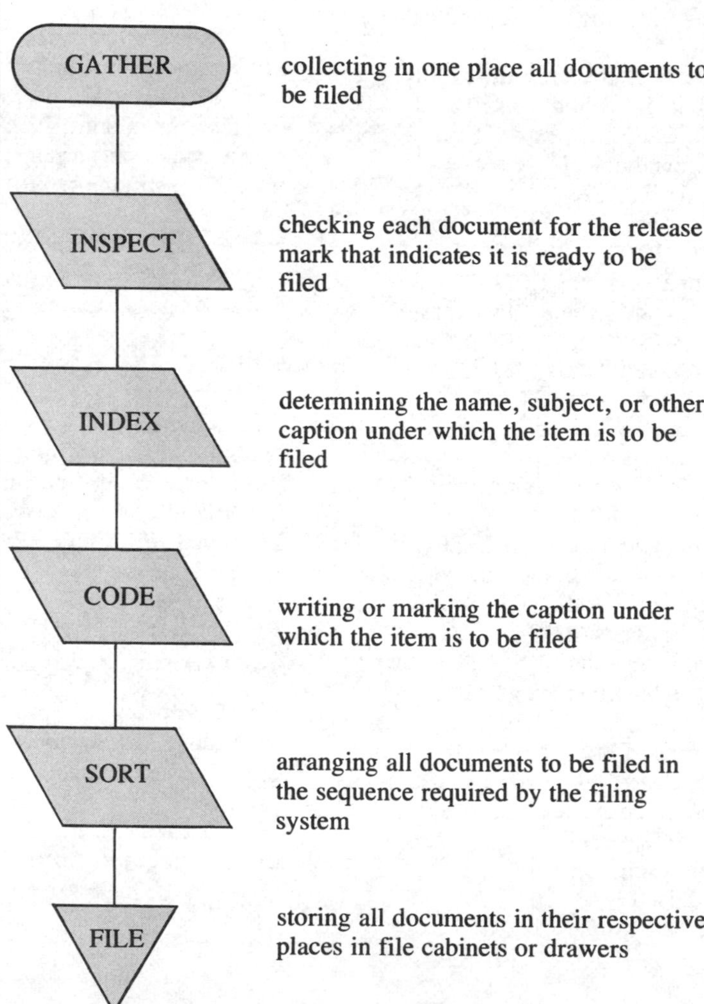
GATHER
collecting in one place all documents to be filed
INSPECT
checking each document for the release mark that indicates it is ready to be filed
INDEX
determining the name, subject, or other caption under which the item is to be filed
CODE
writing or marking the caption under which the item is to be filed
SORT
arranging all documents to be filed in the sequence required by the filing system
FILE
storing all documents in their respective places in file cabinets or drawers

The list below offers general hints that apply to all filing tasks.

1. Follow the prescribed sequence of tasks for each type of filing system to save time and effort during filing.

2. Use spare moments during the day to file or at least sort papers prior to filing.

3. Do not allow papers to accumulate from day to day; papers that are not filed are likely to become lost or misfiled.

4. Do not allow files to be kept in desk drawers. For safety and more efficient office procedures, keep all files in their appropriate places.

5. When a file is removed from the files, an out-card system should be used to indicate who has the file and when it was borrowed.

Alphabetic filing system

12.2 The alphabetic filing system, based on the letters of the alphabet, is a direct method of filing and retrieving. When the file caption is known, the file may be located by simply checking the files under the letter(s) in question. The rules for alphabetic filing are presented in four segments: names of individuals, businesses, institutions, and government agencies.

Names of individuals

12.3 Names of individuals are arranged with the last name first, then the first name or initial, then any middle name or initial. When names are transposed, a comma separates the last name or surname from the rest of the name.

Gomes, Joseph C.
Lau, J. Dennis
Martin, Shirley A. (Mrs.)
Vanderhof, Berthe G. (Ms.)

12.4 Each part of an individual's name is an indexing unit; the more words in the name, the more indexing units there will be. Indexing units are compared letter by letter until a difference is found, to determine where the file will be placed. An individual's last name is the first indexing unit; his or her first name is the second indexing unit; and his or her middle name or initial, if any, is the third indexing unit.

12.5 Abbreviated given names are indexed as though they were spelled out in full.

Chas. D. Thomas	Thomas, Charles D.
Wm. C. Thompson	Thompson, William C.

12.6 Generally, use the last part of an unusual or foreign name as the surname.

Bing Yee	Yee, Bing
Xavier Douglas	Douglas, Xavier

12.7 A surname containing a hyphen is indexed as one word; in other words, the hyphen is disregarded and the name is visualized as one word.

Sylvia Lopez-Tiana	Lopeztiana, Sylvia
Louis C. Lopes-Blanco	Lopesblanco, Louis C.

12.8 When all indexing units of individuals' names are identical, use the cities, provinces, street names, and then house numbers as identifying elements to determine the correct filing sequence.

Kane, Daniel (Amherst)
Kane, Daniel (Saint John, New Brunswick)
Kane, Daniel (St. John's, Newfoundland)

12.9 An initial is an indexing unit and is placed before a word starting with the same letter.

Johnson	James	H.
Johnson	James	Henry
Johnson	S.	R.

12.10 The name of a married woman is usually filed as she has written it. For legal purposes, the name usually consists of given names and husband's surname. If husband's name is known, it is also included.

Pucci, Maria T. (Mrs.)
(Mrs. Anthony G. Pucci)

Other:

Engel, Maria T. (Ms.)
(Mrs. Anthony G. Pucci)

Pucci, Engel, Maria T. (Mrs.)

12.11 A nickname is changed to the person's given name if the given name can be determined. (Note: The legal name of some persons may be a known nickname.)

Bob C. Underwood	Underwood, Robert C.

12.12 A title before or after an individual's complete name is treated as an identifying element; the title is not considered an indexing unit.

Dr. James D. Wise	Wise, James D. (Doctor)

A title preceding an individual's given name or surname alone is indexed as a separate unit as written.

Prince William	Prince William
Lord Beaverbrook	Lord Beaverbrook

12.13 A professional degree following an individual's name is treated as an identifying element; it is not considered an indexing unit.

Louis Wortz, M.D.	Wortz, Louis (M.D.)

12.14 Seniority titles such as Jr., Sr., II, 2d, and III are considered identifying elements only.

Norman Vanderveen, Jr.	Vanderveen, Norman (Jr.)

12.15 In similar but not identical names, the one with the fewest letters is filed first. (Principle: Nothing comes before something.)

Haskin, Samuel
Haskins, David

12.16 A surname containing a prefix is indexed as though it were written as one word. Surname prefixes include *A', D', de, De la, Des, Di, Du, Fitz, La, Le, M', Mac, Mc, O', Van, Van der, Von* and *Von der.*

Sandra O'Hara	Ohara, Sandra
Jerry MacKenzie	Mackenzie, Jerry

Names of businesses

12.17 Company names are generally indexed in the order in which the words are written. Each significant word in the name is indexed as a separate unit.

12.18 When a company name includes an abbreviation, determine what the abbreviation represents. Then index the abbreviation as though it were spelled out, with each word a separate unit.

Harper Mfg. Co.	Harper Manufacturing Company
Mielke Electrical Corp.	Mielke Electrical Corporation

12.19 The article *the* is not an indexing unit. However, to indicate the correct full name of the company, *the* must be written in parentheses. If *the* appears as the first word in the name, it is written in parentheses and placed at the end of the name. If *the* appears in the middle of a name, it is placed in parentheses in its proper position within the name.

The Cove Inn	Cove Inn (The)
Jack the Barber	Jack (the) Barber

12.20 A "coined" business name is formed by joining special combinations of phonetic spellings, trade words, prefixes, or suffixes to create a special-sounding, eye-appealing name.

A trade name identifies goods or services as products of a particular company, distinguishing it from comparable items on the market.

Determine if each word in the name can stand by itself. If so, each significant word in the name would be a separate indexing unit.

Stop-and-Go Markets	Stop (and) Go Markets

If an expression in the name cannot stand alone as a separate word, the name is indexed as one word and one indexing unit to retain the full meaning of the words in the name.

Redi-Maid Cleaners	Redimaid Cleaners

12.21 The compass points *north, east, south,* and *west,* when written by themselves, are separate indexing units.

East Monticello Boutique
South Truro Beach Rentals

12.22 When these words are combined, for the sake of consistency index them as one unit even when they are separated by hyphens or spaces.

South-Eastern Products	Southeastern Products
North West News Service	Northwest News Service

12.23 A compound word is a combination of two or more words forming the name of a business, product, or service. These words may be joined by hyphens, spelled as one word, or left as two words (see 12.20–12.22, Coined Words and Trade Names and Compass Points).

Interprovincial Transportation Lines
Inter-State Packers, Inc.

Interprovincial	Transportation	Lines
Interstate	Packers	Incorporated

12.24 The conjunction (and) and the ampersand symbol (&) are not separate indexing units and are disregarded in filing. However, to retain the complete company name, the word *and* or the ampersand symbol are placed in parentheses.

Benziger Bruce & Glencoe	Benziger Bruce (&) Glencoe
Wongworavit and Associates	Wongworavit (and) Associates

12.25 Each English word in a compound geographic name is indexed as a separate unit.

Mount St. Anne Resorts	Mount Saint Anne Resorts

A non-English compound geographic name is indexed as one entire indexing unit since the prefix cannot stand alone as a separate unit.

La Tuque Minerals	Latuque Minerals
San Simeon Recreation Club	Sansimeon Recreation Club

12.26 Index company names consisting of geographic locations in the order in which the words are written. Geographic names can refer to streets, cities, provinces, or countries.

Thunder Bay Athletic Club	Thunder Bay Athletic Club
Third Avenue Copy Shoppe	Third Avenue Copy Shoppe

12.27

If a name begins with the word *Hotel* or *Motel,* transpose the name so that the main, distinctive word appears as the first indexing unit. Then index names of hotels and motels in the order in which the words are written, with such words as *hotel, motel, lodge,* and *inn* indexed as separate units.

The Chancellor Hotel	Chancellor Hotel (The)
Traveller's Inn	Traveller('s) Inn

12.28 A hyphenated compound company name consists of the surnames of two individuals joined by a hyphen. Each surname is indexed as a separate unit, followed by the other words in the company name.

Lopez-Tiana Secretarial Services	Lopez Tiana Secretarial Services
Luft-Schmidt Appliances	Luft Schmidt Appliances

12.29 Cities, provinces, street names, and building numbers are used as identifying elements when all indexing units of two or more companies are identical.

12.30 The city is used as the first identifying element when the companies' names are identical.

Aqua Products Company (Brandon)
Aqua Products Company (Sturgeon Falls)

12.31 The province or country is used as the second identifying element when the companies' names and cities are identical.

Worldwide Sporting Goods (Hamilton, Bermuda)
Worldwide Sporting Goods (Hamilton, Ontario)

12.32 The street name is used as the third identifying element when the first and second elements are identical.

Hammer Five Record Company (Toronto, Ontario)
Front Street

Hammer Five Record Company (Toronto, Ontario)
Richmond Street

12.33 The building number is used as the last identifying element when all other elements are identical.

Domtar Chemicals Limited (Halifax, Nova Scotia)
Barrington Street (1741)

Domtar Chemicals Limited (Halifax, Nova Scotia)
Barrington Street (1802)

12.34 When a company's name includes the full name (given name, middle name or initial, and surname) of an individual, the individual's name must first be transposed into the proper indexing units: surname, given name, middle name or initial. The other words in the company name are then indexed in the order in which they are written.

Arthur C. Kelley Clothiers
Janice Jackson Fashion Boutique

Jackson	Janice	Fashion	Boutique
Kelley	Arthur	C.	Clothiers

12.35 Names containing numerals as the first indexing unit are listed, arranged, and filed before the alphabetic names. Keeping these names separate from the alphabetic listing enables quicker indexing and filing of information.

The lower numbers would appear before the higher numbers, so that company names containing numerals would be filed numerically in ascending order.

4-Hour Cleaners
6th Avenue Reprographics Centre
People's Jewellers
Weston's Company

When the first indexing unit consists of a number that is spelled out, consider the entire number as one indexing unit and index the entire name in the order in which the words are written.

Three-Fifty Data Corp.	Threefifty	Data	Corporation
Two-Two-Two Club	Twotwotwo	Club	

When a numeral appears within the company's name, spell out the number and consider the entire number as one indexing unit. The entire name is then indexed in the order in which the words are written.

Bergie's 200 Diner	Bergie('s)	Twohundred	Diner
Bonham 211, Inc.	Bonham	Twoeleven	Incorporated

12.36 The rule for forming the possessive of a name that does not end in *s* is to add an apostrophe and *s* (*'s*) to the name. Index the name up to the apostrophe and enclose in parentheses the apostrophe and *s*.

Behrman's Import-Export Co.

Behrman('s)	Import	Export	Company

12.37 Prepositions such as *from, for, to, by, on,* and *in* are not separate indexing units and are disregarded. However, the preposition should be placed in parentheses in its proper position within the name.

Canadian Institute of Banking	Canadian Institute (of) Banking
Fashions by Renee	Fashions (by) Renee

12.38 Index single letters in a company's name as separate indexing units. In some names, there is a space between the letters; in others, a period is placed between the letters; in still others, the letters are written together. The presence of spacing or periods within the name does not affect the indexing order.

K. P. Restaurants
Triple A Drugs
T.T.R. Sportswear
CFRB Radio

K	P	Restaurants		
Triple	A	Drugs		
T	T	R	Sportswear	
C	F	R	B	Radio

12.39 When a company name includes a title and the complete name of an individual, transpose the parts of the individual's name. The title preceding a complete name is an identifying element, not a separate indexing unit. The title is placed in parentheses at the end of the individual's name.

Sir Thomas Drake Caterers
Doctor A. C. Kahoka's Clinic

Drake	Thomas (Sir)	Caterers	
Kahoka('s)	A	C (Doctor)	Clinic

When a title precedes only one name as part of a company name, the title becomes a separate indexing unit, and the individual's name (surname or given) is one indexing unit.

Captain Andres' Inn
Doctor Allesio's Foot Clinic

Captain	Andres(')	Inn	
Doctor	Allesio('s)	Foot	Clinic

Names of institutions

12.40 Institutions include schools, churches, libraries, banks, credit unions, trust companies, and hospitals.

12.41 Index colleges and universities by the distinctive words in names—generally in the order in which the words are written. The words *college*, *university*, and *school* should be indexed as the last unit.

Confederation College of Applied Arts
University of New Brunswick
Ryerson Polytechnical Institute

Confederation	College (of Applied Arts)	
New	Brunswick	University (of)
Ryerson	Polytechnical	Institute

Institution names that include the name of an individual must first be transposed so that the individual's name is in its appropriate indexing order.

Simon Fraser University
John P. Robarts Research Library

Fraser	Simon	University		
Robarts	John	P.	Research	Library

12.42 Names of elementary and secondary schools can be indexed and filed according to the cities in which they are located. When schools have identical names, listing by cities may be preferred. If the name includes the complete name of an individual, that individual's name must first be transposed.

Saskatoon, Klein, Bishop, School
Saskatoon, Vanier, George, Secondary School
Toronto, Vanier, George, Secondary School
Willowdale, York Mills Secondary School

The names of schools can also be indexed and filed in the order in which the words are written.

Bishop Klein School, Saskatoon
George Vanier Secondary School, Saskatoon
George Vanier Secondary School, Toronto
York Mills Secondary School, Willowdale

12.43 Financial institutions include banks, credit unions, insurance companies, and trust companies. They are indexed according to the cities in which they are located; the city name is the first indexing unit, even if it is not part of the institution name.

Any identifying elements such as branch or street names are placed in parentheses after the name.

Royal Bank of Canada, Calgary, Alberta
Royal Bank of Canada, King and Yonge Streets, Toronto

Calgary, Royal Bank of Canada (Alberta)
Toronto, Royal Bank of Canada (King and Yonge Streets)

12.44 Hospitals, sanatoriums (a term increasingly in disuse), extended care or convalescent homes are generally indexed according to the order in which the words are written.

Hospital for Sick Children
Glendale Lodge Extended Care
Niagara Peninsula Sanatorium
St. John's Convalescent Hospital

Sick	Children('s)	Hospital	
Glendale	Lodge	Extended	Care
Niagara	Peninsula	Sanatorium	
Saint	John('s)	Convalescent	Hospital

When a hospital includes the complete name of an individual, the individual's name is transposed into its proper indexing units.

Daniel Freeman Hospital	Freeman	Daniel	Hospital

12.45 Religious institutions include churches, temples, cathedrals, and synagogues. Names of various institutions should be filed according to their denominations, if known, with the denomination being the first indexing unit. (If the denomination is not known, use the first significant word other than *Church*, *Cathedral*, or *Temple* as the first indexing unit.)

St. Alban's Anglican Church
Greatheart Buddhist Monastery
Holy Blossom Temple
Montreal West Presbyterian Church

Anglican	Saint	Alban('s)	Church
Buddhist	Greatheart	Monastery	
Jewish	Holy	Blossom	Temple
Presbyterian	Montreal	West	Church

Government names

12.46 Government bodies or agencies include various departments, commissions, boards, and offices of municipal, provincial, and federal agencies. At each level of government there may be departments, commissions, boards, and offices that are organized or subdivided into bureaus, divisions, or sections. In a few instances a commission or board is one of the offices of a department. The complexity of these governmental functions and titles creates the need for additional filing rules, although standard alphabetic filing rules generally apply.

12.47 Index and code names of federal government agencies with *Canadian Government* as the first two indexing units, followed by the name of the department and the name of the bureau, division, commission, or board.

Family Allowances	Canadian Government Health (and) Welfare (Department of) Family Allowances
Canadian Citizenship	Canadian Government Secretary of State (Department of) Canadian Citizenship
Consumer Fraud Protection	Canadian Government Consumer Affairs (Department of) Consumer Fraud Protection

12.48 Index and code names of municipal government agencies under the name of the city or town as the first indexing unit(s), followed by its identification as a city or town and the name of the department, bureau, division, commission, or board.

Brockville Board of Education	Brockville, City (of), Education (Board of)
Department of City Engineer City of Charlottetown	Charlottetown, City (of), City Engineer (Department of)

12.49 Index and code names of provincial government agencies under the name of the province as the first indexing unit(s), followed by its identification as a province and the name of the department, bureau, division, commission, or board.

Brampton Adult Training Centre,
Ontario Department of
Correctional Services

Ontario, Province (of),
Correctional Services (Department of)
Brampton Adult Training Centre

12.50 Index and code names of agencies in foreign countries under the name of the country and the name of the department, bureau, and division.

Department of Internal Revenue Service United States	United States Internal Revenue Service (Department of)
Ministry of Education of the Republic of China	China (Republic of), Education (Ministry of)

12.51 Hints for filing government names:

1. Disregard for indexing purposes such words as *department, commission, bureau,* and *board* that appear within names of government agencies. However, such titles must be coded on all records and typed on file folders for proper identification.

2. Each significant word in the name of a government agency is a separate indexing unit. The more words there are in a name, the more indexing units it will have.

3. Disregard for indexing purposes words such as *the, and, for, by,* and *on* appearing within names of government agencies. However, such words must be coded on records and typed on file folders for proper identification. (*The* appearing at the beginning of a name is written in parentheses and placed at the end of the name; *the* appearing in the middle of a name is written in parentheses and placed in its proper sequence within the name. Other words are written in parentheses and placed in their proper sequences within the names.)

4. Index and code names of government agencies by the name of the city, province, or country; then by the major department; then by the name of the bureau, division, commission, or board. (These subdivision names vary from city to city and from province to province. Therefore, it is important to refer to the proper sources to determine the names of departments and officials.)

5. Refer to the telephone directories and government directories in 15.12 and Canadian Almanac in 15.2 for listings of municipal, provincial, and federal officials as well as departments and department heads.

6. Do not confuse names of government agencies with names of private organizations that may include the name of a city, town, province, or the word *Canadian*.

Canadian Mines Equipment	Etobicoke City Bakery
New Brunswick Snowmobile Federation	Ontario Professional Carpet Cleaners
Saint John Beverage Ltd.	Victoria Elevator Ltd.

7. Establish a separate file for each government agency, apart from other correspondence files, if an organization does business with one or more government agencies.

8. Establish a separate file for each country, apart from other correspondence files, if an organization does business with one or more foreign governments.

9. Establish files under the name most commonly referred to within an organization; cross reference to other possible names.

Example: Family Allowances (and) Old Age Security
File: Canadian Government, National Health (and) Welfare
(Department of) Family Allowances
Cross Reference: Family Allowances

Cross-reference card should read:
Family Allowances
See: Canadian Government, National Health (and) Welfare
(Department of)

10. Maintain a consistent system of indexing, coding, and filing records for each government agency.

Numeric filing system

12.52 The numeric filing system involves arranging correspondence, cards, business forms, and documents by the number system, which permits quick and easy identification of records in sequential order and prevents the duplication that often occurs in alphabetic systems.

Components

12.53 Numeric filing systems include these elements.

1. Main numeric file, where all records are stored in numeric sequence with numeric guides and folders bearing numeric captions.

2. Miscellaneous alphabetic files, where records are temporarily stored until five or more pieces of correspondence have accumulated for any one correspondent.

3. Alphabetic card index, containing index cards for all customers and correspondents with important information on each company and individual together with the file numbers assigned.

4. Numeric register or log, listing in numeric sequence all numbers assigned to correspondents and the dates files were created.

Rules for consecutive numeric filing

12.54 1. Index each digit in a number as a separate unit. The larger the number, the more indexing units a number will have.

142	1	4	2		
1 411	1	4	1	1	
26 401	2	6	4	0	1

2. Compare each number digit by digit until a difference is found.

3470	3	4	7	0
3465	3	4	6	5
3219	3	2	1	9

3. Compare the second and subsequent indexing units only when the first units are identical.

4. Disregard for indexing purposes the space (or comma) appearing within numbers.

2 546	2	5	4	6
7 002	7	0	0	2

5. Disregard for indexing purposes the hyphens appearing within numbers

12-45-60	1	2	4	5	6	0
20-95-08	2	0	9	5	0	8
67-33-29	6	7	3	3	2	9

Exception: Some numbers are preceded by a numeric prefix. Such a prefix must be retained as a complete unit during the indexing and coding steps.

12-4560	12	4	5	6	0
20-9508	20	9	5	0	8
67-3329	67	3	3	2	9

6. File records in ascending order; that is, a smaller number is always filed before a larger one.

7. File records in chronological sequence when there are several papers for the same correspondent. The most recent correspondence is placed on top of the file.

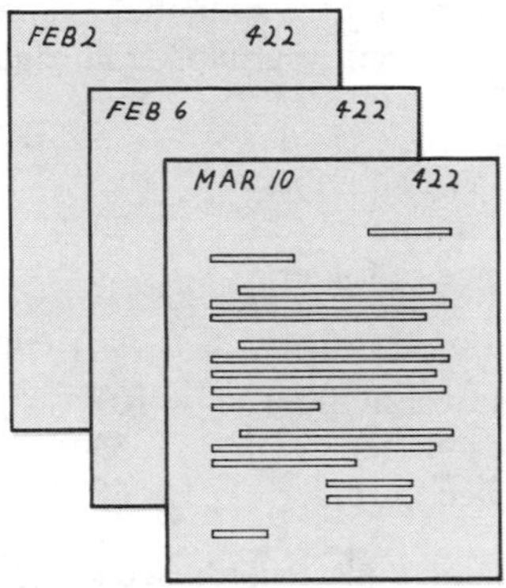

Terminal digit filing

12.55 Terminal digit filing is a numeric filing system in which records are arranged according to the last, or terminal, digits rather than the first units. This system is advantageous for large systems with file numbers of five digits or more.

The advantages of the terminal digit filing system are that files are evenly distributed throughout the system, and file cabinets and drawers can be permanently numbered.

File numbers are assigned in the usual manner—in consecutive sequence as listed in the numeric register—but the numbers are read from right to left. The last two digits—the terminal digits—determine the file drawer number; the middle two digits determine the file folder number in that drawer; and the first digits determine the sequence within the file folder.

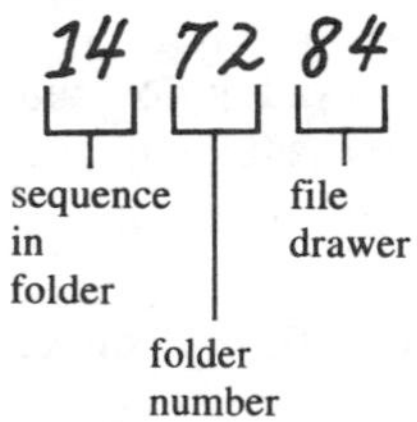

Rules for Terminal-Digit Numeric Filing

12.56 1. Read numbers in groups of two from right to left. (Numbers with more than six digits may be read in groups of three from right to left.)

2. Index each digit in a number as a separate unit, even though the numbers are read in groups from right to left.

497022 becomes	227049		
File drawer number:	22	2	2
Folder number:	70	7	0
Sequence in folder:	49	4	9

6853107 becomes	1075368			
File drawer number:	107	1	0	7
Folder number:	53	5	3	
Sequence in folder:	68	6	8	

3. Index and code records according to the numeric filing rules.

4. File records according to drawer number, folder number, and sequence within the folder.

5. File records in ascending numeric order; that is, a record bearing a smaller number is always filed before a record bearing a larger number—both in terms of folder number and sequence within a folder.

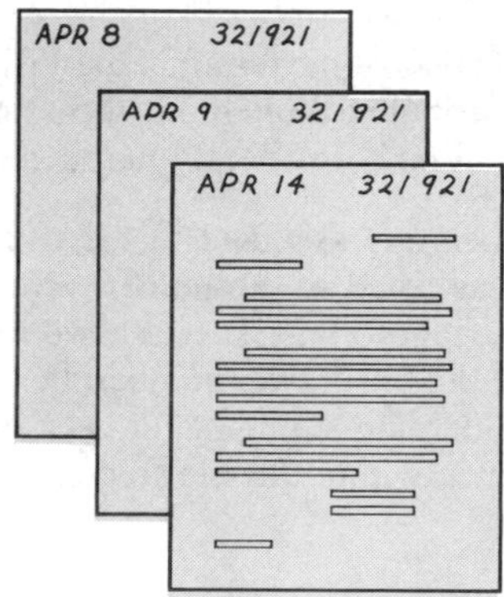

6. File records in chronological order with the most recent item on top, when there is more than one item of correspondence for an individual or company.

Hints for numeric filing, consecutive or terminal digit

12.57 1. All numbers in a group should have the same number of digits to be compared. Numbers that may appear to be identical should be carefully checked; they could be only similar.

1177110 681144092
117710 6811144092

2. Compare only one indexing unit at a time when arranging papers in numeric sequence. Work with one part of a number at a time to avoid confusing the digits.

3. Sort papers alphabetically first so file numbers may be obtained easily and systematically within the alphabetic card index.

4. Sort papers into numeric sequence before filing. This saves significant time during the filing process.

5. Begin by sorting papers into small groups by numbers (rough sorting), then sort into numeric sequence by groups. The larger the group of papers or the larger the range of numbers, the more often sorting must be done. Sorting can be accomplished more easily when working with smaller groups of papers.

6. Code each item of correspondence numerically by writing the file number in the upper right corner of each record. This enables a file worker to file and refile records easily.

1 GLOBAL
2 TELEVISION
3 NETWORK

81 Barber Greene Road
Don Mills, Ontario
M3C 2A2 (416) 446-5311

Global Communications Limited

243701

7. Code each card alphabetically by underlining each indexing unit in the name of the company or individual. This information will stand out so file numbers can be obtained quickly.

Subject filing system

12.58 The subject filing system is based on the arrangement of records by topic names, or subject classifications, rather than by names of individuals, companies, or geographic locations.

This system works best when records are stored and retrieved according to categories or classifications of information. It follows alphabetic filing rules except that the captions on file folders are names of subjects.

Encyclopaedic arrangement

12.59 A subject file with an encyclopaedic arrangement consists of major subject headings with each subject further separated into divisions and subdivisions. Used for larger files, this arrangement is advantageous where small topic divisions are desirable. The components of a subject filing system with an encyclopaedia arrangement are:

1. Main subject files—containing records on various subjects filed alphabetically by subject captions and divided into divisions and subdivisions.

2. Relative index (either an index card file or a typewritten list)—showing all the subject headings/captions and the various classifications or subdivisions under each major subject used within the filing system.

Dictionary arrangement

12.60 A subject file with a dictionary arrangement consists of files set up for the major subjects only, with no breakdown into divisions. This arrangement is advantageous for smaller files, where a person can file or retrieve records without having to check the relative index.

Rules for subject filing

12.61 1. Follow the indexing and coding rules for the alphabetic filing system, except now file by subject names.

2. Each significant word in a subject name is a separate indexing unit.

Sales Records	Sales	Records
Production Schedules	Production	Schedules

3. The major subject heading or caption is the first indexing unit(s), followed by the division heading or caption and the subdivision heading, if any.

4. Index and code items of correspondence by writing the subject captions in the upper right corner of the record.

5. File records in chronological order within each subdivision without regard for grouping correspondence from one individual or company. The most recent correspondence is placed on top of the file.

Hints for subject filing

12.62 1. Use key words for major subject headings.

Production Schedules instead of Schedules for Production
Expense Reports instead of Reports of Expenses

2. Determine major subject headings and add divisions and subdivisions as the file expands.

Major subject heading:	Advertising
Division headings:	Advertising—Agencies
	Advertising—Newspapers
	Advertising—Television

3. Sort records by major subject headings first, then by divisions within the major subject headings.

4. Code records with their subject headings and divisions; this saves time during filing and refiling of papers.

5. File all related papers under one major subject and cross reference where necessary under related topics.

Television Ad Agencies   See Advertising—Television

Geographic filing system

12.63 The geographic filing system is based on the arrangement of records by names of cities, provinces, and/or countries, and then by the name of the individual or company within each geographic location.

This sytem is used when information needs to be filed and retrieved by geographic locations—such as district offices, salespersons' territories, and store locations—rather than by names of individuals, companies, or subjects.

Rules for geographic filing

12.64 1. Index and code with the name of the province as the first indexing unit(s), followed by the name of the city or town, then the name of the individual or company.

Bertelson Art Gallery, Vancouver, B.C.
Tempo Canadian Crafts, Victoria, B.C.

British	Columbia	Vancouver	Bertelson	Art	Gallery
British	Columbia	Victoria	Tempo	Canadian	Crafts

2. Use the street name as an identifying element when the province, city or town, and correspondents' names are identical.

Cheeseboro Electronics, Starbuck Drive, Selkirk, Manitoba
Cheeseboro Electronics, Woodridge Drive, Selkirk, Manitoba

Manitoba Selkirk Cheeseboro Electronics (Starbuck Drive)
Manitoba Selkirk Cheeseboro Electronics (Woodbridge Drive)

3. Code each item of correspondence by circling the names of the province and city or town, then underlining each indexing unit in the name of the correspondent.

4. Index and code miscellaneous correspondence by the name of the city or town, then alphabetically by the name of the correspondent.

5. Sort records by provincial names first, then sort by city or town names.

6. File papers by city or town name, then alphabetically by correspondents' names.

7. File papers within folders in chronological order with the most recent papers on top when there are several items for the same correspondent.

8. File records for an individual correspondent in a separate folder when five or more items have accumulated for that correspondent.

9. Create a separate folder for a city or town when five or more items of correspondence have accumulated for that city or town.

10. File papers in miscellaneous alphabetic folders behind each city or town name until five or more items have been accumulated for the same city or town.

Reading file

12.65 A reading file consists of an extra carbon copy (or photocopy) of each piece of correspondence filed in chronological order with the most recent correspondence on top. The file is kept in a notebook for quick reference.

Correspondence in the reading file is not maintained for more than six months, depending on the volume and the need to refer to previous correspondence. Papers are discarded on a regular basis so the file does not become cumbersome.

Tickler file

12.66 A tickler file or system is a follow-up or reminder file to show what tasks need to be completed, or followed up on, during the month or year.

This file, usually a 12.5 cm × 7.5 cm or 15 cm × 10 cm card file, is arranged chronologically by months and days. The reminder notices are arranged in order behind guides for the months. All notices for the current month are placed in the front of the file behind guides for the days. As each day arrives, notices for that day are removed and acted upon. The guide for that day is moved to the back of the file, where notices may begin to accumulate for subsequent periods of time.

Figure 12-2. Tickler file

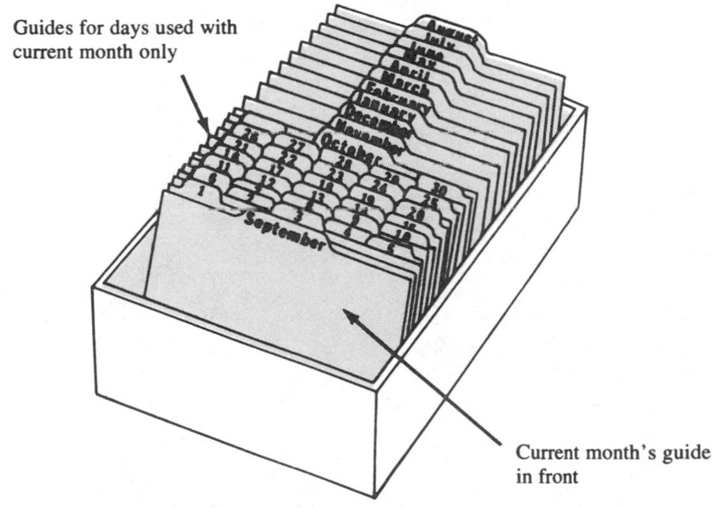

A tickler file may also be maintained in a notebook where information is written about duties or responsibilities that should be performed on certain dates. This record must be maintained on a daily basis, like the tickler file above, and items should be crossed out or initialled to indicate that action has been taken.

Office Procedures 13

Organizing work

13.1 The systematic organization of work responsibilities places an office employee in command of the job. Good organization is knowing how to make the best use of available time; organizing work on a day-to-day basis helps to maintain a high rate of production. Follow these general suggestions.

1. Set aside a small block of time at the end of each day to plan the next day's work. Anticipate important deadlines, prepare for a meeting, plan for additional personnel needs, and be ready for the next day's work.

2. Make a list of the specific jobs or tasks that need to be handled. Such a list helps determine the priority of work to be done and serves as a reminder of work to be completed.

3. Check off each item as the task is completed. Seeing what is left to be done will help keep the work moving along and keep you organized to complete these jobs.

4. Establish a routine for performing routine work to save time, motion, and energy.

5. Prepare a timetable and a list of the routine tasks that must be performed on a daily, weekly, or monthly basis.

6. Use a notebook or a 7.5 cm × 12.5 cm card index file to maintain a record of those papers or correspondence requiring action that have been routed to others in the office.

7. Use a notebook to jot down reminders such as specific tasks to be done; errands to be run; and people to see, call, or write.

8. Place each major job in a separate file folder to keep related papers together.

Information Processing

13.2 A word processing, or information processing, system describes the organized way of changing one person's thoughts or ideas into a form (usually on paper) that others can view. Traditionally, the flow of information in a company was directed by the small group of people who originated the material. Efficiency and control of costs were also left to the discretion of this group. Many companies saw an advantage to be gained in efficiency and in a reduction of time and costs by making standard the methods by which all employers transfer information from one place to another. Employers initiated specific procedures, using skilled personnel and modern electronic equipment, to move information—a word processing system.

The development of word processors and word processing systems has helped to alleviate the repetitive nature of many tasks in the office. Office employees are able to pursue more interesting tasks that provide a fulfilling work experience. The inception of word processing systems has brought about changes in the office environment as well. Through ergonomics (the study of the relationship among people, their work environment, and the equipment they operate) factors such as lighting, seating comfort, eye strain, noise levels, and colour, are now given more consideration when new equipment is installed. There is, however, some concern about possible health hazards due to radiation from the CRT component of word processors. Every operator should make it their business to be well informed about the latest research in this area.

The following chart shows the movement of information through a word processing system.

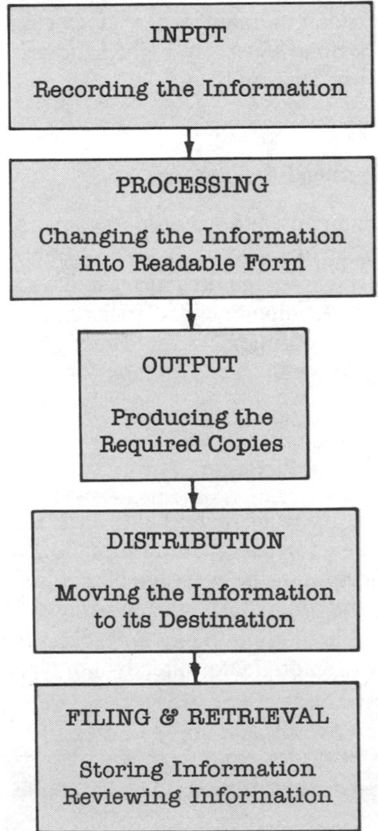

Office employees are pleasantly surprised to learn that many of the skills they use in the "traditional" office—keyboarding, machine transcription, proofreading, filing—can be easily updated and adapted for use in a word processing system.

13.3 **INPUT: Recording the Information**

Options

1. Longhand

Although it is time consuming, many authors (called originators, users, or principals) use handwriting to record their thoughts. This method permits the author to review the material immediately after its composition, but the transcriber often experiences difficulties when trying to decipher the handwriting. As the cost of the originator's time is usually high, handwriting ideas is expensive and should be discouraged.

2. Shorthand dictation

Originators dictate material to someone who records it in a handwritten or machine keyboarded symbolic shorthand. Transcribing shorthand notes requires many skills (see sections 13.11 and 13.12); however, computer aided transcription (CAT) is able to convert machine shorthand notes directly into typed words stored on magnetic media, such as tapes or floppy disks.

3. Machine dictation

Originators using hand-held, desk top, or centralized recording equipment dictate their information onto magnetic media. If a clarification of the message is required, the transcriber can easily replay the originator's spoken words (see sections 13.9 and 13.10). New technology is being developed that will convert the spoken words of an originator directly into typed words stored on magnetic media.

13.4 **Processing: Changing the Information into Readable Form**

Options

1. Text-Editing Equipment

The heart of the information processing system is the electronic text-editing typewriter, more commonly known as a word processor. It is often made up of a keyboard, a separate printer, a display device, and disk drives. It works as follows:

- the information that is keyed into the processor is shown on the screen so that the operator can see what has been recorded before it is produced in print.
- editing, either single letter changes or insertions of whole paragraphs, can be done without retyping the whole document.
- when the document is error-free, the processor can direct an attached printer to produce copies at speeds of over 450 words a minute.
- the processor can store the information internally or transfer the information to floppy disks or other memory devices. This information can be fed back into the word processor at any later time.

A unit such as the one described above, which works independently and uses its own software and storage capabilities, is known as a standalone word processor. Others are joined together in shared systems under the control of a central computer. A company may centralize all its word processing equipment in one location or may decentralize its system and set up mini centres to serve individual departments. Every company will make its own arrangements to meet its own needs.

2. Typewriter and Optical Character Reader (OCR)

In a company with a specialized department it may be advantageous for a transcriber who is familiar with the originator's terminology to use a typewriter equipped with an OCR compatible font to produce the first draft of a document. The originator can review the document and mark any changes on it directly. Then the OCR can scan the first draft and magnetically record the typed words without the operator having to keyboard them into the word processor. The operator (or another operator who is not familiar with the originator's terminology) can then use the word processor to incorporate the changes in the usual way (see above).

13.5 OUTPUT: Producing the Required Copies

Paper Documents

Information keyboarded onto magnetic media need not be printed onto paper immediately, and, in some cases, need never be made into hard copy. (See electronic mail.) When hard copy is needed, however, the printer attached to the word processor can produce it. Printers can make extra copies, but it is inefficient and expensive to use word processing equipment as copying machinery. Copies should be made on photocopiers, offset printers, or by other reprographic means. (See sections 13.13–13.24.)

13.6 DISTRIBUTION: Moving the Information to its Destination

Options

1. Traditional Methods

Paper copies of information may be transferred by carriers (such as the post office) in the usual way. (See chapter 14.) Magnetic media that hold keyboarded data may also be distributed in this way. However, special care must be taken when handling these materials since difficulties will arise in their use if they are bent, scratched, or exposed to adverse temperatures or magnetic fields.

2. Electronically (electronic mail)

(a) On Site

(1) Word processors in one location can relay information to compatible equipment in a different location via telecommunications (e.g., telephone lines or direct wiring). Only at the destination will a hard copy be produced if required. Numerous time and cost-saving benefits can be gained by using these communicating word processors; transfer of information is accomplished in minutes rather than in days.

(2) Hard copies of original documents may be transferred to other locations by using compatible facsimile (or FAX) equipment and the telephone. FAX can reproduce images such as graphs, handwriting, and pictures, as well as the printed word. The cost is determined by the length of time for the transmission over the telephone and the cost of the FAX equipment.

(3) Computers are also being used to store and then forward verbal and video messages from one location to another. Technology in this field is expanding and improving rapidly.

(b) Remote

Outside firms such as CNCP, TWX, and Telex offer message forwarding services that transmit information either from their offices or from installations on the user's premises. See section 14.27 ff. for further information about these services.

13.7 FILING AND RETRIEVAL:

Storing the Information and Reviewing the Information

Options

1. Hard Copies

(a) Conventional Style Cabinets

Commonly used cabinets of three or four drawers hold letter- and legal-sized paper in horizontal folders with tabs at the top. For safety, only one drawer may be opened at a time. Specially designed cabinets are available for unusual-sized documents (e.g., blueprints, computer printouts).

(b) Open Shelf Units

Lateral, open-sided filing shelves hold paper in containers or folders that have colour-coded side labels or tabs for quick identification. Filed documents can be retrieved easily by more than one person at a time. Shelving may extend higher than conventional cabinets as there are no drawers to open; hence, floor space and storage costs are reduced.

2. Magnetic Media

Magnetic media can be irreparably damaged if they are not handled and stored with care. Reputable manufacturers or distributors of these products should be contacted for suggestions on proper storage methods.

3. Micrographics

Paper copy storage may be reduced or eliminated by preserving documents on film. This can be accomplished by using either the paper copies or the electronically stored data of a computer-linked word processor and a computer output microfilm unit (COM). A more advanced method of storing and retrieving micro images (usually microfiche) includes the use of electronic coding on each image, which permits rapid computer assisted retrieval (CAR).

Viewers or readers must be used when information is recalled. Full sized hard copy can be produced if required. Storage space is dramatically diminished when hard copy files are converted to film.

Word Processing Glossary

13.8 administrative secretary — someone who usually performs non-typing tasks in an office: research, travel and meeting arrangements, and telephone communications.

bit — the smallest unit of information used in a computer.

byte — the most common unit of computer storage; a group of bits.

CAR — computer assisted retrieval.

COM — computer output microfilm.

CPU — central processing unit; the part of the computer that coordinates the whole system.

CRT — cathode ray tube; the same as a VDT; the screen on which information is displayed.

chip — a silicon wafer etched with tiny electronic circuits.

correspondence secretary — someone who is trained to operate word processing equipment.

data base — the organized body of information that is systematically recorded, retrieved, and updated.

disk — a flat circular object for magnetic storage of information (also floppy disk).

electronic mail — messages sent between two or more word processors or computers.

hard copy — any document produced on paper (typed, printed, or handwritten).

hardware — the physical components of a computer.

magnetic media — material on which information is recorded, and that can be stored or re-used (tapes, cards, floppy disks).

memory — the computer's storage area for information.

originator — the author of the information; same as a principal.

principal — the author of the information; same as an originator.

software — the instructions that a computer follows.

standalone — machines that operate independently, separate from other equipment.

VDT — video display terminal; the same as a CRT.

Machine dictation

13.9 Machine dictation involves initiating and transmitting information into a dictation machine that records the exact message. Machine dictation also involves transcribing directly from dictation recorded on a tape, belt, card, or disc. A transcription machine is used to transform the spoken message into written form.

Machine dictation-transcription

13.10 1. Follow the operating instructions for using dictation-transcription equipment. Some machines are both dictation and transcription units, while others are separate units.

2. Learn how to handle, process, and store the medium used for dictation—cassette tape, magnetic belt, magnetic card, or magnetic disc.

3. When taking work from a new dictator or word originator, determine his or her preferences for a particular format, use of punctuation, etc.

4. Use a folder with a pocket to separate the dictation on each card, belt, disk, or tape. Any notes or related correspondence can be kept in the folder.

5. When transcription work is done for more than one person, keep separate folders for each person and label them clearly.

6. Separate used cards, belts, tapes, and discs from new ones. (If all dictated materials are to be filed rather than reused immediately, file them immediately after transcription. Label each with the date of dictation, the name of the word originator, and your name.)

7. Organize materials efficiently so that stationery and other papers and supplies are accessible. Return the eraser and other correction devices to the same place after each use.

8. Use the eraser and other correction devices so that mistakes cannot be detected.

9. Learn to work with one margin setting for all letters; learn to adjust the lines between letter parts for shorter or longer letters. See 7.73 and 7.74. (Learn to "read" the indicator strip with each dictation to determine the length of material to be transcribed.)

10. Keep a dictionary, word division manual, or reference manual available for reference.

11. During transcription, have all correspondence to which you need to refer assembled in the same order as the dictation.

12. Listen to the dictated material whenever necessary before transcribing. Familiarize yourself with the contents and any

changes that may have been made during dictation. Be alert to any special notations or instructions that may have been added, either in the middle or at the end of the dictation.

13. Type a rough draft of lengthy or technical material if necessary, so that the word originator has an opportunity to review the material and make any changes.

14. During transcription, try to keep the typewriter moving—use the controls on the transcription machine to stop, start, or replay the dictated material.

15. Do not hesitate to go to the word originator to clarify spellings of names or addresses or to verify other information.

16. Proofread all work before removing it from the typewriter; corrections are easier to make.

Taking shorthand dictation

13.11 To make the most effective use of the time spent during the dictation session, follow these guidelines:

1. Decide on a regular time of day for the dictation session. Most employers and secretaries prefer the morning hours when they are fresh and alert. Dictation after the morning mail delivery is a convenient time.

2. Have all necessary supplies assembled in one place and ready for dictation—notebooks, two pens, a colour pencil, paper clips, and a correspondence folder.

3. Each day, date the notebook at the bottom of the first clean page. This facilitates locating old notes. Marking notes with *a.m.* and *p.m.* is also helpful.

4. Keep a rubber band around the used pages of the notebook so it can be opened to the next clean page.

5. When dictation is taken from more than one person, keep separate notebooks and correspondence folders for each and label them clearly.

6. Use a folder for correspondence to be signed by the dictator. In this way, all correspondence and attachments are kept together for signature.

7. Keep a folder in your desk for all pending work.

8. Keep an extra notebook on your desk to jot down messages or instructions or to take dictation on the spot.

9. Use a pen. It increases dictation speed and ease, and transcription speed is increased because notes are more easily read.

10. During the dictation session, number each letter in your notebook and code it with its related correspondence. Place the correspondence face down in the folder so everything will be in sequence for transcription.

11. Skip two or three lines between each dictated letter for those special notations and instructions that the dictator may mention after the dictation.

12. If the dictator is one to change his or her mind frequently, use only one column of each notebook page. Any changes can be made in the other column without disturbing other notes.

13. Number each insertion made in your notes and indicate its place in your notes by a caret (∧). A red pencil notation can be spotted readily.

14. Do not hesitate to ask the dictator about the spelling of a name or address that may not be in the files.

15. Use a colour pencil (preferably red) to flag important correspondence to be transcribed first or to call attention to special notations. Fold the relevant notebook page so the edge sticks out; then you can find this urgent letter more quickly.

16. If interrupted by the telephone or by a visitor during dictation, you may need to review the last few sentences of your notes before receiving additional dictation.

17. Write down changes, special notations, and instructions. Don't trust your memory.

18. When the dictation session is over, make an effort to transcribe notes immediately. If this cannot be done, review your notes and remind yourself to raise any questions that might require clarification.

Shorthand transcription

13.12 1. As soon after the dictation session as possible, review your notes and locate any priority correspondence that should be transcribed first.

2. Always read through your notes before attempting to transcribe. Insert any necessary punctuation marks and paragraphs if they were not dictated. Obtain correct spelling(s) of proper names, cities, and provinces; obtain correct addresses and postal codes; verify days, dates, and amounts of money.

3. Keep your eyes on the shorthand notes while transcribing. This increases transcription speed.

4. Organize your materials efficiently. Keep stationery and other papers and supplies accessible. Return your eraser and correction materials to the same place after each use.

5. Use the eraser and other correction devices so mistakes cannot be detected.

6. Learn to work with one margin setting for all correspondence; learn to adjust the lines between letter parts for shorter or longer letters. (See 7.73 and 7.74.)

7. Draw a diagonal line through the shorthand notes after the letter is transcribed, so you won't have to read them again.

8. Keep a dictionary, word division manual, or reference manual available.

9. When transcribing, have all correspondence to which you need to refer assembled in the same order as the dictation. (The correspondence should already have been placed face down in the folder used during dictation.)

10. Proofread all work before removing it from the typewriter; corrections are easier to make.

Reprographic processes

13.13 Reproducing information for distribution—by using carbon paper, photocopiers, mimeograph, or offset printing—is an important aspect of the output phase in the word processing cycle.

Each office has its own reprographic processing needs. The following questions should be asked in determining the most appropriate method of reproducing information.

1. What quality of copy is desired?

2. How many copies are required?

3. How much can be spent on materials and labour?

4. How soon must copies be ready?

Carbon paper

13.14 Up to ten legible copies of a document can be made using carbon paper. At least one carbon copy of correspondence for the files is required in most offices, and several carbon copies of documents are often required for distribution to all persons concerned.

It is important that carbon copies be legible and neat, with no wrinkles or creases. Since photocopies may be made from carbon copies later, it is essential that any mistakes be corrected at the time the original is corrected.

Carbon copies are usually prepared on onionskin paper, manifold paper, or coloured paper of a lighter weight than company letterhead stationery.

The grade of carbon paper used depends on the number of copies made at one typing and the number of times carbon is used. Typewriter carbon paper is different from carbon paper used with pen or pencil.

13.15 A carbon pack consists of alternating layers of stationery, carbon paper, and carbon copy paper (called second sheets). A carbon pack is assembled and inserted into the typewriter as follows:

1. Place the second sheet on the desk or on top of the typewriter. Place a sheet of carbon paper, carbon side down, on top of the second sheet. Place the letterhead or other stationery on top.

2. Lift the entire pack up so that the back of the second sheet is facing you. Tap the pack to straighten the sheets.

3. Hold the pack with the back of the second sheet facing you and drop it into the typewriter, using the paper release lever to insert the pack into position.

4. Adjust the carbon copy indicator on the typewriter to loosen the pressure against the cylinder if several carbon copies are made.

5. To remove the carbons from the pack, hold the upper left edge of the entire pack and shake the carbons from the pack. (Most carbon papers are notched in the upper left and lower right corners for ease in removing from packs.)

Hints on Using Carbon Paper

13.16 1. When carbon paper is not in use, place it flat in its box in a cool, dry place.

2. Keep carbon paper carbon-side down on a protective sheet on the desk between uses to prevent carbon from smudging the desk, other papers, or clothing.

3. When inserting and removing a carbon pack from the typewriter, use the paper release lever to prevent typewriter roller marks on the copies and wrinkles or creases on the carbon paper.

4. Keep hands clean—use a non-greasy lotion or cream to prevent carbon from accumulating on the fingers.

5. Use carbon paper that is about 2 cm longer than the paper. It is easier to handle than carbon that is the same size as the stationery.

6. Always use an eraser shield (a plastic or metal guard that fits over the cylinder between the paper and the carbon paper) to prevent wearing out the carbon by rubbing against it during erasing.

7. Use the correct weight of carbon paper for the number of copies being made. Use lightweight carbon paper for several carbon copies; use medium-weight carbon paper for normal typing.

Photocopy process

13.17 Photocopiers make it possible to reproduce copies of an existing record without preparing a master. They are widely used, both for their convenience and the high quality of copies produced.

The most popular photocopying process is the electrostatic dry photocopier. The electrostatic process includes the xerographic or transfer method and the direct method.

13.18 The xerographic or transfer method uses a light-reflection process when an original is "photographed" and the image is transferred from a drum to the copy paper. The image is then fused to the paper by heat.

Advantages

- Copies are easy and fast to make.
- Machine uses regular bond or duplicator paper.

Disadvantages

- Equipment is expensive to operate.
- Photographs, colours, and solid areas cannot always be reproduced.

13.19 Direct method photocopies are made by forming the image directly on the copy paper itself and then fusing the impression by heat.

Advantages

- Machine is fast to operate.
- Most colours can be copied.
- Photographs, halftones, and solid areas can be reproduced.

Disadvantages

- Specially coated paper must be used.
- Copies are easily scratched.

Spirit Duplicating

13.20 Spirit duplicating is an inexpensive method of making fair quality copies.

The spirit duplicator package is made up of a spirit master (a heavy, non-absorbent paper); a protective sheet to separate the master from the carbon; carbon paper coated with dye. Copies are made by attaching the prepared spirit master to the cylinder of the spirit duplicator. Then the master sheet, dye side out, is passed over nonporous paper. The dye is released onto the paper.

Advantages

- low cost
- masters can be typed or handwritten
- masters can be stored and re-used
- there is a variety of colours

Disadvantages

- low quality reproduction
- up to 100 copies can be made
- masters must be prepared
- making corrections is complicated

Stencil (mimeograph) process

13.21 The stencil or mimeograph process is very popular because hundreds and sometimes thousands of good copies, all of equal quality and usually in permanent black ink, can be produced from one stencil.

13.22 The stencil master consists of a waxy sheet of paper that does not absorb ink. When information is typed, drawn, or written on the master, it is actually cut onto the stencil. Electronic stencil-cutting machines transfer and cut information from a typewritten, handwritten, or drawn work, thus eliminating the need to prepare a stencil master.

The mimeograph machine allows the ink to go through the cuttings on the stencil master, and the impression is transferred to the paper copies. Up to 1000 copies can be made from an average stencil; other qualities of stencils provide more copies.

Advantages

- Copies are inexpensive to make in quantities.
- Copies are professional looking and easy to read.
- Corrections are easy to make on the stencil.
- Copies can be reproduced on photocopying machines.
- Stencils can be stored for future use.

Disadvantages

- The ink used is impossible to remove from clothing.
- A specific quality of paper must be used so that the ink is absorbed quickly.
- Correcting the master after it has been used is almost impossible because it is ink laden.
- Storage of the used masters is cumbersome because of their size.
- The size of the master makes it difficult to fit sideways into most typewriters.

Offset printing process

13.23 The offset printing process is more time-consuming than the other processes, but it produces professional-looking copies.

Material is typed, drawn, or written on a paper master, which is then transferred to the plate by a photochemical process. Between 50 and 100 copies can be made with paper plates; up to 10 000 copies can be made with long-run metal plates.

Advantages

- High-quality, professional copies are obtained.
- All copies are of the same quality.
- Printing can be done in various colours.
- The master is filed for future use.

Disadvantages

- Cost of equipment is higher than other processes.
- Special training is needed to operate the machine.
- Cost of supplies and maintenance is higher than other machines.

Hints for Using Reprographic Processes

13.24 1. Do not make more copies than are needed.

2. Use a routing slip with one set of materials rather than preparing copies for everyone.

3. Do not use the photocopying machine indiscriminately.

a. Use only when a single high-quality copy is required.

b. Do not photocopy the same item more than once. Unless a perfect copy is required (which is seldom), a copy that is clear and legible will serve its purpose.

c. Make carbon copies of correspondence rather than photocopies unless a photocopier is easily accessible.

4. Use an appropriate reprographic process for the job, based on the quality of copies needed, quantity needed, cost factor, and time element.

5. If possible, keep a log sheet of everyone using the photocopier—make everyone accountable for its use.

6. Determine the "needs" versus the "wants" of copying. Unless copies are necessary, they only clutter files and take up valuable office space.

Typing hints

Assembling printed letters or forms

13.25 If printed letters or forms must be assembled into sets for typing with carbon paper, collate forms into sets. Staple each set on the top of the page parallel to the top edge so the pack can be inserted easily into the typewriter.

Interleave carbon paper into the pack before typing.

Use spare minutes to assemble small supplies of these sets of letters or forms so they will be available when needed.

Blind carbon copy

13.26 A blind carbon copy of a letter or memorandum is prepared when the writer does not want the addressee to know another person is receiving a copy of the communication (see also 7.53).

1. Type the entire letter or memorandum to the point on the page where the blind carbon copy (bcc or bc) notation is to be typed.

2. Disengage the paper release lever.

3. Pull the original letter and the first carbon paper out of the typewriter with one hand while the other hand holds the remaining pages and carbons in position.

4. Straighten the remaining pack of papers and carbons.

5. Type the blind carbon copy notation in its appropriate place on the page.

or

1. Type the entire letter or memorandum to the point on the page where the blind carbon copy notation is to be typed.

2. Insert a small piece of paper between the original and the type guide of the typewriter.

3. Move the carbon copy indicator back two or three notches to release the tension on the cylinder.

4. Type the blind carbon copy notation in its appropriate place.

Carbon copies

13.27 1. Make carbon copies of correspondence sent out rather than photocopies; they are less expensive and less time consuming.

2. Use the back of incoming letters and memoranda for the carbon copy of a reply to the writer. This results in less paperwork.

Chain feeding envelopes

13.28 Use this method when many envelopes are to be addressed; chain feeding allows a continuous supply of envelopes to be fed into the typewriter.

1. Place a stack of envelopes on the desk, address side down, with the flap end pointing away from you.

2. Pick up each envelope and drop it into the typewriter.

3. Type the first envelope address.

4. Insert a second envelope in the back of the typewriter immediately behind the first envelope.

5. Remove the first envelope using the cylinder knob and/or carriage return (carrier return) to bring the second envelope into typing position.

6. As each envelope is addressed, insert the next one to form a chain.

Composing at the typewriter

13.29 Save time by learning to compose short messages, letters, and memoranda as you type. This involves thinking and organizing thoughts at the typewriter.

1. Decide what needs to be written, and jot down notes as necessary.

2. Organize the ideas in your mind: important points, details, overall form, and the appropriate words.

3. Think and type simultaneously. Try to type the final communication the first time through. If changes are necessary, type them on the page; then use this page as a rough draft as you retype the communication in final form.

Folders

13.30 Use various folders with pockets to keep work together and to ensure privacy.

1. Keep a folder for *WORK TO BE DONE*.
2. Keep a folder for your employer of things *TO BE SIGNED*.

Follow-up correspondence

13.31 When receipt of a follow-up letter or memorandum is necessary, send a photocopy of the original correspondence with a handwritten note mentioning the follow-up. A standard form letter or printed reminder notice may also be used to save typewritten work.

Handling simple inquiries

13.32 Use incoming letters and memoranda to write responses or make simple inquiries. This eliminates dictation and transcription time and the need to create additional papers for the files.

Index cards and labels

13.33 Fold a 1 cm pleat in the centre of a sheet of paper.

Insert the paper into the typewriter so the pleat is visible. Insert the index card or label inside the pleat. Roll the paper backward to type the desired information.

Rough drafts

13.34 1. Type correspondence and business reports in final form at the first typing unless a rough draft is requested or necessary.

2. When material is to be typed from rough drafts that include special headings, indentions, or special features, refer to the files to locate similar projects to obtain the appropriate form and style.

3. If columns of information or figures are to be typed, insert a page from a previously typed table into the typewriter to determine the margin settings and tabulator stops. This eliminates the need to calculate the spacing.

Typing tables

13.35 When high-priority work is to be typed and you are in the middle of typing statistical data in columnar form, jot down the numbers of margin settings, tabulator stops, and other spacing on the page so that you may return to the table quickly.

Using the telephone

13.36 Use the telephone to obtain or to verify information urgently needed or when communication of technical or detailed information can more effectively be conveyed and discussed by telephone. Be sure to take notes of the conversation and date and initial the notes for future reference.

Proofreading

13.37 Proofreading is an essential skill that everyone should develop to ensure that correspondence, reports, and business forms sent within and outside the company will be error free. Proofreading involves four steps.

1. Look at the overall document. Is it attractively placed on the page? Is the general format correct? (If the answers are ''No,'' it is not necessary to proofread further.)

2. Scan the document for obvious mistakes. Are there any typographical errors, errors in spacing, or incorrectly divided words at ends of lines? (If the answer is ''Yes,'' can these errors be easily corrected?)

3. Read the entire document for meaning. Does the information make sense? Is it grammatically correct? (If the answer is "No," how can the information be rewritten?)

4. Verify names, addresses, numbers, and amounts. Are words and names spelled correctly? Are the numbers and amounts correct?

Proofreading Techniques

13.38 1. Concentrate on the material being proofread. If necessary, proofread a second time.

2. Proofread tables, charts, graphs, legal descriptions, measurements, and other technical information with another person. (The person who typed the material should read from the original material while the second person proofreads the typewritten copy.)

3. Place the original and copy side by side and proofread using two fingers—one on the original and the other following the typewritten copy. (As the bottom portion of a page is proofread, one page may be overlapped to make the distance between the original and the copy easier for the eye to read.)

4. Place a light check mark with a pencil in the right margin next to the line where an error exists. (For a lengthy document, it may be more desirable to place a paper clip at the right edge to spot errors on each page.)

5. Try to correct a mistake if it can be corrected in an acceptable manner. Determine how much needs to be corrected and retype the page if necessary.

6. Whenever a page needs to be retyped, do not type by reading from the incorrect sheet. Instead, read from the original. (This prevents compounding errors or making the same mistake again.)

7. When extensive corrections need to be made, use standard proofreading symbols (see section 6.55).

Making corrections

13.39 There are five ways to correct errors on typewritten work: eraser, correction fluid, correction paper, correction tape, and self-correcting typewriter. Each method has its advantages and disadvantages.

Eraser

13.40 The eraser requires the most time and skill. Erasing is a permanent method that involves the use of several tools—an eraser suitable for the type and colour of paper used, an erasing guide, and a plastic or metal eraser shield.

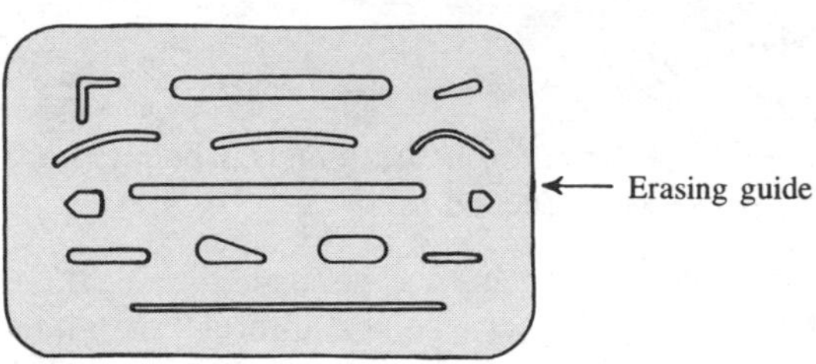

13.41 Before beginning to erase an error, consider whether it can be corrected easily or whether the page should be retyped. For example, it is more efficient to retype the entire page than to spend several minutes erasing several words or a line.

1. Move the carriage (or carrier) to the extreme left or right side. Use the margin release key.

2. Raise the paper bail or pull it forward.

3. Advance the paper several lines to allow space to make the correction. (If the error appears on the top part of the page, advance the paper forward; if the error appears on the bottom part of the page, roll the paper backward.)

4. Place an eraser shield over the letter or word to be erased so that only the letter or word is visible. (See 13.40.)

5. Hold the paper firmly in place with clean fingers so the paper does not slip.

6. Use a typewriter eraser (abrasive) for originals and a pencil eraser (non-abrasive) for carbon copies.

7. Sharpen the eraser to a blunt end, not to a point.

8. Use short, up-and-down strokes while erasing. Brush or blow away eraser crumbs.

9. Roll the paper to its original position, check the alignment of the line of typing, and type the correct letter or word. Strike the correct letter or word again if necessary to obtain an even stroke on the page.

10. Keep erasers clean by rubbing them on a sheet of paper or emery board after each use.

Erasing Original and Carbon Copies

13.42 1. Erase the last carbon copy first, using techniques listed in 13.41.

2. Place an eraser shield behind the next-to-last copy.

3. Erase the next-to-last carbon copy; then remove the eraser shield and place it behind the next carbon copy.

4. Proceed in the same manner to erase all carbon copies.

5. Place the eraser shield behind the original and correct the original.

Correction fluid

13.43 Correction fluid is perhaps the easiest way to correct typing errors. However, this method also takes skill to use, and its uses are limited.

The main advantage of correction fluids is that they can be used to block out a letter, a word, or a line from typewritten, handwritten, or printed material and then the original can be photocopied with no trace of the error on the copies. The original is used as the master and kept in files until additional photocopies are desired.

Correction fluids are available in many colours to match the various colours of paper and card stock in use.

Correction fluids should not be used on original correspondence or reports unless the material is to be photocopied. The fluid does cover up the error, but it can be detected on the page.

Using Correction Fluids

13.44 1. Roll the cylinder forward or backward several lines so the error is visible.

2. Shake the correction fluid well.

3. Remove excess fluid from the brush.

4. Apply sparingly by dotting the fluid over the error.

5. Replace the cap on the bottle to prevent drying up.

6. Allow the fluid to dry thoroughly. (A water-base fluid takes longer to dry than an oil base.)

7. Return the paper to the line of typing and correct the mistake.

Correction paper

13.45 Correction paper is used for making corrections on originals and carbon copies. This chalk-coated paper is available in all colours but is not a permanent correction device.

Correction paper must be used in conjunction with an eraser. A correction made with this chalk-coated paper is detectable on the original as well as any photocopies.

Use correction paper only when the correction involves letters of the same size and shape (e.g., to correct an *e* to an *a*).

Do not use correction paper when the correction involves letters that are different sizes or shapes. Use an eraser to erase all or part of the letter and type the correct letter.

Do not use correction paper when the correction involves a mis-typed letter between two words. Use an eraser, as the letter with the chalk coating is quite detectable.

Using Correction Paper

13.46 1. Backspace to the error.

2. Insert the correction paper over the error between the paper and the card holders on the typewriter.

3. Retype the incorrect letter to coat it with the chalk covering.

4. Remove the correction paper and check to see if the incorrect letter has been completely covered with chalk.

5. Backspace to the error and type the correct letter. Strike it again if necessary to obtain an even type.

Correction tape

13.47 Correction tape is a self-adhesive tape that comes in varied widths used to cover a letter, word, line, or paragraph. This device is used for making corrections on original work that will be photocopied. Do not use correction tape on originals unless they are to be photocopied.

Using Correction Tape

13.48 1. Roll the cylinder forward or backward several lines so the error is visible and so the area of the error rests on the cylinder or against the top of the typewriter. (It may be desirable to remove the paper from the typewriter to make the correction.)

2. Tear off the appropriate length needed to cover the error.

3. Apply the tape over the error. To cover up an entire line, hold both ends of the tape to be sure the line is completely covered.

4. Return the paper to the line of typing and type the correct letter, word, or line.

Self-correcting typewriter

13.49 A self-correcting typewriter contains a special backspace-correction key that backspaces once to the error while changing the typing mode to "correction." The special cartridge contains the adhesive correcting ribbon that literally lifts the error off the page.

The correction made with this special typewriter is permanent.

Using a Self-Correcting Typewriter

13.50 1. Depress the backspace-correction key on the typewriter.

2. Retype the mistyped letter.

3. Type the correct letter.

Maintaining office calendars

13.51 Office calendars should be kept on a regular basis—daily, weekly, and/or monthly. They are essential in planning future events and in reviewing events of the past.

1. Maintain a monthly calendar to show at a glance the month's activities. Being able to look ahead to projects, important meetings, and deadlines increases office efficiency.

2. The secretary should maintain a weekly calendar in some detail to plan for the week's activities. In scheduling appointments and meetings, the secretary can work around other activities of the week.

3. A daily calendar or appointment book is a must for employer and secretary alike. Draw a line through the hours for each activity so you and the employer can anticipate the length of each meeting, schedule other appointments around those meetings, and arrange for work within the office.

4. Use the daily calendar for a tickler file also to remind you or your employer to follow up on a previous matter on a particular day.

5. Go through the calendars at the beginning of each month, or sooner if necessary, and write in standing appointments and meetings.

Scheduling appointments

13.52 Schedule appointments for the employer so they do not conflict with other activities. Some employers prefer to meet with clients at certain specified times, thus freeing other times for conferences and other office tasks.

Keep these guidelines in mind when appointments are being made.

1. Determine which people the employer wishes to see whenever they call for an appointment.

2. Determine which callers may see the employer without an appointment.

3. Determine an appropriate procedure for scheduling appointments and dealing with salespeople.

4. Determine which individuals the employer prefers not to see.

5. Determine whether the employer will accept telephone calls or other interruptions during meetings.

When a caller requests an appointment, these steps should be followed.

1. Determine the purpose of the proposed appointment. Is the matter something that the employer must handle or could someone else—perhaps the secretary—take care of the caller?

2. Determine the approximate length of the proposed visit. Is it something that can be handled in a few minutes, or is a longer conference necessary?

3. Determine whether others will be meeting with the employer and the caller so schedules can be co-ordinated if necessary.

4. Check to see whether the employer wants to make the appointment if she or he is available. In some instances, the matter may be handled over the telephone. If the employer is not available to confirm the appointment, make a tentative appointment with the caller and confirm it later.

5. Check the employer's calendar to determine the best time and date for such a meeting. Try not to schedule too many meetings in succession if possible.

6. Verify the time, date, and place with the caller. If the meeting is to take place somewhere other than the employer's office, verify this information too.

7. Immediately after the appointment has been verified, write it on the employer's calendar as well as on yours.

Preparing for appointments

13.53 To help the employer prepare for the appointment, certain tasks should be performed before the caller arrives.

1. Remind the employer of the day's scheduled appointments.

2. Determine beforehand whether your presence will be needed either at the meeting or at your desk to handle work that may need to be processed.

3. Before each caller arrives gather any necessary correspondence, files, or notes that may be needed during the meeting.

Confirming appointments

13.54 It is sometimes necessary to change the time and/or date of meetings previously arranged. Ideally, an appointment should be changed or cancelled well in advance.

1. All appointments made can be considered confirmed at the time they are made unless the conversation indicates otherwise.

2. Confirm appointments when they involve luncheon dates, meetings out of the city, and meetings arranged several weeks or months ago.

3. When an appointment has to be changed, notify the other persons as soon as possible so other plans can be made and another time or date can be arranged.

4. When a meeting involves several individuals, be sure to notify everyone and verify the new time and date.

5. When in doubt about an appointment, always call the other person(s) to verify the appointment time and date. It is better to be safe than to have the employer miss the meeting.

Planning meetings

13.55 Meetings—regular activities for most employers—enable participants to exchange ideas and establish a common basis for business operations.

Documents prepared for meetings and during meetings include the agenda, the minutes of the meeting, and the resolution.

Agenda

13.56 An agenda is a list of the order of business for a meeting. The person calling the meeting prepares the tentative agenda based on the items to be discussed. An agenda should be distributed to the participants before the meeting begins—or mailed out well in advance if detailed or technical matters are involved.

13.57 An agenda usually includes the following:

- Call to order by presiding officer
- Roll call
- Reading of previous minutes
- Approval of minutes
- Reports of officers
- Reports of standing committees
- Reports of special committees
- Discussion of old business
- Discussion of new business
- Date, time, and place of next meeting
- Adjournment

Minutes

13.58 The record of topics discussed at a meeting, decisions voted upon, and other actions is called the minutes. Taking minutes is more than a skill; it involves careful detail work and an ability to stay alert. The secretary is often called upon to take the minutes.

13.59 Here are some guidelines to follow in taking minutes effectively and accurately.

1. Before the meeting, review the agenda and other materials that will be covered to gain an understanding of what will be discussed (note that the agenda serves as an outline for taking the minutes).

2. Before the meeting begins, jot down participants' names and seating positions. It may be helpful to devise a coding system for each person, to facilitate identification of each speaker.

3. During the meeting, take notes on the important information discussed. Record all motions made and any accompanying discussion. Include the names of individuals who make and second motions. Record motions as they are made. Other points may be summarized.

4. Organize notes, keeping all discussion on any one subject together to simplify transcription of notes.

5. Do not hesitate to interrupt politely to ask for a restatement of the motion or to determine names needed for the minutes.

Resolutions

13.60 A resolution is a statement made by those at the meeting to express a group opinion. Resolutions are often formulated to express sympathy for the loss of a member or colleague, to show appreciation to an individual for the work contributed to the organization, and to recognize an outstanding person in the group.

Processing mail

13.61 With the exception of correspondence marked *Personal* or *Confidential*, incoming mail should be opened, dated, and read as quickly as possible. Correspondence should be answered within 48 to 72 hours of receipt. If an answer cannot be given immediately or if information must be obtained, notify the correspondent by telephone or letter so he or she knows the request is being processed.

Opening mail

13.62 Use a letter opener. If mail often includes cheques, money orders, or other valuable papers, open three sides of the envelopes to be sure everything has been removed.

13.63 Check to see if the writer's return address is included within the letter. If not, copy the address from the envelope onto the letter. Unless the postmark on the envelope is needed for legal purposes, the envelope should be discarded.

13.64 Verify any enclosures that should have been included with the letter. Notify the correspondent if the enclosure is missing.

Sorting mail

13.65 Sort mail into the following categories.

1. Urgent or special mail (registered, airmail, and special delivery)

2. Regular mail (first-class mail, interoffice correspondence to be answered)

3. Routine mail (to be routed to others or answered by the secretary)

4. Bulletins, magazines, advertising circulars, etc.

Distributing mail

13.66 Before placing correspondence or other information on the employer's desk, attach any previous correspondence or files that might be needed in processing the correspondence.

13.67 When mail is to be routed to another office or department for processing, the person who originally receives the mail should be responsible for it. Record in a notebook or card file the following information for all such correspondence.

name of correspondent
date of letter
subject matter
person or office where routed
date routed

Routing slips

13.68 When bulletins, circulars, magazines, or supplements to books are routed on a regular basis to office personnel, use a printed routing slip to expedite the material from person to person.

The routing slips should list the name of everyone in the office who reads the information distributed. One form should be used to route items for everyone to see (containing everyone's name). Another form should be used to route items for a few to see (containing selected names).

Routing slips save time because lists do not have to be handwritten each time and each person sends the material directly to the next person.

Communication Services 14

Courier services

14.1 Courier services can be used to deliver material when speed and security are crucial and when these demands cannot be satisfactorily met by the mail systems. Businesses of all types, large or small, may need the services of a courier regularly or only occasionally.

Material of all sizes and types (manuscripts, computer tapes, legal documents, etc.) is delivered in anything from radio-dispatched taxies to corporate aircrafts. Services are offered within cities, from city to city, and between countries. Very large courier services usually have their own aircraft, but when these are not available, they either charter or use commercial aircraft.

Since courier services transmit material personally and directly from point to point, they always offer proof of delivery slips.

For a listing of courier services, consult the Yellow Pages of local telephone books.

Postal services

14.2 Canada Post is responsible for mail service within Canada. Postal rates and regulations change occasionally, so the post office should be consulted regularly for current information and rate charts.

Postal code procedures

14.3 The use of automated equipment such as the Optical Character Reader (OCR) expedites the handling and delivery of mail, but addresses must be accurate, legible, and complete to avoid errors and delays. (See 7.75-7.81 for correct address procedures.)

The OCR reads the postal code part of the address and translates it into a bar code that can be read by a computer. The OCR works at a speed of 30 000 letters an hour. If your letter does not have the postal code on it, it will be rejected by the OCR.

Correct positioning of the postal code is as important as a correct street address number. It is preferable to type the postal code alone as the last line of the address, but if it is typed on the same line as the city and province, use two spaces to separate the code from the province. (See Figure 14-1 for position of postal code and Figure

14-2 for a map of Canada showing allocation of the first character of the postal code.)

President W. S. Smith, Ph.D.
Athabaska University
14515-122 Avenue
Edmonton, Alberta
T5L 2W4

President W. S. Smith, Ph.D.
Athabaska University
14515-122 Avenue
Edmonton, Alta. T5L 2W4

For correct postal codes, always refer to postal code directories at post offices. The postal code is always the last item in the address.

For mail destined to the U.S., type the Zip code (postal code) one space after the two-letter state abbreviation (see 7.79).

Use the two-letter state abbreviations adopted by the U.S. Postal Service. Refer to the National ZIP Code Directory, which lists codes for every postal delivery zone in the United States. (See 5.18 for postal abbreviations.)

Addressing hints

14.4 Follow these guidelines to ensure that you get the most efficient mail service. See Figure 14-1 for the correct addressing procedures outlined below.

1. Type all envelope addresses—including the return address—in single spacing.

2. Include a complete return address on all mail, including post cards.

3. Include the personal titles *Dr., Miss, Mrs.,* and *Ms.* on all envelopes addressed to individuals.

4. Include the personal titles *Dr., Mrs.* and *Ms.* in the return address of correspondence.

5. An apartment, suite, or room number, when written in full, should precede the street address (see 7.12). When an abbreviated form is used, it should follow the street address (see 7.16).

6. The province may or may not be abbreviated. Abbreviations must follow postal code forms (see 5.17 for postal abbreviations).

7. Type postal notations (such as AIRMAIL, REGISTERED MAIL, SPECIAL DELIVERY, and CERTIFIED MAIL) in the upper left corner of the envelope below the return address. (See also 7.80 and Figure 7-16.)

8. Type addressee notations (such as PERSONAL, CONFIDENTIAL, PLEASE FORWARD, and ATTENTION) in the upper left

corner of the envelope below the return address (see 7.81 and Figure 7-17).

9. Mark the class of mail on the front when oversize kraft envelopes are used; otherwise, they may be processed as fourth class.

10. Always include the postal code on all mail, in the return address as well as in the addressee's address.

Domestic mail classes

14.5 Domestic mail may travel first-class, second-class, third-class, fourth-class, special fourth-class, air mail, or air parcel post.

14.6 First-class mail includes letters, postcards, receipts, invoices, and any other mail that the sender chooses to mail at first-class rates of postage.

Supplementary services available for first-class mail are: certified mail, C.O.D., insurance, registration, and special delivery.

14.7 Second-class mail consists of newpapers as well as magazines that are issued four or more times a year and may only be mailed by a publisher.

14.8 Third-class mail consists of all other mailable matter—such as circulars, books, catalogues, and other printed matter—not included as first- and second-class mail. The mass limitation for third-class mail is 500 g or less.

Third-class mail can be posted in Canada for delivery in or outside Canada as long as it meets post office requirements.

14.9 Fourth-class mail includes mailable articles with a mass greater than 500 g and are posted in Canada for delivery in or outside Canada.

Mass cannot exceed 16 kg. A charge is added on any parcel over 1 m long or more than 2 m in girth (girth equals twice the width plus twice the length). The maximum length for a fourth-class parcel is 2 m and maximum girth is 3 m.

14.10 In Canada, all first-class mail goes air mail.

Figure 14-1. Addressing envelopes

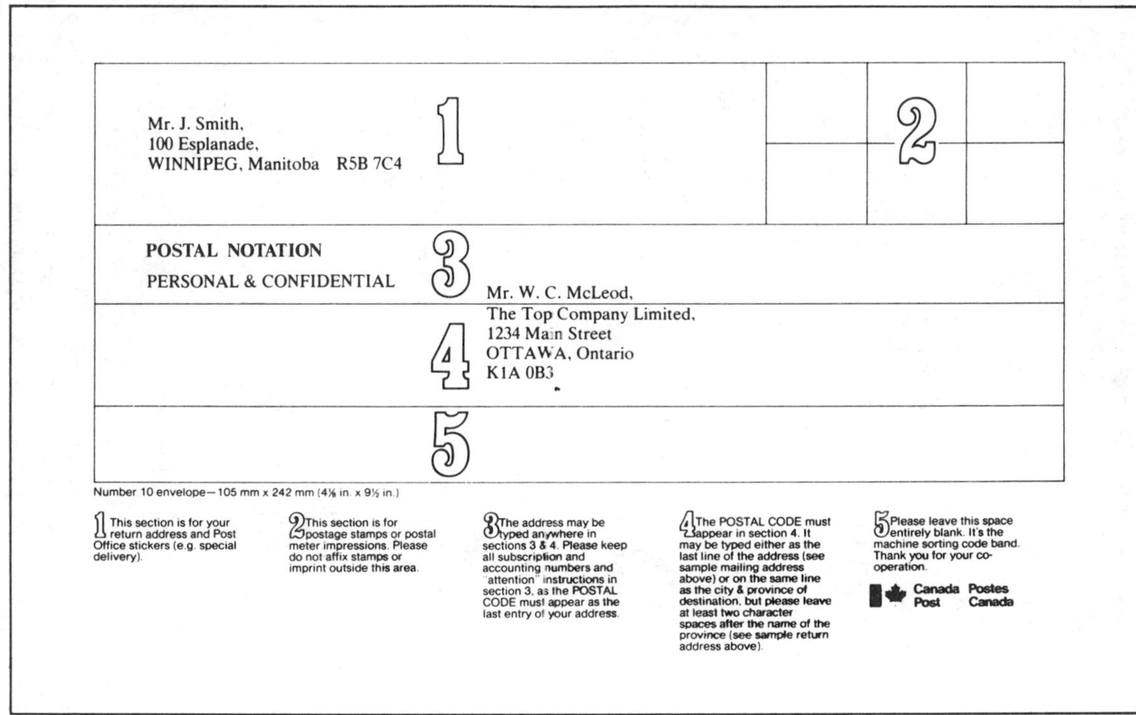

Mr. J. Smith,
100 Esplanade,
WINNIPEG, Manitoba R5B 7C4
1
2
POSTAL NOTATION
PERSONAL & CONFIDENTIAL
3
Mr. W. C. McLeod,
The Top Company Limited,
1234 Main Street
OTTAWA, Ontario
K1A 0B3
4
5
Number 10 envelope—105 mm x 242 mm (4⅛ in. x 9½ in.)
1 This section is for your return address and Post Office stickers (e.g. special delivery).
2 This section is for postage stamps or postal meter impressions. Please do not affix stamps or imprint outside this area.
3 The address may be typed anywhere in sections 3 & 4. Please keep all subscription and accounting numbers and "attention" instructions in section 3, as the POSTAL CODE must appear as the last entry of your address.
4 The POSTAL CODE must appear in section 4. It may be typed either as the last line of the address (see sample mailing address above) or on the same line as the city & province of destination, but please leave at least two character spaces after the name of the province (see sample return address above).
5 Please leave this space entirely blank. It's the machine sorting code band. Thank you for your co-operation.
Canada Post
Postes Canada

Figure 14-2. Allocation of the first character of the postal code

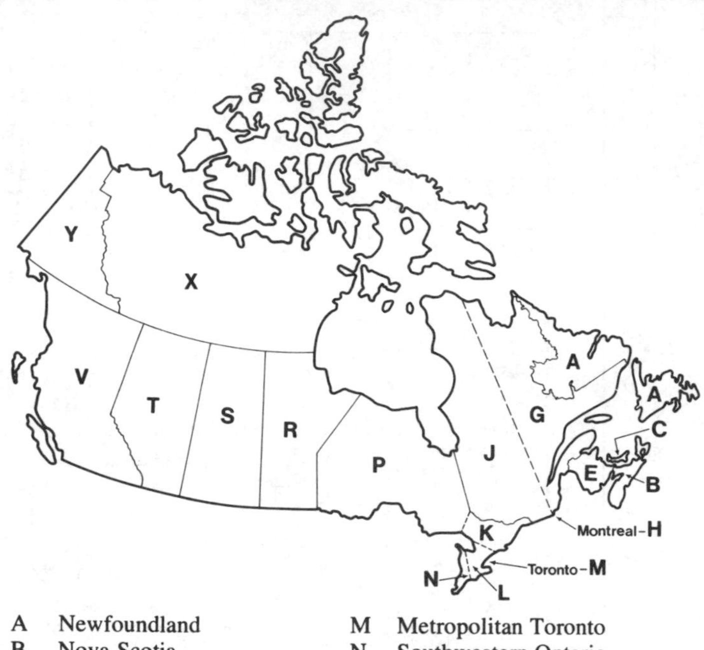

A	Newfoundland	M	Metropolitan Toronto
B	Nova Scotia	N	Southwestern Ontario
C	Prince Edward Island	P	Northern Ontario
E	New Brunswick	R	Manitoba
G	Quebec East	S	Saskatchewan
H	Montreal Metropolitan	T	Alberta
J	Quebec West	V	British Columbia
K	Eastern Ontario	X	Northwest Territories
L	Central Ontario	Y	Yukon

International mail

14.11 International mail does not include CAPO (Canadian Army Post Office) or CFPO (Canadian Fleet Post Office) addresses. Mail sent overseas may be letters, letter packages, printed matter, small packages of merchandise or samples, or parcel post. There are three classes of international mail.

14.12 Surface mail rates for letters are based on each gram up to 500 g, with higher rates based on total mass.

14.13 Aerogrammes are printed on special lightweight stationery that folds into a self-envelope. They provide an economical means of overseas communication. No enclosures are allowed.

14.14 Air parcel post rates vary from country to country. There are specific mass and dimension limitations as well as ways of packing goods for shipment. Goods sent abroad must meet customs regulations of both Canada and the destination country.

Mailing hints

14.15 Follow these suggestions to ensure the quickest arrival of mail.

1. Mail early in the day for the most efficient handling.

2. Write or print legibly all envelope addresses.

3. Mark any postal notation clearly, in the appropriate place on the envelope.

4. Use the correct amount of postage. When in doubt about the mass of a letter or package, have it measured at the post office.

5. Do not label a letter or package air mail if the destination is within Canada since all first-class mail is sent by air anyway.

6. Use special delivery service only when extra speed is desirable.

7. Use preprinted mailing labels (or other addressing devices) for regular correspondents or customers.

8. When return receipt is essential, use registration plus acknowledgement and/or certified mail.

Other postal services

14.16 Post office box rentals are available at most post offices and postal stations for the convenience of individuals and businesses. These boxes provide privacy for the renter and are convenient when it may not be desirable to have mail delivered to a home or business address. Mail is delivered to the post office box number where it may be picked up by the renter, even when the post office is closed. Box rental rates vary according to the classification of the post office and the size of the box.

14.17 Postal money orders provide a means of sending money through the mail safely. They may be purchased and redeemed at any post office.

14.18 Priority Post provides businesses with high-speed intercity delivery of important papers and products when time is crucial. Consult the customer service representative of Canada Post for information on the different options that involve postal employees picking up shipments, taking them to the airport, and delivering them to the addressee.

14.19 Telepost is an electronic message communications service offered by Canada Post in conjunction with CNCP Telecommunications. A telepost message, given to a CN or CP telegraph office in Canada, is transmitted electronically to a post office near the addressee, put in an envelope by Canada Post, and processed for the next scheduled delivery as first class mail (see 14.34).

14.20 Business reply mail simplifies the addressee's task when the sender needs a response. The sender obtains a special permit from Canada Post and guarantees the postage on all replies returned, based on first-class mail rates plus an additional fee for the service (there is no charge for the permit itself).

Preprinted envelopes designating business reply mail must state: No postage stamp necessary if mailed in Canada. Postage will be paid by (name and address of firm or organization).

14.21 First-, third- and fourth-class material may be sent on a cash-on-delivery (C.O.D.) basis. The addressee pays for the postage plus the value of the goods, up to a maximum of $200, contained in the letter or parcel. The amount collected by the mail carrier is sent to the sender by a postal money order.

The C.O.D. fee, paid by the sender, includes insurance against loss, damage, and failure to collect payment from the addressee.

14.22 Certified mail provides proof of delivery to the sender. The addressee's signature is obtained on delivery, a proof of delivery card is returned to the sender and a record of the delivery is kept by Canada Post. This service is useful for valuable documents or other items for which a record of delivery and receipt are needed. There is no insurance value, since certified mail carries no liability for lost mail.

14.23 First-, third- and fourth-class mail can be insured against loss or damage to contents. Maximum liability is $1000, with fees based on the value of the contents.

14.24 Registered mail offers protection for valuable papers, stocks, bonds, jewellery, money, etc., up to $10 000, with liability limited to the value declared by the sender. This is available for domestic first-class and air mail.

The customer is provided with a receipt at the time of mailing and the post office keeps a record of the mailing. Return receipt is available at extra cost.

14.25 All first-class mail may be sent special delivery, which means mail is delivered to the addressee as soon as possible upon arrival at the local post office (with limitations in distance and time). Use special delivery only when extra speed is desirable.

A special delivery service fee is charged in addition to the regular postage.

14.26 Intelpost, Canada Post's and Teleglobe/CNCP Telecommunications' high-speed, electronic document transmission service uses satellite and microwave technology with the latest high-speed facsimile equipment. In seconds any document, plan, drawing, design graphic, or other item that can be photocopied (up to legal size) can be sent and received in any one of 13 Intelpost Centres in Canada, Europe, and the U.S.

Telecommunications services

14.27 Modern telecommunications services are provided in Canada by two major sources, the members of the TransCanada Telephone System, and CNCP Telecommunications.

Business use various telecommunications services to transmit messages and data when speed and a written record are essential. A written record is often required for legal purposes, or when offices are closed because of time-zone differences (the written message is delivered later), or in cases of international communication where a written message facilitates translation.

Written telecommunications messages are usually cheaper to send than long distance telephone calls. Other savings are achieved because only essential information is sent.

Written messages can be sent as telegrams, cablegrams and by teletypewriter. Computers and other business machines communicate over various private and shared transmission networks.

Computer Communications Group Services

14.28 The Computer Communications Group (CCG) is the specialist data communications arm of the TransCanada Telephone System (TCTS). CCG has developed a variety of computer terminals and networks for data communications, including: *Teletypewriter Exchange Service (TWX)*, a network of 59 000 teletype stations throughout Canada and the United States, and a total of 400 000 listings in 302 countries; *Multicom Network*, a pay-as-you-use network that transmits voice or data at speeds of up to 4800 bits per second between specified customer locations; the *Datacom* family of keyboard terminals, which transmit or receive data or messages; *Vucom*, a series of visual display terminals; *Vutran*, a transaction terminal about the size of a regular telephone, used in financial and retail industries for credit card authorization, cheque verification/guarantee, bank balance inquiry and electronic funds transfer; the *Dataroute Network*, a nationwide, digital data network providing private line services at speeds of up to 56 000 bits per second, with different rates for day, night and 24-hour use; the *Datapac Network*, a nationwide packet-switched data network used by many customers at the same time, just as the telephone network is; and *Envoy 100*, a public store and forward messaging service.

Telex

14.29 The most widely-used CNCP service is *Telex*, which has some 50 000 teletypewriter terminals in offices across Canada. These terminals, which have a typewriter-like keyboard, can exchange written information instantaneously with each other, or with more than a million other Telex terminals around the world. Telex terminals can receive messages while unattended, so that messages can be received even after offices have closed for the day. There are a number of service features that improve the utility of Telex: *Tel-Tex*, which permits a Telex subscriber to send messages to non-Telex subscribers in Canada and the U.S. The sender transmits a message to the public service message centre nearest the addressee and it is then handled as a full rate telegram at a flat rate regardless of length of message. *MATS* or *Multiple Access Telex Service*, enables subscribers to send a common text to a number of Telex or Tel-Tex locations with a single transmission. *Maritime Satellite Telex Operation*, available to specially equipped ships in the Atlantic and Pacific regions. *DataTelex* involves a dial-and-type record communications service that can be used to send teleprinter transmissions of up to 250 words a minute.

Infotex

14.30 CNCP also provides a service called *Infotex*, which links communicating word processors with each other and with the Telex network. This Infotex service will be able to accommodate the new international Teletex service of communicating word processors which is now under development. Infotex will also be able to provide such features of the integrated electronic office of the future as electronic mailboxes, access to distant data banks, and input and output from electronic files.

The rapid development of new telecommunications and computer technology means that in future offices will handle in electronic form much of the information now processed in the form of words, numbers and graphics on paper. Infotex is designed to provide the basis for this office of the future.

CNCP has several services designed to handle private line voice and computer data. These include *Broadband Exchange Service*, an analog service that provides transmission of computer data, facsimile, and private line voice traffic; *Infodat*, a private-line digital service for computer data, and *Infoswitch*, a packet and circuit switched network with three options—*Infocall, Infogram* and *Infoexchange*—to meet a wide range of requirements. It is used in such applications as instant reservations, credit verifications, banking transactions, and inventory control from remote locations as well as for the transmission of computer data in bulk.

CNCP offers a range of terminals called *Infomodes* on its data services and *Telemodes* for Telex service. These include such features as micro-processors, electronic memories and cathode ray tube screens.

Telegrams

14.31 Telegrams were once the main method of sending written record communications. Now, however, most large businesses use other, more effective methods of sending written record communications (see 14.27-14.30).

Telegrams sent to overseas destinations are called cablegrams.

In Canada telegrams and cablegrams are handled by CNCP Telecommunications, which provides service by telephone throughout Canada on a 24-hour basis. Local telephone directories list local and after-hour toll-free telephone numbers to major public message centres. Telegrams and cablegrams are sent by calling these numbers and dictating the message to be sent. There are different types of telegrams each involving different rates.

14.32 A full rate telegram receives priority and will be sent immediately. Where possible, the message is telephoned to the addressee at the destination and a printed copy is mailed as confirmation. The rate is based on a minimum of 15 words with an additional charge for each additional word. Thus brevity in the message is important. Rates vary from time to time, and should be checked at the time the message is being sent.

14.33 A night letter service is offered at a lower rate. Messages are accepted during the day for transmission overnight for next day delivery. The rate is based on a minimum charge of 50 words with an additional charge for each additional 25 words.

14.34 Telepost service is offered jointly by CNCP Telecommunications and the Canada Post. The subscriber simply phones the nearest CNCP public service message centre listed in the phone book and dictates the message as he or she would a telegram. The message is transmitted to the Post Office Telepost Centre nearest the receiver for delivery in the next scheduled mail delivery. Telex subscribers can send Telepost messages via their Telex machines. In the U.S. there is similar service called Mailgram.

14.35 Additional services are available to telegram senders on payment of a supplementary charge. These include messenger service (where available), confirmation copies to the sender, and confirmation of delivery. Telegrams can also be sent collect.

Money orders

14.36 Money can also be sent by wire. To transfer money, the sender must go to the nearest CNCP Telecommunications office with cash, certified cheque, or money order to cover both the amount to be sent and the charge for the service. This cannot be arranged over the telephone.

Cablegrams

14.37 These international telegrams are filed with CNCP Telecommunications although the overseas transmission is provided by Teleglobe Canada and other connecting international telecommunications companies. There are four classes of service but some countries will not accept all classes.

1. Urgent cablegrams receive top priority. Rates are based on a minimum of seven words with double the full rate charge for each additional word.

2. Full rate cablegram is the next priority. Rates are based on a minimum of seven words with a charge for each additional word.

3. A letter telegram follows the full rate cablegram in priority. It offers an overnight service with messages being accepted up to midnight for transmission the next day. Rates are based on a 22-word minimum with each additional word charged at one-half that of the full-rate cablegram. This service is not available to all countries.

4. Social telegrams are personal or social messages destined for British Commonwealth countries. The rates are half that of the letter telegram and are based on a minimum of ten words.

Telephone services

14.38 The telephone is the most commonly used communication device in modern business. It is considered a necessity; the farthest sections of the country and the world are accessible by telephone. Correct use of the telephone saves time and reduces correspondence and travel costs.

Using the telephone effectively

14.39 Follow the suggestions below to make your business calls as efficient, productive, and gracious as possible.

1. Speak distinctly to be understood. Pronounce your words carefully.

2. Take your time and speak slowly. Telephone speech should be neither too fast nor too slow.

3. Speak directly into the mouthpiece. Your voice is carried most clearly when you hold the transmitter directly in front of your mouth without touching the mouthpiece.

4. Use your normal tone of voice. A loud voice may irritate the person on the telephone and disturb those nearby. A weak voice can be equally annoying because the listener must strain to hear what is being said and may ask for frequent repetition.

5. Make your voice interesting, pleasant, and helpful.

6. Plan your conversation. Jot down notes on the topics to be discussed. This saves time for both the caller and the person called and creates a better impression of the caller.

7. Be sure you have the correct number. Keep an up-to-date list of frequently called numbers and use the telephone directory to locate others (call directory assistance—information—only if a number is not listed in the directory).

8. Place your own calls whenever possible instead of having another person call for you.

9. Let the telephone ring long enough to give the person called sufficient time to get to the telephone and answer.

10. Identify yourself and the name of the person or department to whom you wish to speak.

11. If the person called is not available, leave your name and telephone number, the time you can be reached, and a message or request to expedite the return of the call.

12. Always keep a note pad handy for messages. Indicate the name and number of the caller and the message. Obtaining the nature of the call helps the caller gather necessary information when the call is returned.

13. Always verify dates, numbers, amounts, and addresses over the telephone. Never hesitate to ask someone to repeat information.

14. Spell out any names that may be difficult to understand or to spell. Clarify each letter by giving a well-known word that begins with the same letter.

15. Pronounce numbers carefully.

16. Apologize for errors or delays but be sincere and natural.

17. Use the hold button when you must leave the line for even a few minutes. The telephone is very sensitive and can transmit extraneous office noises and conversations.

18. Suggest a time when the caller may call you again if you will be out of the office part of the day.

19. Do not argue with a caller, especially one who is upset or disturbed. Allow the caller to let off steam before you ask questions or try to solve the problem.

20. Check the time difference before calling across the nation. A three o'clock call from British Columbia would be received at seven o'clock in the Maritimes; a three o'clock call from British Columbia would be received at six o'clock in Ontario. (See Figure 14-3.)

21. Let the caller hang up the receiver before you do. If you are the caller, put the receiver down gently.

Long-distance calls

14.40 Long-distance calls are those made to any telephone outside the local service area. Special charges called toll charges are based on the distance of the call, length of time the line is used, type of call made, and the time of day the call is placed.

Before making a long-distance call to a business in another town, always check the phone directory to see if the business has an INWATS (code 800) or Zenith number (see 14.44 and 14.45). If it does, you can call toll free.

Figure 14-3. Time zones and telephone area codes

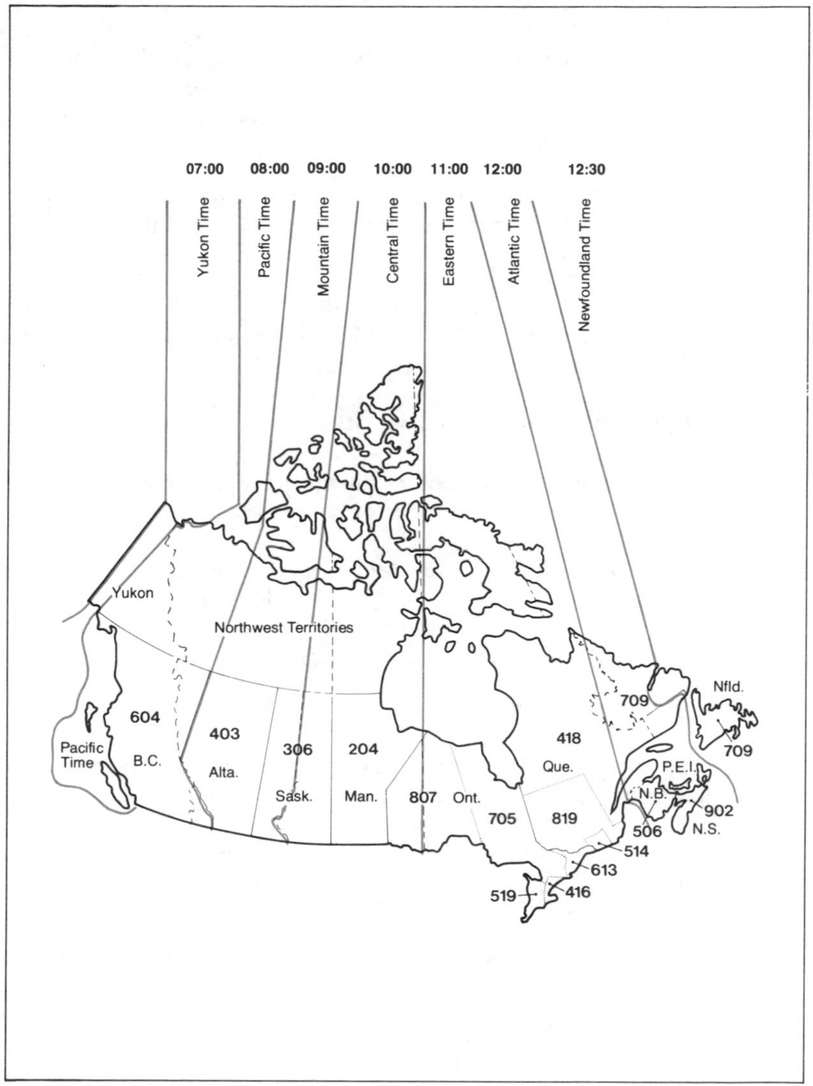

Direct distance dialling (DDS)

14.41 To facilitate long-distance calls, most telephones have been equipped for Direct Distance Dialling (DDS) service.

Direct Distance Dialling permits you to dial directly from your office or home to telephones in almost any town or city in Canada, the United States, as well as many overseas countries.

Area, country and city codes

14.42 DDS is made possible by the development of special switching apparatus and by the identification of dialling areas by area codes, country codes and city codes. These codes, when dialled before the seven figures of a telephone number, create a number that is not duplicated anywhere else.

Consult the code maps and listings in the front pages of telephone directories for correct numbers in Canada, the United States, and overseas.

For overseas calls, allow at least 30 seconds for the ringing to start. After numbers are dialled, an operator will answer and assist you in completing the type of call desired.

Other long-distance call services

14.43 Consult the front pages of the directory for proper telephone procedures for the different kinds of services available.

14.44 INWATS (Incoming Wide Area Telecommunications Service) is a service that permits the caller to dial long-distance from certain places without being charged. In the phone directory, an INWATS service is listed in the following way:

Burgundy Importers 1-800-929-3876

To call an INWATS number in Canada, always dial 1, then the code 800 and the special number of the customer having this service.

14.45 Zenith calls are a service used by some businesses and organizations to permit calls from certain long-distance points without a charge.

In the phone directory, a Zenith service is listed in the following way:

Brandzel International
From telephones in Toronto
No charge to calling party
Ask Operator for . . . . . . Zenith 56969

A Zenith number requires the services of an operator and cannot be called directly like an INWATS number.

14.46 When given the names and telephone numbers of several persons in several places, the operator can arrange a conference call in which everyone can speak and be heard by all the others.

14.47 Marine calls reach ships with radio telephone service. To make a marine call, dial "0" and ask for the marine operator.

14.48 Mobile calls provide access to automobiles and trucks equipped with manual mobile telephone service. To make a mobile call, dial "0" and ask for the mobile operator.

14.49 Telephone companies across Canada have a credit card system available to both companies and individuals. This system enables users to make credit card calls.

In most cases the credit card number consists of the telephone number plus a numerical code of three digits followed by a letter.

The Great Soup Company 449-6832-476-A

Employees of companies or individuals who have telephone credit cards may place long-distance calls and charge them to their credit card numbers by the following methods:

1. When calling from hometown to anywhere in North America except Alaska, use DDS (see 14.41).

Dial 0 + Area Code + Number
Toronto to Lincoln, Nebraska: 0 + 402 + 781-9289

When the operator cuts in, give the credit card number and the call is completed.

2. When calling from hometown to overseas, use DDS (see 14.41).

Dial 01 + Country Code + Routing (City Code) + Local Number
Toronto to London, England: 01 + 44 + 1 + 963-4200

3. When calling from outside of hometown to anywhere in North America or overseas, call the operator and advise of the calling destination and give the credit card number. The operator will indicate whether a DDS call can be made or not.

Guidelines for handling calls

14.50 When receiving calls:

1. Answer the telephone promptly—by the end of the first or second ring if possible.

2. Greet the caller pleasantly and identify the office and yourself.

3. Jot down the appropriate information. Do not trust telephone information to memory.

4. Let the caller conclude the conversation.

14.51 When transferring calls:

1. Transfer a call only when it is necessary.

2. Be tactful with the individual, especially when she or he might have reached the incorrect number.

3. Explain why the transfer of the call is necessary; then indicate what you are going to do: "I will transfer you to our Sales Department. One moment, please."

4. Be sure the caller is willing to be transferred. It may be advisable for the caller to note the complete telephone number so he or she can place the call directly at a later time.

14.52 When placing calls on hold:

1. Explain why you would like the caller to hold and determine if the caller would care to wait.

2. Depress the hold button.

3. Check back on the caller periodically so the caller knows he or she has not been forgotten and that you are aware the person is still waiting on the line.

4. If the caller has waited more than a reasonable length of time, obtain his or her name and telephone number.

14.53 If the employees in the office are responsible for answering calls in each other's absence, be sure to tell the person in charge of the telephones when you will return to the office.

When answering calls for others:

1. Take calls for others as efficiently and as courteously as you would expect them to take your calls.

2. Identify the office and yourself.

3. Inform the caller that the person called is not available. Offer to help the caller.

4. Note the caller's name and number.

5. Give the message promptly to the person called.

References 15

Introduction

15.1 References and source materials with which office managers, secretaries, and other office workers should be familiar are almanacs, biographical books, dictionaries and word books, directories, encyclopaedias, indexes, secretarial handbooks and textbooks, and such general references as atlases and the postal code directory.

The public library is an excellent source of information on all reference material.

Almanacs

15.2 An almanac is a collection of historical, social, economic, and political facts published on an annual basis. It includes names of government officials and departments; data about each province, Canada, and foreign nations; memorable dates and holidays; and facts of interest about many other subjects.

Canada Year Book. Canadian Government Publishing Centre. Supply and Services Canada.

Canadian Almanac and Directory. Toronto: Copp Clark Publishing Co.

Canadian Annual Review. Toronto: University of Toronto Press.

Corpus Almanac. Toronto: Corpus Publishers Services Ltd.

Information Please Almanac, Atlas, and Yearbook. New York: Simon & Schuster, Inc.

Contains information on such diversified topics as geography, politics, sports, taxes, vital statistics, and social and political conditions.

World Almanac and Book of Facts. Garden City, N.Y.: Doubleday & Co., Inc.

Contains information on economic, social, educational, and political events.

Biographical books

15.3 Biographical books supply factual data about prominent men and women, noting such information as their background, age, parentage, schools attended, occupation or profession, marital status, affiliations, achievements, and honours.

Canadian Who's Who. Toronto: Who's Who Canadian Publications.

Biographies are entered by merit. Published every three years.

Current Biography. New York: The H.W. Wilson Co. Monthly and cumulated year.

Covers such celebrities as kings, prime ministers, presidents, and radio, television, film, stage, and sports personalities. The yearly cumulation is entitled *Current Biography Yearbook.*

Webster's Biographical Dictionary. Springfield, Mass.: G. & C. Merriam Co.

Useful for identifying persons of any nationality from any period of history.

Who's Who. New York: St. Martin's Press, Inc. Annually.

Listing of internationally famous men and women, primarily British.

Who's Who in America. Chicago: Marquis–Who's Who, Inc. Biennially.

Biographies of best-known living men and women in all lines of useful and reputable achievement.

Who's Who in Canada. Toronto: International Press Ltd. Annually.

Who's Who in Commerce and Industry. Chicago: Marquis-Who's Who, Inc. Biennially.

Biographical data of outstanding business professionals throughout the world.

Dictionaries

15.4 Dictionaries are published in various sizes, from the abridged small pocket editions to the large unabridged volumes. Abridged dictionaries contain information about the more common words, while unabridged dictionaries give authoritative information about virtually every word in the English language. Both volumes are indispensable tools for written and oral communication.

Cassell's New Spelling Dictionary. London, England: Cassell & Company Ltd.

Dictionary of Canadian English. Toronto: Gage Educational Publishing Limited.

Funk & Wagnall's Standard College Dictionary. New York: Harcourt Brace Jovanovich, Inc.

The Original Roget's Thesaurus of English Words and Phrases. New York: St. Martin's Press, Inc.

The Oxford English Dictionary. New York: Oxford University Press.

Roget's International Thesaurus of Words and Phrases. New York: Crowell Collier and Macmillan, Inc.

Webster's Eighth New Collegiate Dictionary. Springfield, Mass.: G. & C. Merriam Co.

Webster's New Dictionary of Synonyms. Springfield, Mass.: G. & C. Merriam Co.

Directories and indexes

15.5 A directory is an alphabetical listing (in booklet or book form) of names and addresses of people within a particular community or a given business, industry, or profession.

An index gives listings of the titles and contents of books and periodicals on particular subjects.

Both are helpful in verifying the spelling of an individual's name, finding an address or a telephone number of a person or company, identifying a company's officers, products and/or services. They are also helpful in seeking information on the sources available for a variety of subjects.

Advertising

15.6 ***CARD*** (Canadian Advertising Rates and Data). Toronto: Statistics Canada and Maclean Hunter Research Bureau. Monthly.

Furnishes rates and data for an extensive list of advertising media including aerial advertising, airport displays, newspapers, magazines and all other kinds of publications as well as radio, TV, and taxicabs.

National List of Advertisers. Toronto: Maclean Hunter Limited. Monthly.

Mathew's List. Beaconsfield, Quebec: Robbie and Neil Oakley Publishing Company.

Contains a complete survey of the national daily media, and their equipment facilities, people, and features.

Standard Directory of Advertising Agencies (American). Skokie, Illinois: National Register Publishing Co.

Associations

15.7 ***Directory of Associations in Canada.*** Toronto: University of Toronto Press.

A listing of societies, federations, alliances, clubs and unions, and any associations that are voluntary, non-government and non-profit.

Encyclopaedia of Associations. Detroit, Michigan: Gales Research.

A guide to American and international organizations running the gamut from athletic societies to zoological associations.

Books and periodicals

15.8 ***Ayer Directory of Publications.*** Philadelphia: Ayer Press. Annually.

Covers daily and weekly newspapers and magazines (consumer, business, technical, trade, and farm) in both the U.S. and Canada.

Books in Print. New York: R.R. Bowker Company.

An author-title-subject index to the Publishers' Trade List Annual. Consists of six volumes of all hardbound, paperback, trade, text, adult, and juvenile books published and distributed in the U.S.

Canadiana. Ottawa.

Lists everything printed in Canada.

Canadian Books in Print. Toronto: University of Toronto Press. Annually.

Canadian Periodical Index. Ottawa: Canadian Library Association and National Library of Canada. Monthly.

Cassell's Directory of Publishing. Toronto: Longman Canada Limited. Annually.

Cumulative Book Index. New York: The H. W. Wilson Company. Monthly.

A listing of currently published books in the English language.

Readers' Guide to Periodical Literature. New York: The H. W. Wilson Company. Semimonthly. September-June; Monthly, July-August.

15.9 Business, industrial, financial

Business Education Index. New York: Delta Pi Epsilon Fraternity and Gregg Division, McGraw-Hill Book Co. Annually.

Canadian Key Business Directory. Toronto: Dun & Bradstreet Canada Ltd. Annually.

Lists businesses alphabetically, by geographical location, line of business and by D-U-N-S Numbers (Data Universal Numbering System, which comprises the key element of Dun & Bradstreet's marketing services).

Canadian Trade Index. Montreal: Canadian Manufacturers' Association. Annually.

A comprehensive list of Canadian manufacturers.

Directory of Directors. Toronto: Maclean Hunter Ltd. Annually.

Up-to-date listing of Canadian businessmen with their executive positions and directorships. Also, listing of key Canadian companies with the names of Canadian and foreign executives and directors.

Dun & Bradstreet Reference Book. Toronto: Dun & Bradstreet Canada Ltd.

Reference book of corporate management. Lists credit ratings of Canadian businesses. Annually.

Financial Post Surveys. Toronto: Maclean Hunter Ltd. Annually.

Financial Post provides five separate annual surveys on the newest facts on Canada's (consumer) markets, industries, funds, mines, and energy resources.

Fortune Directory. New York: *Fortune* Magazine.

Contains listings of major industrial firms in the U.S. with their sales and assets.

Fraser's Canadian Trade Directory. Toronto: Maclean Hunter Ltd. Annually.

A complete guide to Canadian manufacturers and industries.

Kelly's Directory of Merchants, Manufacturers and Shippers of the World. London, England: Kelly's Directory Ltd.

Moody's Investor Services, Inc. New York.

Moody's publishes six separate manuals that cover bonding and finance, industry, public utility and transportation, and government.

Scotts' Industrial Directory (for the Atlantic Provinces, Quebec, Ontario, and Western Provinces). Oakville, Ontario: Penstock Publishers.

City directories

15.10 City directories are compiled, published, and sold commercially for most of the cities of Canada and the United States. Each directory lists names, addresses, and business of all residents.

Customs and tariffs directories

15.11 ***Canadian Customs Tariff Book.*** Canadian Government.

McGoldrick's Canadian Customs and Excise Tariffs. Toronto: McGoldrick's.

McGoldrick's lists all custom and excise tariffs on thousands of items and includes Canadian and American custom brokers.

Government directories

15.12 ***Canada Year Book.*** Canadian Government.

Canadian Almanac and Directory. Toronto: Copp Clark Publishing Co.

Corpus Administrative Index. Toronto: Corpus Publishing Services.

Corpus lists officials, departments, and department heads of every provincial government administration. It is updated four times a year.

Directory of Municipal Governments (Canadian). Toronto: Bureau of Municipal Research.

Government of Canada Telephone Directory. Ottawa: Printing and Publishing Centre, Supply and Services Canada.

Encyclopaedias

15.13 Encyclopaedias provide authoritative information on a great number of subjects and topics arranged in alphabetic order and discussed briefly in articles written by specialists in the various fields. Many encyclopaedias are illustrated with pictures, graphs, maps, and charts.

Specialized encyclopaedias that relate to a particular field or subject are found in school and public libraries, and in the libraries of professional and technological societies or organizations.

Columbia Encyclopedia. New York: Columbia University Press.

Encyclopaedia Britannica (30 volumes). Chicago: Encyclopaedia Britannica, Inc.

Encyclopaedia Canadiana. Toronto: Grolier Ltd.

Encyclopedia Americana (30 volumes). New York: Grolier Incorporated.

Secretarial handbooks and textbooks

15.14 For the secretarial or clerical worker who must be familiar with a wide range of information and skills, the following selected list of reference sources should be consulted. Such handbooks and textbooks provide the latest office procedures and techniques.

Anderson, Ruth I., Dorothy E. Lee, Allien A. Russon, Jacquelyn A. Wentzell, and Helen M. S. Horack. ***The Administrative Secretary: Resource.*** New York: Gregg Division, McGraw-Hill Book Co.

Bate, Marjorie D., and Mary C. Casey. ***Legal Office Procedures.*** New York: McGraw-Hill Book Co.

Bredow, Miriam. ***Medical Office Procedures.*** New York: McGraw-Hill Book Co.

Hanna, J. Marshall, Estelle L. Popham, and Rita Sloan Tilton. ***Secretarial Procedures and Administration.*** Cincinnati: South-Western Publishing Co.

House, Clifford R., and Apollonia M. Koebele. ***Reference Manual for Office Personnel.*** Cincinnati: South-Western Publishing Co.

Sabin, William A. ***Reference Manual for Secretaries and Typists SI Metric***. 2d Canadian edition. Toronto: McGraw-Hill Ryerson Limited.

Smith, P., P. Hay-Ellis, and M.A. McConnell. ***Pitman Office Handbook.*** Toronto: Copp Clark Pitman.

Sparling, Allan E. ***Office Procedures.*** Toronto: McGraw-Hill Ryerson Limited.

Swartz, Elsie E. ***Procedures for the Legal Secretary.*** Toronto: Holt, Rinehart and Winston.

Taintor, Sarah, and Kate M. Monroe. ***Secretary's Handbook.*** New York: Macmillan Co., Inc.

Westgate, Douglas. ***Office Procedures 2000.*** Toronto: Gage Educational Publishing Limited.

General references

15.15 Important additional reference sources include books that give correct legal procedures and citations; postal and shipping rates; hotel, travel, geographic information; grammar and style usage; and information on key topics and quotations.

Grammar and style references

15.16 Bernstein, Theodore M. ***The Careful Writer: A Modern Guide to English Usage.*** New York: Atheneum.

Fowler, H. W. ***A Dictionary of Modern English Usage.*** 2d ed. revised by Sir Ernest Gowers. New York: Oxford University Press.

Londo, Richard J. ***Common Sense in Business Writing.*** New York: Macmillan Publishing Co. Inc.

The Chicago Manual of Style. 13 ed. Chicago. The University of Chicago Press.

A standard reference for anyone who prepares typewritten copy for the printer.

Perrin, Porter G. ***Writer's Guide and Index to English.*** 4th ed. Chicago: Scott, Foresman and Company.

Consists of two parts: a writer's guide, which discusses general English topics; and an index to English, which gives details on grammar and usage arranged alphabetically.

Hotel, travel, and geographic references

15.17 Travel information and road maps may be obtained from provincial travel bureaus, various automobile associations, and oil companies.

Business Traveller's Handbook: A Guide to the United States and Canada. New York: Paddington Press, Ltd.

This series is intended to answer any question a business traveller might have—hotels, airflights, etc. Other books in the series are: ***A Guide to Europe; the Middle East; Latin America; Africa; Asia, Australia and the Pacific.***

Commercial Atlas & Marketing Guide. Chicago: Rand McNally & Co. Annually.

Fodor's Canada. Toronto: General Publishing Co. Ltd. Annually. This book gives background information and practical information (hotels, transportation, restaurants) on Canada.

Hotel and Motel Red Book. New York: American Hotel Association Directory Corporation. Annually.

Lists hotels and motels alphabetically by city and state, gives information about number of rooms, location, telephone numbers, and rates.

National Directory of Addresses and Telephone Numbers. New York: Bantam. Annually. A listing of the 50 000 most wanted telephone numbers in the U.S.

Rand McNally Commercial Atlas & Marketing Guide. Chicago: Rand McNally & Co. Annually.

Gives general information for the U.S., population and reference maps for Canada, and reference maps and general information for the world.

15.18 **Legal work references**

A Uniform System of Citation. Cambridge, Mass.: The Harvard Law Review.

A manual of citation, rules and style.

Banks, Margaret A. ***Using a Law Library: a Guide for Students and Lawyers in the Common Law Provinces of Canada.*** Agincourt, Ontario: The Carswell Co. Ltd.

Samuels, J. W. ***Legal Citation for Canadian Lawyers.*** Toronto: Butterworth & Co. (Canada) Ltd.

A brief study on the subject that does not include complete lists of abbreviations.

Yogis, J. A. ***Legal Writing and Research Manual.*** Toronto: Butterworth & Co. (Canada) Ltd.

A useful manual with various sections devoted to the subject of citation.

Postal and shipping references

15.19 ***Bullinger's Postal Shipper's Guide for the United States, Canada, and Newfoundland.*** Westwood, N.J.: Bullinger's Guides, Inc.

Contains names of post office and railroad stations on the railroad or steamer lines, and the delivery express for every town. Also lists railroads and water lines with their terminal points.

A Canada Postal Standards and Code Manual.

Canadian Postal Code Directories.

Directory of Post Offices. Washington: U.S. Postal Service.

Dun & Bradstreet Exporters' Encyclopaedia. New York: Dun & Bradstreet, Inc. Annually.

International Mail. Washington: U.S. Government Printing Office.

Leonard's Guide. New York: G. R. Leonard & Co., Inc.

Includes information on Canadian and foreign parcel post as well as shipper's guide for freight, express, and parcel post.

15.20 **Quotations**

Bartlett's Familiar Quotations. 14th ed. Toronto: Little, Brown Canada Ltd.

Canadian Quotations and Phrases, Literary and Historical. Toronto: McClelland & Stewart Limited.

Colombo's Canadian Quotations. Edmonton: Hurtig Publishers.

The Oxford Dictionary of Quotations. 2d ed. Toronto: Oxford University Press.

Year book

15.21 ***The Statesman's Year Book.*** Toronto: Macmillan Co. of Canada Ltd.

This book gives current topical information on key areas in every country such as industrial production, government, labour unions, newspapers, radio and TV stations, etc.

Word List

A

aard-vark
abaci
aba-cus
abaft
aban-don
abase
abash
abate
abater
ab-at-toir
abbé
ab-bess
ab-bey
ab-bre-vi-ate
ab-bre-vi-a-tion
ab-di-ca-ble
ab-di-cate
ab-di-ca-tion
ab-di-ca-tor
ab-do-men
ab-duct
ab-duc-tion
ab-duc-tor
abed
ab-er-rance
ab-er-rancy
ab-er-rant
ab-er-rated
ab-er-ra-tion
abet
abet-ted
abet-ting
abet-tor
or abet-ter
abey-ance
abey-ant
ab-hor
ab-horred
ab-hor-rence
ab-hor-rent
ab-hor-ring
abid-ance
abide
abil-i-ties
abil-ity
ab-ject
ab-jec-tion
ab-jure
ab-jurer
ab-late
ab-la-tion
ab-la-tive
ablaze
able
abler
ablest
able—bodied
ab-luted
ab-lu-tion
ab-ne-gate
ab-ne-ga-tion
ab-nor-mal-i-ties
ab-nor-mal-ity
aboard
abode
abol-ish
abol-isher
abo-li-tion
abo-li-tion-ism
abo-li-tion-ist
A—bomb
abomi-na-ble
abomi-na-bly
abomi-nate
abomi-na-tion
abomi-na-tor
ab-origi-nal
ab-orig-ine
abort
aborter
abor-tion
abor-tion-ist
abor-tive
abound
about—face *(n.)*
above-board
ab-ra-ca-dabra
abrade
abrader
abra-sion
abra-sive
abreast
abridge
abridge-ment
or abridg-ment
abroad
ab-ro-gate
ab-ro-ga-tion
abrupt
abrup-tion
ab-scess
ab-scis-sa
ab-scond
ab-sence
ab-sent
ab-sen-tee
ab-sen-tee-ism
ab-sent-minded
ab-sinthe
or ab-sinth
ab-so-lute
ab-so-lu-tion
ab-so-lut-ism
ab-solve
ab-solver
ab-sorb
ab-sorb-abil-ity
ab-sorb-able
ab-sorber
ab-sor-bance
ab-sor-ben-cies
ab-sor-bency
ab-sor-bent
or ab-sor-bant
ab-sorp-tance
ab-sorp-tion
ab-stain
ab-ste-mi-ous
ab-sten-tion
ab-sten-tious
ab-sti-nence
ab-sti-nent
ab-stract
ab-strac-tion
ab-strac-tion-ism
ab-strac-tive
ab-struse
ab-surd
ab-surd-ism

ab-surdi-ties
ab-surd-ity
abun-dance
abun-dant
abus-able
abuse
abu-sive
abut
abut-ted
abut-ting
abys-mal
abyss
abys-sal
aca-de-mia
aca-demic
or **aca-demi-cal**
acade-mi-cian
acade-mies
acad-emy
ac-cede
cf. **ex-ceed**
ac-cel-er-ate
ac-cel-era-tion
ac-cel-era-tive
ac-cel-era-tor
ac-cent
ac-cen-tual
ac-cen-tu-ate
ac-cen-tu-a-tion
ac-cept
cf. **ex-cept**
ac-cept-abil-ity
ac-cept-able
ac-cep-tance
ac-cess
cf. **ex-cess**
ac-ces-si-bil-ity
ac-ces-si-ble
ac-ces-si-bly
ac-ces-sion
ac-ces-sory
or **ac-ces-sary**
ac-ces-so-ries
or **ac-ces-sa-ries**
ac-ci-dent
ac-ci-den-tal
ac-claim
ac-cla-ma-tion
ac-cli-mate
ac-cli-ma-tion
ac-cli-ma-ti-za-tion
ac-cli-ma-tize
ac-cliv-ity
ac-co-lade
ac-com-mo-date
ac-com-mo-da-tion
ac-com-mo-da-tive
ac-com-pa-ni-ment
ac-com-pa-nist
ac-com-pany
ac-com-plice
ac-com-plish
ac-com-plish-able
ac-cord
ac-cor-dance
ac-count
ac-count-abil-ity
ac-coun-tancy
ac-coun-tant
ac-credit
ac-crete
ac-crual
ac-crue
ac-cul-tur-ate
ac-cul-tu-ra-tion
ac-cu-mu-late
ac-cu-mu-la-tion
ac-cu-mu-la-tive
ac-cu-mu-la-tor
ac-cu-ra-cies
ac-cu-racy
ac-cu-rate
ac-cursed
or **ac-curst**
ac-cusal
ac-cu-sa-tion
ac-cu-sa-tive
ac-cu-sa-tory
ac-cuse
ac-cus-tom
ac-cus-tom-ation
ace
ac-er-bate
acer-bic
acer-vate
ace-tate
acety-lene
ache
achiev-able
achieve
achiever
acid
acid-i-fi-ca-tion
acid-ify
acid-ity
ack-ack
ac-knowl-edge-able
ac-knowl-edge-ment
or **ac-knowl-edg-ment**
acme
aco-lyte
acne
acous-tic
acous-ti-cal
ac-ous-ti-cian
ac-quaint
ac-quain-tance
ac-quain-tance-ship
ac-qui-esce
ac-qui-es-cence
ac-qui-es-cent
ac-quir-able
ac-quire
ac-qui-si-tion
ac-qui-si-tional
ac-quis-i-tive
ac-quit
ac-quit-tal
ac-quit-ted
ac-quit-ting
acre
acre-age
acre—foot *(n.)*
ac-rid
ac-ri-mo-ni-ous
ac-ri-mo-nies
ac-ri-mony
ac-ro-bat
ac-ro-batic
ac-ro-nym
ac-ro-pho-bia

acropo-lis
across
across—the—board *(adj.)*
acrylic
act
ac-tion
ac-ti-vate
ac-ti-va-tion
ac-ti-va-tor
ac-tive
ac-tiv-ism
ac-tiv-is-tic
ac-tivi-ties
ac-tiv-ity
ac-tor
ac-tress
ac-tual
ac-tu-al-i-ties
ac-tu-al-ity
ac-tu-al-iza-tion
ac-tu-al-ize
ac-tu-ar-ial
ac-tu-ar-ies
ac-tu-ary
ac-tu-ate
ac-tua-tion
ac-tua-tor
acu-ities
acu-ity
acu-men
acu-punc-ture
acute
acuter
acut-est
ad-age
ada-gio
ada-mant
adapt
cf. **adept**
cf. **adopt**
adapt-abil-ity
adapt-able
ad-ap-ta-tion
adapter
or **adap-tor**
adap-tive
ad-denda *(n. pl.)*
ad-den-dum
ad-dict
ad-dic-tion
ad-dic-tive
ad-di-tion
ad-di-tive
ad-dress
ad-dress-able
ad-dressed
ad-dressee
ad-dresser
ad-duce
ad-duct
ade-noid
adept
cf. **adapt**
cf. **adopt**
ade-qua-cies
ade-quacy
ade-quate
ad-here
ad-her-ence
cf. **ad-her-ents**
ad-her-ent
ad-he-sion
ad-he-sive
ad hoc
adia-batic
adieu
adieus
or **adieux** *(n. pl.)*
ad in-fi-ni-tum
adios
ad-ja-cent
ad-jec-tive
ad-join
ad-journ
ad-judge
ad-ju-di-cate
ad-ju-di-ca-tive
ad-ju-di-ca-tor
ad-junct
ad-ju-ra-tion
ad-jure
ad-just
ad-just-able
ad-juster
or **ad-jus-tor**
ad-ju-tant
ad—lib
ad—libbed
ad—libbing
ad-min-is-ter
ad-min-is-tra-ble
ad-min-is-trate
ad-min-is-tra-tion
ad-min-is-tra-tive
ad-min-is-tra-tor
ad-mi-ra-ble
ad-mi-ra-bly
ad-mi-ra-tion
ad-mire
ad-mirer
ad-mis-si-bil-ity
ad-mis-si-ble
ad-mis-sion
ad-mis-sive
ad-mit
ad-mit-tance
ad-mit-ted
ad-mit-ting
ad-mon-ish
ad-mon-isher
ad-mo-ni-tion
ad nau-seam
adobe
ado-les-cence
ado-les-cent
adopt
cf. **adapt**
cf. **adept**
adopt-abil-ity
adopt-able
adopter
adop-tion
adop-tive
ador-able
ado-ra-tion
adore
adorer
adorn
ad-re-nal
adroit
ad-sorb

ad-sorb-able
ad-sorp-tion
ad-sorp-tive
adu-late
adu-la-tion
adult
adul-ter-ate
adul-ter-a-tion
adul-terer
adul-ter-ess
adul-ter-ous
adul-tery
adult-hood
ad-vance
ad-van-tage
ad-van-ta-geous
ad-vec-tion
Ad-vent
ad-ven-ture
ad-ven-turer
ad-ven-ture-some
ad-ven-tur-ess
ad-ven-tur-ous
ad-verb
ad-ver-bial
ad-ver-sar-ies
ad-ver-sary
ad-verse
ad-ver-si-ties
ad-ver-sity
ad-vert
cf. avert
ad-ver-tise
ad-ver-tiser
ad-vice *(n.)*
cf. ad-vise *(v.)*
ad-vis-abil-ity
ad-vis-able
ad-vise
cf. ad-vice
ad-vi-ser
or ad-visor
ad-vis-ory
ad-vo-cacy
ad-vo-cate
ad-vo-ca-tor
adze
or adz
aer-ate
aera-tion
aera-tor
aer-ial
aer-i-al-ist
aero-bat-ics
aero-naut
aero-nau-tics
aero-plane
aero-sol
aero-space
aero-sphere
aes-thetic
aes-theti-cal
af-fa-bil-ity
af-fa-ble
af-fa-bly
af-fect
cf. ef-fect
af-fect-abil-ity
af-fect-able
af-fec-ta-tion
af-fec-tion
af-fec-tion-ate
af-fec-tive
af-fi-da-vit
af-fili-ate
af-fili-ation
af-fini-ties
af-fin-ity
af-firm
af-fir-ma-tion
af-fir-ma-tive
af-fix
af-fix-a-tion
af-flict
af-flic-tion
af-flic-tive
af-flu-ence
af-flu-en-cies
af-flu-ency
af-flu-ent
cf. ef-flu-ent
af-ford
af-ford-able
af-for-est
af-for-es-ta-tion
af-fray
af-front
aflame
afore-men-tioned
afore-said
afore-thought
afraid
A—frame
aft
after
after—hours *(adj.)*
af-ter-noon
after—shave *(n.)*
af-ter-ward
again
against
agate
age
ag-ing
or age-ing
agen-cies
agency
agenda
agent
ag-glom-er-ate
ag-glom-era-tion
ag-glu-ti-nate
ag-glu-ti-na-tion
ag-gran-dize
ag-gra-vate
ag-gra-va-tion
ag-gre-gate
ag-gre-ga-tion
ag-gre-ga-tive
ag-gres-sion
ag-gres-sive
ag-gres-sor
ag-grieve
aghast
ag-ile
agili-ties
agil-ity
agi-tate
agi-ta-tion
agi-ta-tor

agi-ta-tive
aglow
ag-nos-tic
ag-nos-ti-cism
ago
agog
ago-nies
ago-nist
ago-nis-tic
ago-nize
ag-ony
agrar-ian
agrari-an-ism
agree
agree-able
ag-ri-cul-ture
ag-ri-cul-tur-al-ist
agron-omy
ague
ahead
aid
cf. **aide**
aide—de—camp
aides—de—camp
(n. pl.)
ail
aim
air
cf. **heir**
air base
air-borne
air—condition *(v.)*
air con-di-tioner *(n.)*
air-plane
aisle
cf. **isle**
ajar
akimbo
akin
ala-bas-ter
a la carte
a la mode
alac-rity
alarm
alarm-ist
al-beit
al-bum
al-che-mist
al-chemy
al-co-hol
al-co-holic
al-co-hol-ism
al-cove
al-der-man
alert
al-falfa
algae
al-ge-bra
al-ge-braic
al-ge-bra-ically
ALGOL
or **Al-gol**
al-go-rithm
alias
al-ibi
alien
alien-ate
alien-ation
align
or **aline**
al-i-men-tary
cf. **el-e-men-tary**
al-i-mony
alive
al-kali
al-ka-line
al-ka-lin-ity
all
cf. **awl**
all—Canadian *(n.) (adj.)*
all—around *(adj.)*
al-lay
al-le-ga-tion
al-lege
al-le-giance
al-le-gori-cal
al-le-gory
al-le-luia
or **hal-le-lu-jah**
al-ler-gic
al-lergy
al-le-vi-ate
al-ley
cf. **ally**
al-li-ance
al-lied
al-lo-cate
al-lo-ca-tion
all—or—nothing *(adj.)*
al-lot
al-lot-ted
al-lot-ting
al-low
al-low-able
al-low-ance
al-loy
all right *(adj.)*
cf. **al-right** *(adv.) (adj.)*
all—star *(n.)*
al-lude
al-lure
al-lu-sion
cf. **il-lu-sion**
al-lu-sive
cf. **elu-sive**
ally
cf. **al-ley**
alma ma-ter
al-ma-nac
al-mighty
al-most
alms
alone
along
aloof
aloud
al-paca
al-pha-bet
al-pha-beti-cal
al-pha-bet-ize
al-ready
cf. **all ready**
al-right *(adv.) (adj.)*
cf. **all right** *(adj.)*
al-tar
cf. **al-ter**
al-ter-able
al-ter-ation
al-ter-ca-tion
al-ter ego
al-ter-nate

al-ter-na-tion
al-ter-na-tive
al-ter-na-tor
al-time-ter
al-ti-tude
al-ti-tu-di-nal
al-to-gether
cf. **all to-gether**
al-tru-ism
al-tru-ist
al-tru-is-tic
alu-mi-nate
cf. **il-lu-mi-nate**
alu-mi-num
alu-mi-nize
alumna
alum-nae *(n. pl.)*
alum-nus
al-ways
amal-gam-ate
amal-gam-ation
ama-teur
ama-teur-ish
ama-teur-ism
ama-tive
ama-tory
amaze
ama-zon
am-bas-sa-dor
am-bas-sa-do-rial
am-bas-sa-dor-ship
am-ber
am-bi-dex-ter-ity
am-bi-dex-trous
am-bi-gu-ities
am-bi-gu-ity
am-bigu-ous
am-bi-tion
am-bi-tious
am-biva-lence
am-biva-lent
am-ble
am-bu-lance
am-bu-lant
am-bu-late
am-bu-la-tory
am-bus-cade
am-bush
ame-lio-rate
ame-lio-ra-tion
ame-lio-ra-tive
ame-lio-ra-tory
ame-na-ble
ame-na-bly
amend
amend-able
ame-ni-ties
ame-nity
ami-able
amia-bly
ami-ca-ble
amid
or **amidst**
am-mo-nia
am-mu-ni-tion
am-ne-sia
am-nes-ties
am-nesty
amoeba
amoe-bas
or **amoe-bae** *(n. pl.)*
among
amoral
amo-rous
amor-phous
am-or-tiz-able
am-or-tize
amount
amour
am-per-age
am-pere
am-per-sand
am-phib-ian
am-phib-i-ous
am-phi-the-atre
am-ple
am-ply
am-pli-fi-ca-tion
am-pli-fied
am-pli-fier
am-plify
am-pli-tude
am-pu-tate
am-pu-tee
amu-let
amuse
anach-ro-nism
anach-ro-nis-tic
or **ana-chronic**
or **anach-ro-nous**
an-aes-the-sia
an-aes-thetic
ana-gram
an-al-ge-sia
an-al-ge-sic
analo-gist
analo-gize
analo-gous
analo-gies
ana-logue
or **ana-log**
anal-ogy
ana-lyse
analy-ses
analy-sis
ana-lyst
ana-lytic
an-ar-chism
an-ar-chist
an-ar-chy
anath-ema
anathe-ma-tize
anat-omy
an-ces-tor
an-ces-tral
an-ces-tress
an-ces-try
an-chor
an-chor-age
an-cho-vies
an-chovy
an-cient
an-cil-lary
and
and-iron
and/or *(conj.)*
an-droid
an-ec-dot-age
an-ec-dotal
an-ec-dote
ane-mia

ane-mic
anem-one
an-es-the-sia
an-es-the-si-olo-gist
an-es-the-si-ol-ogy
an-es-thetic
anes-the-tist
anes-the-tize
an-eu-rysm
anew
an-gel
an-ger
an-gina
angle
an-gler
an-gli-cize
Anglo—Saxon
an-grier
an-gri-est
an-grily
an-gry
an-guish
an-gu-lar
ani-mal
ani-mal-ism
ani-mal-is-tic
ani-mate
ani-ma-tion
ani-mos-i-ties
ani-mos-ity
an-kle
an-kle-bone
an-nal-ist
an-nex
an-nexa-tion
an-ni-hi-late
an-ni-hi-la-tion
an-ni-ver-sa-ries
an-ni-ver-sary
anno Do-mini
an-no-tate
an-no-ta-tion
an-no-ta-tor
an-nounce
an-nouncer
an-noy
an-noyer
an-nual
an-nu-ities
an-nu-ity
an-nul
an-nulled
an-nul-ling
an-nun-cia-tion
an-ode
anoint
anoma-lous
anoma-lies
anom-aly
anon
ano-nym-ity
anony-mous
an-orak
an-other
an-swer
an-swer-able
ant
ant-acid
an-tago-nism
an-tago-nist
an-tago-nis-tic
an-tago-nize
ant-arc-tic
an-te-bel-lum
an-te-cede
an-te-ced-ence
cf. **an-te-ced-ents**
an-te-ced-ent
an-te-date
an-te-lope
an-tenna
an-ten-nas
or **an-ten-nae**
an-te-rior
cf. **in-te-rior**
an-them
an-thol-o-gies
an-thol-ogist
an-thol-ogy
an-thra-cite
an-thro-poid
an-thro-pol-o-gist
an-thro-pol-ogy
an-thro-po-log-i-cal
an-ti-air-craft
an-ti-bi-otic
an-tic
An-ti-christ
an-tici-pate
an-tici-pa-tion
an-tici-pa-tive
an-tici-pa-tory
an-ti-cli-mac-tic
an-ti-cli-max
an-ti-clock-wise
an-ti-dotal
an-ti-dote
an-ti-freeze
an-ti-his-ta-mine
an-ti-pasto
an-tipa-thies
an-tipa-thy
an-ti-quar-ian
an-ti-quate
an-tique
an-tiq-ui-ties
an-tiq-uity
an-ti—Sem-itism *(n.)*
an-ti-sep-tic
an-ti-so-cial
an-tith-eses *(n. pl.)*
an-tith-esis
an-ti-toxin
ant-ler
ant-onym
anxi-eties
anxi-ety
anx-ious
any
any-body
A—OK
A 1
apart
apart-heid
apa-thetic
apa-thy
ape
ape—man *(n.)*
aperi-tif
ap-er-ture
apex

apexes
or **api-ces** *(n. pl.)*
aphid
apho-rism
aph-ro-dis-iac
api-ary
apiece
aplenty
aplumb
apoca-lypse
apo-gee
Apollo
apolo-getic
apolo-gies
apolo-gize
apol-ogy
apo-plexy
apos-tle
ap-os-tolic
apos-tro-phe
apoth-e-car-ies
apoth-e-cary
ap-pal
or **ap-pall**
ap-pa-ra-tus
ap-pa-ra-tus *(n. pl.)*
or **ap-pa-ra-tuses**
ap-parel
ap-par-ent
ap-pa-ri-tion
ap-peal
ap-pear
ap-pear-ance
ap-pease
ap-pel-late
ap-pel-la-tion
ap-pend
ap-pend-age
ap-pen-dec-to-mies
ap-pen-dec-tomy
ap-pen-di-ci-tis
ap-pen-dix
ap-pen-dixes
or **ap-pen-dices** *(n. pl.)*
ap-per-ceive
ap-per-cep-tion
ap-pe-tite
ap-pe-tizer
ap-plaud
ap-plause
ap-ple
ap-pli-ance
ap-pli-ca-ble
ap-pli-ca-bil-ity
ap-pli-cant
ap-pli-ca-tion
ap-point
ap-poin-tee
ap-por-tion
ap-po-site
ap-po-si-tion
ap-praise
ap-pre-cia-ble
ap-pre-cia-bly
ap-pre-ci-ate
ap-pre-ci-a-tion
ap-pre-cia-tive
ap-pre-hend
ap-pre-hen-si-ble
ap-pre-hen-si-bly
ap-pre-hen-sion
ap-pre-hen-sive
ap-pren-tice
ap-prise
cf. **ap-prize**
ap-proach
ap-proach-able
ap-pro-bate
ap-pro-ba-tion
ap-propri-ate
ap-pro-pri-a-tion
ap-proval
ap-prove
ap-proxi-mate
ap-proxi-ma-tion
apron
ap-ro-pos
apt
ap-ti-tude
aqua-cade
aqua-naut
aquar-ium
Aquar-ius
aquatic
aq-ue-duct
ara-ble
ar-bi-ter
ar-bi-tra-ble
ar-bi-trarily
ar-bi-trary
ar-bi-trate
ar-bi-tra-tion
ar-bi-tra-tive
ar-bi-tra-tor
ar-bo-re-tum
ar-bour
arc
ar-cade
arch
ar-chae-ol-o-gist
or **ar-che-ol-o-gist**
ar-chae-ol-ogy
or **ar-che-ol-ogy**
ar-chaic
arch-di-o-cese
arch-duch-ess
arch-duchy
arch-duke
arch-ene-mies
arch-en-emy
ar-cher
ar-chery
ar-chi-pel-ago
ar-chi-tect
ar-chi-tec-tural
ar-chi-tec-ture
ar-chive
arc-tic
ar-dent
ar-dour
ar-du-ous
area
cf. **aria**
area code *(n.)*
arena
ar-gu-able
argue
ar-guer
ar-gu-ment
ar-gu-men-ta-tion
ar-gu-men-ta-tive

aria
cf. area
arid
arid-ity
arise
ar-is-toc-ra-cies
ar-is-toc-racy
aris-to-crat
aris-to-cratic
arith-me-tic
ar-ith-met-i-cal
ark
arm
ar-mada
ar-ma-ment
ar-ma-ture
arm-chair
ar-mies
ar-mi-stice
ar-mour
ar-mour-ies
ar-moury
army
aroma
around
around—the—clock *(adj.)*
arouse
ar-raign
ar-range
ar-ray
ar-rear
ar-rest
ar-rival
ar-rive
ar-ro-gance
ar-ro-gant
ar-row
ar-se-nal
ar-se-nate
ar-se-nic
ar-son
ar-te-rio-scle-ro-sis
ar-ter-ies
ar-tery
ar-te-sian well *(n.)*
ar-thritic
ar-thri-tis
ar-ti-choke
ar-ti-cle
ar-ticu-late
ar-ticu-la-tion
ar-ti-fact
ar-ti-fi-cial
ar-ti-fi-cial-i-ties
ar-ti-fi-ci-al-ity
ar-til-lery
ar-ti-san
art-ist
ar-tis-tic
art-istry
art-work
Aryan
as-bes-tos
as-cend
as-cend-able
or as-cend-ible
as-cen-dance
or as-cen-dence
as-cen-dancy
or as-cen-dency
as-cent
cf. as-sent
as-cer-tain
as-cetic
ascor-bic acid
as-cot
as-cribe
asex-ual
ash
ashamed
ashen
Asian
Asi-atic
aside
asi-nine
asi-nin-ity
ask
askance
or askant
askew
asleep
asp
as-pect
as-perse
as-per-sion
as-phalt
as-phyx-i-ate
as-pic
as-pi-rant
as-pi-ra-tion
as-pire
as-pi-rin
as-sail
as-sail-ant
as-sas-sin
as-sas-si-nate
as-sas-si-na-tion
as-sas-si-na-tor
as-sault
as-saulter
as-say
cf. es-say
as-sem-blage
as-sem-ble
as-sem-bly
as-sent
cf. as-cent
as-sert
as-ser-tion
as-ser-tive
as-sess
as-sess-able
as-ses-sor
as-set
as-sev-er-ate
as-sev-era-tion
as-sev-era-tive
as-si-du-ity
as-sidu-ous
as-sign
as-sig-na-tion
as-signee
as-signer
as-simi-late
as-simi-la-tion
as-simi-la-tor
as-sist
as-sis-tance
cf. as-sis-tants
as-so-ci-ate
as-so-cia-tion

as-so-cia-tive
as-sort
as-suage
as-sua-sive
as-sume
as-sum-abil-ity
as-sum-able
as-sump-tion
as-sump-tive
as-sur-ance
as-surer
or as-suror
as-ter-isk
astern
as-ter-oid
asthma
as-tig-matic
astig-ma-tism
as-ton-ish
as-tound
astrad-dle
as-tral
astride
as-tro-dome
as-trol-ogy
as-tro-naut
as-tro-nav-i-ga-tion
as-tron-o-mer
as-tro-nom-i-cal
as-tron-omy
as-tute
asun-der
asy-lum
asym-met-ric
asym-met-ri-cal
asym-me-try
at all
cf. atoll
athe-ism
athe-ist
athe-is-tic
athe-is-ti-cal
ath-lete
ath-letic
at-las
at-mos-phere
at-mos-pheric
atoll
cf. at all
atom
atom bomb
atomic
at-om-ize
atone
atop
atro-cious
atroci-ties
atroc-ity
at-ro-phy
at-tach
at-ta-ché
at-tack
at-tain
at-tar
at-tempt
at-tend
at-ten-dance
cf. at-ten-dants
at-ten-tion
at-ten-tive
at-tenu-ate
at-tenu-ation
at-test
at-tes-ta-tion
at-tic
at-tire
at-ti-tude
at-ti-tu-di-nal
at-ti-tu-di-nize
at-tor-nies
at-tor-ney
attorney—at—law
attorneys—at—law
(n. pl.)
at-tract
at-trac-tion
at-trac-tive
at-trib-ute
at-trib-ut-able
at-tribu-tion
at-tribu-tive
at-tri-tion
at-tune
atypi-cal
au-burn
auc-tion
auc-tion-eer
au-da-cious
au-dac-ity
au-di-ble
au-di-ence
au-dio
au-di-ol-ogy
au-dio-vi-sual
au-dit
au-di-tion
au-di-tor
au-di-to-rium
au-di-tory
au-ger
aught
cf. ought
aug-ment
au gra-tin
au-gust
au jus
auld lang syne
aunt
au-ral
cf. oral
au re-voir
au-ri-cle
cf. or-a-cle
aus-pice
aus-pi-cious
aus-tere
aus-ter-i-ties
aus-ter-ity
au-then-tic
au-then-ti-ca-tion
au-then-tic-ity
au-thor
au-thori-tar-ian
au-thori-tar-i-an-ism
au-thori-ta-tive
au-thori-ties
au-thor-ity
au-thori-za-tion
au-thor-ize
au-thor-ship
au-to-bio-graphi-cal

au-to-bi-og-ra-phy
au-to-bi-og-ra-pher
au-toc-racy
au-to-crat
au-to-cratic
au-to-crati-cal
au-to-graph
au-to-mate
au-to-matic
au-to-ma-tion
au-toma-tism
au-toma-ti-za-tion
au-toma-ton
au-to-mo-bile
au-to-mo-tive
au-tono-mous
au-tono-mies
au-ton-omy
au-topsy
au-tumn
aux-il-ia-ries
aux-il-iary
avail
avail-abil-ity
avail-able
ava-lanche
ava-rice
ava-ri-cious
avast
avenge
avenger
ave-nue
aver
av-er-age
averse
aver-sion
averred
aver-ring
avert
cf. **ad-vert**
avi-ary
avia-tion
avia-tor
avid
avo-cado
avo-ca-tion
avoid
avoid-able
avoid-ance
av-oir-du-pois
avouch
avow
avowal
await
awake
awaken
aware
away
cf. **aweigh**
awe
aweigh
cf. **away**
aw-ful
awk-ward
awl
cf. **all**
awry
axe
or **ax**
axes (pl. of *ax* and *axis*)
cf. **axis**
ax-iom
axi-om-atic
axis
axle
aye
cf. **eye**
azi-muth
azure

B

bab-ble
babies *(n. pl.)*
baby
baby—sitter *(n.)*
bac-ca-lau-re-ate
bache-lor
bache-lor-hood
ba-cil-lus
back
back-fire
back-ground
back-lash
back-stage
back-track
ba-con
bac-te-ria *(n. pl.)*
bac-te-rial
bac-te-ri-ol-o-gist
bac-te-ri-ol-ogy
bac-te-rium *(n. sing.)*
bad
bade
badger
bad-min-ton
bad—mouth *(v).*
baf-fle
ba-gel
bag-gage
bag-ging
baggy
bag-pipe
bail
cf. **bale**
bai-liff
bai-li-wick
bait
bake
baker
bak-er-ies
bak-ery
bal-ance
bal-co-nies
bal-cony
bald
bale
cf. **bail**
balk
balky
ball
cf. **bawl**
bal-lad
ball—and—socket joint *(n.)*
bal-last
ball bear-ing *(n.)*
bal-let
bal-lis-tic
bal-loon

bal-lot
ball—point
bal-ly-hoo
balm
balm-ier
balmi-est
balsa
bal-sam
bal-us-trade
bam-boo
ban
ba-nana
band
band-age
ban-dana
or **ban-danna**
ban-do-lier
or **ban-do-leer**
band saw *(n.)*
bang
ban-gle
ban-ish
ban-is-ter
or **ban-nis-ter**
banjo
banjos
or **ban-joes** *(n. pl.)*
bank
bank note
bank-roll
bank-rupt
bank-rupt-cies
bank-ruptcy
ban-ner
ban-quet
ban-tam
ban-zai
bap-tism
bap-tize
bar
barb
bar-bar-ian
bar-bari-an-ism
bar-baric
bar-ba-rism
bar-bar-ity
bar-ba-rous
bar-be-que
bar-ber
bar-ber-shop
bar-bi-tu-rate
bare
cf. **bear**
bare-leg-ged
bar-gain
barge
bark
bari-tone
bar mitz-vah
barn
bar-na-cle
barn dance *(n.)*
barn-storm
ba-rome-ter
baro-met-ric
baron
cf. **barren**
bar-on-ess
bar-onet
bar-rage
bar-rel
bar-ren
cf. **baron**
bar-ri-cade
bar-rier
bar-ris-ter
bar-ter
basal
base
base-ball
based
cf. **baste**
base hit *(n.)*
bash
ba-sic
ba-sin
bas-ket
bas mitz-vah
bass
bas-si-net
baste
cf. **based**
bas-tion
bat
batch
bate
bath *(n).*
bathe *(v.)*
bathy-sphere
ba-ton
bat-ted
bat-ter
bat-ter-ies
bat-tery
bat-ting
bat-tle
bawl
cf. **ball**
Bayes-ian
bayo-net
ba-zaar
cf. **bi-zarre**
be *(v.)*
cf. **bee** *(n.)*
beach
cf. **beech**
bea-con
beam
bear
cf. **bare**
bear-able
beard
bearer
beast
beat
cf. **beet**
beaten
beat-nik
beau
cf. **bow**
beaux
or **beaus**
beau-te-ous
beau-ti-ful
beau-tify
be-came
be-cause
bed
bed-ded
bed-ding
be-devil

bed-lam
be-drag-gle
bed-rid-den
bee *(n.)*
cf. **be** *(v.)*
beech
cf. **beach**
beefy
bee-hive
beer
cf. **bier**
beet
cf. **beat**
bee-tle
be-fit-ting
be-fore
be-fore-hand
be-friend
be-fud-dle
beg
be-gan
beg-gat
begged
beg-ging
be-gin
be-gin-ner
be-gin-ning
be-gone
be-gun
be-grudge
be-guile
be-guiler
be-half
be-have
be-hav-iour
be-hav-ioural
be-hav-iour-ism
be-held
be-hest
be-hind
behind—the—scenes *(adj.)*
be-hold
be-holden
be-holder
beige
be-labour
be-lated
be-lay
belch
bel-fries
bel-fry
be-lie
be-lief
be-liev-able
be-liev-ably
be-lieve
be-liever
be-lit-tle
be-lit-tler
bell
cf. **belle**
bell—bottoms *(n.)*
bell-boy
belle
cf. **bell**
bell-hop
bel-lig-er-ence
bel-lig-er-ency
bel-lig-er-ent
bel-low
bell-wether
be-long
be-loved
below
be-med-aled
or **be-med-alled**
be-moan
be-muse
bench
bench mark *(n.)*
bench war-rant *(n.)*
bend
be-neath
bene-dic-tion
bene-dic-tory
bene-fac-tor
be-nefic
be-nefi-cence
be-nefi-cent
bene-fi-cial
bene-fi-cia-ries
bene-fi-ciary
bene-fi-ci-ate
bene-fit
bene-fited
or **bene-fit-ted**
be-nevo-lence
be-nevo-lent
be-nign
be-nig-nancy
be-nig-nant
ben-zene
ben-zi-dine
ben-zine
be-queathal
be-quest
be-rate
be-reave
be-reaved
or **be-reft**
be-ret
ber-ries
berry
ber-serk
berth
cf. **birth**
be-seech
be-set
be-set-ting
be-side *(prep.)*
be-sides *(adv.)*
be-siege
be-smear
be-smirch
be-spec-ta-cled
best
bes-tial
bes-ti-al-i-ties
bes-ti-al-ity
best man *(n.)*
be-stow
best seller *(n.)*
bet
beta
be-to-ken
be-tray
be-trayal
be-trayer
be-troth
be-trothal

bet-ter
bet-tor
be-tween
be-twixt
bevel
bev-er-age
be-ware
be-wil-der
be-witch
be-yond
bias
bib
bi-ble
bib-li-cal
bib-lio-graphic
bib-lio-graph-i-cal
bib-li-og-ra-phies
bib-li-og-ra-phy
bi-cen-te-nary
bi-cen-ten-nial
bi-ceps
bicker
bi-cy-cle
bid
bid-den
bid-ding
bide
bi-en-nial
bier
cf. **beer**
bi-fo-cal
bi-fur-cate
bi-fur-ca-tion
biga-mous
biga-mist
big-amy
big-ger
big-gest
bigot
big-otry
bi-kini
bi-lat-eral
bi-lat-er-al-ism
bile
bilge
bi-lin-gual
bi-lin-gual-ism
bil-ious
bilk
bill
bill-board
bil-let
billet—doux
billets—doux *(n. pl.)*
bil-lion
bil-lion-aire
bil-low
bi-modal
bi-monthly
bin
bi-nary
bind
binder
bind-er-ies
bind-ery
binge
bin-oc-u-lar
bi-no-mial
bio-de-grad-able
bio-graph-i-cal
bio-graphic
bi-og-ra-phies
bi-og-ra-phy
bio-logic
bio-log-i-cal
bi-olo-gist
bi-op-sies
bi-opsy
bi-par-ti-san
bi-par-ti-san-ism
bi-par-ti-san-ship
birch
birch-bark
bird
birth
cf. **berth**
birth-day
birth-rate
bis-cuit
bi-sect
bi-sec-tor
bi-sex-ual
bishop
bish-op-ric
bi-son
bit
bite
bit-ter
bi-tu-men
bi-tu-mi-nous
bi-vari-ate
biv-ouac
bi-weekly
bi-zarre
cf. **ba-zaar**
black
black-mail
black-mar-ket
black-out
black-top
blade
blame
blanch
bland
blank
blan-ket
blare
blasé
blas-pheme
blas-phemer
blas-phe-mous
blas-phe-mies
blas-phemy
blast
blast-off *(n.)*
bla-tant
blaze
bleach
bleach-able
bleak
blear-ily
blear-i-ness
bleary
bled
bleed
bleeder
blem-ish
blend
blender
bless

blessed
or **blest**
blew
cf. **blue**
blight
blimp
blind
blind-fold
blink
bliss
bliss-fully
blis-ter
blis-tery
blithe
blithe-some
blitz
blitz-krieg
bliz-zard
bloat
blob
bloc
cf. **block**
block-ade
block-age
blond
blonde
blood
blood-ier
bloodi-est
blood-hound
blood-stain
bloody
bloom
blos-som
blot
blotch
blotchy
blot-ted
blot-ter
blot-ting
blouse
blow
blown
blud-geon
blue
cf. **blew**
blue book
blue chip
blue—collar *(adj.)*
blu-ing
or **blue-ing**
bluer
bluff
blu-ish
blun-der
blun-derer
blunt
blur
blurb
blurred
blur-ring
blurry
blush
boar
cf. **bore**
board
cf. **bored**
boarder
board-walk
boast
bob
bob-bin
bode
bod-ice
bod-ies
bod-ily
body
bog
bogged
bog-ging
boggy
bo-gus
bo-he-mian
boil
boiler
bois-ter-ous
bold
bo-lo-gna
bol-she-vism
bol-ster
bolt
bomb
bom-bard
bom-bar-dier
bomber
bona fide
bo-nanza
bond
bond-able
bond-age
bone
bon-fire
bon-ier
boni-est
bon-net
bo-nus
bon vi-vant
bon voy-age
bony
boogie—woogie
book
book-end
book-keeper
book-keep-ing
book-let
book-mo-bile
Bool-ean
boom
boo-mer-ang
boon
boon-docks
booster
boot
boo-tee
or **bootie**
cf. **booty**
bo-rax
bor-der
bore
cf. **boar**
bored
cf. **board**
bore-dom
born
cf. **borne**
bor-ough
cf. **burro**
cf. **bur-row**
bor-row
bo-som
boss

boss-ier
bossi-est
boss-ism
bossy
bo-tani-cal
bota-nist
bot-any
both
bother
both-er-some
bot-tle
bot-tle-neck
bot-tom
bot-tom-most
botu-lism
bou-doir
bough
cf. bow
bought
bouil-lon
cf. bul-lion
boul-der
bou-le-vard
bounce
bounc-ier
bounci-est
bouncy
bound
bound-aries
bound-ary
bounder
boun-te-ous
boun-ti-ful
boun-ties
bounty
bou-quet
bour-geois
bour-geoi-sie
bout
bou-tique
bou-ton-niere
bow
cf. beau
bow-ery
bowl
box
boxes
box-car
boy
cf. buoy
boy-cott
boy-friend
boy scout
boy-sen-berry
brace
brace-let
bracket
brack-ish
brad
brag
brag-ga-do-cio
brag-gart
bragged
brag-ger
braid
braille
brain
brain—picking *(n.)*
brain-storm
brain-wash
brake
cf. break
bram-ble
bran
branch
brand
bran-dish
brandy
brash
brass
bras-sard
bras-siere
bra-vado
bra-va-does
or bra-va-dos
brave
brav-ery
bravo
brawl
brawn
bra-zen
bra-zier
breach
breaches
cf. breeches
bread
cf. bred
breadth
break
cf. brake
break-able
break-age
break-down
breaker
break-wa-ter
breast
breath
breathe
breath-tak-ing
bred
cf. bread
breed
breeder
breeze
breez-ier
breezi-est
breez-ily
breezi-ness
breezy
breth-ren
brev-ity
brew
brew-er-ies
brew-ery
bribe
brib-ery
bric—a—brac
brick
brick-layer
bridal
cf. bridle
bride-groom
brides-maid
bridge
bridge-head
bridge-work
bridle
cf. bridal
brief
brief-case

brier
brig
bri-gade
brig-and
briga-dier
bright
brighten
bril-liance
bril-liancy
bril-liant
brim
brimmed
brim-ming
brine
bring
brin-ier
brin-i-est
brink
brink-man-ship
briny
brisk
bris-tle
brit-tle
brit-tler
brit-tlest
broach
broad
broad-cast
broad-caster
broaden
broader
broad—minded *(adj.)*
bro-cade
bro-chure
broi-der
broi-dery
broil
broiler
broke
bro-ken
broken—down *(adj.)*
bro-ken-hearted
bro-ker
bro-ker-age
bron-chial
bron-chi-tis
bron-cho-pneu-mo-nia
bron-cho-scope
bron-chi *(n. pl.)*
bron-chus
bronco
bronze
brooch
brood
brook
broom
broom-stick
broth
brother
brother—in—law
brothers—in—law *(n. pl.)*
brought
brow
brow-beat
brown
browse
browser
bru-cel-lo-sis
bruise
bruit
cf. **brute**
brunch
bru-net
or **bru-nette**
brunt
brush
brush-fire
brusque
bru-tal
bru-tali-ties
bru-tal-ity
bru-tal-iza-tion
bru-tal-ize
brute
cf. **bruit**
brut-ish
bub-ble
bub-ble gum
bub-blier
bub-bli-est
bub-bly
buc-ca-neer
buck
bucket
buckle
buck-shot
buck-skin
buck-tooth
buck-wheat
bu-colic
bud
bud-ded
Bud-dha
Bud-dhism
Bud-dhist
bud-dies
bud-ding
buddy
budge
bud-get
buff
buf-falo
buf-fa-loes *(n. pl.)*
or **buf-falo**
or **buf-fa-los**
buffer
buf-fet
buf-foon
buf-foon-er-ies
buf-foon-ery
bug
bug-a-boo
buggy
bu-gle
bu-gler
build
builder
built
built—up *(adj.)*
bulb
bul-bous
bulge
bulk
bulkier
bulki-est
bulki-ness
bulky
bull
bull-dog
bull-doze
bull-dozer

bull-fight
bul-le-tin
bul-lion
cf. **bouil-lon**
bul-lied
bul-lies
bull-ish
bull-pen
bull's—eye
bully
bul-wark
bum-ble
bum-bler
bump
bumper
bump-ier
bump-i-est
bump-kin
bump-tious
bumpy
bunch
bunco
or **bunko**
bun-dle
bun-ga-low
bun-gle
bun-gler
bun-ion
bunk
bunker
bunt
buoy
cf. **boy**
buoy-ance
buoy-ancy
buoy-ant
bur-den
bur-den-some
bu-reau
bu-reau-cra-cies
bu-reau-cracy
bu-reau-cratic
bu-reau-cra-ti-za-tion
bu-reau-cra-tize
bur-glar
bur-glar-ies
bur-glar-ize
bur-glary
bur-go-mas-ter
burial
bur-ied
bur-lap
bur-lesque
burn
burner
bur-nish
burr
burred
burrer
burro
cf. **bor-ough**
cf. **bur-row**
bursa
bur-sar
bur-si-tis
burst
bury
bus
cf. **buss**
buses *(n. pl.)*
or **bus-ses**
bush
bushel
bush-ier
bushi-est
bushy
bus-ied
bus-ier
bus-ily
busi-ness
busi-ness-like
busi-ness-man
busi-ness-woman
buss
cf. **bus**
bust
bus-tle
busy
but
cf. **butt**
bu-tane
butcher
butch-er-ies
butch-ery
but-ler
butt
cf. **but**
butte
but-ter
but-ter-fly
but-tock
but-ton
but-ton-hole
but-tress
buxom
buy
cf. **by**
buyer
buzz
buzzer
by
cf. **buy**
by—line *(n.)*
by-pass
by-stander

C

cab
cab-bage
ca-bal-lero
ca-bana
caba-ret
cabin
cabi-net
ca-ble
ca-ble-gram
cable TV
ca-cao
cache
cf. **cash**
cac-tus
ca-daver
cad-die
or **caddy**
ca-dence
ca-denza
ca-det
cadre
ca-du-ceus

Cae-sar-ean
or ce-sar-ean
or ce-sar-ian
café
caf-e-te-ria
caf-feine
cage
cagey
or cagy
ca-jole
ca-lami-ties
ca-lam-ity
cal-cif-er-ous
cal-ci-fi-ca-tion
cal-ci-fied
cal-cify
cal-cium
cal-cu-la-ble
cal-cu-late
cal-cu-la-tion
cal-cu-la-tor
cal-en-dar
calf
cali-bre
or cali-ber
cali-brate
cal-li-per
or cali-per
cal-lis-then-ics
or cal-is-then-ics
calk
cal-lous *(adj.)*
cal-lus *(n.)*
calm
ca-loric
calo-rie
or cal-ory
ca-lypso
cameo
cam-era
cam-ou-flage
cam-paign
cam-paigner
cam-phor
camp-site
camp-stool
cam-pus
can
ca-nal
can-apé
cf. can-opy
can-cel
can-cel-la-tion
or can-cel-ation
can-cer
can-de-la-bra
can-did
can-di-dacy
can-di-date
can-dle
can-dor
can-dies
can-died
cane
ca-nine
can-ing
can-is-ter
or can-nis-ter
can-ker
can-na-bis
canned
can-ni-bal
can-ni-bal-ism
can-ni-bal-is-tic
can-ning
can-non
cf. canon
can-nily
can-ni-ness
canny
ca-noe
canon
cf. can-non
cano-pied
can-opy
cf. can-apé
can-ta-loupe
can-tan-ker-ous
can-teen
can-ter
cf. can-tor
can-tina
can-vas
cf. can-vass
can-yon
cap
ca-pa-bil-i-ties
ca-pa-bil-ity
ca-pa-ble
ca-pac-ity
ca-per
cap-il-lary
cap-i-tal
capi-tal-ism
capi-tal-ist
capi-tal-is-tic
capi-tal-iza-tion
capi-tal-ize
ca-pit-u-late
ca-pit-u-la-tion
capped
cap-ping
ca-price
ca-pri-cious
cap-size
cap-stan
cap-sule
cap-tain
cap-tion
cap-ti-vate
cap-ti-va-tion
cap-ti-va-tor
cap-tiv-ity
cap-ture
ca-rafe
cara-mel
carat
or karat
cf. car-rot
cf. caret
car-bine
car-bo-hy-drate
car-bon
car-bu-re-tor
car-cass
car-diac
car-di-nal
ca-reen
ca-reer
ca-ress

caret
cf. carat
or karat
cf. car-rot
cargo
car-goes
or car-gos
car-hop
cari-ca-ture
car-nal
car-na-tion
car-ni-val
car-niv-o-rous
ca-rouse
car-pen-ter
car-pen-try
car-pet
car-port
car-riage
car-ried
car-rier
car-ries
car-rot
cf. carat
or karat
cf. caret
carry
carte blanche
car-ti-lage
car-tog-ra-phy
car-ton
car-toon
car-toon-ist
car-tridge
carve
carver
cas-cade
cash
cf. cache
cash-ier
cash-mere
cas-ket
cas-sette
cast
cf. caste
cas-ti-gate
cas-tle
cas-trate
ca-sual
ca-su-al-ties
ca-su-alty
cata-comb
cata-logue
or cata-log
cata-loguer
or cata-loger
cata-lyst
cata-pult
cata-ract
ca-tas-tro-phe
cata-strophic
catch
catcher
catchup
or cat-sup
or ketchup
catchy
cate-chism
cate-go-ries
cate-gory
cater
ca-the-dral
cathe-ter-ize
cath-ode
catho-lic
cf. Catho-lic
Ca-tholi-cism
cat—o'—nine—tails *(n.)*
cat-sup
or catchup
or ketchup
cat-tle
cau-cus
causal
cau-sal-ity
cau-sa-tion
cause-way
caus-tic
cau-ter-ize
cau-tion
cau-tious
cav-al-cade
cava-lier
cav-alry
cave
cave—in
cave-man
cav-ern
cav-ern-ous
cav-iar
or cavi-are
cavi-ties
cav-ity
ca-vort
cease
ce-dar
cede
cf. seed
ceil-ing
cele-brate
cele-bra-tion
ce-leb-rity
cel-ery
ce-les-tial
celi-bate
cell
cf. sell
cel-lar
cf. seller
cel-lo-phane
cel-lu-lose
ce-ment
ceme-ter-ies
ceme-tery
cen-ser
cf. cen-sor
cen-sor-ship
cen-sure
cen-sus
cent
cf. scent
cf. sent
cent-are
cen-ten-nial
cen-ti-grade
cen-ti-me-tre
cen-tral
cen-tral-iza-tion
cen-tral-ize
cen-tre
cen-tre-piece

cen-trifu-gal
cen-tu-ries
cen-tury
ce-ramic
ce-real
cf. se-rial
ce-re-bral
cere-mo-nial
cere-mo-nies
cere-mo-ni-ous
cere-mony
cer-tain
cer-tainty
cer-tifi-cate
cer-ti-fi-ca-tion
cer-ti-fied
ces-sa-tion
ces-sion
cf. ses-sion
chafe
chaff
cha-grin
chain
chain—reaction *(n.)*
chain—smoke *(v.)*
chair
chair lift
chair-man
chair-woman
chaise lounge
chal-ice
cf. chal-lis
chalk
chal-lenge
chal-lenger
chal-lis
cf. chal-ice
cha-me-leon
cham-ber
cham-ber-maid
cham-bray
cham-ois
or chammy
cham-pagne
cham-pion
chan-cel-lery
or chan-cel-lory
chan-cel-lor
chan-de-lier
change
change-able
change-over *(n.)*
chan-nel
Cha-nu-kah
or Ha-nuk-kah
chaos
cha-otic
chap
chap-ar-ral
chapel
chap-eron
or chap-er-one
chap-lain
chapped
chap-ping
char
char-ac-ter-is-tic
char-ac-ter-iza-tion
char-ac-ter-ize
cha-rade
char-coal
charge
charge-able
charge—a—plate *(n.)*
or charge plate
charger
char-iot
cha-ris-ma
or char-ism
cha-ris-mata *(pl.)*
or char-isms
charmer
char-ter
char-treuse
chase
chased
cf. chaste
chaser
chas-ing
chasm
chas-sis
chaste
cf. chased
chas-ten
chas-tise
chas-tity
chat
châ-teau
châ-teaux
or châ-teaus *(pl.)*
chatted
chat-tel
chat-ter
chat-ting
chatty
chauf-feur
chau-vin-ism
chau-vin-ist
cheap
cf. cheep
cheat
cheater
cf. chee-tah
check
check-er-board
check-mate
check-out *(n.)*
check out *(v.)*
cheep
cf. cheap
cheer
cheer-ier
cheer-i-ness
cheerio
cheer-leader
cheese
chees-ier
cheesi-ness
cheesy
chef
chemi-cal
chem-is-try
che-nille
cher-ish
cher-ries
cherry
cherub
che-ru-bic
cher-u-bim
or cher-ubs *(pl.)*
chess

chest
chest-ier
chesty
chev-ron
chew
chew-able
chewy
chi-can-ery
chick
chicken
chicken pox
chick-pea *(n.)*
chide
chief
chief-tain
chif-fon
child
child-birth
child-hood
child-ish
chil-dren
chili
or **chile**
or **chilli**
cf. **chilly**
chill
chill-ier
chilly
cf. **chili**
or **chile**
or **chilli**
chime
chim-ney
chim-pan-zee
china
chin-chil-la
chip
chipped
chip-per
chip-ping
chi-ro-prac-tic
chi-ro-prac-tor
chisel
chis-elled
or **chis-eled**
chit-chat
chiv-al-rous
chiv-alry
chlo-ride
chlo-ri-nate
chlo-ri-na-tion
chlo-rine
chlo-ro-form
chlo-ro-phyll
chock
chock—full *(adj.)*
choc-o-late
choice
choir
cf. **quire**
chol-era
cho-les-terol
choose
chop
chop—chop *(adv.)*
chopped
chop-ping
choppy
chop-stick
chop suey
cho-ral
cf. **cho-rale**
or **cho-ral**
chord
cf. **cord**
chordal
chore
cho-re-og-ra-pher
cho-re-og-ra-phy
cho-ris-ter
chorus
chose
cho-sen
chow-der
chrome
chronic
chroni-cle
chro-no-log-i-cal
chro-nol-o-gies
chro-nol-ogy
chub-bier
chub-bi-ness
chubby
chuckle
chunk
chunk-ier
church
church-goer
chute
cf. **shoot**
ci-ca-trix
ci-ca-tri-ces *(pl.)*
ci-der
ci-gar
cig-a-rette
or **cig-a-ret**
cin-der
cin-ema
cin-na-mon
ci-pher
circa
cir-cle
cir-cuit
cir-cu-itous
cir-cu-lar
cir-cu-lar-ize
cir-cu-late
cir-cu-la-tion
cir-cu-la-tory
cir-cum-fer-ence
cir-cum-lo-cu-tion
cir-cum-nav-i-gate
cir-cum-scribe
cir-cum-spect
cir-cum-stance
cir-cum-stan-tial
cir-cum-stan-ti-ate
cir-cum-vent
cir-cum-ven-tion
cir-cus
cir-rho-sis
cis-tern
cita-del
ci-ta-tion
cite
cf. **sight**
cf. **site**
citi-zen
citi-zenry
cit-ron
cit-rus

ci-ties
city
city-scape
civic
civic—minded *(adj.)*
civil
ci-vil-ian
ci-vil-ity
civi-li-za-tion
civi-lize
civil rights *(pl. only)*
claim
claim-able
claim-ant
claimer
clair-voy-ance
clair-voy-ant
clam-mier
clammy
clamour
clam-or-ous
clan
clan-des-tine
claret
clari-fi-ca-tion
clari-fied
clar-ify
clari-net
clar-ity
clasp
class
clas-sic
clas-si-cal
clas-si-cism
clas-si-cist
clas-si-fi-ca-tion
clas-si-fied
clas-si-fier
clas-sify
class-room
clause
cf. claws
claus-tro-pho-bia
claws
cf. clause
clean
clean—cut *(adj.)*
cleaner
clean-li-ness
cleanse
cleanser
clear
clear—cut *(adj.)*
clear-headed
cleav-age
cleave
cleaver
clem-ency
clench
cleric
cleri-cal
clerk
clue
or clew
cli-ché
click
cf. clique
cli-en-tele
cliff—hanger *(n.)*
cli-mate
cli-matic
cli-max
climb
climb-able
clinch
clincher
cling
clingy
clinic
clini-cal
clip
clipped
clip-per
clip-ping
clique
cf. click
cloak
clois-ter
close
cf. clothes
closer
closet
clo-sure
cloth
clothe
clothed
or clad
clothes
cf. close
cloth-ing
cloud
cloudy
clown
club
clubbed
club-bing
clum-sier
clum-si-ness
clumsy
clus-ter
clutch
clut-ter
coach
co-agu-late
co-agu-la-tion
co-ali-tion
coarse
cf. course
coarsen
coarser
coast
coaster
coax
co-ax-ial
co-balt
CO-BOL
or Co-bol
co-caine
cock-ier
cocki-ness
cocky
co-co-nut
co-coon
co-deine
codi-cil
codi-fi-ca-tion
codi-fied
cod-ify
coed
co-edu-ca-tion
co-ef-fi-cient

co-er-cion
co-ex-ist
co-ex-is-tence
co-ex-is-tent
cof-fee
cof-fer
cof-fin
cogi-tate
cog-nac
cog-ni-tive
cog-ni-zant
co-habit
co-habi-tant
co-habi-ta-tion
co-her-ence
co-her-ent
co-he-sion
co-he-sive
co-hort
coif-fure
coin-age
co-in-cide
co-in-ci-dence
co-in-ci-den-tal
co-itus
col-an-der
cold—blooded *(adj.)*
cold-hearted
cole-slaw
colic
coli-seum
col-labo-rate
col-labo-ra-tion
col-labo-ra-tor
col-lapse
col-laps-ible
col-lar
col-lat-eral
col-league
col-lect
col-lect-ible
col-lec-tion
col-lec-tive
col-lec-tiv-ism
col-lege
col-le-gian
col-le-giate
col-lide
col-li-sion
cf. **col-lu-sion**
col-lo-quial
col-lo-qui-al-ism
col-lo-quies
col-lo-quy
col-lu-sion
cf. **col-li-sion**
col-lu-sive
co-logne
co-lon
colo-nel
cf. **ker-nel**
co-lo-nial
colo-nies
colo-nist
colo-ni-za-tion
colo-nize
col-ony
co-los-sal
col-os-seum
col-our
col-umn
col-um-nist
coma
cf. **comma**
co-ma-tose
com-bat
com-bat-ant
com-bat-ive
com-bi-na-tion
com-bine
com-bus-ti-ble
com-bus-tion
co-me-dian
co-me-di-enne
come-dies
com-edy
come-lier
comely
come—on *(n.)*
come on *(v.)*
comet
com-fort
com-fort-able
com-forter
comic
comi-cal
comma
cf. **coma**
com-mand
com-man-dant
com-man-deer
com-mander
com-mander in chief
com-memo-rate
com-memo-ra-tion
com-memo-ra-tive
com-mence
com-mend
com-mend-able
com-men-da-tion
com-men-da-tory
com-men-su-ra-ble
com-men-su-ra-bly
com-men-su-rate
com-ment
com-men-tar-ies
com-men-tary
com-men-ta-tor
com-merce
com-mer-cial
com-mer-cial-ism
com-mer-cial-iza-tion
com-mer-cial-ize
com-mis-er-ate
com-mis-er-a-tion
com-mis-sar
com-mis-sary
com-mis-sion
com-mis-sioner
com-mit
com-mit-tal
com-mit-ted
com-mit-tee
com-mit-tee-man
com-mit-tee-woman
com-mit-ting
com-mode
com-modi-ties
com-mod-ity
common—law *(adj.)*
com-mon law *(n.)*

com-mon-wealth
com-mu-nal
com-mune
com-mu-ni-ca-ble
com-mu-ni-cate
com-mu-ni-ca-tion
com-mu-ni-ca-tive
com-mu-nion
com-mu-nism
com-mu-nist
com-mu-nis-tic
com-mu-ni-ties
com-mu-nity
com-mu-ta-tion
com-mute
com-muter
com-pact
com-pan-ion
com-pan-ion-able
com-pa-nies
com-pany
com-pa-ra-ble
com-para-tive
com-pare
com-pari-son
com-part-ment
com-pass
com-pas-sion
com-pas-sion-ate
com-pati-bil-ity
com-pati-ble
com-pel
com-pelled
com-pel-ling
com-pen-sate
com-pen-sa-tion
com-pen-sa-tor
com-pen-sa-tory
com-pete
com-pe-tence
com-pe-ten-cies
com-pe-tency
com-pe-tent
com-pe-ti-tion
com-peti-tive
com-peti-tor
com-pi-la-tion
com-pile
com-pla-cence
cf. **com-plai-sance**
com-pla-cency
com-pla-cent
com-plain
com-plain-ant
com-plainer
com-plai-sance
cf. **com-pla-cence**
com-plai-sant
com-plected
com-ple-ment
cf. **com-pli-ment**
com-ple-men-tary
com-plete
com-ple-tion
com-plex
com-plex-ion
com-plex-ity
com-pli-ance
com-pli-cate
com-pli-ca-tion
com-plic-ity
com-pli-ment
cf. **com-ple-ment**
com-pli-men-tary
com-plied
com-ply
com-po-nent
com-pose
com-poser
com-pos-ite
com-po-si-tion
com-po-sure
com-pound
com-pre-hend
com-pre-hen-si-ble
com-pre-hen-sion
com-pre-hen-sive
com-press
com-pres-sion
com-pres-sor
com-prise
com-pro-mise
com-pro-miser
com-pul-sion
com-pul-sive
com-pul-sory
com-punc-tion
com-pu-ta-tion
com-pute
com-puter
com-put-er-ize
com-rade
com-rad-ery
con-cave
con-ceal
con-ceal-able
con-cede
con-ceit
con-ceiv-able
con-ceive
con-cen-trate
con-cen-tra-tion
con-cen-tric
con-cept
con-cep-tual
con-cern
con-cert
con-certo
con-ces-sion
con-ces-sion-aire
con-cili-ate
con-cili-a-tion
con-cili-a-tor
con-cilia-tory
con-cise
con-clave
con-clude
con-clu-sion
con-clu-sive
con-coct
con-coc-tion
con-comi-tant
con-crete
con-cur
con-curred
con-cur-rence
con-cur-ring
con-cus-sion
con-demn
con-dem-na-tion

con-dens-able
or con-dens-ible
con-den-sa-tion
con-dense
con-denser
con-de-scend
con-de-scen-sion
con-di-ment
con-di-tion
con-di-tional
con-dole
con-do-lence
con-done
con-du-cive
con-duct
con-duc-tive
con-duc-tor
con-duit
cone
con-fec-tion
con-fec-tion-ary
con-fec-tion-ery
con-fed-er-acy
con-fed-er-ate
con-fed-er-a-tion
con-fer
con-feree
con-fer-ence
con-ferred
con-fer-ring
con-fess
con-fes-sion
con-fes-sional
con-fes-sor
con-fetti
con-fi-dant
cf. con-fi-dent
con-fi-dante
con-fide
con-fi-dence
con-fi-dent
cf. con-fi-dant
con-fi-den-tial
con-fine
con-firm
con-fir-ma-tion
con-fis-cate
con-fis-ca-tion
con-fla-gra-tion
con-flict
con-fluent
con-form
con-form-ance
con-for-ma-tion
con-form-ist
con-form-ity
con-found
con-front
con-fron-ta-tion
con-fuse
con-fu-sion
con-geal
con-genial
con-ge-ni-al-ity
con-geni-tal
con-gest
con-ges-tion
con-ges-tive
con-glom-er-ate
con-glom-era-tion
con-gratu-late
con-gratu-la-tion
con-gratu-la-tory
con-gre-gate
con-gre-ga-tion
con-gre-ga-tional
con-gru-ence
con-gru-ent
con-gru-ity
con-gru-ous
co-ni-fer
co-nif-er-ous
con-jec-tural
con-jec-turer
con-ju-gal
con-ju-gate
con-ju-ga-tion
con-junc-tion
con-junc-tive
con-jure
con-jurer
or con-juror
con-nect
con-necter
or con-nec-tor
con-nec-tion
con-nec-tive
con-niv-ance
con-nive
con-niver
con-nois-seur
con-no-ta-tion
con-note
con-nu-bial
con-quer
con-queror
con-quest
con-quis-ta-dor
con-quis-ta-do-res
con-science
con-sci-en-tious
con-scio-na-ble
con-scious
con-script
con-se-crate
con-se-cra-tion
con-se-cra-tor
con-secu-tive
con-sen-sus
con-sent
con-senter
con-se-quence
con-se-quent
con-se-quen-tial
con-ser-va-tion
con-ser-va-tion-ist
con-ser-va-tism
con-ser-va-tive
con-serve
con-sider
con-sid-er-able
con-sid-er-ate
con-sid-er-ation
con-sign
con-sign-able
con-signee
con-signor
con-sist
con-sis-tence
con-sis-tency

con-sis-tent
con-so-la-tion
con-sole
con-soli-date
con-soli-da-tion
con-sommé
con-so-nance
con-so-nant
con-spicu-ous
con-spir-a-cies
con-spir-acy
con-spire
con-sta-ble
con-stabu-lary
con-stant
con-stancy
con-stel-la-tion
con-ster-na-tion
con-stitu-en-cies
con-stitu-ency
con-stitu-ent
con-sti-tute
con-sti-tu-tion
con-sti-tu-tional
con-sti-tu-tion-al-ity
con-strain
con-straint
con-strict
con-stric-tion
con-stric-tive
con-stric-tor
con-struct
con-struct-ible
con-struc-tion
con-struc-tive
con-struc-tor
con-stru-able
con-strue
con-sul
con-sul-ate
con-sular
con-sult
con-sul-tant
con-sul-ta-tion
con-sume
con-sumer
con-sum-mate
con-sum-ma-tion
con-sump-tion
con-sump-tive
con-tact
con-ta-gion
con-ta-gious
con-tain
con-tainer
con-tami-nate
con-tami-na-tion
con-tami-na-tor
con-tem-plate
con-tem-pla-tion
con-tem-po-ra-ne-ous
con-tem-po-rary
con-tempt
con-tempt-ible
con-temp-tu-ous
con-tend
con-tender
con-tent
con-ten-tion
con-test
con-test-able
con-test-ant
con-text
con-tex-tual
con-ti-gu-ity
con-tigu-ous
con-ti-nence
cf. con-ti-nents
con-ti-nen-tal
con-tin-gency
con-tin-ent
con-tin-ual
con-tinu-ance
con-tinu-ation
con-ti-nu-ity
con-tinu-ous
con-tort
con-tor-tion
con-tor-tion-ist
con-tour
con-tra-band
con-tra-cep-tion
con-tra-cep-tive
con-tract
con-tract-ible
con-trac-tion
con-trac-tor
con-tra-dict
con-tra-dict-able
con-tra-dic-tion
con-tra-dictor
con-tra-dic-tory
con-trail
con-trari-ness
con-trary
con-trast
con-trast-able
con-tra-vene
con-trib-ute
con-tri-bu-tion
con-trib-u-tor
con-trib-u-tory
con-trite
con-tri-tion
con-triv-ance
con-trive
con-triver
con-trol
con-trol-la-ble
con-trolled
con-trol-ler
or comp-trol-ler
con-trol-ling
con-tro-ver-sial
con-tro-versy
con-tu-sion
con-va-lesce
con-va-les-cence
con-va-les-cent
con-vec-tion
con-vene
con-ve-nience
con-ve-nient
con-vent
con-ven-tion
con-ven-tional
con-verge
con-ver-gence
con-ver-gent
con-ver-sant
con-ver-sa-tion

con-ver-sa-tional
con-verse
con-ver-sion
con-vert
con-verter
or **con-ver-tor**
con-vert-ibil-ity
con-vex
con-vey
con-vey-ance
con-veyor
or **con-veyer**
con-vict
con-vic-tion
con-vince
con-vincer
con-viv-ial
con-viv-ial-ity
con-vo-ca-tion
con-voy
con-vulse
con-vul-sion
con-vul-sive
cool
coolly
coop
cf. **coupe**
co-op-er-ate
co-op-era-tion
co-op-era-tive
co-or-di-nate
co-or-di-nat-ing
co-or-di-na-tor
cope
co-pi-lot
co-pi-ous
cop—out *(n.)*
cop-per
copu-late
cop-ies
copy
copy-holder
co-quette
or **co-quet**
co-quet-tish
coral
cf. **choral**
cf. **chor-ale**
coral snake
cord
cf. **chord**
cord-age
cor-dial
cor-dial-ity
cor-don
core
cf. **corps.**
co-re-late
co-re-la-tion
co-re-spon-dent
cf. **cor-re-spon-dent**
cor-nea
cor-nu-co-pia
coro-nary
coro-na-tion
coro-ner
cor-po-ral
cor-po-rate
cor-po-ra-tion
corps
cf. **core**
cor-pu-lence
cor-pu-lent
cor-pus-cle
cor-ral
cor-ralled
cor-ral-ling
cor-rect
cor-rect-able
cor-rec-tion
cor-rec-tive
cor-rec-tor
cor-re-late
cor-re-la-tion
cor-re-spond
cor-re-spon-dence
cor-re-spon-dent
cf. **co-re-spon-dent**
cor-ri-dor
cor-robo-rate
cor-robo-ra-tion
cor-robo-rative
cor-robo-ra-tor
cor-rode
cor-ro-sion
cor-ro-sive
cor-ru-gate
cor-rupt
cor-rupter
or **cor-rup-tor**
cor-rupt-ible
cor-rupt-ibil-ity
cor-rup-tion
cor-sage
cor-tege
or **cor-tège**
cor-ti-sone
co-sine
cf. **co-sign**
cos-metic
cos-me-tolo-gist
cos-me-tol-ogy
cos-mic
cos-mo-naut
cos-mo-poli-tan
co—star
cost—of—living index *(n.)*
couch
cou-gar
cough
coun-cil
cf. **coun-sel**
coun-cil-lor
or **coun-cilor**
coun-sel-lor
or **coun-selor**
coun-sellor—at—law
coun-sellors—at—law
count-able
count-down
coun-te-nance
counter
coun-ter-ac-tion
coun-ter-clock-wise
coun-ter-es-pio-nage
coun-ter-feit
coun-tri-fied
or **coun-try-fied**
coun-try
coup
coup de grace

coup d'état
coupe
cf. **coop**
coups de grace *(pl.)*
coups d'état *(pl.)*
cou-ple
cou-pon
cour-age
cou-ra-geous
cou-rier
course
cf. **coarse**
court
court-house
cour-te-ous
cour-te-san
cour-tesy
court—martial
courts—martial *(pl.)*
cousin
cove
co-ven
cov-enant
cover
cov-er-all *(n.)*
cover—all *(adj.)*
co-vert
cover—up *(n.)*
cov-et-ous
cow-ard
cow-ard-ice
cow-ard-li-ness
cow-boy
cow-hand
cow-hide
coy
co-zier
crab
crabbed
crab-bing
crack
crack-down *(n.)*
crack down *(v.)*
cracker—barrel
crack—up *(n.)*
crack up *(v.)*
cra-dle
craft
craft-ier
crafty
cram
crammed
cram-ming
crane
cra-nium
crank
crank-ier
cranky
crash dive *(n.)*
crash hel-met *(n.)*
crash—land *(v.)*
crate
crater
crave
cra-ven
crawl
crayon
craze
cra-zier
cra-zi-ness
crazy
creak
cf. **creek**
creak-ier
creak-ily
cream
cream-ery
crease
cre-ate
cre-ation
cre-ative
cre-ator
crea-ture
cre-dence
cre-den-tial
credi-ble
credi-bil-ity
credit
cred-it-abil-ity
cred-it-ably
credit card *(n.)*
credi-tor
credo
credu-lous
creed
creek
cf. **creak**
cre-scendo
cres-cent
crest
cre-vasse
crev-ice
crew
crew cut *(n.)*
crib
crib-bage
cribbed
cribber
crib-bing
crick
cricket
crime
crimi-nal
crimi-nolo-gist
crimi-nol-ogy
crim-son
cringe
crin-kle
crip-ple
cri-ses *(pl.)*
cri-sis *(sing.)*
crisp
crisp-ier
crispy
criss-cross
cri-te-ria *(pl.)*
or **cri-te-rions**
cri-te-rion *(sing.)*
critic
criti-cal
criti-cism
criti-cize
criti-cizer
cri-tique
croak
cro-chet
crock-ery
croco-dile
cro-nies
crony

crop
cropped
crop-ping
cro-quet
cf. **cro-quette**
cross
cross—country *(n.)*
cross—examination *(n.)*
cross—examine
cross—reference
cross-road
crou-pier
cru-cial
cru-ci-ble
cru-ci-fied
cru-ci-fix
cru-ci-fix-ion
cru-cify
crude
cruder
cru-dity
cruel
cru-el-ties
cru-elty
cruise
cruiser
crumb
crum-ble
cf. **crum-ple**
crummy
or **crumby**
crunch
cru-sade
cru-sader
crus-ta-cean
crutch
crux
cried
cries
cry
cryp-tic
cryp-to-gram
crys-tal
crys-tal-line
crys-tal-li-za-tion
crys-tal-lize
or **crys-tal-ize**

cub-by-hole
cube
cubic
cu-bi-cal
cf. **cu-bi-cle**
cub-ism
cub-ist
cuck-old
cud-dle
cud-dly
cue
cf. **queue**
cui-sine
cuff link
cul—de—sac
cu-li-nary
cull
cul-mi-nate
cul-mi-na-tion
cul-pa-ble
cul-prit
cult
cul-ti-va-ble
or **cul-ti-vat-able**
cul-ti-vate
cul-ti-va-tion
cul-ti-va-tor
cul-tural
cul-ture
cul-vert
cum-ber-some
cum laude
cum-mer-bund
cu-mu-late
cu-mu-la-tion
cu-ne-ate
cun-ning
Cu-pid
cur-able
cure
cure—all *(n.)*
cur-dle
cur-few
cu-rio
cu-ri-os-ity
cu-ri-ous
curl

curler
curl-i-cue
or **curly-cue**
curl-ier
cur-rant
cf. **cur-rent**
cur-ren-cies
cur-rency
cur-ric-u-lums
or **cur-ric-ula** *(pl.)*
cur-ric-u-lar
cur-ric-u-lum
curry
curse
cur-sive
cur-sory
curt
cur-tail
curt-sied
or **curt-seyed**
curt-sies
or **curt-seys**
curtsy
or **curt-sey**
cur-va-ceous
or **cur-va-cious**
cur-va-ture
cush-ion
cus-tard
cus-to-dial
cus-to-dian
cus-tody
cus-tom
cus-tom-arily
cus-tom-ary
custom—built *(adj.)*
cus-tomer
custom—made
custom—tailor
cut
cut—and—dry
or **cut—and—dried** *(adj.)*
cut-lery
cut-off *(n.) (adj.)*
cu-ti-cle
cut-lass
cut-ter

cut-ting
cy-ana-mide
cya-nide
cy-ber-netic
cy-cle
cy-clic
cy-cli-cal
cy-clist
cyl-in-der
cy-clone
cy-clonic
cy-lin-dri-cal
cym-bal
cf. **sym-bol**
cynic
cyni-cal
cyni-cism
cyst
czar
cza-rina
czar-ism

D

dab-ble
dab-bler
dachs-hund
Da-cron
dag-ger
da-guerreo-type
dahlia
daily
dain-tier
dain-tily
dain-ti-ness
dainty
dair-ies
dairy
dais
dai-sies
daisy
dal-li-ance
dal-lied
dal-lier
dally
dam
cf. **damn**
dam-age
damned
dam-ming
dam-na-ble
dam-na-tion
damp
dampen
damper
dam-sel
dance
dancer
dan-de-lion
dan-ger
dan-ger-ous
dan-gle
dare
dare-devil
darer
dark
Dark Ages
darken
darn
dart
Dar-win
Dar-win-ian
Dar-win-ism
data *(pl.)*
or **da-tums**
da-ta-ma-tion
date
datum *(sing.)*
date
daub
daugh-ter
daunt-less
daw-dle
daw-dler
dawn
day—care *(adj.)*
daze
cf. **days**
daz-zle
daz-zler
D day
dea-con
dea-con-ess
dead
deaden
dead-line
dead-li-ness
dead-lock
deaf
deafen
deaf—mute *(n.)*
deal
dealer
dealt
dean
dear
cf. **deer**
dearth
death
death-bed
de-ba-cle
de-bark
de-bar-ka-tion
de-base
de-baser
de-bat-able
de-bate
de-bater
de-bauch
de-baucher
de-bauch-er-ies
de-bauch-ery
de-ben-ture
de-bili-tate
debit
debo-nair
de-bris *(sing. pl.)*
debt
debtor
de-bug
de-but
debu-tante
de-cade
deca-dence
deca-dent
de-cal
de-canter
de-capi-tate
de-capi-ta-tion

de-cay
de-cease
de-ce-dent
de-ceit
de-ceive
de-ceiver
de-cel-er-ate
de-cel-er-a-tion
de-cency
de-cent
de-cen-tral-iza-tion
de-cen-tral-ize
de-cep-tion
de-cep-tive
deci-bel
de-cide
de-cid-u-ous
deci-mal
deci-mal point
deci-mate
deci-ma-tion
de-ci-pher
de-ci-pher-able
de-ci-sion
de-ci-sive
deck
de-claim
de-clam-a-tory
dec-la-ra-tion
de-clara-tive
de-clare
de-clas-si-fied
de-clas-sify
de-clin-able
de-cline
de-code
dé-col-le-tage *(n.)*
dé-col-le-té *(adj.)*
de-com-pos-able
de-com-pose
de-com-po-si-tion
de-con-ges-tant
de-con-tami-nate
dé-cor
or de-cor
deco-rate
deco-ra-tion
deco-ra-tive
deco-ra-tor
de-co-rum
de-coy
de-crease
de-cree
de-crepit
de-cry
dedi-cate
dedi-ca-tion
de-duce
de-duc-ible
de-duct
de-duct-ible
de-duc-tion
de-duc-tive
deem
deep
deepen
deep—freeze *(v.)*
deep—six *(v.)*
deep six *(n.)*
deer
cf. dear
de-face
de facto
defa-ma-tion
de-fama-tory
de-fame
de-famer
de-fault
de-faulter
de-feat
de-feat-ism
de-feat-ist
defe-cate
de-fect
de-fec-tion
de-fec-tor
de-fec-tive
de-fence
or de-fense
de-fend
de-fend-able
de-fend-ant
de-fen-si-bil-ity
de-fen-si-ble
de-fen-sive
de-fer
def-er-ence
def-er-en-tial
de-ferred
de-fer-ring
de-fi-ance
de-fi-ant
de-fi-cien-cies
de-fi-cient
defi-cit
de-fied
de-fier
de-file
de-filer
de-fin-able
de-fine
defi-nite
defi-ni-tion
de-fini-tive
de-flate
de-fla-tion
de-fla-tor
de-flect
de-flec-tor
de-flo-ra-tion
de-flower
de-fo-liant
de-fo-li-ate
de-for-est
de-for-es-ta-tion
de-form
de-for-ma-tion
de-formi-ties
de-form-ity
de-fraud
de-fray
de-fray-able
de-funct
defy
de-gen-er-acy
de-gen-er-ate
de-gen-era-tion
de-grad-able
deg-ra-da-tion
de-grade
de-gree

de-hu-man-ize
de-hu-mid-ify
de-hy-drate
de-hy-dra-tion
de-icer
dei-fi-ca-tion
dei-fied
de-ify
de-ism
de-ist
de-is-tic
dei-ties
de-ity
de-jected
de-jec-tion
de-lec-ta-ble
dele-gate
dele-ga-tion
de-lete
de-le-tion
dele-te-ri-ous
de-lib-er-ate
de-lib-er-a-tion
deli-ca-cies
deli-cacy
deli-cate
deli-ca-tes-sen
de-li-cious
de-lin-eate
de-lin-ea-tion
de-lin-ea-tor
de-lin-quency
de-lin-quent
de-liri-ous
de-lir-ium
de-liver
de-liv-er-able
de-liv-er-ance
de-liv-erer
de-liv-er-ies
de-liv-ery
de-lude
de-lu-sion
de-lu-sive
del-uge
de-luxe
delve

dem-a-gogue
or dem-a-gog
de-mand
de-mar-ca-tion
or de-mar-ka-tion
de-mean
de-mented
de-men-tia
de-men-tia prae-cox
de-merit
de-mili-ta-ri-za-tion
de-mili-ta-rize
de-mise
demi-tasse
de-mo-bi-li-za-tion
de-mo-bi-lize
de-moc-racy
dem-o-crat
demo-cratic
de-moc-ra-ti-za-tion
de-moc-ra-tize
de-mol-ish
demo-li-tion
de-mon
or dae-mon
de-monic
or de-mon-i-cal
de-mon-stra-ble
dem-on-strate
dem-on-stra-tion
dem-on-stra-tor
de-mor-al-iza-tion
de-mor-al-ize
de-mor-al-izer
de-mote
de-mo-tion
de-mur
cf. de-mure
de-murred
de-murer
de-nial
denim
de-nomi-na-tion
de-nomi-na-tional
de-nomi-na-tor
de-note
de-nounce

dense
den-si-ties
den-sity
den-tal
den-ti-frice
den-tist
den-ture
de-nun-cia-tion
de-nied
deny
de-odor-ant
de-odor-ize
de-odor-izer
de-part
de-part-men-tal
de-par-ture
de-pend
de-pend-abil-ity
de-pend-able
de-pen-dant
de-pen-dence
or de-pen-dance
de-pen-den-cies
de-pen-dency
de-pen-dent
de-pict
de-plete
de-ple-tion
de-plor-able
de-plore
de-ploy
de-port
de-por-ta-tion
de-pose
de-posit
de-posi-tary
cf. de-posi-tory
de-pos-i-tor
dep-o-si-tion
de-pot
de-prave
de-prav-ity
dep-re-cate
dep-re-ca-tion
dep-re-ca-tory
de-pre-cia-ble
de-pre-ci-ate

de-pre-cia-tion
de-press
de-pres-sant
de-pres-sion
dep-ri-vation
de-prive
depth
depu-ties
depu-tize
dep-uty
de-rail
de-range
dere-lect
der-e-lic-tion
de-ride
deri-lict
de-riv-able
deri-va-tion
de-riv-a-tive
de-rive
de-roga-tory
der-rick
der-ri-ere
or **der-ri-ère**
der-rin-ger
de-scend
de-scend-ible
de-scent
de-scen-dant
or **de-scen-dent**
de-scrib-able
de-scribe
de-scriber
de-scrip-tion
de-scrip-tive
dese-crate
dese-crater
or **dese-cra-tor**
de-seg-re-gate
de-seg-re-ga-tion
de-sen-si-tize
de-sert
cf. **des-ert**
cf. **des-sert**
de-serter
de-ser-tion
de-serve
de-sign
de-signer
des-ig-nate
des-ig-na-tion
de-sir-abil-ity
de-sir-able
de-sire
de-sir-ous
de-sist
deso-late
deso-la-tion
de-spair
des-per-ado
des-per-ate
des-pera-tion
de-spi-ca-ble
de-spise
de-spite
de-spoil
de-spoiler
de-spond
de-spon-dence
de-spon-dency
des-pot
des-potic
des-po-tism
des-sert
cf. **de-sert**
cf. **des-ert**
des-sert-spoon
des-ti-na-tion
des-ti-nies
des-tiny
des-ti-tute
des-ti-tu-tion
de-stroy
de-stroyer
de-struc-ti-bil-ity
de-struc-ti-ble
de-struc-tion
de-struc-tive
des-ul-tory
de-tach
de-tach-able
de-tail
de-tain
de-tect
de-tect-able
de-tec-tion
de-tec-tor
de-ten-tion
de-ter
de-ter-gent
de-te-rio-rate
de-te-rio-ra-tion
de-ter-min-able
de-ter-mi-nant
de-ter-mi-nate
de-ter-mi-na-tion
de-ter-mine
de-ter-rence
de-ter-rent
de-test
de-test-able
de-throne
deto-na-ble
deto-nate
de-tour
de-toxi-fi-ca-tion
de-toxi-fied
de-tox-ify
de-tract
de-trac-tion
de-trac-tive
de-trac-tor
de-train
det-ri-ment
det-ri-men-tal
de-valu-ate
de-valu-ation
de-value
dev-as-tate
dev-as-ta-tion
de-velop
de-vel-op-able
de-vel-oper
de-vi-ance
de-vi-ate
de-vi-a-tion
de-vi-a-tor
de-vice
devil
dev-il-ish

dev-iltry
or dev-ilry
de-vi-ous
de-vis-able
de-vise
de-viser
de-vi-sor
de-void
de-volve
de-vote
devo-tee
de-vo-tion
de-vour
de-vourer
de-vout
dew
cf. do
cf. due
dew point
dex-ter-ity
dex-ter-ous
dex-trose
dia-be-tes
dia-betic
dia-bolic
dia-bol-i-cal
di-ag-nose
di-ag-no-ses
di-ag-no-sis
di-ago-nal
dia-gram
dia-gram-matic
dial
dia-lect
dia-lec-tic
dia-lec-ti-cal
dia-logue
or dia-log
di-al-y-sis
di-ame-ter
dia-met-ric
dia-mond
dia-per
dia-phragm
di-ar-rhoea
or di-ar-rhea
dia-ries
di-ary
dia-stolic
diced
di-chot-omy
dic-ing
dic-tate
dic-ta-tion
dic-ta-tor
dic-ta-tor-ship
dic-tion
dic-tio-nar-ies
dic-tio-nary
die
cf. dye
die—hard *(adj.)*
die-hard *(n.)*
die—off *(n.)*
die out *(v.)*
die-sel
diet
di-eti-tian
or di-eti-cian
di-etary
dif-fer
dif-fer-ence
dif-fer-ent
dif-fer-en-tial
dif-fer-en-ti-ate
dif-fer-en-ti-a-tion
dif-fi-cult
dif-fi-cul-ties
dif-fi-dence
dif-fi-dent
dif-fuse
dif-fu-sion
dig
di-gest
di-gest-ible
di-ges-tion
di-ges-tive
digged
dig-ging
digi-tal
dig-ni-fied
dig-nify
dig-ni-tar-ies
dig-ni-tary
dig-nity
di-gress
di-gres-sion
di-gres-sive
dike
di-lapi-date
di-lapi-da-tion
di-late
di-lemma
dil-et-tante
dil-et-tantes
or dil-et-tanti
dili-gence
dili-gent
dil-ly-dally
di-lute
di-lu-tion
di-men-sion
di-men-sional
di-min-ish
di-min-ish-able
dimi-nu-tion
di-minu-tive
dim-ple
dim-wit *(n.)*
dim—witted *(adj.)*
diner
cf. din-ner
dinga-ling *(n.)*
dinghies
din-ghy
din-gier
dingy
din-ner-ware
di-no-saur
di-oc-e-san
dio-cese
di-orama
diph-the-ria
diph-thong
di-ploma
di-plo-macy
dip-lo-mat
dip-lo-matic
dip-lo-mati-cally
dire
di-rect

di-rec-tion
di-rec-tional
di-rec-tive
di-rec-tor
di-rec-to-ries
di-rec-tory
dirge
di-ri-gi-ble
dirt
dirt farmer
dirt-ier
dirty
dis-abili-ties
dis-abil-ity
dis-able
dis-ad-van-tage
dis-ad-van-ta-geous
dis-agree
dis-agree-able
dis-al-low
dis-ap-pear
dis-ap-pear-ance
dis-ap-point
dis-ap-prove
dis-arm
dis-ar-ma-ment
dis-ar-range
dis-ar-ray
dis-as-ter
dis-as-trous
dis-avow
dis-avowal
dis-band
dis-bar
dis-barred
dis-bar-ring
dis-be-lief
dis-be-lieve
dis-burse
cf. dis-perse
disc
disc brake
dis-cern
dis-cern-ible
or dis-cern-able
dis-charge
dis-charge-able
dis-ci-ple
disc jockey *(n.)*
dis-claim
dis-claimer
dis-close
dis-clo-sure
dis-colour
dis-col-our-ation
dis-com-bobu-late
dis-com-fort
dis-con-nect
dis-con-so-late
dis-con-tent
dis-con-tinue
dis-con-tinu-ance
dis-cord
dis-cord-ance
dis-cord-ant
dis-co-theque
dis-count
dis-counter
dis-cour-age
dis-course
dis-cour-te-ous
dis-cour-tesy
dis-cover
dis-cov-er-able
dis-cov-erer
dis-cov-er-ies
dis-cov-ery
dis-credit
dis-cred-it-able
dis-creet
cf. dis-crete
dis-crep-an-cies
dis-crep-ancy
dis-cre-tion
dis-cre-tion-ary
dis-crimi-nate
dis-crimi-na-tion
dis-crimi-na-tive
dis-crimi-na-tor
dis-cursive
dis-cus
dis-cuss
dis-cuss-able
or dis-cuss-ible
dis-cus-sant
dis-cus-sion
dis-dain
dis-ease
dis-em-bark
dis-em-bar-ka-tion
dis-em-body
dis-en-gage
dis-favour
dis-fran-chise
dis-grace
dis-grun-tle
dis-guise
dis-gust
dish-cloth
dis-hearten
dis-hon-est
dis-hon-esty
dis-honour
dis-hon-our-able
dish-washer
dis-il-lu-sion
dis-in-cli-na-tion
dis-in-cline
dis-in-fect-ant
dis-in-herit
dis-in-te-grate
dis-in-te-gra-tion
dis-in-te-gra-tor
dis-in-ter
dis-in-ter-est
disk
dis-lik-able
dis-like
dis-lo-cate
dis-lo-ca-tion
dis-lodge
dis-loyal
dis-loy-alty
dis-mal
dis-man-tle
dis-may
dis-mem-ber
dis-miss
dis-missal
dis-mount
dis-obe-di-ence

dis-obe-di-ent
dis-obey
dis-or-der
dis-order-li-ness
dis-or-ga-nize
dis-ori-ent
dis-ori-en-tate
dis-ori-en-ta-tion
dis-own
dis-par-age
dis-pari-ties
dis-par-ity
dis-pas-sion-ate
dis-patch
dis-patcher
dis-pel
dis-pelled
dis-pel-ling
dis-pens-able
dis-pens-abil-ity
dis-pen-sa-ries
dis-pen-sary
dis-pen-sa-tion
dis-pense
dis-penser
dis-perse
cf. dis-burse
dis-persal
dis-perser
dis-pers-ible
dis-per-sion
dis-place
dis-play
dis-please
dis-pos-able
dis-posal
dis-pose
dis-po-si-tion
dis-pos-sess
dis-pos-ses-sion
dis-pos-ses-sor
dis-pro-por-tion
dis-pro-por-tional
dis-pro-por-tion-ate
dis-prove
dis-pu-ta-ble
dis-pute
dis-quali-fi-ca-tion
dis-quali-fied
dis-qual-ify
dis-re-gard
dis-repu-ta-ble
dis-re-pute
dis-re-spect
dis-robe
dis-rupt
dis-rupter
dis-rup-tion
dis-rup-tive
dis-sat-is-fac-tion
dis-sat-is-fac-tory
dis-sat-is-fied
dis-sat-isfy
dis-sect
dis-sec-tion
dis-semi-nate
dis-semi-na-tion
dis-semi-na-tor
dis-sen-sion
dis-sent
dis-senter
dis-sen-tient
dis-ser-ta-tion
dis-ser-vice
dis-si-dence
dis-si-dent
dis-si-pate
dis-si-pater
dis-si-pa-tion
dis-sol-uble
dis-solve
dis-solv-able
dis-taff
dis-tance
dis-tant
dis-taste
dis-tem-per
dis-tend
dis-till
dis-til-late
dis-til-la-tion
dis-tiller
dis-till-ery
dis-tinct
dis-tinc-tion
dis-tinc-tive
dis-tin-guish
dis-tin-guish-able
dis-tort
dis-tor-tion
dis-traught
dis-tress
dis-trib-ute
dis-tri-bu-tion
dis-tribu-tor
dis-trict
dis-trust
dis-turb
dis-turb-ance
dis-unity
ditch-dig-ger
ditto
di-ur-nal
dive
dive—bomb *(v.)*
dive—bomber *(n.)*
diver
di-verge
di-ver-gence
di-ver-gent
di-verse
di-ver-si-fi-ca-tion
di-ver-si-fied
di-ver-sion
di-ver-sion-ary
di-ver-sity
di-vert
di-verter
di-vest
di-vid-able
di-vide
divi-dend
di-vider
di-vine
diving bell *(n.)*
divining rod *(n.)*
di-vis-ible
di-vi-sion
di-vi-sive
di-vi-sor
di-vorce

di-vorcé
di-vorcée
di-vot
di-vulge
diz-zier
diz-zily
diz-zi-ness
dizzy
do
cf. **dew**
cf. **due**
doc-ile
do-cil-ity
dock
docket
dock-yard
doc-tor
doc-trine
doc-trinal
docu-ment
docu-men-tary
docu-men-ta-tion
dod-der
dodge
dodger
dodo
dodos
or **dodoes**
doe
cf. **dough**
dog
dog-cart
dog—ear *(n.)*
dog—eared *(adj.)*
dog—eat—dog *(adj.)*
dog-face
dog-gie bag
dog-house
dogma
dog-matic
dog-ma-tism
dog-ma-tist
dog-ma-ti-za-tion
dog-ma-tize
dog-ma-tizer
do—gooder *(n.)*
dog-tag
dol-drums
dole
dol-lar
dol-phin
do-main
do-mes-tic
do-mes-ti-cally
do-mes-ti-cate
do-mes-ti-ca-tion
do-mi-cile
domi-nance
domi-nant
domi-nate
domi-na-tion
domi-na-tor
domi-neer
do-min-ion
dom-ino
domi-noes
or **domi-nos**
do-nate
do-na-tion
don-ny-brook
doo-dle
dooms-day
door
door-bell
door-knob
door-step
door—to—door *(adj.)*
door-way
dopey
or **dopy**
dor-mant
dor-mer
dor-mi-to-ries
dor-mi-tory
dor-sal
dos-age
dose
do—si—do
dot-age
dou-ble
double—breasted *(adj.)*
double—cross *(v.)*
double—dealing *(n.)*
double—header *(n.)*
double—talk *(n.)*
dou-bloon
dou-bly
doubt
dough
cf. **doe**
dough-nut
douse
dove-tail
dow-ager
dowd-ier
dowdi-ness
dowdy
dowel
down
down—and—out *(adj.)*
down-fall
down-grade
down-hearted
dow-ries
dowry
dowse
drab
draft
draftee
cf. **drafty**
draft-ier
drafty
cf. **draftee**
drag-net
dragon
drain
drain-age
drama
dra-matic
dra-ma-tist
dra-ma-ti-za-tion
dra-ma-tize
drape
dra-per-ies
dra-pery
dras-tic
dras-ti-cally
draw
draw-back
drawl
drawn

dread
dream
dreamed
or **dreamt**
dreamer
dream-ier
dreamy
drea-rier
dreary
dredge
drench
dresser
dress-maker
dressy
drib-ble
dried
drift
drill
driller
drink
drink-able
drinker
drip
dripped
drip-ping
drive—in *(n.)*
drivel
driz-zle
droll
drone
drool
droop
drop-let
drought
or **drouth**
drown
drowse
drows-ier
drows-ily
drows-ing
drudge
drudg-ery
drug
drugged
drug-ging
drug-gist
drug-store
drum
drum-beat
drum major
drummed
drum-mer
drum-ming
drunk
drunk-ard
drunken
dry
dry cell
dry—clean *(v.)*
dryer
or **drier**
dual
cf. **duel**
du-al-ity
du-bi-ous
duct
dud
dude
due
cf. **dew**
cf. **do**
duel
cf. **dual**
du-eller
du-el-list
duet
dumb
dum-found
or **dumb-found**
dum-mies
dummy
dump
dunce
dun-geon
dun-nage
dupe
du-plex
du-pli-cate
du-pli-ca-tion
du-plic-ity
du-ra-ble
du-ra-bil-ity
du-ress
dusk-ier
duski-ness
dusky
du-ties
du-ti-ful
duty
dwarf
dwarf-ish
dwell
dweller
dwelt
or **dwelled**
dwin-dle
dye
cf. **die**
dyed—in—the—wool *(adj.)*
dy-namic
dy-na-mite
dy-namo
dy-nas-ties
dy-nasty
dys-tro-phy

E

ea-ger
ea-ger bea-ver
ea-gle
ear
ear-ache
ear-drum
ear-lier
early
ear-mark
ear-muffs
earn
cf. **urn**
ear-nest
ear-phone
ear-ring
ear-shot
earth
earthen
earth-en-ware
earth-quake
earth-ward

earth-worm
earthy
ease
ea-sel
ease-ment
eas-ier
easy
easy-go-ing
eat
eat-able
eaves-drop
ebb
ebb tide *(n.)*
ebony
ec-cen-tric
ec-cen-trici-ties
ec-cen-tric-ity
ec-cle-si-as-ti-cal
eche-lon
echo
ec-lec-tic
eclipse
eclip-tic
eco-log-ical
ecolo-gist
ecol-ogy
eco-nomic
eco-nomi-cal
econo-mist
econo-mize
econo-mizer
econ-omy
ec-sta-sies
ec-stasy
ec-static
ec-to-morph
ec-to-mor-phic
ec-to-plasm
ec-zema
edge
edge-wise
or edge-ways
eddy
edema
edgy
ed-ible
edict
edi-fi-ca-tion
edi-fice
edi-fied
ed-ify
edit
edi-tion
edi-tor
edi-to-rial
edi-to-ri-al-ize
edu-ca-ble
edu-cate
edu-ca-tion
edu-ca-tive
ee-rie
or eery
ee-rily
ef-face
ef-face-able
ef-facer
ef-fect
cf. af-fect
ef-fec-tive
ef-fec-tual
ef-fec-tu-ate
ef-fer-vesce
ef-fer-ves-cence
ef-fer-ves-cent
ef-fi-ca-cious
ef-fi-cacy
ef-fi-ciency
ef-fi-cient
ef-fi-gies
ef-figy
ef-flu-ent
cf. af-flu-ent
ef-fort
ef-fron-tery
egali-tar-ian
egg
egg-beater
egg-nog
egg-plant
egg-shell
ego
ego-cen-tric
ego-ism
ego-ist
ego-tism
ego-tist
ego-tis-tic
ego—trip *(n.)*
egress
ei-der
ei-der-down
eight
eight ball
eight-een
eighth
eighti-eth
eighty
ei-ther
ejec-tion
ejec-tor
eke
eke out *(v.)*
elabo-rate
elabo-ra-tion
elabo-ra-tive
elapse
elas-tic
elas-tic-ity
elate
ela-tion
el-bow
el-bow grease
el-bow room
elder
elect
elect-able
elec-tion
elec-tive
elec-tor
elec-toral
elec-tor-ate
elec-tric
elec-tri-cal
elec-tric eye
elec-tri-cian
elec-tric-ity
elec-tri-fi-ca-tion
elec-tri-fied
elec-trify
elec-trode
elec-tron

elec-tronic
ele-gance
ele-ment
ele-men-tal
ele-men-tary
cf. ali-men-tary
ele-phant
ele-phan-tine
ele-vate
ele-va-tion
ele-va-tor
eleven
elf
elfin
elf-ish
elicit
cf. il-licit
eli-gi-bil-ity
eli-gi-ble
Eli-jah
elimi-nate
elimi-na-tion
Eli-sha
elite
elixir
el-lipse
el-lip-ses
el-lip-sis
el-lip-ti-cal
elo-cu-tion
elo-cu-tion-ist
elon-gate
elon-ga-tion
elope
eloper
elo-quence
elo-quent
else-where
elu-ci-date
elu-ci-da-tion
elude
elu-sion
cf. al-lu-sion
cf. il-lu-sion
elu-sive
cf. al-lu-sive
elves

ema-ci-ate
ema-cia-tion
eman-ci-pa-tion
eman-ci-pa-tor
emas-cu-late
emas-cu-la-tion
em-balm
em-balmer
em-bank-ment
em-bargo
em-bar-goes
em-bark
em-bar-ka-tion
em-bar-rass
em-bas-sies
em-bassy
em-bat-tle
em-bed
em-bed-ded
em-bed-ding
em-bel-lish
em-bez-zle
em-bez-zler
em-bit-ter
em-blem
em-bod-ied
em-bodi-ment
em-body
em-bo-lism
em-brace
em-brace-able
em-bra-sure
em-broi-der
em-broi-derer
em-broi-dery
em-broil
em-bryo
em-bry-onic
em-cee
em-er-ald
emerge
emer-gence
emer-gen-cies
emer-gency
emer-gent
emer-ita
emer-iti *(pl.)*

emeri-tus
emer-sion
emi-grant
cf. im-mi-grant
emi-grate
émi-gré
or emi-gré
emi-nent
cf. im-mi-nent
emi-nent do-main
em-is-sar-ies
em-is-sary
emis-sion
emis-sive
emit
emit-ted
emit-ter
emit-ting
emol-lient
cf. emol-u-ment
emote
emo-tion
emo-tion-al-ism
em-pa-thic
em-pa-thize
em-pa-thy
em-peror
em-phases *(pl.)*
em-pha-sis
em-pha-sized
em-phatic
em-pire
em-piri-cal
em-piri-cism
em-piri-cist
em-ploy
em-ploy-able
em-ployee
or em-ploye
em-ployer
em-power
em-press
emp-tied
emp-ties
emp-ti-ness
empty
empty—handed *(adj.)*

emu-late
cf. **im-mo-late**
emu-la-tion
emul-si-fied
emul-sify
emul-sion
en-able
en-act
enamel
en-chant
en-chan-tress
en-cir-cle
en-close
en-clo-sure
en-code
en-core
en-coun-ter
en-cour-age
en-croach
en-cum-ber
en-cum-brance
en-cyc-li-cal
en-cy-clo-pae-dia
or **en-cy-clo-pe-dia**
en-cy-clo-pae-dic
or **en-cy-clo-pe-dic**
en-dan-ger
en-dear
en-deavour
en-dors-able
en-dorse
en-dor-see
en-dorser
en-dow
en-dur-ance
en-dur-able
en-dure
end zone
en-ema
ene-mies
en-emy
en-er-getic
en-er-geti-cally
en-er-gies
en-er-gize
en-er-gizer
en-ergy
en-fee-ble
en-fold
en-force
en-force-able
en-forcer
en-fran-chise
en-gage
en-gen-der
en-gine
en-gi-neer
Eng-lish
en-gorge
en-grave
en-graver
en-gross
en-gulf
en-hance
enigma
en-join
en-joy
en-joy-able
en-large
en-larger
en-lighten
en-list
en-liven
en masse
en-mi-ties
en-mity
en-no-ble
enor-mity
enor-mous
enough
en-quire
en-quiry
en-rage
en-rapt
en-rap-ture
en-rich
en-rol
or **en-roll**
en-rollee
en route
en-sconce
en-sconced
en-sem-ble
en-shrine
en-sign
en-slave
en-snare
en-sue
en-tail
en-tan-gle
en-ter
en-ter-prise
en-ter-tain
en-thral
or **en-thrall**
en-throne
en-thuse
en-thu-si-asm
en-thu-si-ast
en-thu-si-as-tic
en-tice
en-tire
en-tirety
en-ti-ties
en-ti-tle
en-tity
en-tomb
en-to-mol-ogy
en-tou-rage
en-train
en-trance
cf. **en-trants**
en-trap
en-treat
en-treat-ies
en-treaty
en-tree
or **en-trée**
en-trench
en-tre-pre-neur
en-tries
en-trust
en-twine
enu-mer-ate
enu-mera-tion
enu-mera-tive
enu-mera-tor
enun-ci-ate
enun-cia-tion
en-velop
cf. **en-ve-lope**

en-vi-able
en-vied
en-vies
en-vi-ous
en-vi-ron
en-vi-ron-men-tal
en-vi-ron-men-tal-ist
en-vi-rons
en-vis-age
en-vi-sion
en-voy
envy
en-zyme
épée
ephem-eral
epic
epi-cure
epi-demic
epi-lepsy
epi-lep-tic
epi-logue
epis-co-pal
Epis-co-pa-lian
epi-sode
epis-tle
epi-taph
epi-thet
epit-ome
epito-mize
ep-och
ep-ochal
equal
equal-ity
equal-iza-tion
equal-ize
equal-izer
equa-nim-ity
equate
equa-tion
equa-tor
equa-to-rial
eques-trian
eques-tri-enne
equi-lat-eral
equi-lib-rium
equine
equi-nox

equip
equipped
equip-ping
eq-ui-ta-ble
eq-uity
equiva-lence
equiva-lent
equivo-cal
equivo-cate
eradi-cate
eradi-ca-tion
eradi-ca-tor
erase
eras-able
eraser
era-sure
erect
erec-tion
erec-tor
ergo
erode
Eros
ero-sion
erotic
eroti-cism
er-rand
er-rant
er-rata *(pl.)*
er-ratic
er-ra-tum *(sing.)*
er-ro-ne-ous
er-ror
er-satz
erst-while
eru-dite
eru-di-tion
erupt
erup-tion
cf. ir-rup-tion
es-ca-late
es-ca-la-tion
es-ca-la-tor
es-ca-pade
es-cape
es-ca-pee
es-carp-ment
es-chew

es-cort
es-crow
eso-teric
es-pe-cial
es-pio-nage
es-pla-nade
es-pouse
es-prit de corps
es-say
cf. as-say
es-say-ist
es-sence
es-sen-tial
es-sen-ti-al-ity
es-tab-lish
es-tate
es-teem
es-thete
es-thetic
es-thet-ics
es-ti-ma-ble
es-ti-ma-tion
es-ti-ma-tor
es-tro-gen
es-tu-ary
et al
et cet-era
etch
eter-nal
eter-nity
ether
ethe-real
ethic
ethi-cal
eth-nic
eti-quette
Eu-cha-rist
eu-lo-gize
eu-logy
eu-phe-mism
eu-pho-ni-ous
eu-phony
Eur-asian
eu-reka
eu-tha-na-sia
evacu-ate
evacu-ation

evac-uee
evade
evad-able
evader
evalu-ate
evalu-ation
evalu-ator
evan-ge-lism
evan-ge-list
evapo-rate
evapo-ra-tion
evapo-ra-tor
eva-sion
eva-sive
eve
evec-tion
cf. evic-tion
eve-ning
event
even-tide
even-tual
even-tu-al-ity
ev-er-last-ing
ev-er-more
every
ev-ery-body
ev-ery-day
ev-ery-thing
ev-ery-where
evict
evic-tion
cf. evec-tion
evi-dence
evi-dent
evil
evil-doer
evil eye *(n.)*
evil—minded *(adj.)*
evoke
evo-lu-tion
evo-lu-tion-ary
evolve
ewe
cf. yew
cf. you
ex-ac-er-bate
ex-act
ex-ag-ger-ate
ex-ag-gera-tion
ex-ag-gera-tor
ex-alt
ex-al-ta-tion
ex-ami-na-tion
ex-am-ine
ex-am-iner
ex-am-ple
ex-as-per-ate
ex-as-pera-tion
ex-ca-vate
ex-ca-va-tion
ex-ca-va-tor
ex-ceed
cf. ac-cede
ex-cel
ex-celled
ex-cel-lence
ex-cel-lency
ex-cel-lent
ex-cel-ling
ex-cept
cf. ac-cept
ex-cep-tion
ex-cep-tion-able
ex-cerpt
ex-cess
cf. ac-cess
ex-ces-sive
ex-change
ex-change-able
ex-cise
ex-cit-able
ex-cite
ex-citer
ex-claim
ex-clama-tory
ex-clud-able
ex-clude
ex-cluder
ex-clu-sion
ex-clu-sive
ex-com-mu-ni-cate
ex-com-mu-ni-ca-tion
ex-creta
ex-cre-tion
ex-cru-ci-ate
ex-cru-ci-at-ing
ex-cus-able
ex-cuse
exe-cra-ble
exe-crate
exe-cra-tion
exe-cra-tive
exe-cute
exe-cu-tion
exe-cu-tioner
ex-ecu-tive
ex-ecu-tor
ex-em-plary
ex-em-plify
ex-emp-tion
ex-er-cise
cf. ex-or-cise
ex-ert
ex-er-tion
ex-ha-la-tion
ex-hale
ex-haust
ex-haust-ible
ex-haus-tion
ex-haus-tive
ex-hibit
ex-hi-bi-tion
ex-hi-bi-tion-ism
ex-hi-bi-tion-ist
ex-hibi-tor
ex-hila-rate
ex-hila-ra-tion
ex-hort
ex-hor-ta-tion
ex-horter
ex-hume
exi-gence
exi-gency
exi-gent
ex-ist
ex-ist-ence
ex-ist-ent
ex-is-ten-tial
ex-is-ten-tial-ism
ex-is-ten-tial-ist
exo-dus

ex of-fi-cio
ex-on-er-ate
ex-on-era-tion
ex-or-bi-tance
ex-or-bi-tant
ex-or-cise
cf. ex-er-cise
ex-otic
ex-pand
ex-panse
ex-pan-si-ble
ex-pan-sion
ex-pan-sive
cf. ex-pen-sive
ex-pa-tri-ate
ex-pa-tria-tion
ex-pect
ex-pect-ance
ex-pect-ant
ex-pec-ta-tion
ex-pe-di-ency
ex-pe-di-ence
ex-pe-di-ent
ex-pe-dite
ex-pe-diter
ex-pe-di-tion
ex-pe-di-tion-ary
ex-pe-di-tious
ex-pel
ex-pel-la-ble
ex-pelled
ex-pel-ler
ex-pel-ling
ex-pend
ex-pend-able
ex-pender
ex-pendi-ture
ex-pense
ex-pen-sive
cf. ex-pan-sive
ex-pe-ri-ence
ex-peri-ment
ex-peri-men-tal
ex-peri-men-ta-tion
ex-peri-menter
ex-pert
ex-pert-ise
ex-pert-ism
ex-pi-ate
ex-pia-tion
ex-pi-ra-tion
ex-pi-ra-tory
ex-pire
ex-plain
ex-pla-na-tion
ex-plana-tory
ex-ple-tive
ex-plic-able
ex-plicit
ex-plode
ex-ploit
ex-ploit-able
ex-ploi-ta-tion
ex-ploiter
ex-plo-ra-tion
ex-plora-tory
ex-plore
ex-plorer
ex-plo-sion
ex-plo-sive
ex-po-nent
ex-port
ex-port-able
ex-por-ta-tion
ex-porter
ex-pose *(v.)*
ex-posé *(n.)*
ex-poser
ex-po-si-tion
ex-posi-tive
ex post facto
ex-pos-tu-late
ex-po-sure
ex-pound
ex-pounder
ex-press
ex-press-age
ex-press-ible
ex-pres-sion
ex-pres-sion-ism
ex-pres-sive
ex-press-way
ex-pro-pri-ate
ex-pro-pria-tion
ex-pro-pria-tor
ex-pul-sion
ex-pul-sive
ex-punge
ex-pur-gate
ex-qui-site
ex-scind
ex-tant
cf. ex-tent
ex-tem-po-ral
ex-tem-po-ra-ne-ous
ex-tem-po-rary
ex-tem-pore
ex-tem-po-ri-za-tion
ex-tem-po-rize
ex-tem-po-rizer
ex-tend
ex-tend-ible
ex-ten-sible
ex-ten-sion
ex-ten-sive
ex-tent
cf. ex-tant
ex-tenu-ate
ex-tenu-ation
ex-tenu-ator
ex-te-rior
ex-ter-mi-nate
ex-ter-mi-na-tion
ex-ter-mi-na-tor
ex-ter-nal
ex-tinct
ex-tinc-tion
ex-tin-guish
ex-tin-guish-able
ex-tin-guisher
ex-tir-pate
ex-tol
or ex-toll
ex-tolled
ex-tol-ler
ex-tor-sion
cf. ex-tor-tion
ex-tort
ex-tor-tion
cf. ex-tor-sion
ex-tor-tioner

ex-tor-tion-ist
ex-tra
ex-tract
ex-tract-able
or **ex-tract-ible**
ex-trac-tion
ex-trac-tive
ex-trac-tor
ex-tra-cur-ricu-lar
ex-tra-dit-able
ex-tra-dite
ex-tra-di-tion
ex-tra-ne-ous
ex-tra-or-di-nary
ex-trapo-late
ex-tra-sen-sory
ex-tra-ter-res-trial
ex-trava-gance
ex-trava-gant
ex-trava-ganza
ex-treme
ex-trem-ism
ex-trem-ist
ex-trem-ity
ex-tri-ca-ble
ex-tri-cate
ex-tri-ca-tion
ex-trin-sic
ex-tro-vert
ex-trude
ex-tru-sion
exu-ber-ance
exu-ber-ant
exu-ber-ate
ex-ude
ex-ult
ex-ult-ant
ex-ul-ta-tion
eye
cf. **aye**
eyeball—to—eyeball *(adj.)*
eye bank *(n.)*
eye-let
eye-sore
eye-wit-ness

F

fa-ble
fab-ric
fab-ri-cate
fab-ri-ca-tion
fab-ri-ca-tor
fabu-lous
fa-çade
or **fa-cade**
facet
cf. **fau-cet**
face
face—lifting *(n.)*
face—saver *(n.)*
fa-ce-tious
face—to—face *(adj.)*
fa-cial
fac-ile
fa-cili-tate
fa-cili-ta-tion
fa-cili-ties
fa-cil-ity
fac-sim-ile
fac-tion
fac-tual
fac-to-ries
fac-tory
fac-ul-ties
fac-ulty
fad
fad-dish
fad-dist
fade
fag-got
or **fagot**
fahr-en-heit
fail
fail—safe *(adj.)*
fail-ure
faint
cf. **feint**
faint-hearted
fair
cf. **fare**
fair—minded *(adj.)*
fair-way
fair-ies
fairy
fairy-land
fait ac-com-pli *(n.)*
faith
fake
fak-ery
fal-la-cious
fal-lacy
fal-la-cies
fal-li-ble
fal-li-bil-ity
fall-out *(n.)*
fall out *(v.)*
false
false-hood
fal-setto
fal-si-fi-ca-tion
fal-si-fied
fal-sify
fal-ter
fa-mil-ial
fa-mil-iar
fa-mil-iar-ity
fa-mil-iar-iza-tion
fa-mil-iar-ize
fami-lies
fam-ily
fam-ine
fam-ish
fa-mous
fa-natic
fa-nati-cal
fa-nati-cism
fan-cied
fan-cier
fancy
fancy—free *(adj.)*
fan-cy-work *(n.)*
fan-fare
fan-fold
fan—jet
fan-ta-sia
fan-ta-sies
fan-ta-size
fan-tasy
far

far-away
farce
far-ci-cal
fare
cf. fair
fare-well
far-fetched
far—flung
farm
farmer
farm-hand
farm-house
farm-yard
far—off *(adj.)*
far—out *(adj.)*
far-sighted
far-ther
far-ther-most
far-thest
fas-ci-nate
fas-ci-na-tion
fas-cism
fas-cist
fash-ion
fash-ion-able
fas-ten
fast—food *(adj.)*
fas-tidi-ous
fast—talk *(v.)*
fa-tal
fa-tal-ism
fa-tal-ist
fa-tal-is-tic
fa-tal-ity
fate
cf. fete
or fête
fa-ther
fa-ther-hood
fa-ther-land
fathers—in—law
fathom
fath-om-able
fa-tigue
fat—soluble *(adj.)*
fat-ten
fat-ter
fatty
fatu-ous
fau-cet
cf. facet
fault
fault-finder
fault-ier
faun (deity)
cf. fawn (deer)
faux pas
fa-vour
fa-vour-able
fa-vour-ite
fa-vour-it-ism
faze
cf. phase
fe-alty
fear
fear-some
fea-si-ble
fea-si-bil-ity
feast
feat
cf. feet
feather
feath-er-weight
fea-ture
fe-cund
fe-cun-dity
fed-eral
fed-er-al-ism
fed-er-al-ist
fed-er-al-iza-tion
fed-er-al-ize
fed-er-ate
fed-er-a-tion
fe-dora
fee-ble
fee-ble-minded *(adj.)*
fee-bly
feed-back *(n.)*
feet
cf. feat
feign
feint
cf. faint
fe-lici-tate
fe-lici-ta-tion
fe-lici-ties
fe-lici-tous
fe-line
fel-low
fel-low-ship
felon
felo-nies
fe-lo-ni-ous
fel-ony
felt
fe-male
femi-nine
femi-nin-ity
femme fa-tale *(n.)*
fence
fend
fender
fer-ment
fer-men-ta-tion
fe-ro-cious
fer-ret
fer-ried
ferry
fer-ry-boat
fer-tile
fer-til-ity
fer-til-iza-tion
fer-til-ize
fer-til-izer
fer-vent
fer-vid
fer-vour
fes-cue
fes-ti-val
fes-tive
fes-tivi-ties
fes-tiv-ity
fes-toon
fe-tal
fetch
fete
or fête
cf. fate
fetid
fe-tish
or fe-tich

fe-tish-ism
or **fe-tich-ism**
fe-tus
feud
feu-dal
feu-dal-ism
fe-ver
fe-ver-ish
fi-ancé
fi-an-cée
fi-asco
fi-as-cos
fiat
fib
fibbed
fib-ber
fib-bing
fi-bre
or **fi-ber**
fi-brous
fiche
cf. **fish**
fickle
fic-tion
fic-tional
fic-ti-tious
fi-deli-ties
fi-del-ity
fidget
fidg-eti-ness
fid-gety
fi-du-cia-ries
fi-du-ciary
fief
fief-dom
field
fielder
field goal *(n.)*
fiend
fiend-ish
fierce
fiercer
fierc-est
fi-ery
fi-esta
fif-teen
fif-teenth
fif-ti-eth
fif-ties
fifty
fifty—fifty *(adj.)*
fig-ment
fig-ura-tive
fig-ure
fig-ure-head
fila-ment
fil-ial
fili-bus-ter
film
film-strip
fil-ter
fil-ter-able
or **fil-tra-ble**
filth
filth-ier
filthi-ness
filthy
fil-trate
fil-tra-tion
fi-na-gle
fi-na-gler
fi-nal
fi-nale
fi-nal-ist
fi-nal-ity
fi-nal-ize
fi-nance
fi-nan-cial
fin-an-cier
finder
fin-er-ies
fin-ery
fi-nesse
fin-est
fine—tooth comb *(n.)*
fin-ger
fin-ger-nail
fin-ger-print
fin-icky
or **fini-cal**
fin-ish
fin-isher
fi-nite
fir
cf. **fur**
fire
fire-arm
fire-ball
fire-bomb
fire-cracker
fire en-gine *(n.)*
fire es-cape *(n.)*
fire ex-tin-guisher *(n.)*
fire-fly
fire-man
fire-place
fire-power
fire-proof
fire-side
fire-trap
fire-wood
first
first aid *(n.)*
first base *(n.)*
first-born
first class *(n.)*
first—rate *(adj.)*
fis-cal
fish
cf. **fiche**
fish *(pl.)*
or **fishes**
fish—and—chips
(n. pl.)
fish-ery
fis-sion
fis-sion-able
fis-sure
fist
fisti-cuffs
five—and—ten *(n.)*
fix
fix-ate
fixa-tion
fix-ture
fiz-zle
flab-ber-gast
flab-bier
flab-bi-ness
flabby

flac-cid
flag
flag-el-late
flagged
flag-ging
flagon
flag-stone
flair
cf. **flare**
flak
flake
flak-ier
flaki-ness
flaky
flam-boy-ance
flam-boy-ant
flame
flam-ma-ble
flange
flank
flare
cf. **flair**
flare—up *(n.)*
flan-nel
flash
flash-bulb
flash-cube
flash flood
flash-gun
flash-ier
flashi-ness
flash-light
flask
flat
flat-boat
flat-car
flat—footed *(adj.)*
flat-ten
flat-ter
flat-tish
flat-top
flat-tery
flaunt
fla-vour
flaw
flea
cf. **flee**

flea market *(n.)*
fleet
flesh
flesh and blood *(n.)*
flesh—coloured
flesh-ier
fleshi-ness
flew
cf. **flu**
cf. **flue**
flex
flexi-ble
flex-ion
flib-ber-ti-gib-bet
flick
flier
or **flyer**
flies
flight
flight-ier
flighti-ness
flighty
flim-flam
flim-sier
flim-si-ness
flimsy
fling
flint
flip
flip—flop *(n.) (v.)*
flip-pancy
flip-pant
flipped
flip-per
flirt
flir-ta-tion
flir-ta-tious
flirter
flit-ter
float
flock
floe
cf. **flow**
flog
flood
flood-gate
flood-light

floor
floor show *(n.)*
floor-walker
flop
flop-house
flopped
flop-pier
flop-pi-ness
floppy
flora
flo-ral
floras
or **flo-rae** *(n. pl.)*
flo-rist
florid
floss
flo-ta-tion
flo-tilla
flot-sam
flounce
floun-der
flour
cf. **flower**
flour-ish
flout
flow
cf. **floe**
flow-chart
flow-diagram
flower
cf. **flour**
flow-er-pot
flow-ery
flown
flu
cf. **flew**
cf. **flue**
fluc-tu-ate
fluc-tua-tion
flu-ency
flu-ent
fluff
fluff-ier
fluffi-ness
fluffy
fluid
flu-id-ity

fluke
fluky
or flukey
flume
flung
flunkey
or flunky
fluo-res-cence
fluo-res-cent
fluori-date
fluori-da-tion
fluo-ride
flur-ries
flurry
flush
flus-ter
flute
flut-ist
flut-ter
flux
fly
fly-able
fly ball *(n.)*
fly—by—night *(adj.)*
flyer
or flier
fly-wheel
foal
foam
foam-ier
fob
fo-cal
fo-cus
fo-cuses
or foci
fod-der
foe
fog
fogged
fog-gier
fog-gi-ness
fog-ging
fog-horn
foi-ble
foist
fold
fo-li-age
fo-li-ate
fo-lio
folk
folk dance
folk-lore
folk music
folk-sier
folk-singer
folksy
folk-tale
fol-li-cle
fol-low
follow—through *(n.)*
follow—up *(adj.) (n.)*
fol-low up *(v.)*
fol-lies
folly
fo-ment
fond
fon-dle
fon-due
food stamp
fool
fool-har-di-ness
fool-hardy
fool-proof
fool's gold
fool's par-a-dise
foot
foot-age
foot-ball
foot-can-dle
foot—drag-ging *(n.)*
foot-hold
foot-lights
foot-loose
foot-note
foot-path
foot-print
foot sol-dier
foot-sore
foot-stool
fop
fop-pish
fop-pish-ness
for-age
foray
for-bid
or for-bade
or for-bad
for-bear-ance
for-bid-den
for-bid-ding
for-bore
for-borne
force
for-ceps
forc-ing
ford
fore
cf. four
fore-arm
fore-bear
or for-bear
fore-bode
fore-cast
fore-clo-sure
fore-fa-ther
forego
fore-ground
fore-head
for-eign
for-eign af-fairs
for-eign—born *(adj.)*
for-eigner
fore-man
fore-most
fore-noon
fo-ren-sic
fore-see
fore-sight
for-est
fore-stall
for-ester
for-estry
fore-tell
for-ever
for-ever-more
fore-warn
fore-word
for-feit
for-fei-ture
for-gave
forge

for-ger-ies
for-gery
for-get
forget—me—not
for-get-ta-ble
for-get-ting
for-giv-able
for-give
for-giver
forgo
or forego
for-lorn
for-mal
form-al-de-hyde
for-mal-ism
for-mal-ist
for-mali-ties
for-mal-ity
for-mal-iza-tion
for-mal-ize
for-mat
for-ma-tion
for-ma-tive
for-mer
for-mi-da-ble
for-mula
for-mu-las
or for-mu-lae
for-mu-late
for-sake
for-saken
for-sook
fort
cf. forte
for-ti-fi-ca-tion
for-tify
forth
cf. fourth
forth-right
forth-with
for-ti-eth
for-ti-tude
fort-night
FOR-TRAN
or For-tran
for-tui-tous
for-tu-ity
for-tu-nate
for-tune
for-tune—teller
forty
forty—niner
fo-rum
for-ward
fos-sil
fos-ter
fought
foul
cf. fowl
foul line *(n.)*
foul—up *(n.)*
foul up *(v.)*
found
foun-da-tion
founder
found-ries
foundry
foun-tain
foun-tain-head
foun-tain pen *(n.)*
four
cf. fore
four—dimensional *(adj.)*
four-fold
four—footed *(adj.)*
four—poster
four-score
four-some
four-teen
fourth
cf. forth
fowl
cf. foul
fox
foxes *(n. pl.)*
fox-ier
fox-hole
fox-tail
fox—trot *(n.) (v.)*
foxy
foyer
fra-cas
frac-tion
frac-ture
frag-ile
fra-gil-ity
frag-ment
frag-men-tary
frag-men-ta-tion
fra-grance
fra-grant
frail
frail-ties
frailty
frame
frame—up *(n.)*
frame-work
franc
cf. frank
fran-chise
fran-chi-see
frank-furter
fran-tic
fra-ter-nal
fra-ter-nity
fra-ter-ni-za-tion
fra-ter-nize
frat-ri-cide
fraud
fraudu-lence
fraudu-lent
fraught
fray
fraz-zle
freak
freak-ish
freckle
free
free-dom
free enterprise
free—fall *(n.)*
free—for—all *(n.)*
free-hand
free—lance *(v.)*
(adj.)
freer
free love
free-thinker
free-way
free-will *(adj.)*
freeze

freezer
freight
fren-zied
frenzy
fre-quence
fre-quency
fre-quent
fresh
freshen
fresh-wa-ter *(adj.)*
fret
fret-ted
fret-ting
friar
cf. **fryer**
fric-as-see
fric-tion
friend
friend-lier
friend-li-ness
fright
frighten
frigid
fri-gid-ity
frilly
fringe
fringe benefit *(n.)*
Fris-bee
frisk
frisk-ier
friski-ness
frisky
frit
frit-ter
fri-vol-ity
frivo-lous
frock
frog-man
frolic
frol-icked
frol-ick-ing
frol-ic-some
front
front-age
fron-tal
fron-tier
fron-tiers-man
fron-tis-piece
front office
frost
frost-bite
frost-ier
frosty
froth
froth-ier
frown
frowzy
or **frowsy**
froze
fro-zen
fruc-tose
fru-gal
fruit
fruit fly
frui-tion
fruity
frump
frus-trate
frus-tra-tion
fuch-sia
fuddy—duddy *(n.)*
fudge
fuel
fu-gi-tive
ful-crum
ful-fil
or **ful-fill**
full
full-back
full—blooded *(adj.)*
full—dress *(adj.)*
fum-ble
fu-mi-gate
fu-mi-ga-tion
fu-mi-ga-tor
func-tion
func-tional
fun-da-men-tal
fun-da-men-tal-ism
fun-da-men-tal-ist
fu-neral
fu-ne-real
fun-gi-cide
fun-gus
fungi *(n. pl.)*
or **fun-guses**
fun-nel
fun-nier
funny
funny bone
fur
cf. **fir**
fu-ri-ous
furl
fur-long
fur-lough
fur-nace
fur-nish
fur-ni-ture
fu-ror
furred
fur-rier
fur-row
furry
fur-ther
fur-ther-ance
fur-ther-more
fur-ther-most
fur-thest
fur-tive
fury
fuse
cf. **fuze**
fu-se-lage
fu-sil-lade
fu-sion
fuss
fuss-ier
fussy
fu-tile
fu-til-ity
fu-ture
fu-tur-is-tic
fu-tu-rity
fuze
cf. **fuse**
fuzz
fuzz-ier
fuzzi-ness
fuzzy

G

gab-ar-dine
gab-fest
ga-ble
gad-get
gad-ge-teer
gage
cf. gauge
gai-ety
gaily
gain
gait
cf. gate
gala
gal-axy
gale
gall
gal-lant
gal-lantry
gal-leon
gal-ler-ies
gal-lery
gal-ley
gal-lon
gal-lop
gal-lows
ga-lore
gal-va-ni-za-tion
gal-va-nize
gam-bit
gam-ble
cf. gam-bol
gam-bler
game
gamut
gang
gang-plank
gan-grene
gan-gre-nous
gang-ster
gap
gape
ga-rage
garb
gar-bage
gar-ble
gar-çon
gar-den
gar-dener
gar-de-nia
gar-gle
gar-goyle
gar-ish
gar-land
gar-lic
gar-ment
gar-ner
gar-nish
gar-nishee
gar-ri-son
gar-rotte
gar-ru-lous
gas
gas-eous
gases *(n. pl.)*
gash
gas-ket
gas mask
gaso-line
or gaso-lene
gasp
gassed
gas-sing
gas sta-tion
gassy
gas-tric
gas-tro-in-tes-ti-nal
gas-tro-nomic
gate
cf. gait
gate-way
gather
gath-erer
gaud-ier
gaudi-ness
gaudy
gauge
cf. gage
gauge-able
gauger
gaunt
gaunt-let
gauze
gave
gavel
gawk
gawk-ier
gawki-ness
gay
gayer
gaze
ga-zebo
ga-zelle
gazer
ga-zette
gaz-et-teer
gear
gear-shift
gee
geese
gee—whiz *(adj.)*
Gei-ger counter
gei-sha
gela-tin
or gela-tine
geld
gem
Gem-ini
gen-darme
gen-der
gen-eral
gen-er-al-ist
gen-er-al-ity
gen-er-al-iza-tion
gen-er-al-ize
gen-er-ate
gen-era-tion
gen-era-tive
gen-era-tor
ge-neric
gene-sis
ge-netic
ge-nius
geno-cide
gen-teel
gen-tile
gen-til-ity
gen-tle
gen-tle-man
gen-tle-woman

gen-try
genu-flect
genu-ine
ge-nus
geo-desic
ge-og-ra-pher
geo-graphic
geo-graphi-cal
ge-og-raphy
ge-olo-gist
ge-ol-ogy
geo-met-ric
geo-met-ri-cal
ge-om-e-try
geo-phys-i-cist
geo-phys-ics
geri-at-ric
germ
germ cell
ger-mi-cidal
ger-mi-cide
ger-mi-nate
ger-mi-na-tion
germ warfare
ge-stalt
ge-stapo
ges-tate
ges-ta-tion
ges-ture
ge-sund-heit
get
get-away
get—to-gether *(n.)*
get—up *(n.)*
get up *(v.)*
gey-ser
ghast-lier
ghast-li-ness
ghastly
ghetto
ghet-tos *(n. pl.)*
or **ghet-toes**
ghost
ghost-lier
ghost—write *(v.)*
ghoul
gi-ant
gib-ber
gib-ber-ish
gib-bet
gid-di-ness
giddy
gift
gi-gan-tic
gig-gle
gig-gler
gig-gly
gig-olo
gild
cf. **guild**
gilt
cf. **guilt**
gilt—edged
or **gilt—edge** *(adj.)*
gim-mick
gin-ger
gin-ger ale
gin-ger-bread
gin-ger-li-ness
gin-gerly
ging-ham
gi-raffe
gird
girded
or **girt**
girder
gir-dle
girl
girl-ish
girl-friend
girth
gist
give
give—and—take *(n.)*
give-away *(n.)*
give away *(v.)*
given
gla-cial
gla-cier
glad
glad—hand *(v.)*
gladi-ator
glam-orize
or **glam-our-ize**
glam-or-ous
glam-our
or **glamor**
glance
gland
glan-du-lar
glare
glass
glass-ier
glassi-ness
glass-ware
glassy
glau-coma
glaze
gleam
glean
glee
glee club *(n.)*
glen
glib
glide
glider
glide path *(n.)*
glim-mer
glimpse
glint
glis-ten
glit-ter
glit-tery
gloat
gloater
global
globe
globe—trotter *(n.)*
globu-lar
glob-ule
gloom
gloom-ier
gloomi-ness
gloomy
glo-ri-fi-ca-tion
glo-ri-fied
glo-rify
glo-ri-ous
gloss
glos-sa-ries
glos-sary

glossi-est
glossy
gloss-ies
glow
glue
gluey
glum
glum-mer
glut
glut-ted
glut-ting
glut-tony
glyc-erin
or glyc-er-ine
gnarl
gnash
gnat
gnaw
gnome
go—ahead *(n.)*
goal
goat
go—between
gob-ble
gob-let
gob-lin
god-child
god-dess
god-fa-ther
god-for-saken
god-mother
god-par-ent
god-send
god-son
goi-tre
or goi-ter
gold
golden
golden rule
gold—filled *(adj.)*
gold-fish
gold leaf
gold rush
golf
gon-dola
gone
gong
gon-or-rhoea
good—bye
or goodbye
good—for—nothing *(adj.)*
good—hearted
good—looking *(adj.)*
goof
goose
goose flesh
gore
gor-geous
gori-est
gory
gos-ling
gos-pel
gos-sip
gos-sipy
got
got-ten
gouge
gouger
gourd
gour-met
gov-ern
gov-ern-ance
gov-ern-ess
gov-er-nor
gown
grab
grabbed
grab-bing
grabby
grace
gra-cious
gra-da-tion
grade
grade school
grad-ual
gradu-ate
gradu-ation
graf-fiti *(n. pl.)*
graf-fito *(n. sing.)*
graft
grain
gram
gram-mar
gram-mar-ian
gram-mar school
gram-mati-cal
grand
grand-child
grand-daugh-ter
grand duch-ess
gran-dee
gran-deur
grand-fa-ther
gran-dilo-quence
gran-di-ose
grand jury
grand-mother
grange
gran-ite
grant
granu-lar
granu-late
granu-la-tion
gran-ule
grape
grape-fruit
grape-shot
grape-vine
graph
graphic
graph-ite
grap-nel
grap-ple
grasp
grasp-able
grasper
grass
grass-hop-per
grass-ier
grass-land
grass—roots
grassy
grate
cf. great
grati-fi-ca-tion
grati-fied
grat-ify
gra-tis
grati-tude
gra-tu-itous
gra-tu-ity

grave
gravel
graven
grave-stone
grave-yard
gravi-tate
gravi-ta-tion
grav-ity
gra-vies
gravy
graze
grease
greas-ier
greasi-ness
greasy
great
cf. **grate**
great—aunt
great circle
great-uncle
greed
greed-ier
greed-ily
greedi-ness
greedy
green
green-back
green-house
green thumb *(n.)*
greet
greeter
gre-gari-ous
grem-lin
gre-nade
grena-dier
grew
grey
or **gray**
grey-hound
grey-ish
or **gray-ish**
grid
grid-dle
grid-iron
grief
griev-ance
grieve
griev-ous
grill
cf. **grille**
grim
gri-mace
grime
grim-ier
grimi-ness
grimy
grin
grind
grinder
grind-stone
gringo
grinned
grin-ning
grip
cf. **grippe**
gripe
gripped
grip-ping
gris-li-est
grisly
gris-tle
grit
griz-zled
griz-zly
griz-zly bear
groan
gro-cer
gro-cer-ies
gro-cery
grog
grog-gier
grog-gi-ness
groggy
groin
grom-met
groom
groove
grope
gross
gro-tesque
grotto
grouch
grouchi-est
grouchy
ground
ground floor
ground rule
ground-work
group
group ther-apy
grouse
grout
grove
grovel
growl
grown—up *(adj.) (n.)*
growth
grub
grubbed
grub-bier
grub-bi-ness
grub-bing
grubby
grub-stake
grudge
gruel
gru-el-ling
grue-some
gruff
grum-ble
grum-bler
grump-ier
grumpi-ness
grumpy
grunt
guar-an-tee
guar-an-teed
guar-an-ties
guar-an-tor
guar-anty
guard-house
guard-ian
guess
guess-work
guest
guf-faw
guid-ance
guide
guide-book
guild
cf. **gild**

guile
guil-lo-tine
guilt
cf. **gilt**
guilt-ier
guilti-ness
guilty
guinea pig
gui-tar
gulf
gull
gul-let
gul-li-ble
gul-lies
gully
gulp
gump-tion
gun
gun-boat
gun-fire
gung ho *(adj.)*
gun-ner
gun-nery
gun-pow-der
gur-gle
guru
gush
gusher
gush-ier
gushy
gust-ier
gusto
gusty
gut
gut-ter
gut-tural
guz-zle
gym-na-sium
gym-nast
gym-nas-tic
gy-nae-col-ogy
gyp-sum
gyp-sies
gypsy
gy-rate
gy-ra-tion
gy-ro-scope

H

ha-beas cor-pus
hab-er-dasher
hab-er-dash-ery
habit
hab-it-able
ha-bi-tant
ha-bi-tat
habi-ta-tion
habit—forming *(adj.)*
ha-bit-ual
ha-bit-u-ate
ha-bi-tué
hack-saw
Ha-des
hae-mo-glo-bin
or **he-mo-glo-bin**
haem-or-rhage
or **hem-or-rhage**
hag
hag-gard
hag-gle
hag-gler
hail
cf. **hale**
Hail Mary
hail-stone
hail-storm
hair
cf. **hare**
hair-breadth
hair-cut
hair-dresser
hair-ier
hair-line
hair-piece
hair-pin
hair—raising *(adj.)*
hair-split-ting
hair-spring
hair-styl-ist
hair—trigger *(adj.)*
hair trigger *(n.)*
hairy
hale
cf. **hail**

half
half—and—half *(n.)*
half-back
half—baked *(adj.)*
half—breed *(n.)*
half brother *(n.)*
half—caste *(n.)*
half—cocked *(adj.)*
half—dollar *(n.)*
half-hearted *(adj.)*
half hour
half nel-son
half note
half sis-ter
half-way
half—wit *(n.)*
hali-to-sis
hall
cf. **haul**
hal-le-lu-jah
or **al-le-luia**
hall-mark
hall-way
hal-low
Hal-low-een
hal-lu-ci-nate
hal-lu-ci-na-tion
hal-lu-ci-na-tory
hal-lu-ci-no-gen
hal-lu-ci-no-sis
halo
halt
hal-ter
halve
ham-burger
ham-let
ham-mer
hammer—and—tongs *(adj.)*
ham-mock
ham-per
ham-string
hand
hand-bag
hand-ball
hand-bill
hand-book

hand-cuff
handi-cap
handi-craft
handi-work
hand-ker-chief
hand-ker-chiefs
or **hand-ker-chieves**
han-dle
hand-made
cf. **hand-maid**
hand—me—down *(adj.)*
hand-shake
hand-some
hand—to—mouth *(adj.)*
hand-work
hand-writ-ing
hand-writ-ten
hand-wrote
hand-ier
handy
handy-man
hang
hangar
cf. **hanger**
hang—up *(n.)*
hang up *(v.)*
hank
han-ker
hanky—panky *(n.)*
Ha-nuk-kah
or **Cha-nu-kah**
hap-haz-ard
hap-less
hap-pen
hap-pier
hap-pily
hap-pi-ness
happy
happy-go-lucky
hara—kiri
ha-rangue
ha-rass
har-bin-ger
har-bour
hard
hard—and—fast *(adj.)*
hard—bitten *(adj.)*
hard—boiled *(adj.)*
hard—core *(adj.)*
harden
hard—headed *(adj.)*
hard—hearted *(adj.)*
hard—hitting *(adj.)*
har-dier
hard-ship
hard-ware
hard-wood
hardy
hare
cf. **hair**
hare-brained
harem
har-lot
har-lotry
harm
har-monic
har-mon-ica
har-mo-ni-ous
har-mo-nize
har-mo-nizer
har-mony
har-ness
harp
harp-ist
har-poon
har-pooner
har-ried
harsh
har-vest
has
has—been *(n.)*
hash
hash-ish
has-sle
haste
has-ten
hast-ier
hast-ily
hasti-ness
hasty
hatch
hatcher
hatch-er-ies
hatchet
hatch-way
hate
ha-tred
haugh-tier
haugh-tily
haughty
haul
cf. **hall**
haunch
haunt
ha-ven
havoc
hawk
hawk-eye
haw-ser
hay
hay fe-ver
hay-loft
hay-stack
hay-wire
haz-ard
haz-ard-ous
haze
hazer
ha-zier
ha-zi-ness
hazy
H—bomb
head
head-ache
head-dress
header
head-first
head-hunter
head—hunting *(n.)*
head-light
head-line
head-long
head-mas-ter
head-mis-tress
head—on *(adj.)*
head-quar-ters
head-strong
head-waiter
head-way
heady

heal
cf. **heel**
health
health-ier
healthi-est
healthi-ness
healthy
heap
hear
cf. **here**
heard
cf. **herd**
hear-say
hearse
heart
heart-ache
heart-beat
heart-break
heart-burn
hearten
heart-felt
heart-ier
heart-rend-ing
heart-sick
heart—to—heart *(adj.)*
hearty
heat
heater
hea-then
hea-then-ish
heat wave *(n.)*
heave
heaven
heav-en-li-ness
heav-ier
heav-ily
heavi-ness
heavy
heavy-weight
He-brew
heckle
heck-ler
hec-tic
hedge
he-do-nism
he-do-nist
he-do-nis-tic
hee-bie—jee-bies
heed
heel
cf. **heal**
heft
heft-ier
hefty
he-ge-mony
heifer
height
heighten
hei-nous
heir
cf. **air**
heir ap-pa-rent
heirs ap-pa-rent
(n. pl.)
heir-ess
heir-loom
heist
he-li-cop-ter
he-li-port
he-lium
hell
hell—bent *(adj.)*
hell-cat
hel-lion
hell-ish
helm
hel-met
help-ful
helter—skelter *(adj.)*
hem
hemmed
hem-ming
hemi-sphere
hem-line
hence
hence-forth
hence-for-ward
hench-man
hepa-ti-tis
her-ald
her-aldry
herb
her-ba-ceous
herb-age
her-biv-o-rous
Her-cu-lean *(adj.)*
herd
cf. **heard**
herder
here
cf. **hear**
here-af-ter
hereby
he-redi-tary
he-red-ity
herein
hereon
her-esies
her-esy
her-etic
he-reti-cal
heri-tage
her-mit
her-mit-age
her-nia
hero
he-roic
her-oin
cf. **her-o-ine**
hero worship *(v.)*
her-self
hesi-tance
hesi-tancy
hesi-tant
hesi-tate
hesi-ta-tion
het-ero-ge-ne-ity
het-ero-ge-ne-ous
het-ero-sex-ual
hew
cf. **hue**
hex
hexa-gon
hex-ag-o-nal
hia-tus
hi-ba-chi
hi-ber-nate
hi-ber-na-tion
hic-cup
or **hic-cough**
hid-den

hide
hid-eous
hide-out
hie
cf. **high**
hi-er-ar-chi-cal
hi-er-ar-chies
hi-er-ar-chy
hi-ero-glyphic
high
cf. **hie**
high—and—mighty *(adj.)*
high-born
high-brow
higher—up
high fi-del-ity
high—frequency
high—grade *(adj.)*
high—handed *(adj.)*
high—hat *(v.)*
high jump
high-light
high mass
high-ness
high—pitched *(adj.)*
high—pressure *(adj.)*
high school
high—sounding *(adj.)*
high—spirited *(adj.)*
high—strung *(adj.)*
high—toned *(adj.)*
high-way
hi-jack
hike
hiker
hi-lari-ous
hi-lar-ity
hill
hill-billy
hill-side
hill-top
hilly
hilt
him
cf. **hymn**

him-self
hind
hin-der
hind-most
hind-quar-ter
hin-drance
hind-sight
Hindu
hinge
hint
hip-pie
hip-po-drome
hip-po-pota-mus
hip-po-pota-muses
or **hip-po-pot-ami** *(n. pl.)*
hire
hir-sute
hiss
hist
his-to-gram
his-to-rian
his-toric
his-tori-cal
his-tory
his-tri-onic
hit—and—miss *(adj.)*
hit—and—run *(adj.) (v.)*
hitch
hitch-hike
hither
hith-erto
hit—or—miss *(adj.)*
hives
hoard
cf. **horde**
hoarder
hoarse
hoax
hob-bies
hob-ble
hobby
hob-by-horse
hob-by-ist
hob-gob-lin
hob-nail
hob-nob

hob-nobbed
hob-nob-bing
hobo
ho-bos
or **ho-boes**
hock
hockey
hock-shop
ho-cus
hocus—pocus *(n.)*
hod
hodge-podge
Hodg-kin's disease
hoe
hoe-down
hog
hogged
hog-ging
hog-gish
hogs-head
hog—tie *(n.)*
hog-wash
hoi pol-loi
hoist
hoity—toity *(n.)*
hokey
hokum
hold
holder
hold off *(v.)*
hold on *(n.)*
hold-out *(n.)*
hold-over *(n.)*
hole
cf. **whole**
holi-day
ho-li-ness
Hol-ler-ith *(n.)*
hol-low
hol-low-ware
or **hol-lo-ware**
holly
ho-lo-caust
ho-loga-mous
ho-lo-gram
ho-lo-graph
ho-lo-phras-tic

ho-lo-zoic
hol-stein
hol-ster
holy
Holy Com-mu-nion
holy day
Holy Father
Holy Ro-man Em-pire
Holy See
Holy Spirit
Holy Week
hom-age
hom-bre
hom-burg
home
home-com-ing
home eco-nom-ics
home econ-o-mist
home-land
home-lier
home-li-est
home-like
home-made
home-maker
ho-meo-path
ho-me-op-a-thy
ho-meo-pathic
Ho-meric
home run
home-sick
home-site
home-spun
home-stead
home-stretch
home-ward
home-work
homey
or homy
ho-mi-cidal
homi-cide
hom-ier
homi-est
ho-mog-e-ne-ity
ho-mo-ge-neous
ho-mog-e-ni-za-tion
ho-molo-gous
homo-lo-graphic
hom-onym
ho-mo-phone
ho-mopho-nous
ho-mo sa-pi-ens
hone
hon-est
hon-esty
honey
hon-ey-bee
hon-ey-comb
hon-ey-dew
hon-ey-moon
honk
honky—tonk *(n.) (adj.)*
honour
hon-our-able
hono-rar-ium
hono-rar-iums
or hono-raria
hon-or-ary
hon-or-ific
hood
hood-lum
hood-wink
hooey
hoo-ray
hop
hopped
hop-ping
horde
cf. hoard
ho-ri-zon
hori-zon-tal
hor-monal
hor-mone
horn
hor-net
horo-scope
hor-ren-dous
hor-ri-ble
hor-ri-bly
hor-rid
hor-ri-fied
hor-rify
hor-ror
hor-ror struck *(adj.)*
hors d'oeuvre
hors d'oeuvres *(n. pl.)*
horse
horse-back
horse-fly
horse-hair
horse-hide
horse-man
horse-power
horse-shoe
horse-whip
horse-woman
horsy
or horsey
hor-ti-cul-ture
hor-ti-cul-tural
hor-ti-cul-tur-ist
ho-sanna
hose
ho-siery
hos-pi-ta-ble
hos-pi-ta-bly
hos-pi-tal
hos-pi-tal-ity
hos-pi-tal-iza-tion
hos-pi-tal-ize
host
hos-tage
hos-tel
host-ess
hos-tile
hos-til-i-ties
hos-til-ity
hot
hot air *(n.)*
hot-bed
hot—blooded *(adj.)*
hot-cake
hot dog
ho-tel
hot-head
hot-house
hot line *(n.)*
hour
cf. our
hour-long *(adj.)*
house
house-boat

house-breaker
house-bro-ken
house-clean
house-coat
house-fly
house-hold
house-keep-er
house-maid
house party
house-top
house-wares
house-warm-ing
house-wife
house-wives
house-work
hovel
hover
how-ever
how-it-zer
howl
how—to *(adj.)*
hub
hub-bub
huckle-berry
huck-ster
hud-dle
hue
cf. **hew**
huff
huffy
hug
hugged
hug-ging
huge
hulk
hull
hul-la-ba-loo
hum
hu-man
hu-mane
hu-man-ism
hu-man-is-tic
hu-mani-tar-ian
hu-mani-tari-an-ism
hu-man-ity
hum-ble
hum-bly
hum-bug
hum-drum
hu-mid
hu-midi-fied
hu-midi-fier
hu-mid-ify
hu-mid-ity
hu-mili-ate
hu-mili-ation
hu-mil-ity
hummed
hum-ming
hu-mor-esque
hu-mor-ist
hu-mor-ous
hu-mour
hump
hump-back
hump-ier
humpty—dumpty
humpy
hu-mus
hunch
hunch-back
hun-dred
hun-dreds *(n. pl.)*
hun-dred-weight
hun-ger
hun-ger strike
hun-grily
hun-gry
hunk
hunt
hunter
hur-dle
hurdy—gurdy
hurl
hurler
hur-rah
or **hur-ray**
hur-ri-cane
hur-ried
hur-ries
hurry
hurt
hus-band
hus-bandry
hush
hush—hush *(adj.)*
husk
husker
hus-kier
hus-ki-ness
hus-kies *(n. pl.)*
husky
hus-tle
hut
hutch
huzza
or **huz-zah**
hy-brid
hy-drant
hy-drate
hy-drau-lic
hy-dro-dy-nam-ics
hy-dro-elec-tric
hy-dro-gen
hy-dro-gen bomb
hy-drom-eter
hy-dro-pon-ics
hy-ena
hy-giene
hy-gienic
hy-gien-ist
hymn
cf. **him**
hym-nal
hymn-book
hy-per-ac-tive
hy-per-bola
hy-per-bole
hy-per-bolic
hy-per-crit-i-cal
hy-phen
hy-phen-ate
hy-phen-ation
hyp-no-ses *(n. pl.)*
hyp-no-sis
hyp-notic
hyp-no-tism
hyp-no-tist
hyp-no-tize
hy-po-chon-dria
hy-po-chon-driac

hy-poc-ri-sies
hy-poc-risy
hypo-crite
hypo-crit-i-cal
hy-po-der-mic
hy-pos-ta-tize
hy-pot-e-nuse
hy-pothe-sis
hy-pothe-ses *(n. pl.)*
hy-pothe-size
hy-po-theti-cal
hys-te-ria
hys-teric
hys-ter-ical

I

ibid
ibi-dem
ice
ice age *(n.)*
ice-berg
ice-boat
ice-bound
ice-box
ice-breaker
ice—cold *(adj.)*
ice cream *(n.)*
Ice-lan-dic *(adj.)*
ice—skate *(v.)*
ice skate *(n.)*
ici-cle
icon
icono-clasm
icono-clast
icono-clas-tic
icy
ID card
ideal
ide-al-ism
ide-al-ist
ide-al-is-tic
ide-al-ity
ide-al-iza-tion
ide-al-ize
idem
iden-ti-cal
iden-ti-fi-able
iden-ti-fi-ably
iden-ti-fi-ca-tion
iden-ti-fied
iden-ti-fier
iden-ti-ties
iden-tity
ideo-logi-cal
ide-olo-gies
ide-olo-gist
ide-ol-ogy
idi-ocies
id-iocy
id-iom
idi-omatic
idio-syn-crasy
id-iot
idi-otic
idle
cf. **idol**
idler
idol
cf. **idle**
idola-ter
idola-trous
idola-try
idol-ize
idyll
or **idyl**
idyl-lic
ig-loo
ig-ne-ous
ig-nit-able
ig-nite
ig-no-ble
ig-no-mini-ous
ig-no-miny
ig-no-ra-mus
ig-no-rance
ig-no-rant
ig-nore
ikon
ill
ill—advised *(adj.)*
ill-bred
il-le-gal
il-le-gal-ity
il-le-gal-ize
il-legi-bil-ity
il-legi-ble
il-legi-bly
il-le-giti-macy
il-le-giti-mate
ill—fated *(adj.)*
ill—favoured *(adj.)*
ill—gotten *(adj.)*
il-licit
cf. **elicit**
il-lit-er-acy
il-lit-er-ate
ill—mannered
il-logic
il-logi-cal
il-lu-mi-nate
cf. **alu-mi-nate**
il-lu-mi-na-tion
il-lu-sion
cf. **al-lu-sion**
cf. **elu-sion**
il-lu-sion-ary
il-lu-sive
il-lu-sory
il-lus-trate
il-lus-tra-tion
il-lus-tra-tive
il-lus-tra-tor
il-lus-tri-ous
ill will *(n.)*
im-age
im-agery
imagi-nable
imagi-nary
imagi-na-tion
imagi-na-tive
imag-ine
im-bal-ance
im-be-cile

im-be-cilic
im-be-cili-ties
im-be-cil-ity
im-bibe
im-bi-bi-tion
im-bri-cate
im-bri-ca-tion
im-bro-glio
im-brue
im-brute
im-bue
imi-ta-ble
imi-tate
imi-ta-tion
imi-ta-tive
imi-ta-tor
im-macu-lacy
im-macu-late
Im-macu-late Con-cep-tion
im-ma-nent
im-ma-te-rial
im-ma-ture
im-ma-tu-rity
im-meas-ur-able
im-me-di-acy
im-me-di-ate
im-medi-ca-ble
im-me-mo-rial
im-mense
im-men-si-ties
im-men-sity
im-men-su-ra-ble
im-merge
im-mer-gence
im-merse
im-mers-ible
im-mer-sion
im-mi-grant
cf. **em-i-grant**
im-mi-grate
im-mi-gra-tion
im-mi-nent
cf. **emi-nent**
im-miti-ga-ble
im-mo-bile
im-mo-bil-ity
im-mo-bi-li-za-tion
im-mo-bi-lize
im-mod-er-acy
im-mod-er-ate
im-mod-era-tion
im-mod-est
im-mod-esty
im-mo-late
cf. **emu-late**
im-mo-la-tion
im-mo-la-tor
im-moral
im-mor-al-ist
im-mo-ral-ity
im-mor-tal
im-mor-tal-ity
im-mor-tal-ize
im-mov-able
im-mova-bil-ity
im-mune
im-mu-ni-ties
im-mu-nity
im-mu-ni-za-tion
im-mu-nize
im-mu-nol-ogy
im-mure
im-mu-ta-ble
imp
im-pact
im-pac-tion
im-pac-tor
or **im-pacter**
im-pair
im-pala
im-pale
im-part
im-par-tial
im-par-ti-al-ity
im-pass-abil-ity
im-pass-able
cf. **im-pas-si-ble**
im-passe
im-pas-si-bil-ity
im-pas-sioned
im-pas-sive
im-pas-siv-ity
im-pa-tience
im-pa-tient
im-peach
im-peach-able
im-pec-ca-bil-ity
im-pec-ca-ble
im-pec-ca-bly
im-pe-cu-ni-os-ity
im-pe-cu-nious
im-pede
im-pedi-ment
im-pedi-menta
im-pelled
im-pel-ler
im-pel-ling
im-pend
im-pen-dent
im-pene-tra-bil-ity
im-pene-tra-ble
im-pene-tra-bly
im-peni-tence
im-peni-tent
im-pera-tive
im-per-ceiv-able
im-per-cep-ti-bil-ity
im-per-cep-ti-ble
im-per-cep-ti-bly
im-per-cep-tive
im-per-fect
im-per-fec-tion
im-pe-rial
im-pe-ri-al-ism
im-pe-ri-al-ist
im-peril
im-per-ish-able
im-pe-rium
im-per-ma-nence
im-per-ma-nency
im-per-ma-nent
im-per-me-abil-ity
im-per-me-able
im-per-meably
im-per-mis-si-bil-ity
im-per-mis-si-ble
im-per-mis-si-bly
im-per-sonal
im-per-son-ate
im-per-son-ation
im-per-son-ator

im-per-ti-nence
im-per-ti-nen-cies
im-per-ti-nency
im-per-ti-nent
im-per-turb-abil-ity
im-per-turb-able
im-per-turb-ably
im-per-vi-ous
im-petu-osi-ties
im-petu-os-ity
im-petu-ous
im-pi-eties
im-pi-ety
im-pinge
im-pi-ous
imp-ish
im-placa-bil-ity
im-plac-able
im-pla-ca-bly
im-plant
im-plau-si-bil-ity
im-plau-si-ble
im-plau-si-bly
im-ple-ment
im-pli-cate
im-pli-ca-tion
im-pli-ca-tive
im-plicit
im-plied
im-plode
im-plore
im-ply
im-po-lite
im-poli-tic
im-po-liti-cal
im-pon-der-able
im-pon-der-ably
im-pone
im-port
im-por-tance
im-por-tant
im-por-ta-tion
im-porter
im-por-tune
im-pose
im-po-si-tion
im-pos-si-bil-ity
im-pos-si-ble
im-pos-si-bly
im-pos-tor
im-pos-ture
im-po-tence
im-po-tency
im-po-tent
im-pound
im-pov-er-ish
im-prac-ti-ca-bil-ity
im-prac-ti-ca-ble
im-prac-ti-ca-bly
im-prac-ti-cal
im-prac-ti-cal-ity
im-pre-cate
im-pre-ca-tion
im-pre-ca-tory
im-pre-cise
im-preg-na-bil-ity
im-preg-na-ble
im-preg-na-bly
im-preg-nate
im-press-ibil-ity
im-press-ible
im-press-ibly
im-pres-sion
im-pres-sion-abil-ity
im-pres-sion-able
im-pres-sion-ably
im-pres-sion-ism
im-pres-sion-ist
im-pres-sion-is-tic
im-pres-sive
im-press-ment
im-prest
im-pri-ma-tur
im-pri-mis
im-print
im-prison
im-pris-on-able
im-proba-bil-ity
im-prob-able
im-prob-ably
im-promptu
im-proper
im-pro-pri-eties
im-pro-pri-ety
im-prov-abil-ity
im-prov-able
im-prov-ably
improve
im-provi-dence
im-provi-dent
im-pro-vi-sa-tion
im-pro-vise
im-pru-dence
im-pru-dent
im-pu-dent
im-pu-dic-ity
im-pugn
im-puis-sance
im-puis-sant
im-pulse
im-pul-sion
im-pul-sive
im-pu-nity
im-pure
im-pu-ri-ties
im-pu-rity
im-put-abil-ity
im-put-able
im-pute
in
cf. **inn**
in-abil-ity
in ab-sen-tia
in-ac-ces-si-bil-ity
in-ac-ces-si-ble
in-ac-ces-si-bly
in-ac-cu-ra-cies
in-ac-cu-racy
in-ac-cu-rate
in-ac-tion
in-ac-ti-vate
in-ac-tive
in-ade-qua-cies
in-ade-quacy
in-ade-quate
in-ad-mis-si-bil-ity
in-ad-mis-si-ble
in-ad-mis-si-bly
in-ad-ver-tence
in-ad-ver-ten-cies
in-ad-ver-tency

in-ad-ver-tent
in-ad-vis-abil-ity
•in-ad-vis-able
in-ad-vis-ably
in-alien-abil-ity
in-alien-able
in-alien-ably
in-al-ter-abil-ity
in-al-ter-able
in-al-ter-ably
in-amo-rata
in-ane
in-ani-mate
inani-ties
ina-ni-tion
inan-ity
in-ap-pli-ca-bil-ity
in-ap-pli-ca-ble
in-ap-pli-ca-bly
in-ap-pre-cia-tive
in-ap-proach-able
in-ap-pro-pri-ate
in-apt
in-ar-ticu-late
in-ar-tis-tic
in-as-much as *(conj.)*
in-at-ten-tion
in-at-ten-tive
in-au-di-bil-ity
in-au-di-ble
in-au-di-bly
in-au-gu-ral
in-au-gu-rate
in-au-gu-ra-tion
in-aus-pi-cious
in-bred
Inca
in-cal-cu-la-ble
in-can-des-cence
in-can-des-cent
in-can-ta-tion
in-can-ta-tory
in-ca-pa-bil-ity
in-ca-pa-ble
in-ca-pa-bly
in-ca-paci-tate
in-ca-paci-ta-tion
in-ca-paci-ta-tor
in-ca-paci-ties
in-ca-pac-ity
in-car-cer-ate
in-car-cera-tion
in-car-nate
in-car-na-tion
in-cau-tion
in-cau-tious
in-cen-di-ary
in-cense
in-cen-tive
in-cep-tion
in-ces-sant
in-cest
in-ces-tu-ous
inch
in-ci-dence
cf. in-ci-dents
in-ci-dent
in-ci-den-tal
in-cin-er-ate
in-cin-era-tor
in-cipi-ent
in-ci-pit
in-cise
in-ci-sion
in-ci-sive
in-ci-sor
in-ci-ta-tion
in-cite
cf. in-sight
in-clem-ency
in-clem-ent
in-clin-able
in-cli-na-tion
in-cline
in-close
in-clud-able
or in-clud-ible
in-clu-sion
in-clu-sive
in-co-erc-ible
in-cogi-tant
in-cog-nita
in-cog-nito
in-cog-ni-zance
in-cog-ni-zant
in-co-her-ence
in-co-her-ent
in-com-bus-ti-bil-ity
in-com-bus-ti-ble
in-come
in-com-men-su-ra-bil-ity
in-com-men-su-ra-ble
in-com-men-su-ra-bly
in-com-men-su-rate
in-com-mu-ni-ca-bil-ity
in-com-mu-ni-ca-ble
in-com-mu-ni-ca-bly
in-com-mu-ni-cado
in-com-mu-ni-ca-tive
in-com-mut-able
in-com-mut-ably
in-com-pa-ra-bil-ity
in-com-pa-ra-ble
in-com-pa-ra-bly
in-com-pati-bil-i-ties
in-com-pati-bil-ity
in-com-pati-ble
in-com-pati-bly
in-com-pe-tence
in-com-pe-tency
in-com-pe-tent
in-com-plete
in-com-pre-hen-si-bil-ity
in-com-pre-hen-si-ble
in-com-pre-hen-si-bly
in-com-pre-hen-sion
in-com-put-able
in-con-ceiv-abil-ity
in-con-ceiv-able
in-con-ceiv-ably
in-con-clu-sive
in-con-gru-ity
in-con-gru-ous
in-con-se-quence
in-con-se-quen-tial
in-con-sid-er-able
in-con-sid-er-ably
in-con-sid-er-ate
in-con-sist-ence
in-con-sist-ency
in-con-sist-ent

in-con-sol-able
in-con-sol-ably
in-con-so-nance
in-con-so-nant
in-con-stancy
in-con-stant
in-con-spic-u-ous
in-con-test-able
in-con-tro-vert-ibil-ity
in-con-tro-vert-ible
in-con-tro-vert-ibly
in-con-ven-ience
in-con-ven-iency
in-con-ven-ient
in-con-vinc-ible
in-cor-po-rate
in-cor-po-ra-tion
in-cor-rect
in-cor-ri-gi-bil-ity
in-cor-ri-gi-ble
in-cor-ri-gi-bly
in-cor-rupt-ible
in-crease
in-credi-bil-ity
in-cred-ible
in-cred-ibly
in-cre-du-lity
in-credu-lous
in-cre-ment
in-cre-men-tal
in-crimi-nate
in-crimi-na-tion
in-crimi-na-tory
in-crus-ta-tion
in-cu-bate
in-cu-ba-tion
in-cu-ba-tor
in-cul-cate
in-cul-ca-tion
in-cul-ca-tor
in-cul-pa-ble
in-cum-ben-cies
in-cum-bency
in-cum-bent
in-cum-ber
in-cur
in-cur-able
in-curred
in-cur-ring
in-cur-sion
in-debted
in-de-cency
in-de-cent
in-de-ci-pher-able
in-de-ci-sion
in-de-ci-sive
in-de-co-rum
in-deed
in-de-fati-ga-bil-ity
in-de-fati-ga-ble
in-de-fati-ga-bly
in-de-fin-able
in-defi-nite
in-del-ible
in-deli-cacy
in-dem-ni-fi-ca-tion
in-dem-ni-fied
in-dem-nify
in-dem-ni-ties
in-dem-nity
in-dent
in-den-ta-tion
in-den-ture
in-de-pend-ence
cf. **in-de-pen-dents**
in-de-scrib-able
in-de-struc-ti-ble
in-de-struc-ti-bly
in-de-ter-mi-na-ble
in-de-ter-mi-na-bly
in-de-ter-mi-nacy
in-de-ter-mi-nate
in-de-ter-mi-na-tion
in-dex
in-dexes
or **in-di-ces**
in-di-cate
in-di-ca-tion
in-dica-tive
in-di-ca-tor
in-di-cia
in-dict
cf. **in-dite**
in-dict-able
in-dicter
or **in-dictor**
in-dif-fer-ence
in-dif-fer-ent
in-di-gence
in-dige-nous
in-di-gent
in-di-gest-ibil-ity
in-di-gest-ible
in-di-ges-tion
in-dig-nant
in-dig-na-tion
in-dig-ni-ties
in-dig-nity
in-digo
in-di-rect
in-dis-cern-ible
in-dis-creet
cf. **in-dis-crete**
in-dis-cre-tion
in-dis-crimi-nate
in-dis-pen-sa-bil-ity
in-dis-pen-sa-ble
in-dis-pen-sa-bly
in-dis-pose
in-dis-po-si-tion
in-dis-pu-ta-ble
in-dis-pu-ta-bly
in-dis-solu-ble
in-dis-tinct
in-dis-tinc-tive
in-dis-tin-guish-abil-ity
in-dis-tin-guish-able
in-dis-tin-guish-ably
in-dite
cf. **in-dict**
in-diter
in-di-vert-ible
in-di-vert-ibly
in-di-vid-ual
in-di-vidu-al-ism
in-di-vidu-al-ist
in-di-vidu-al-ity
in-di-vidu-al-iza-tion
in-di-vidu-al-ize
in-doc-ile
in-do-cil-ity

in-doc-tri-nate
in-doc-tri-na-tion
in-doc-tri-na-tor
in-do-lence
in-do-lent
in-domi-ta-bil-ity
in-domi-ta-ble
in-domi-ta-bly
In-do-nesian
in-door *(adj.)*
in-doors *(adv.)*
in-du-bi-ta-bil-ity
in-du-bi-ta-ble
in-du-bi-ta-bly
in-duce
in-duc-ibil-ity
in-duc-ible
in-duct
in-duc-tance
in-ductee
in-duc-tion
in-duc-tive
in-duc-tor
in-dulge
in-dul-gence
in-dulger
in-du-rate
in-du-ra-tion
in-du-ra-tive
in-dus-trial
in-dus-tri-al-ism
in-dus-tri-al-ist
in-dus-tri-al-iza-tion
in-dus-tri-al-ize
in-dus-tries
in-dus-tri-ous
in-dus-try
ine-bri-ant
ine-bri-ate
ine-bria-tion
in-ebri-ety
in-ed-ible
in-ed-ited
in-edu-ca-bil-ity
in-edu-ca-ble
in-ef-fa-bil-ity
in-ef-fa-ble
in-ef-fa-bly
in-ef-fec-tive
in-ef-fec-tual
in-ef-fec-tu-al-ity
in-ef-fi-ca-cious
in-ef-fi-cacy
in-ef-fi-ciency
in-ef-fi-cient
in-elas-tic
in-eli-gi-bil-ity
in-eli-gi-ble
in-ept
in-epti-tude
in-equal-ity
in-eq-ui-ta-ble
in-eq-ui-ta-bly
in-eq-ui-ty
cf. **in-iq-uity**
in-eradi-ca-bil-ity
in-eradi-ca-ble
in-eradi-ca-bly
in-er-rancy
in-er-rant
in-ert
in-er-tia
in-es-cap-able
in-es-cap-ably
in-es-ti-ma-ble
in-es-ti-ma-bly
in-evi-ta-bil-ity
in-evi-ta-ble
in-evi-ta-bly
in-ex-act
in-ex-cus-able
in-ex-haust-ible
in-ex-haust-ibly
in-exo-ra-ble
in-ex-pen-sive
in-ex-pe-ri-ence
in-ex-pi-able
in-ex-plic-abil-ity
in-ex-tin-guish-able
in-ex-tri-ca-ble
in-fal-li-bil-ity
in-fal-li-ble
in-fa-mies
in-fa-mous
in-famy
in-fancy
in-fant
in-fan-ti-cide
in-fan-tile
in-fan-til-ism
in-fan-til-ity
in-fan-try
in-fan-try-man
in-fatu-ate
in-fatu-ation
in-fect
in-fec-tor
in-fec-tion
in-fec-tious
in-fec-tive
in-fe-lici-tous
in-fe-lici-ties
in-fe-lic-ity
in-fer
in-fer-ence
in-fer-en-tial
in-fe-rior
in-fe-ri-or-ity
in-fer-nal
in-ferno
in-ferred
in-fer-ring
in-fer-tile
in-fest
in-fes-ta-tion
in-fi-del
in-fi-deli-ties
in-fi-del-ity
in-field *(n.)*
in-fight-ing *(n.)*
in-fil-trate
in-fil-tra-tion
in-fil-tra-tive
in-fil-tra-tor
in-fi-nite
in-fi-ni-tesi-mal
in-fin-ity
in-firm
in-fir-ma-ries
in-fir-mary
in-fix

in-flame
in-flam-ma-bil-ity
in-flam-ma-ble
in-flam-ma-bly
in-flam-ma-tion
in-flam-ma-tory
in-flat-able
in-flate
in-fla-tion-ary
in-fla-tion-ism
in-flect
in-flec-tion
in-flex-ible
in-flict
in-flic-tion
in-flu-ence
in-flu-en-tial
in-flu-enza
in-flux
in-form
in-for-mal
in-for-mali-ties
in-for-mal-ity
in-form-ant
in-forma-tive
in-former
in-frac-tion
in-fra-red
in-fre-quency
in-fre-quent
in-fringe
in-fu-ri-ate
in-fuse
in-fus-ible
in-fu-sion
in-ge-nious
in-gé-nue
or **in-ge-nue**
in-ge-nui-ties
in-ge-nu-ity
in-genu-ous
in-gest
in-gest-ible
in-ges-tive
in-got
in-grain
in-grate
in-gra-ti-ate
in-gra-tia-tion
in-gra-tia-tory
in-grati-tude
in-gre-di-ent
in-gress
in—group *(n.)*
in-growth
in-grown
in-gur-gi-tate
in-gur-gi-ta-tion
in-habit
in-hab-it-able
in-hab-it-ant
in-hal-ant
in-ha-la-tion
in-ha-la-tor
in-hale
in-her-ent
in-herit
in-her-it-able
in-her-it-ance
in-heri-tor
in-hibit
in-hi-bi-tion
in-hibi-tor
or **in-hib-iter**
in-hos-pi-ta-ble
in—house *(adj.)*
in-hu-man
cf. **in-hu-mane**
in-hu-man-ity
in-imi-cal
in-imi-ta-ble
in-imi-ta-bly
in-iq-ui-tous
in-iq-uity
cf. **in-eq-uity**
ini-tial
ini-tial-ize
ini-ti-ate
ini-tia-tion
ini-tia-tive
ini-tia-tor
ini-tia-tory
in-ject
in-jec-tion
in-jec-tor
in-ju-di-cious
in-junc-tion
in-jure
in-ju-ries
in-ju-ri-ous
in-jury
in-jus-tice
ink
ink-ling
ink-stand
ink-well
in-laid
in-land
in—law *(n.)*
in-lay
in-let
in lo-co pa-ren-tis
in-mate
in me-mo-riam *(prep.)*
in-most
inn
cf. **in**
in-nards
in-nate
in-ner
inner city *(n.)*
in-ner-most *(n.)*
in-ner-spring
in-ner-vate
in-ner-va-tion
in-ning
inn-keeper
in-no-cence
in-no-cen-cies
in-no-cency
in-no-cent
in-nocu-ous
in-no-vate
in-no-va-tion
in-no-va-tive
in-no-va-tor
in-no-va-tory
in-nu-endo
in-nu-en-does
in-nu-mer-able
in-nu-mer-ably

in-ocu-late
in-ocu-la-tion
in-of-fen-sive
in-op-er-able
in-op-era-tive
in-op-por-tune
in-or-di-nate
in-or-ganic
in-os-cu-late
in-os-cu-la-tion
in-pa-tient
in—person *(adj.)*
in per-so-nam
in—print *(adj.)*
in—process *(adj.)*
in pro-pria per-sona *(adv.)*
in-put
in-quest
in-quire
in-quirer
in-quir-ies
in-quiry
in-qui-si-tion
in-quisi-tive
in-road *(n.)*
in-sa-lu-bri-ous
in-sa-lu-brity
in-sane
in-sani-tary
in-sani-ta-tion
in-sani-ties
in-san-ity
in-sa-tia-bil-ity
in-sa-tia-ble
in-sa-tia-bly
in-sa-tiate
in-scribe
in-scriber
in-scrip-tion
in-scrip-tive
in-scroll
in-scru-ta-bil-ity
in-scru-ta-ble
in-scru-ta-bly
in-seam
in-sect
in-sec-ti-cidal
in-sec-ti-cide
in-sec-ti-fuge
in-sec-tivo-rous
in-se-cure
in-se-cu-rity
in-sem-inate
in-semi-na-tion
in-sen-si-bil-ity
in-sen-si-ble
in-sen-si-bly
in-sen-si-tive
in-sen-si-tiv-ity
in-sen-tient
in-sepa-ra-bil-ity
in-sepa-ra-ble
in-sepa-ra-bly
in-sert
in-ser-tion
in—service *(adj.)*
in-set
in-shore
in-side
in-sider
in-sidi-ous
in-sight
cf. **in-cite**
in-sig-nia
in-sig-nifi-cance
in-sig-nifi-cancy
in-sig-nifi-cant
in-sin-cere
in-sin-cer-ity
in-sinu-ate
in-sinu-a-tion
in-sipid
in-si-pid-ity
in-sist
in-sis-tence
in-sis-ten-cies
in-sis-tency
in-so-bri-ety
in-so-cia-bil-ity
in-so-cia-ble
in-so-cia-bly
in-so-far *(adv.)*
in-so-late
in-so-la-tion
in-sole
in-so-lence
in-so-lent
in-solu-bil-ity
in-solu-bi-li-za-tion
in-solu-bi-lize
in-solu-ble
in-solu-bly
in-solv-able
in-solv-ably
in-sol-vency
in-sol-vent
in-som-nia
in-som-niac
in-so-much as *(conj.)*
in-sou-ci-ance
in-sou-ci-ant
in-spect
in-spec-tion
in-spec-tor
in-spi-ra-tion
in-spi-ra-tional
in-spire
in-sta-bil-ity
in-sta-ble
in-stall
in-stal-la-tion
in-stance
in-stancy
in-stant
in-stan-ta-neous
in-stead
in-step
in-sti-gate
in-sti-ga-tion
in-sti-ga-tor
in-stil
or **in-still**
in-stinct
in-stinc-tive
in-sti-tute
in-sti-tu-tion
in-sti-tu-tional
in-sti-tu-tion-al-iza-tion
in-sti-tu-tion-al-ize
in-struct
in-struc-tion

in-struc-tive
in-struc-tor
in-stru-ment
in-stru-men-tal
in-stru-men-tal-ism
in-stru-men-tal-ist
in-stru-men-tal-ity
in-stru-men-ta-tion
in-sub-or-di-nate
in-sub-or-di-na-tion
in-sub-stan-tial
in-suf-fer-able
in-suf-fi-cience
in-suf-fi-ciency
in-suf-fi-cient
in-su-lant
in-su-late
in-su-la-tion
in-su-la-tor
in-su-lin
in-sult
in-su-per-able
in-su-per-ably
in-sup-port-able
in-sup-port-ably
in-sup-press-ible
in-sur-abil-ity
in-sur-able
in-sure
in-surer
in-sur-gence
in-sur-gen-cies
in-sur-gency
in-sur-gent
in-sur-mount-able
in-sur-mount-ably
in-sur-rec-tion
in-tact
in-take
in-te-ger
in-te-gral
in-te-grate
in-te-gra-tion
in-teg-rity
in-tel-lect
in-tel-lec-tion
in-tel-lec-tive
in-tel-lec-tual
in-tel-lec-tu-al-ism
in-tel-lec-tu-al-ity
in-tel-lec-tu-al-iza-tion
in-tel-lec-tu-al-ize
in-tel-li-gence
in-tel-li-gent
in-tel-li-gent-sia
in-tel-li-gi-bil-ity
in-tel-li-gi-ble
in-tel-li-gi-bly
in-tem-per-ance
in-tem-per-ate
in-tend
in-tense
in-ten-si-fi-ca-tion
in-ten-si-fier
in-ten-sify
in-ten-sion
cf. in-ten-tion
in-ten-si-ties
in-ten-sity
in-ten-sive
in-tent
in-ten-tion
cf. in-ten-sion
in-ten-tional
in-ter
in-ter-act
in-ter-ac-tant
in-ter-ac-tion
in-ter-ac-tive
in-ter-atomic
in-ter-breed
in-ter-ca-lary
in-ter-ca-late
in-ter-cede
in-ter-ceder
in-ter-cel-lu-lar
in-ter-cept
in-ter-cepter
in-ter-cep-tion
in-ter-cep-tor
in-ter-ces-sion
in-ter-ces-sional
in-ter-ces-sor
in-ter-ces-sory
in-ter-change
in-ter-changer
in-ter-change-able
in-ter-change-ably
in-ter-col-le-giate
in-ter-co-lum-nia-tion
in-ter-com
in-ter-com-mu-nion
in-ter-con-ti-nen-tal
in-ter-course
in-ter-de-nomi-na-tional
in-ter-de-part-men-tal
in-ter-de-pen-dence
in-ter-de-pen-dency
in-ter-de-pen-dent
in-ter-dict
in-ter-dic-tion
in-ter-dis-ci-plin-ary
in-ter-est
in-ter-face
in-ter-faith
in-ter-fere
in-ter-fer-ence
in-terim
in-te-rior
cf. an-te-rior
in-ter-ject
in-ter-jec-tion
in-ter-jec-tor
in-ter-jec-tory
in-ter-lace
in-ter-leaf
in-ter-li-brary
in-ter-lo-cu-tion
in-ter-locu-tor
in-ter-locu-tory
in-ter-lope
in-ter-loper
in-ter-lude
in-ter-mar-riage
in-ter-marry
in-ter-me-di-acy
in-ter-me-di-ary
in-ter-me-di-ate
in-ter-mezzo
in-ter-mi-na-ble
in-ter-mi-na-bly

in-ter-min-gle
in-ter-mis-sion
in-ter-mit
in-ter-mit-tence
in-ter-mit-tent
in-ter-mit-ter
in-ter-mix
in-tern
in-ternal
internal—combustion
engine
in-ter-na-tional
in-ter-na-tion-al-ism
in-ter-na-tion-al-ist
in-ter-na-tion-al-iza-tion
in-ter-na-tion-al-ize
in-ter-ne-cine
in-ternee
in-ter-nist
in-ter-of-fice
in-ter-pel-late
in-ter-pene-trate
in-ter-pene-tra-tion
in-ter-per-sonal
in-ter-phase
in-ter-play
in-ter-po-late
in-ter-po-la-tion
in-ter-po-la-tive
in-ter-po-la-tor
in-ter-pret
in-ter-preter
in-ter-pre-tive
in-ter-ra-cial
in-ter-re-late
in-ter-re-la-tion
in-ter-ro-gate
in-ter-ro-ga-tion
in-ter-roga-tive
in-ter-ro-ga-tor
in-ter-rupt
in-ter-rupter
in-ter-rupt-ible
in-ter-rup-tion
in-ter-scho-las-tic
in-ter-sect
in-ter-sec-tion
in-ter-ses-sion
in-ter-space
in-ter-sperse
in-ter-state
in-ter-twine
in-ter-val
in-ter-vene
in-ter-ve-nor
or in-ter-vener
in-ter-ven-tion
in-ter-view
in-ter-weave
in-ter-wo-ven
in-ter-zonal
in-tes-tacy
in-tes-tate
in-tes-ti-nal
in-tes-tine
in-ti-macy
in-ti-mate
in-ti-mater
in-ti-ma-tion
in-timi-date
in-timi-da-tion
in-timi-da-tor
in-tol-er-abil-ity
in-tol-er-able
in-tol-er-ably
in-tol-er-ance
in-tol-er-ant
in-to-nate
in-to-na-tion
in-to-na-tional
in-tone
in toto
in-toxi-cant
in-toxi-cate
in-toxi-ca-tion
in-trac-ta-bil-ity
in-trac-ta-ble
in-trac-ta-bly
in-tra-mu-ral
in-tra-mus-cu-lar
in-tran-si-gence
in-tran-si-gent
in-tra-state
in-tra-ve-nous
in-trepid
in-tri-ca-cies
in-tri-cacy
in-tri-cate
in-tri-gant
or in-tri-guant
in-trigue
in-trin-sic
in-tro-duce
in-tro-duc-tion
in-tro-duc-tory
in-tro-spect
in-tro-spec-tion
in-tro-spec-tive
in-tro-ver-sion
in-tro-vert
in-trude
in-truder
in-tru-sion
in-tru-sive
in-tu-itive
in-un-date
in-un-da-tion
in-ure
in-vade
in-va-lid
in-vali-date
in-vali-da-tion
in-vali-da-tor
in-valu-able
in-vari-ance
in-vari-ant
in-va-sion
in-va-sive
in-vec-tive
in-veigh
in-veigher
in-vei-gle
in-vei-gler
in-vent
in-ven-tion
in-ven-tive
in-ven-tor
in-ven-to-ries
in-ven-tory
in-verse
in-ver-sion

in-vert
in-ver-te-brate
in-verter
in-vert-ible
in-vest
in-ves-ti-gate
in-ves-ti-ga-tion
in-ves-ti-ga-tional
in-ves-ti-ga-tive
in-ves-ti-ga-tor
in-ves-ti-ga-tory
in-ves-ti-ture
in-vet-er-acy
in-vet-er-ate
in-vi-abil-ity
in-vi-able
in-vidi-ous
in-vigo-rate
in-vigo-ra-tion
in-vigo-ra-tor
in-vin-ci-bil-ity
in-vin-ci-ble
in-vin-ci-bly
in-vio-la-ble
in-vio-la-bly
in-vio-lacy
in-vio-late
in-vis-ibil-ity
in-vis-iblc
in-vi-ta-tion
in-vi-ta-tional
in-vite
in-vi-tee
in-vo-ca-tion
in-voice
in-voke
in-vol-un-tar-ily
in-vol-un-tari-ness
in-vol-un-tary
in-volve
in-vul-ner-able
in-ward
or in-wards
io-dine
ion
iono-sphere
ipso facto
iras-ci-bil-ity
iras-ci-ble
iras-ci-bly
irate
ire
iri-des-cence
iri-des-cent
irk
irk-some
iron
Iron Age *(n.)*
iron-bound
iron-clad
Iron Cur-tain
ironic
iro-nies
iron-stone
iron-ware
iron-work
Iro-quois
ir-ra-di-ate
ir-ra-dia-tion
ir-ra-dia-tive
ir-ra-dia-tor
ir-radi-ca-ble
ir-radi-ca-bly
ir-ra-tional
ir-ra-tion-al-ism
ir-ra-tio-nal-ist
ir-ra-tio-nal-is-tic
ir-ra-tion-al-ity
ir-re-al-ity
ir-re-claim-able
ir-rec-on-cil-abil-ity
ir-rec-on-cil-able
ir-rec-on-cil-ably
ir-re-cov-er-able
ir-re-cov-er-ably
ir-re-deem-able
ir-re-deem-ably
ir-re-duc-ibil-ity
ir-re-duc-ible
ir-re-duc-ibly
ir-refu-ta-bil-ity
ir-refu-ta-ble
ir-refu-ta-bly
ir-re-gard-less
ir-regu-lar
ir-regu-lari-ties
ir-regu-lar-ity
ir-rela-tive
ir-rele-vance
ir-rele-van-cies
ir-rele-vancy
ir-rele-vant
ir-re-li-gion
ir-re-li-gious
ir-re-mov-able
ir-repa-ra-ble
ir-repa-ra-bly
ir-re-place-abil-ity
ir-re-place-able
ir-re-place-ably
ir-re-press-ible
ir-re-proach-able
ir-re-proach-ably
ir-re-sist-ible
ir-reso-lute
ir-re-spec-tive
ir-re-spon-si-ble
ir-re-spon-si-bly
ir-re-spon-sive
ir-rev-er-ence
ir-rev-er-ent
ir-re-vers-ible
ir-revo-ca-ble
ir-revo-ca-bly
ir-ri-gate
ir-ri-ga-tion
ir-ri-ga-tor
ir-ri-ta-bili-ties
ir-ri-ta-bil-ity
ir-ri-ta-ble
ir-ri-tant
ir-ri-tate
ir-ri-ta-tion
ir-rupt
ir-rup-tion
cf. erup-tion
Is-lam
Is-lamic
is-land
is-lander

isle
cf. **aisle**
iso-bar
iso-late
iso-la-tion
iso-la-tion-ism
iso-la-tion-ist
iso-met-ric
iso-therm
iso-tope
iso-topic
Is-rael
Is-raeli
Is-raelis *(n. pl.)*
Is-ra-el-ite
is-su-ance
is-sue
isth-mus
italic
itali-cize
itch
item
item-iza-tion
item-ize
it-er-ate
it-era-tion
itin-er-ant
itin-er-ary
it-self
ivied
ivo-ries
ivory
ivy

J

jab
jabbed
jab-bing
jab-ber
jab-ber-wocky
jack
jackal
jacket
Jack Frost *(n.)*
jack-ham-mer
jack—in—the—box *(n.)*
jack—in—the—boxes *(n. pl.)*
jack-knife
jack—of—all—trades *(n.)*
jacks—of—all—trades *(n. pl.)*
jack—o'—lantern
jack-pot
jack-rab-bit
Jack-so-nian
jack-straw
jade
jag
jagged
jag-ging
jag-uar
jai alai
jail
jail-bird
jail-break
jailer
or **jailor**
Jain
Jain-ism
ja-lopy
jal-ou-sie
jam
cf. **jamb**
jam-ba-laya
jam-bo-ree
jammed
jam-mer
jam-ming
jam session
jan-gle
jan-gled
jan-gling
jan-is-sary
or **jan-i-zary**
jan-is-saries *(n. pl.)*
jan-i-tor
jan-i-to-rial
Jan-sen-ism
Jan-sen-ist
Jan-sen-is-tic
Jap-a-nese
jape
jar
jar-di-niere
jar-gon
jar-gon-ize
jarred
jar-ring
jas-mine
jaun-dice
jaunt
jaun-tier
jaun-ti-est
jaun-tily
jaun-ti-ness
jav-e-lin
jaw
Jay-cee
jay-walk
jazz
jazz-ier
jazzi-est
jazz-ily
jazzi-ness
J—bar lift *(n.)*
jeal-ous
jeans
jeep
jeer
Je-ho-vah
jell
jel-lied
jelly
jel-ly-fish
jeop-ar-dize
jeop-ardy
Jer-e-miah
jerk
jerk-ier
jerki-est
jerk-ily
jerki-ness
jerky
jer-ri-can
jer-sey
Je-ru-sa-lem
jest
jester
Je-suit
Je-sus

jet air-plane
jet—black
jet engine
jet-port
jet—propelled
jet pro-pul-sion
jet-sam
jet set *(n.)*
jet stream
jet-ti-son
jet-ti-son-able
jetty
jeu-nesse do-rée
Jew
jewel
jew-elled
or jew-eled
jew-el-ler
or jew-eler
jew-ellery
Jew-ish
jew's harp
or jews' harp
jez-e-bel
jib
jibbed
jib-ber
jib-bing
jibe
jiffy
jig
jigged
jig-ger
jig-ging
jig-gle
jig-gly
jig-saw
jilt
jim—dandy
jim-mies *(n. pl.)*
jimmy
jin-gle
jin-gled
jin-gler
jin-gling
jingo
jin-go-ism
jin-go-ist
jin-go-is-tic
jinx
jit-ney
jit-ter
jit-ter-bug
jit-tery
jive
job
jobbed
job-ber
job-bing
job-holder
job—hopping
job lot
jockey
jo-cose
jocu-lar
jocu-lar-ity
jo-cund
jodh-purs
jog
jogged
jog-ger
jog-ging
jog-gle
john-ny-cake
Johnny—on—the—spot *(n.)*
joie de vivre
join
joiner
joint
joist
joke
joker
jol-lier
jol-li-est
jol-li-fi-ca-tion
jol-li-ties
jolly
jolt
jot
jot-ted
jot-ter
jot-ting
jounce
jounc-ier
jounci-est
jouncy
jour-nal
jour-nal-ese
jour-nal-ism
jour-nal-ist
jour-nal-is-tic
jour-ney
jour-ney-man
joust
jo-vial
jo-vi-al-ity
jowl
joy
joy-ous
joy-ride
ju-bil-ant
ju-bi-la-tion
ju-bi-lee
Ju-dah
Ju-daic
or Ju-da-ical
Ju-da-ism
Judas
Judeo—Christian
judge
judge-ment
or judg-ment
ju-di-ca-tory
ju-di-ca-ture
ju-di-cial
ju-di-ciary
ju-di-cious
judo
jug
jug-gle
jug-gler
jug-gling
jugu-lar
juice
juic-ier
juici-est
juici-ness
juicy
ju-jitsu
or jiu-jitsu

juke box *(n.)*
ju-li-enne
jum-ble
jumbo
jump
jump suit *(n.)*
jumpy
junc-tion
junc-ture
jun-gle
ju-nior
junk
jun-ket
junkie
or junky
junk mail *(n.)*
junk-yard
junta
Ju-pi-ter
ju-rid-i-cal
or ju-ridic
juries
ju-ris-dic-tion
ju-ris-dic-tional
ju-ris-pru-dence
ju-ris-pru-dent
ju-ris-pru-den-tial
ju-rist
ju-ris-tic
ju-ror
jury
ju-ry-man
jus-tice
jus-tice of the peace *(n.)*
jus-ti-cia-bil-ity
jus-ti-cia-ble
jus-ti-fi-abil-ity
jus-ti-fi-able
jus-ti-fi-ably
jus-ti-fi-ca-tion
jus-ti-fi-ca-tory
jus-ti-fied
jus-ti-fier
jus-tify
jut
jut-ted
jut-ting
ju-ve-nile
jux-ta-pose
jux-ta-po-si-tion

K

kai-ser
kale
ka-lei-do-scope
ka-lei-do-scopic
or ka-lei-do-scopi-cal
ka-mi-kaze
kan-ga-roo
karat
cf. car-rot
cf. caret
ka-rate
kat-zen-jam-mer
kava
kayak
kayo
kayoed
ka-zoo
keel
keel-boat
keel-haul
keep
keeper
keep-sake
ke-loid
kelp
ken-nel
kept
ker-chief
ker-chiefs
or ker-chieves *(n. pl.)*
ker-nel
cf. colo-nel
kero-sene
ketchup
or cat-sup
ket-tle
ket-tle-drum
key
key-board
key club *(n.)*
key-hole
key-note
key-stroke
key word
khaki
kib-butz *(sing.)*
kib-but-zim *(pl.)*
kib-butz-nik
ki-bitz
ki-bitzer
ki-bosh
kick
kick-back
kicker
kick-off
kick-stand
kick-up *(n.)*
kick up *(v.)*
kid
kid-ded
kid-der
kid-ding
kid-nap
kid-napped
kid-nap-per
or kid-naper
kid-nap-ping
kid-ney
kid-skin
kill
killer
kill-joy
kiln
kilo
kilo-cy-cle
ki-lo-gram
ki-lo-hertz
ki-lo-me-tre
kilo-watt
kilowatt—hour *(n.)*
kilt
kil-ter
ki-mono
kin
kind
kin-der-gar-ten
kin-der-gart-ner

kind-hearted
kin-dle
kind-lier
kind-li-est
kind-li-ness
kin-dling
kin-dred
ki-ne-mat-ics
kine-scope
ki-ne-sics
ki-net-ics
kin-folk
king
king-bird
king-dom
king-fish
king-lier
king-li-est
king-li-ness
king-maker
king-pin
king—size
or **king—sized** *(adj.)*
kink
kink-ier
kins-folk *(n. pl.)*
kin-ship
kins-man
kins-woman
ki-osk
kis-met
kiss
kit
kitchen
kitch-en-ette
kitch-en-ware
kith
kit-ten
kit-ten-ish
kitty
kitty—corner
or **kitty—cornered**
kiwi
klep-to-ma-nia
klep-to-ma-niac
kludge
knack
knap
cf. **nap**
knap-sack
knave
cf. **nave**
knavery
knavish
knead
cf. **need**
knee
cf. **née or nee**
knee action *(n.)*
knee-cap
knee—deep *(adj.)*
knee-hole
kneel
knell
knew
cf. **new**
knick-ers
knick-knack
knife
knife—edge
knight
cf. **night**
knight—errant
knight-hood
knit
cf. **nit**
knob
knock
knock-down
knocker
knock—knee
knock—out *(n.)*
knock out *(v.)*
knock-wurst
cf. **knack-wurst**
knoll
knot
knot-hole
knot-ted
knot-ting
knotty
know
know-how
know—it—all *(n.)*
knowl-edge-abil-ity
knowl-edge-able
knowl-edge-ably
known
know—nothing *(n.)*
knuckle
ko-peck
or **ko-pek**
Ko-ran
ko-sher
kow-tow
kraal
Krem-lin
Krishna
Krish-na-ism
Kriss Krin-gle
krona
krone
kro-nen
kudo
kum-quat
kung fu
kwashi-or-kor

L

la-bel
la-belled
or **la-beled**
la-bel-ling
or **la-beling**
lab-o-ra-to-ries
labo-ra-tory
la-bo-ri-ous
la-bour
la-bourer
la-bour-sav-ing
laby-rinth
lace
lac-er-ate
lac-er-a-tion
lac-ier
laci-est
lack

lacka-dai-si-cal
lackey
la-conic
lac-quer
la-crosse
lac-tate
lad-der
lad-der—back
lade
laden
la-dies
ladies—in—waiting
la-dle
lady
la-dy-bug
lady—in—waiting
la-dy-like
la-dy-ship
lag
la-ger
lagged
lag-ging
lag-gard
la-goon
laid
lair
laissez—faire *(n.)*
la-ity
lake
lamb
lam-baste
or **lam-bast**
lamb-skin
lame
lame-brain
lame-duck
lamer
lam-est
la-ment
la-men-ta-ble
la-men-ta-bly
lam-en-ta-tion
lami-nate
lami-na-tion
lamp
lamp-black
lam-poon
lam-prey
lance
lancer
land
land-fall
land-fill
land grant
land-holder
land-ing craft
land-ing gear
land-ing strip
land-lady
land-locked
land-lord
land-lub-ber
land-mark
land-owner
land-scape
land-slide
lan-guage
lan-guid
lan-guish
lan-guor
lank
lank-ier
lanki-est
lanki-ness
lanky
lano-lin
lan-tern
lan-yard
lap
la-pel
lapped
lap-ping
lapse
lar-ce-nist
lar-ce-nous
lar-ceny
lard
larder
large
large—scale *(adj.)*
lar-iat
lark
larva
lar-vae
or **larvas** *(n. pl.)*
lar-vi-cide
la-ryn-geal
lar-yn-gitic
lar-yn-gi-tis
la-ryn-ges *(n. pl.)*
lar-ynx
la-sa-gna
las-civi-ous
lase
la-ser
lash
lass
lasso
las-sos
or **las-soes** *(n. pl.)*
last
last—ditch *(adj.)*
last straw
last word
latch
latch-key
latch-string
late
late-comer
later
lat-est
la-ten-cies
la-tency
lat-erad
lat-eral
lat-est
la-tex
lath
cf. **lathe**
lather
lati-tude
lati-tu-di-nal
la-trine
lat-ter
Latter—day Saint *(n.)*
lat-tice
lat-tice-work
laud
laud-able
lau-da-num
lau-da-tion

lau-da-tive
lauda-tory
laugh
laugh-able
laugh-ably
laugh-ing-stock
laugh-ter
launch
launcher
laun-der
laun-derer
laun-dries
laun-dro-mat
laundry
laun-dry-man
laun-dry-woman
lau-re-ate
lau-rel
lava
la-va-liere
or **la-val-liere**
la-va-tion
lav-ato-ries
lav-atory
lave
lav-en-der
lav-ish
law
law—abiding *(adj.)*
law-breaker
law-maker
law-man
lawn
lawn mower
law-suit
law-yer
lax
laxa-tive
lax-ity
lay
cf. **lei**
lay-away
lay down
layer
lay-ette
lay-off
lay-out
la-zier
la-zi-est
la-zily
la-zi-ness
lazy
la-zy-ish
la-zy Su-san
lea
cf. **lee**
leach
lead
leaden
leader
leaf
leaf-age
leaf-ier
leafi-est
leaf-let
league
leak
leak-age
leak-ier
leaki-est
leaki-ness
leaky
lean
cf. **lien**
lean—to *(n.)*
leap
leapt
or **leaped**
leap-frog
leap year
learn
learned
or **learnt**
learner
lease
leash
least
least-ways
least-wise
leather
leath-er-like
leath-ery
leave
leaven
leaves *(n. pl.)*
le-bens-raum
lecher
lech-er-ous
lech-ery
leci-thin
lec-tern
lec-tor
lec-ture
le-der-ho-sen
ledge
led-ger
lee
cf. **lea**
leech
leer
leery
lee-ward
lee-way
left
left—handed *(adj.)*
left—hander *(n.)*
left-ist
left-over *(adj.) (n.)*
left wing *(n.)*
left—winger *(n.)*
leg
lega-cies
leg-acy
le-gal
legal age *(n.)*
le-gal-ese
le-gal-ism
le-gal-ist
le-gal-i-ties
le-gal-ity
le-gal-iza-tion
le-gal-ize
leg-ate
leg-a-tee
le-ga-tion
le-ga-tor
legend
leg-end-ary
leg-er-de-main
legged
leg-ging

leg-horn
leg-ibil-ity
leg-ible
leg-ibly
le-gion
le-gion-ar-ies
le-gion-ary
le-gion-naire
leg-is-late
leg-is-la-tion
leg-is-la-tive
leg-is-la-tor
leg-is-la-to-rial
leg-is-la-ture
le-giti-macy
le-giti-mate
le-giti-ma-tion
le-giti-ma-tize
le-giti-mism
le-giti-mist
leg-room
le-gume
le-gu-mi-nous
leg-work
lei
cf. **lay**
lei-sure
lemon
lem-on-ade
lend
lender
lend—lease *(n.)*
length
lengthen
length-ier
length-ways
length-wise
lengthy
le-nience
le-nien-cies
le-niency
le-nient
Le-nin-ism
leni-tive
len-ity
lens
len-til

leop-ard
leo-tard
leper
lep-re-chaun
lep-ro-sar-ium
lep-rosy
lep-rous
le-sion
less
les-see
lessen
cf. **les-son**
lesser
cf. **les-sor**
lest
let
let-down
le-thal
le-thar-gic
leth-argy
let-ter
let-terer
let-ter-head
letter—perfect *(adj.)*
let-ter-press
let-tuce
leu-ke-mia
leu-ke-mic
levee
cf. **levy**
level
lev-elled
or **lev-eled**
level—headed
lev-el-ling
or **lev-el-ing**
lever
lev-er-age
le-vi-a-than
lev-ied
levi-tate
levi-ta-tion
lev-ity
levy
cf. **levee**
lewd
lexi-cog-ra-pher

lexi-cog-ra-phy
lexi-con
li-abili-ties
li-abil-ity
li-able
li-ais-ing
li-ai-son
liar
li-ba-tion
li-bel
li-bel-lant
or **li-bel-ant**
li-belled
or **li-beled**
li-bel-lee
or **li-belee**
li-bel-ling
or **li-bel-ing**
li-bel-lous
or **li-bel-ous**
lib-eral
lib-er-al-ism
lib-er-al-ist
lib-er-al-is-tic
lib-er-ali-ties
lib-er-al-ity
lib-er-al-iza-tion
lib-er-al-ize
lib-er-al-izer
lib-er-ate
lib-er-a-tion
lib-er-a-tor
lib-er-tar-ian
lib-er-tine
lib-er-tin-ism
lib-er-ties
lib-erty
li-bidi-nous
li-bido
li-bra
li-brar-ian
li-brar-ies
li-brary
lice
li-cence
li-cens-able
li-cense

li-censer
or li-cencer
li-cen-tious
licit
lie
cf. lye
lief
liege
lien
cf. lean
lieu
lieu-ten-an-cies
lieu-ten-ancy
lieu-ten-ant
life
life—and—death
or life—or—death
life belt
life-blood
life-boat
life buoy
life-guard
life-like
life-long
life pre-server
lifer
life-saver
life—size
or life—sized *(adj.)*
life-time
life-work
lift
lift—off *(n.)*
lift truck
liga-ment
li-gate
li-ga-tion
liga-ture
light
lighted
or lit
light bulb
lighten
ligh-ter
lighter—than—air (adj.)
light-face
light—fingered
light—footed
light—handed
light—headed
light-ning
cf. light-en-ing
light-weight
lig-ne-ous
lig-nite
lik-able
or like-able
like
like-lier
like-li-est
like-li-hood
like-wise
li-lac
lil-li-put
lil-li-pu-tian *(adj.)*
lilt
lily
lily—livered
lily of the val-ley
lily—white
limb
lim-ber
limbo
lime
lime-ade
lime-light
lim-er-ick
lime-stone
limit
limi-ta-tion
limp
lim-pid
lin-age
line
lin-eage
lin-eal
lin-ear
line-backer
line-man
linen
liner
lines-man
lineup
lin-ger
lin-gerer
lin-ge-rie
lingo
lin-gual
lin-guist
lin-guis-tic
lini-ment
link
link-age
linkup
li-no-leum
li-no-type
lin-seed
lint
lin-tel
linter
lion
li-on-ess
li-on-hearted
li-on-iza-tion
li-on-ize
li-on-izer
lion's share
lip
li-pase
lipped
lip-ping
lippy
lip—read
lip—reader
lip service
lip-stick
li-quate
li-qua-tion
liq-ue-fac-tion
liq-ue-fi-abil-ity
liq-ue-fi-able
liq-ue-fier
liq-ue-fy
li-queur
cf. li-quor
liq-uid
liq-ui-date
liq-ui-da-tion
liq-ui-da-tor
li-quid-ity
liq-uid-ize

li-quor
cf. **li-queur**
lira
lisp
lis-some
or **lis-som**
list
list-en
lis-tener
lit
lit-any
lit-er-acy
lit-eral
lit-er-al-ism
lit-er-ari-ness
lit-er-ary
lit-er-ate
lit-era-tion
lit-era-ture
lithe
lithe-some
litho-graph
li-tho-gra-pher
litho-graphic
li-thog-ra-phy
litho-sphere
liti-gant
liti-gable
liti-gate
liti-ga-tion
li-ti-gious
lit-mus
li-tre
lit-ter
lit-tera-teur
lit-ter-bag
lit-ter-bug
lit-terer
lit-ter-mate
lit-tle
lit-tler
lit-tlest
or **least**
Little League
lit-to-ral
li-tur-gi-cal
lit-ur-gist

liv-abil-ity
or **live-abil-ity**
liv-able
or **live-able**
live
live—in *(adj.)*
live-lier
live-li-est
live-li-hood
live-long
liver
liv-er-ies
liv-er-wurst
liv-ery
live-stock
live wire
livid
li-vid-ity
liv-ing room
liv-ing stan-dard
living wage
liz-ard
llama
load
cf. **lode**
loader
loaf
loafer
loam
loan
loath
loathe
loather
loath-some
loaves *(n. pl.)*
lob
lobbed
lob-bied
lob-bing
lobby
lob-by-ist
lobe
lo-bot-omy
lob-ster
lo-cal *(adj.)*
cf. **lo-cale** *(n.)*
lo-cal-ism

lo-cal-i-ties
lo-cal-ity
lo-cal-iza-tion
lo-cal-ize
lo-cate
lo-ca-tion
lo-ca-tor
loc cit
loci
lock
locked—in *(adj.)*
locker
locket
lock jaw
lock-out
lock-smith
lockup
loco
lo-co-mo-tion
lo-co-mo-tive
lo-cus
lo-cust
lode
cf. **load**
lodge
lodger
loess
loft
loft-ier
lofti-est
lofti-ness
lofty
log
loga-rithm
logged
log-ger
log-ger-head
log-ging
logic
logi-cal
lo-gi-cian
lo-gis-tic
loin
loin-cloth
loi-ter
loll

lol-li-pop
or lol-ly-pop
lone
lone-lier
lone-li-est
lone-li-ness
loner
lone wolf
long
longer
long—distance
lon-gev-ity
long-hair *(n.)*
long—hair
or long—haired *(adj.)*
long-hand
long haul *(n.)*
long—haul *(adj.)*
long-horn
long-house
long-ish
lon-gi-tude
lon-gi-tu-di-nal
long johns *(n.)*
long—lived *(adj.)*
long—playing *(adj.)*
long—range *(adj.)*
long-shore-man
long shot *(n.)*
long—standing *(adj.)*
long—suffering *(n.) (adj.)*
long—term *(adj.)*
long—winded *(adj.)*
look
look—alike *(n.)*
looker—on
look-out
loom
loon
loony
or loo-ney
loop
loop-hole
loose
cf. lose
loose—jointed *(adj.)*
loose—leaf *(adj.)*

loosen
looser
loot
lop
lope
lop—eared *(adj.)*
lopped
lop-ping
lop-sided
lo-qua-cious
lo-quac-ity
lo-ran
lord
lore
lor-gnette
lor-ries
lorry
lose
cf. loose
losa-ble
loser
loss
lost
lot
lo-thario
lo-tion
lot-ter-ies
lot-tery
lo-tus
loud
loud-mouth
loud-speaker
lounge
lounger
louse
lous-ier
lousi-est
lousy
lout
lout-ish
lou-vre
or lou-ver
lov-able
or love-able
lov-ably
love
love affair

love beads
love-bird
love feast
love knot
love-lier
love-li-est
love-li-ness
lover
love seat
love-sick
loving cup
loving—kindness
low
low-born
low-brow
low—down *(adj.)*
lower
low-est
low—grade *(adj.)*
low—key
or low—keyed *(adj.)*
low-land
low-lier
low-li-est
low-li-ness
loyal
loy-al-ist
loy-al-ties
loy-alty
loz-enge
lub-ber
lu-bri-cant
lu-bri-cate
lu-bri-ca-tion
lu-bri-ca-tor
lu-bri-cious
lu-bri-to-rium
lu-cent
lu-cid
lu-cid-ity
Lu-ci-fer
luck
luck-ier
lucki-est
luck-ily
lucki-ness
lucky

lu-cra-tive
lu-cre
lu-di-crous
lug
lug-gage
lugged
lug-ging
lu-gu-bri-ous
luke-warm
lull
lul-la-bied
lul-laby
lum-bago
lum-bar
lum-ber
lum-berer
lum-ber-jack
lu-men
lu-mi-naire
lu-mi-nance
lu-mi-nary
lu-mi-nes-cence
lu-mi-nes-cent
lu-mi-nif-er-ous
lu-mi-nist
lu-mi-nos-i-ties
lu-mi-nos-ity
lu-mi-nous
lum-mox
lump
lump-ier
lumpi-est
lumpi-ness
lumpy
lu-na-cies
lu-nacy
lu-nar
lu-nar eclipse *(n.)*
lu-nate
lu-na-tic
lu-na-tion
lunch
lun-cheon
lun-cheon-ette
lunch-room
lunch-time
lu-nette
lung
lunge
lung-fish
lu-ni-so-lar
lu-ni-tidal
lurch
lurcher
lure
lurer
lu-rid
lurk
lurker
lus-cious
lush
lust
lus-tre
or lus-ter
lus-trate
lus-tra-tion
lus-tre-ware
lus-trous
lute
lu-te-nist
or lu-ta-nist
Lu-theran
lux
lux-ate
lux-a-tion
luxu-ri-ance
luxu-ri-ant
luxu-ri-ate
luxu-ri-ous
luxu-ries
lux-ury
ly-cée
ly-ceum
lye
cf. lie
lymph
lym-phoid
lynch
lynch law
lynx
lyre
cf. liar
lyric
lyri-cal
lyri-cism
lyri-cist
lyr-ist

M

ma-ca-bre
mac-adam
mac-ad-am-ize
maca-roni
mace
mac-er-ate
mac-era-tion
mac-era-tor
ma-chete
Ma-chia-vel-lian
machi-nate
machi-na-tion
machi-na-tor
ma-chine
ma-chine gun
ma-chinery
ma-chine shop
ma-chine tool
ma-chin-ist
mack-erel
macki-naw
mack-in-tosh
or mac-in-tosh
mac-ramé
macro
mac-ro-cosm
mac-ro-cos-mic
mac-ro-eco-nom-ics
mac-ro-scopic
mad
madam
ma-dame
mad-cap
mad-den
mad-der
made
cf. maid
mad-emoi-selle

mes-de-moi-selles
(n. pl.)
made—up *(adj.)*
mad-house
mad-man
Ma-donna
mad-ri-gal
ma-dri-lene
mad-woman
mael-strom
maestros
Ma-fia
ma-fi-oso
maga-zine
mag-got
magic
magi-cal
mag-is-te-rial
mag-is-trate
Magna Charta
or Magna Carta
magna cum laude
mag-na-nim-i-ties
mag-na-nim-ity
mag-nani-mous
mag-nate
cf. mag-net
mag-ne-sia
mag-ne-sium
mag-net
cf. mag-nate
mag-netic
mag-ne-tism
mag-ne-ti-za-tion
mag-ne-tize
mag-ne-tizer
mag-neto
mag-ne-tom-e-ter
mag-nific
mag-ni-fi-ca-tion
mag-nif-i-cence
mag-nif-i-cent
mag-ni-fied
mag-ni-fier
mag-nify
mag-ni-tude
mag-num
ma-ha-ra-jah
or ma-ha-raja
ma-ha-rani
or ma-ha-ra-nee
ma-hog-any
maid
cf. made
maiden
maid-en-hood
maid—in—waiting
maids—in—waiting
(n. pl.)
maid-ser-vant
mail
cf. male
mail-abil-ity
mail-able
mailbag
mail-box
mail or-der *(n.)*
mail—order house
maim
main
cf. mane
main-land
main-line
main-mast
main-spring
main-stay
main-stream
main-tain
main-tain-abil-ity
main-tain-able
main-tainer
main-te-nance
main-top
mai-son-ette
mai-tre d'
mai-tre d'hô-tel
maitres d'hô-tel *(n. pl.)*
ma-jes-tic
maize
cf. maze
maj-es-ties
maj-esty
ma-jor
major—domo
ma-jori-ties
ma-jor-ity
make
make—do *(adj.)*
make-ready
make-shift
make-up *(n.)*
mal-ad-ap-ta-tion
mal-adapted
mal-adap-tive
mal-ad-justed
mal-ad-jus-tive
mal-ad-just-ment
mala-dies
mal-adroit
mal-ady
mal-aise
mal-ap-ro-pos
ma-laria
ma-lar-key
mal-con-tent
mal de mer
male
cf. mail
male-dic-tion
male-dic-tory
male-fac-tion
male-fac-tor
ma-lefic
ma-lefi-cence
ma-lefi-cent
ma-levo-lence
ma-levo-lent
mal-fea-sance
mal-for-ma-tion
mal-formed
mal-func-tion
mal-ice
ma-li-cious
ma-lign
ma-lig-nance
ma-lig-nan-cies
ma-lig-nancy
ma-lig-nant
ma-lig-nity
ma-lin-ger
ma-lin-gerer

mall
cf. **maul**
mal-lard
mal-lea-bil-ity
mal-lea-ble
mal-let
mal-nour-ished
mal-nu-tri-tion
mal-odor-ous
mal-po-si-tion
mal-prac-tice
mal-prac-ti-tio-ner
malt
Mal-thu-sian
malt-ose
mal-treat
mam-mal
mam-mary
mam-moth
man
man—about—town *(n.)*
mana-cle
man-age
man-age-abil-ity
man-age-able
man-age-ably
man-ager
mana-ge-rial
man—at—arms
man-da-rin
man-date
man-da-tor
man-da-tory
man-do-lin
man-drel
or **man-dril**
mane
cf. **main**
man—eater
ma-nege
or **ma-nège**
man-ga-nate
man-ga-nese
mange
man-ger
mang-ier
mangi-est
man-gle
man-gler
man-han-dle
man-hole
man-hood
man—hour
ma-nia
ma-niac
ma-ni-a-cal
mani-cure
mani-cur-ist
mani-fest
mani-fes-tant
mani-fes-ta-tion
mani-festo
mani-fes-toes
or **mani-fes-tos**
mani-fold
mani-kin
or **man-ni-kin**
ma-nila
ma-nipu-la-bil-ity
ma-nipu-la-ble
ma-nipu-lat-able
ma-nipu-late
ma-nipu-la-tion
ma-nipu-la-tive
ma-nipu-la-tor
ma-nipu-la-tory
man-kind
man—made
man-ne-quin
man-ner
man-ner-ism
ma-noeu-vre
ma-noeu-vra-bil-ity
ma-noeu-vra-ble
ma-noeu-vrer
man—of—war *(n.)*
manor
manse
man-ser-vant
man-sion
man-slaugh-ter
man-tel
man-tel-piece
man-tilla
man-tle
man-ual
manu-fac-ture
manu-fac-turer
manu-script
many
many-fold *(adv.)*
many—sided *(adj.)*
Mao-ism
Mao-ist
map
ma-ple
map-maker
map-ping
ma-raca
mar-a-schino
mara-thon
ma-raud
ma-rauder
mar-ble
mar-ble-ize
mar-bly
march
marcher
mar-chesa
mar-chese
mar-chio-ness
Mardi Gras
mare
mar-ga-rine
mar-gin
mar-ginal
mari-juana
or **mari-huana**
ma-rimba
ma-rina
mari-nate
ma-rine
mari-ner
mari-o-nette
mari-tal
mari-time
mark
mark-down
marker
mar-ket
mar-ket-able

mar-keter
mar-ket-place
markup
marl
mar-ma-lade
mar-mo-real
ma-roon
mar-quee
mar-quis
or **mar-quess**
mar-quises
or **mar-quesses**
mar-riage
mar-riage-able
mar-ried
mar-row
marry
Mars
marsh
mar-shal
cf. **mar-tial**
marsh-land
marsh-mal-low
marsh-ier
marsh-iest
marshy
mar-su-pial
mart
mar-tial
cf. **mar-shal**
mar-tian
mar-ti-net
mar-tyr
mar-tyr-dom
mar-vel
mar-velled
mar-vel-lous
Marx-ian
Marx-ism
Marx-ist
mas-cara
mas-cu-line
mas-cu-lin-ity
mash
mask
cf. **masque**
mas-och-ism
mas-och-ist
mas-och-is-tic
Ma-sonic
masque
cf. **mask**
mas-quer-ade
mass
mas-sa-cre
mas-sa-crer
mas-sage
mass com-mu-ni-ca-tion
mas-seur
mas-seuse
mas-sive
mass me-dium
mass media *(n. pl.)*
mast
mas-tec-tomy
mas-ter
master—at—arms
masters—at—arms *(n. pl*
mas-ter bath
mas-ter bed-room
mas-ter-piece
mas-ter plan
mas-tery
mas-tic
mas-ti-cate
mas-ti-ca-tion
mas-ti-ca-tor
mas-tiff
mast-odon
mas-toid
mat
mata-dor
match
matcher
match-book
match-maker
mate
ma-te-rial
ma-te-ri-al-ism
ma-te-ri-al-iza-tion
ma-te-ri-al-ize
ma-te-riel
ma-ter-nal
ma-ter-ni-ties
ma-ter-nity
math
mathe-mat-ics
mathe-mat-i-cal
mathe-ma-ti-cian
mathe-ma-ti-za-tion
mati-née
or **mati-nee**
ma-tri-arch
ma-tri-ar-chal
ma-tri-ar-chies
ma-tri-ar-chy
ma-tri-cidal
ma-tri-cide
ma-tricu-late
ma-tricu-lant
ma-tricu-la-tion
ma-tri-lin-eal
mat-ri-mo-nial
mat-ri-mony
ma-trix
ma-tri-ces *(n. pl.)*
ma-tron
mat-ted
mat-ter
matter—of—fact *(adj.)*
mat-ting
mat-tock
mat-tress
matu-rate
matu-ra-tion
matu-ra-tional
ma-tura-tive
ma-ture
ma-turer
ma-tu-rity
ma-tu-ti-nal
matzo
mat-zoth *(n. pl.)*
maud-lin
maul
cf. **mall**
mau-so-leum
mav-er-ick
mawk-ish
maxi-coat
maxim

maxi-mi-za-tion
maxi-mize
maxi-mizer
maxi-mum
maxi-mums
or **maxi-ma** *(n. pl.)*
maxi-skirt
may
maybe
May-day
cf. **May Day**
may-hem
may-on-naise
mayor
may-oral
may-or-alty
may-pole
maze
cf. **maize**
meadow
mead-ow-land
mead-ow-lark
mea-gre
or **mea-ger**
meal
meal-time
mealy-mouthed
mean
me-an-der
meant
mean-time
mean-while
mea-sles
mea-slier
mea-sli-est
mea-sly
mea-sur-abil-ity
mea-sur-able
mea-sur-ably
mea-sure
mea-surer
meat
cf. **meet**
cf. **mete**
meat-ball
meat by—product *(n.)*
meat-ier
mecca
me-chanic
me-chani-cal
mecha-ni-cian
mecha-nism
mecha-nist
mecha-nis-tic
mecha-ni-za-tion
mecha-nize
medal
cf. **med-dle**
med-al-ist
or **med-al-list**
me-dal-lic
me-dal-lion
med-dle
cf. **medal**
me-dia
me-dial
me-dian
me-diant
me-di-ate
me-di-a-tion
me-di-a-tive
me-di-a-tor
me-di-a-tory
medic
medi-cal
medi-cate
medi-ca-tion
medi-care
me-dic-i-nal
medi-cine
med-ico
me-di-ae-val
or **me-di-eval**
me-di-aeval-ism
me-di-aeval-ist
me-dio-cre
me-di-oc-ri-ties
me-di-oc-rity
medi-tate
medi-ta-tion
medi-ta-tive
medi-ta-tor
Medi-ter-ra-nean
me-dium
me-di-ums *(n. pl.)*
or **me-dia**
med-ley
meek
meer-schaum
meet
cf. **meat**
cf. **mete**
mega-cy-cle
mega-lo-ma-nia
mega-lo-ma-niac
mega-lo-ma-nia-cal
mega-lopo-lis
mega-phone
mega-ton
mel-an-cho-lia
mel-an-cho-liac
mel-an-cholic
mel-an-chol-ies
mel-an-choly
mela-noma
melba toast
meld
me-lee
me-lio-rate
me-lio-ra-tion
me-lio-ra-tive
me-lio-rism
me-lio-rist
mel-low
me-lo-deon
me-lodic
me-lo-di-ous
melo-dist
melo-dize
melo-drama
melo-dra-matic
melo-dra-ma-tize
melo-dies
mel-ody
melon
melt
melt-able
mem-ber
mem-ber-ship
mem-brane
mem-bra-nous

me-mento
me-men-tos *(n. pl.)*
or me-men-toes
memo
mem-oir
memo-ra-bilia
memo-ra-bil-ity
memo-ra-ble
memo-ra-bly
memo-ran-dum
memo-ran-dums
or memo-randa *(n. pl.)*
me-mo-rial
me-mo-ri-al-ist
me-mo-ri-al-ize
memo-ri-za-tion
memo-ries
memo-rize
memo-rizer
mem-ory
men-ace
me-nag-erie
mend
men-da-cious
men-dac-ity
mender
me-nial
men-in-gi-tis
meno-pause
men-strual
men-stru-ate
men-stru-a-tion
men-tal
men-tali-ties
men-tal-ity
men-tion
men-tion-able
men-tor
menu
mer-can-tile
mer-can-til-ism
mer-ce-nar-ies
mer-ce-nary
mer-chan-dise
mer-chant
mer-cu-rial
mer-cury
mer-cies
mer-ci-ful
mer-ci-less
mer-cury
mercy
mere
merge
merger
me-rid-ian
me-ringue
me-rino
merit
meri-toc-racy
mer-it-ocratic
meri-to-ri-ous
mer-maid
mer-man
mero-mor-phic
mer-rier
mer-ri-est
mer-rily
mer-ri-ment
merry
merry—go—round *(n.)*
mer-ry-mak-ing *(n.)*
mesa
mes-cal
mes-ca-line
mes-dames *(n. pl.)*
mesh
mes-mer-ism
mes-mer-ize
mes-mer-izer
me-so-morph
me-so-mor-phic
Me-so-zoic
mes-quite
mes-sage
mes-sen-ger
mess hall *(n.)*
mes-siah
mess kit *(n.)*
Messrs. *(n. pl.)*
mess-mate
messy
mes-tizo
met
me-tabo-lism
metal
cf. met-tle
me-tal-lic
met-al-lur-gi-cal
met-al-lur-gist
met-al-lurgy
meta-mor-phic
meta-mor-phism
meta-mor-phose
meta-mor-pho-ses *(n. pl.)*
meta-mor-pho-sis
meta-phor
meta-physic
meta-physi-cal
meta-plasm
meta-plas-mic
meta-psy-chol-ogy
me-tas-ta-sis
me-tas-ta-size
meta-tar-sus
meta-zoan
mete
cf. meat
cf. meet
me-teor
me-te-oric
me-te-or-ite
me-te-or-oid
me-teo-ro-log-i-cal
me-teo-rol-o-gist
me-teo-rol-ogy
me-ter
metha-done
metha-nol
method
me-thodi-cal
or me-thodic
Meth-od-ism
Meth-od-ist
meth-od-ologi-cal
meth-od-olo-gist
meth-od-ol-ogy
Me-thu-se-lah
me-ticu-lous
met-ric
met-ri-cal

met-ric sys-tem *(n.)*
met-ro-nome
me-tropo-lis
met-tle
cf. metal
mew
Mexi-can
me-zu-zah
or me-zuza
mez-za-nine
mezza voce
mezzo
mezzo forte
mezzo—soprano
mica
mi-cro
mi-crobe
mi-cro-beam
mi-cro-bio-logic
mi-cro-bio-logi-cal
mi-cro-bi-ol-ogy
mi-cro-bus
mi-cro-cap-sule
mi-cro-cir-cuit
mi-cro-code
mi-cro-com-puter
mi-cro-copy
mi-cro-cosm
mi-cro-cos-mic
mi-cro-cul-ture
mi-cro-den-si-tom-e-ter
mi-cro-eco-nom-ics
mi-cro-elec-trode
mi-cro-elec-tron-ics
mi-cro-fiche
mi-cro-fiche *(n. pl.)*
or mi-cro-fiches
mi-cro-film
mi-cro-groove
mi-cro-inch
mi-crom-e-ter
mi-cro-or-gan-ism
mi-cro-phone
mi-cro-phon-ics
mi-cro-pho-tog-ra-phy
mi-cro-phy-sics
mi-cro-print
mi-cro-pro-gram-ming
mi-cro-reader
mi-cro-scale
mi-cro-scope
mi-cro-scopic
mi-cro-sec-ond
mi-cro-spec-tro-pho-
tome-ter
mi-cro-sphere
mi-cro-sur-gery
mi-cro-wave
mid
mid-air
Mi-das
mid-day
mid-dle
mid-dle—aged *(adj.)*
mid-dle—class *(adj.)*
mid-dle ear *(n.)*
mid-dle-man
middle—of—the—road
(adj.)
mid-dle-weight
middy
mid-field
midget
midi
mid-land
mid-night
mid-point
mid-riff
mid-sec-tion
mid-ship-man
midst
mid-stream
mid-sum-mer
mid-town
mid-way
mid-week
mid-wife
mid-win-ter
mid-year
might
cf. mite
might-ier
mighti-est
mighti-ness
mighty
mi-graine
mi-grant
mi-grate
mi-gra-tion
mi-gra-tional
mi-gra-tor
mi-gra-tory
mi-kado
mike
mild
mil-dew
mile
mile-age
miler
mile-post
mile-stone
mi-lieu
mili-tant
mili-tancy
mili-tarily
mili-ta-rism
mili-ta-ris-tic
mili-ta-ri-za-tion
mili-ta-rize
mili-tary
mili-tate
mi-li-tia
milk
milk-fish
milk glass *(n.)*
milk-maid
milk-man
milk shake *(n.)*
milk-sop
milk-weed
mill
mil-le-nar-ian
mil-le-nary
mil-len-nium
mil-len-ni-ums
or mil-len-nia *(n. pl.)*
miller
mil-let
mil-li-gram
mil-li-li-tre
mil-li-me-tre

mil-li-nery
mil-lion
mil-lions
mil-lion-aire
mil-li-roent-gen
mil-li-sec-ond
mill-pond
mill-stone
mill-wright
mim-eo-graph
mimic
mim-icked
mim-ic-ries
mim-icry
mine-able
or min-able
mince
mincer
mince-meat
mince pie
mind
mind—blowing *(adj.)*
mind—expanding *(adj.)*
mine
miner
mine-layer
min-eral
min-er-al-iz-able
min-er-al-iza-tion
min-er-al-ize
min-er-al-izer
min-er-al-ogi-cal
min-er-alo-gist
min-er-al-ogy
min-estrone
mine-sweeper
min-gle
mini
min-ia-ture
min-ia-tur-iza-tion
min-ia-tur-ize
mini-bike
mini-bus
mini-car
mini-com-puter
mini-mal
mini-max
mini-mi-za-tion
mini-mize
mini-mizer
mini-mum
mini-mums
or mini-ma *(n. pl.)*
mini-mum wage
min-ion
min-is-cule
mini-skirt
mini-state
min-is-ter
min-is-te-rial
min-is-trant
min-is-tra-tion
min-is-tries
min-is-try
mini-track
mink
min-now
mi-nor
mi-nor-i-ties
mi-nor-ity
Mi-no-taur
min-strel
mint
mint-age
minu-end
min-uet
mi-nus
mi-nus-cule
min-ute
cf. mi-nute
min-ute-man
mi-nu-tia
mi-nu-tiae *(n. pl.)*
minx
mira-cle
mi-racu-lous
mi-rage
mire
mirk
mir-ror
mirth
mis-ad-ven-ture
mis-aligned
mis-al-li-ance
mis-ap-pli-ca-tion
mis-ap-ply
mis-ap-pre-hend
mis-ap-pre-hen-sion
mis-ap-pro-pri-ate
mis-ap-pro-pria-tion
mis-be-got-ten
mis-be-have
mis-be-hav-iour
mis-be-lieve
mis-cal-cu-late
mis-cal-cu-la-tion
mis-car-riage
mis-car-ried
mis-carry
mis-cast
mis-ce-ge-na-tion
mis-cel-la-nea
mis-cel-la-neous
mis-cel-la-nies
mis-cel-lany
mis-chance
mis-chief
mis-chie-vous
mis-clas-sify
mis-con-ceive
mis-con-cep-tion
mis-con-duct
mis-con-struc-tion
mis-con-strue
mis-count
mis-cre-ant
mis-deal
mis-deed
mis-de-meanor
miser
mis-er-able
mis-er-ably
mis-er-ies
mis-ery
mis-fea-sance
mis-file
mis-fire
mis-for-tune
mis-give
mis-gov-ern
mis-guide

mis-han-dle
mis-hap
mish-mash
mis-in-form
mis-in-ter-pret
mis-in-ter-pre-ta-tion
mis-judge
mis-la-bel
mis-lay
mis-man-age
mis-no-mer
mi-sog-a-mist
mi-sog-amy
mis-place
mis-play
mis-print
mis-pri-sion
mis-pro-nounce
mis-pro-nun-cia-tion
mis-quote
mis-read
mis-rule
miss
mis-sal
cf. **mis-sile**
missed
cf. **mist**
mis-shape
mis-shapen
mis-sile
cf. **mis-sal**
mis-sion
mis-sion-ar-ies
mis-sion-ary
mis-sive
mis-spell
mis-spend
mis-spent
mis-state
mis-step
mist
cf. **missed**
mis-tak-able
mis-take
mis-taken
mis-ter
mis-time
mis-tle-toe
mis-took
mis-trans-late
mis-treat
mis-tress
mis-trial
mis-trust
mis-un-der-stand
mis-us-age
mis-use
mite
cf. **might**
mi-tre
or **mi-ter**
miti-gate
miti-ga-tion
mitt
mit-ten
mitz-vah
mitz-voth *(n. pl.)*
mix
mixed—media
mixed—up *(adj.)*
mixer
mix-ture
mne-monic
moan
moat
mob
mobbed
mo-bile
mo-bile home *(n.)*
mo-bil-ity
mo-bi-li-za-tion
mo-bi-lize
mob-ster
moc-ca-sin
mock
mocker
mock-ery
mock—up *(n.)*
mod
modal
cf. **model**
mode
mod-er-ate
mod-er-a-tion
mod-era-tor
mod-ern
mod-ern-ist
mod-ern-is-tic
mod-ern-iza-tion
mod-ern-ize
mod-est
mod-esty
modi-cum
modi-fi-ca-tion
modi-fier
modish
modu-la-bil-ity
modu-lar
modu-late
modu-la-tion
modu-la-tor
modu-la-tory
mod-ule
mo-dus ope-randi
modi ope-randi *(n. pl.)*
mo-hair
moist
moisten
mois-ture
mo-lar
mo-las-ses
mold
mold-able
molder
mold-ier
moldi-est
moldy
mole
mo-lecu-lar
mo-lecu-lar-ity
mole-cule
mole-hill
mo-lest
mo-les-ta-tion
mo-lester
mol-li-fi-ca-tion
mol-lify
mol-lusc
or **mol- usk**
molly-cod-dle
molt

mol-ten
mo-lyb-de-num
mo-ment
mo-men-tarily
mo-men-tary
mo-men-tous
mo-men-tum
mo-menta *(n. pl.)*
or mo-men-tums
mon-arch
mo-nar-chi-cal
or mo-nar-chic
mon-ar-chies
mon-ar-chist
mon-ar-chis-tic
mon-ar-chy
mon-as-te-rial
mon-as-tery
mo-nas-tic
mo-nas-ti-cism
mon-atomic
mon-au-ral
mon-ax-ial
mone-tar-ily
mone-tary
mone-ti-za-tion
mone-tize
money
moneys *(n. pl.)*
or mon-ies
mon-ey-lender
mon-ey—maker *(n.)*
mon-ger
Mon-gol
Mon-go-lian
mon-gol-ism
mon-goose
mon-gooses *(n. pl.)*
mon-grel
mo-ni-tion
moni-tor
moni-to-rial
monk
mon-key
mon-key wrench *(n.)*
mono-chro-matic
mon-o-cle

mo-nog-a-mist
mo-noga-mous
mo-nog-amy
mono-gram
mono-grammed
mono-graph
mono-lin-gual
mono-lith
mono-lithic
mono-logue
or mono-log
mono-logu-ist
or mo-no-lo-gist
mo-no-mial
mono-mor-phic
mono-nu-cle-o-sis
mono-pho-nic
mono-plane
mo-nopo-list
mo-nopo-lis-tic
mo-nopo-lize
mo-nop-oly
mono-rail
mono-so-dium glu-ta-mate *(n.)*
mono-syl-labic
mono-syl-la-bic-ity
mono-syl-la-ble
mono-the-ism
mono-the-ist
mono-the-is-tic
or mono-the-is-ti-cal
mono-tone
mono-tonic
mo-noto-nous
mo-not-ony
mono-type
mon-ox-ide
mon-sei-gneur
mes-sei-gneurs *(n. pl.)*
mon-sieur
mon-si-gnor
mon-si-gnors *(n. pl.)*
or mon-si-gnori
mon-soon
mon-ster
mon-stros-i-ties

mon-stros-ity
mon-strous
mon-tage
Mon-tes-so-rian
month
monu-ment
monu-men-tal
monu-men-tal-ize
mooch
mood
mood-ier
moodi-est
moody
moon
moon-beam
moon-light
moon-lit
moon-stone
moon-struck
moor
cf. more
moor-age
moose
moot
mop
mopped
mop-pet
mop-ping
mop—up *(n.)*
mop up *(v.)*
moral
mo-rale
mor-al-ism
mor-al-ist
mor-al-is-tic
mo-ral-i-ties
mo-ral-ity
mor-al-iza-tion
mor-al-ize
mor-al-izer
mora-to-rium
mora-to-ri-ums *(n. pl.)*
or mora-to-ria
mo-ray
mor-bid
mor-bid-ity
mor-da-cious

mor-dac-ity
mor-dancy
mor-dant
more
cf. **moor**
more or less
more-over
mo-res
morgue
mori-bund
mori-bun-dity
Mor-mon
Mor-mon-ism
morn
morn-ing
cf. **mourn-ing**
mo-rocco
mo-ron
mo-rose
mo-ros-ity
mor-phine
mor-row
mor-sel
mor-tal
mor-tal-ity
mor-tar
mor-tar-board
mort-gage
mort-gager
or **mort-gagor**
mor-ti-cian
mor-ti-fi-ca-tion
mor-ti-fied
mor-tify
mor-tise
or **mor-tice**
mor-tu-ar-ies
mor-tu-ary
mo-saic
Mos-lem
mosque
mos-quito
mos-qui-toes *(n. pl.)*
or **mos-qui-tos**
moss
moss-back
moss-ier
mossi-est
mossy
most
mote
mo-tel
moth
moth-ball
moth—eaten *(adj.)*
mother
moth-er-hood
moth-er-house
mother—in—law
mothers—in—law *(n. pl.)*
moth-er-land
moth-er-li-ness
mother—of—pearl *(n.)*
moth-proof
mo-tif
cf. **mo-tive**
mo-tile
mo-tion
mo-ti-va-te
mo-ti-va-tion
mo-ti-va-tor
mo-tive
cf. **mo-tif**
mot-ley
mo-tor
mo-tor-bike
mo-tor-boat
mo-tor bus
mo-tor-cade
mo-tor-car
mo-tor court
mo-tor-cy-cle
mo-tor home
mo-tor inn
mo-tor-ist
mo-tor-iza-tion
mo-tor-ize
mo-tor lodge
mo-tor-man
mo-tor pool
mo-tor scooter
mo-tor-truck
mo-tor ve-hi-cle
mot-tle
motto
mot-toes *(n. pl.)*
or **mot-tos**
mound
mount
moun-tain
moun-tain ash
moun-tain dew
moun-tain-eer
moun-tain-ous
moun-tain-side
moun-tain-top
moun-te-bank
mourn
mourn-ing
cf. **morn-ing**
mourner
mouse
mouse-trap
mous-saka
mousse
mous-tache
or **mus-tache**
or **mus-ta-chio**
mousy
or **mousey**
mouth
mouth-piece
mouth—to—mouth *(adj.)*
mou-ton
mov-able
or **move-able**
mover
movie
mov-ie-dom
mov-ie-goer
mov-ie-maker
mow
Mr.
Mrs.
Ms.
much
mu-cif-er-ous
mu-ci-lage
mu-ci-lag-i-nous
muck
muck-rake

mu-cous
mud
mud-dier
mud-di-est
muddy
mud-guard
mud-slinger
muff
muf-fin
muf-fle
muf-fler
mug
mugged
mug-ger
muk-luk
mu-latto
mu-lat-toes
mul-berry
mulch
mule
mule-teer
mul-ish
mull
mul-let
mul-ti-col-oured
mul-ti-cul-tural
mul-ti-di-men-sional
mul-ti-di-rec-tional
mul-ti-dis-ci-plin-ary
mul-ti-fac-eted
mul-ti-fari-ous
mul-ti-lat-eral
mul-ti-lay-ered
mul-ti-level
or **mul-ti-lev-eled**
mul-ti-lin-gual
mul-ti-lin-gual-ism
mul-ti-me-dia
mul-ti-mil-lion-aire
mul-ti-nu-clear
mul-ti-par-tite
mul-ti-party
mul-ti-phase
mul-ti-pha-sic
mul-ti-ple
mul-ti-plex
mul-ti-pli-able
mul-ti-plic-able
mul-ti-pli-cand
mul-ti-pli-cate
mul-ti-pli-ca-tion
mul-ti-pli-ca-tive
mul-ti-plici-ties
mul-ti-plic-ity
mul-ti-plier
mul-ti-ply
mul-ti-po-lar
mul-ti-pro-cess-ing
mul-ti-pro-ces-sor
mul-ti-pro-gram-ming
mul-ti-pronged
mul-ti-pur-pose
mul-ti-ra-cial
mul-ti-sen-sory
mul-ti-stage
mul-ti-sto-ried
mul-ti-story
mul-ti-syl-labic
mul-ti-tude
mul-ti-tu-di-nous
mul-tiva-lence
mul-ti-va-lent
mul-ti-val-ued
mul-ti-vari-ate
mum
mum-ble
mum-bler
mumbo jumbo
mum-mer
mum-mi-fi-ca-tion
mum-mi-fied
mum-mify
munch
mun-dane
mu-nici-pal
mu-nici-pal-i-ties
mu-nici-pal-ity
mu-nifi-cent
mu-ni-tion
mu-ral
mur-der
mur-der-ous
mu-ri-atic acid
murk
murk-ier
murki-est
murk-ily
murki-ness
mur-mur
mus-ca-tel
mus-cle
cf. **mus-sel**
muscle—bound *(adj.)*
Mus-co-vite
mus-cu-lar
mus-cu-lar-ity
mus-cu-lar dys-tro-phy
muse
mu-seum
mush
mush-room
mu-sic
mu-si-cal
mu-si-cale
mu-si-cian
mu-si-co-log-i-cal
mu-si-col-o-gist
mu-si-col-ogy
mus-ket
mus-ke-teer
mus-ketry
musk—ox *(n.)*
musk-rat
mus-lin
mus-sel
cf. **mus-cle**
must
mus-tang
mus-tard
mus-ter
mus-tier
mus-ti-est
mus-ti-ness
mu-ta-ble
mu-ta-bly
mu-tant
mu-tate
mu-ta-tion
mu-ta-tive
mute
mu-ti-late

mu-ti-la-tion
mu-ti-la-tor
mu-ti-neer
mu-ti-nous
mu-ti-nies
mu-tiny
mutt
mut-ter
mut-ton
mu-tual
mu-tu-al-ism
mu-tu-al-ist
mu-tu-al-is-tic
mu-tu-al-ity
mu-tu-al-iza-tion
mu-tu-al-ize
muu-muu
muz-zle
muz-zler
my
my-co-flora
my-col-ogy
my-co-plasma
my-co-sis
my-eli-tis
my-elo-fi-bro-sis
myo-car-dial
myo-car-dio-graph
myo-pia
myo-pic
myr-iad
myrrh
myr-tle
my-self
mys-te-rious
mys-tery
mys-tic
mys-ti-cal
mys-ti-cism
mys-ti-fi-ca-tion
mys-ti-fied
mys-ti-fier
mys-tique
myth
mythi-cal
mythi-cize
my-thol-ogy

N

nab
nabbed
na-celle
na-cre
na-cre-ous
na-dir
nag
nagged
nag-ging
nail
nail-brush
nail file
na-ïve
or **na-ive**
na-ïveté
or **na-ivete**
na-ked
name
name—calling *(n.)*
name-plate
name-sake
nano-gram
nano-sec-ond
nap
cf. **knap**
na-palm
nape
naph-tha
naph-thene
nap-kin
nar-cis-sism
nar-cis-sist
nar-co-sis
nar-cotic
nar-co-tize
nar-rate
nar-ra-tion
nar-ra-tive
nar-ra-tor
nar-row
na-sal
na-scent
nas-tur-tium
nas-tier
nas-ti-est
nasty
na-tal
na-tali-ties
na-tal-ity
na-tant
na-ta-tion
na-tion
na-tional
na-tion-al-ism
na-tion-al-ist
na-tion-al-is-tic
na-tion-ali-ties
na-tion-al-ity
na-tion-al-iza-tion
na-tion-al-ize
na-tion-hood
na-tion-wide
na-tive
na-tiv-ism
na-tivi-ties
na-tiv-ity
natty
natu-ral
natu-ral-ism
natu-ral-ist
natu-ral-iza-tion
natu-ral-ize
na-ture
naugh-tier
naugh-ti-est
naughty
nau-sea
nau-se-ate
nau-seous
nau-ti-cal
nau-ti-lus
na-val
cf. **na-vel**
nave
cf. **knave**
na-vel
cf. **na-val**
navi-ga-bil-ity
navi-ga-ble
navi-gate
navi-ga-tion
navi-ga-tor

navy
nay
cf. neigh
nazi
Na-zi-ism
near
nearby
near-sighted
neat
neb-ula
nebu-los-ity
nebu-lous
nec-es-sar-ily
nec-es-sary
ne-ces-si-tate
ne-ces-si-ties
ne-ces-sity
neck
neck-er-chief
neck-lace
neck-line
neck-tie
ne-crol-o-gist
nec-ro-mancy
ne-cropo-lis
nec-ropsy
ne-cro-sis
nec-tar
née
or nee
cf. knee
need
cf. knead
need-ier
needi-est
nee-dle
ne'er—do—well *(adj.) (n.)*
ne-fari-ous
ne-gate
ne-ga-tion
ne-ga-tor
nega-tive
nega-tiv-ism
nega-tiv-ist
ne-glect
ne-glecter
neg-li-gee
or neg-ligé
neg-li-gence
neg-li-gent
neg-li-gi-ble
neg-li-gi-bly
ne-go-tia-bil-ity
ne-go-tia-ble
ne-go-tiant
ne-go-tiate
ne-go-tia-tion
ne-go-tia-tor
neigh
cf. nay
neigh-bour
neigh-bour-hood
nei-ther
neme-sis
neon
neo-phyte
neo-plasm
nephew
nepo-tism
Nep-tune
nerve
nervier
nervi-est
nervy
nest
nester
nes-tle
nest-ling
net
net-ted
net-ting
net-tle
net-work
neu-ral
neu-rolo-gist
neu-rol-ogy
neu-ron
neu-ropa-thy
neu-ro-physi-ol-ogy
neu-ro-psy-chi-at-ric
neu-ro-sen-sory
neu-ro-sis
neu-ro-sur-geon
neu-ro-sur-gery
neu-ro-tic
neu-roti-cism
neu-ter
neu-tral
neu-tral-ity
neu-tral-iza-tion
neu-tral-ize
neu-tron
never
nev-er-the-less
new
cf. knew
new-born
new-comer
new-fan-gled
news-cast
news dealer
news-let-ter
news-mag-a-zine
news-pa-per
news-print
news-reel
news-room
news-stand
news-wor-thy
newsy
next
Ni-ag-ara
nib
nice
nice-ties
niche
nick
nickel
nick-nack
nick-name
nico-tine
niece
nifty
nig-gard
nigh
night
cf. knight
night-cap
night-clothes
night-club
night court

night-fall
night-gown
night-mare
night-owl
night-time
ni-hil-ism
ni-hil-ist
Nike
nil
nim-ble
nim-blest
nim-bus
nin-com-poop
nine
nine-fold
nine-teen
nine-teenth
nineties
ninety
nip
nip-ping
nip-ple
nippy
nir-vana
ni-sei
nit
cf. **knit**
ni-trate
ni-tric
nitro
ni-tro-gen
ni-tro-glyc-erin
or **ni-tro-glyc-er-ine**
ni-trous
nitty—gritty *(n.)*
nit-wit
no
cf. **know**
Noah
nob
nob-bier
nob-bi-est
no-bil-ity
no-ble
no-bly
nobody
noc-tur-nal
noc-turne
nocu-ous
nod
node
nod-ule
no—fault *(adj.)*
nog-gin
noise
noise-maker
nois-ier
nois-i-est
noisy
no—load *(adj.)*
nolo con-ten-dere
no-mad
no-madic
no—man's—land *(adj.)*
nom de plume
no-men-cla-ture
nomi-nal
nomi-nate
nomi-na-tion
nomi-na-tive
nomi-na-tor
nomi-nee
non-ad-di-tive
no-na-ge-nar-ian
non-aligned
non-bus-i-ness
non-ca-lo-ric
non-cha-lance
non-com-ba-tant
non-com-mit-tal
non com-pos men-tis
non-con-duc-tor
non-con-form-ist
non-con-form-ity
non-credit
non-de-script
none
non-en-force-able
non-en-tity
none-the-less
non-ex-is-tence
non-fat
non-fic-tion
non-flam-ma-ble
non—food *(adj.)*
non-in-ter-ven-tion
non-me-tal-lic
non-par-ti-san
non-plus
non-pro-duc-tive
non-pro-fes-sional
non-profit
non-pro-lif-era-tion
non-re-fund-able
non-resi-dent
non-re-sis-tance
non-re-stric-tive
non-re-turn-able
non-sched-uled
non-sec-tar-ian
non-sense
non se-qui-tur
non-skid
non-stop
non-union
noo-dle
nook
noon
noon-day
noon-time
no—par
or **no—par—value**
nor-mal
nor-malcy
nor-mal-iza-tion
nor-mal-ize
nor-ma-tive
north
north-bound
north-east
north-easter
north-east-ern
north-ern
north-land
north pole
North Star
north-ward
north-west
nose
nose-bleed
nose cone

nose dive
nose-gay
nose—piece
nosey
or nosy
no-show
nos-tal-gia
nos-tal-gic
nos-tril
not
cf. knot
nota bene
no-ta-ble
no-ta-bly
no-ta-ri-za-tion
no-ta-rize
no-tary pub-lic
no-tate
notch
note
note-book
note-pa-per
note-wor-thy
noth-ing
no-tice
no-tice-able
no-tice-ably
no-ti-fi-ca-tion
no-ti-fied
no-tify
no-tion
no-to-ri-eties
no-to-ri-ety
no-to-ri-ous
noun
nour-ish
novel
nov-el-ette
nov-el-ist
nov-el-ize
nov-el-ties
nov-elty
no-vena
nov-ice
no-vi-tiate
no-vo-caine
nowa-days
nox-ious
noz-zle
nub
nu-bile
nu-clear
nu-cleus
nude
nug-get
nui-sance
null
nul-li-fi-ca-tion
nul-lify
numb
num-ber
nu-mer-able
nu-meral
nu-mer-ate
nu-mera-tion
nu-mera-tor
nu-meric
nu-meri-cal
nu-mer-ol-ogy
nu-mer-o-logi-cal
nu-mer-ous
nu-mis-matic
nu-mis-ma-tist
num-skull
nup-tial
nurse
nurse-maid
nurs-ery
nurse's aide
nur-ture
nut
nu-tri-ent
nu-tri-ment
nu-tri-tion
nu-tri-tional
nu-tri-tion-ist
nu-tri-tious
nu-tri-tive
nutty
nuz-zle
ny-lon
nymph

O

oaf
oak
oaken
oar
cf. or
cf. ore
oa-ses *(n. pl.)*
oa-sis
oat
oath
ob-bli-gato
ob-du-racy
ob-du-rate
obe-di-ence
obe-di-ent
obei-sance
obei-sant
obe-lisk
obese
obe-sity
obey
ob-fus-cate
ob-fus-ca-tion
obitu-ary
ob-ject
ob-jec-tion
ob-jec-tion-able
ob-jec-tive
ob-jec-tor
ob-late
ob-la-tion
ob-li-gate
ob-li-ga-tion
ob-liga-tory
oblige
oblique
oblit-er-ate
oblit-era-tion
oblit-era-tive
oblit-era-tor
obliv-ion
obliv-i-ous
ob-long
ob-lo-quy
ob-nox-ious

oboe
ob-scene
ob-sceni-ties
ob-scen-ity
ob-scur-ant
ob-scure
ob-scu-ri-ties
ob-scu-rity
ob-se-qui-ous
ob-se-quies
ob-serv-able
ob-ser-vance
ob-ser-va-tion
ob-ser-va-tory
ob-serve
ob-server
ob-sess
ob-ses-sion
ob-ses-sive
ob-sid-ian
ob-so-lesce
ob-so-les-cence
ob-so-les-cent
ob-so-lete
ob-sta-cle
ob-stet-ric
ob-ste-tri-cian
ob-sti-nacy
ob-sti-nate
ob-strep-er-ous
ob-struct
ob-struc-tion
ob-struc-tor
ob-tain
ob-tru-sion
ob-tru-sive
ob-tund
ob-tu-rate
ob-tuse
ob-verse
ob-vert
ob-vi-ate
ob-vi-ous
oc-ca-sion
oc-ca-sional
Oc-ci-dent
oc-ci-den-tal
oc-clude
oc-clu-sion
oc-cult
oc-cult-ism
oc-cu-pancy
oc-cu-pant
oc-cu-pa-tion
oc-cu-pa-tional
oc-cu-pied
oc-cupy
oc-cur
oc-curred
oc-cur-rence
oc-cur-rent
oc-cur-ring
ocean
ocean-ar-ium
ocean-front
oce-anic
ocean-og-ra-pher
ocean-og-ra-phy
oce-lot
ochre
or ocher
oc-ta-gon
oc-tago-nal
oc-tane
oc-tave
oc-tavo
oc-tet
oc-to-ge-nar-ian
oc-to-pod
oc-to-pus
oc-to-roon
ocu-lar
ocu-list
odd
odd-ball
oddi-ties
odd-ity
ode
cf. owed
odi-ous
odium
odo-graph
odome-ter
odon-tolo-gist
odon-tol-ogy
odor-ant
odor-if-er-ous
odor-ize
odor-ous
odour
Odys-seus
od-ys-sey
Oe-di-pus
off
of-fal
off and on *(adv.)*
off-beat
off—colour
or off—coloured *(adj.)*
of-fence
or of-fense
of-fend
of-fen-sive
of-fer
of-fer-tory
off-hand
of-fice
of-fice-holder
of-fi-cer
of-fi-cial
of-fi-cial-dom
of-fi-ci-ary
of-fi-ci-ate
of-fi-cious
off—key *(adj.)*
off—line *(adj.)*
off-set
off-shoot
off-shore
off-side
off-spring
off—the—record *(adj.)*
ogive
ogle
ogre
ohm
ohm-me-ter
oil
oil-can
oil-ier
oili-est

oily
oint-ment
old
olden
old—fashioned *(adj.)*
old—timer *(n.)*
oleo
oleo-mar-ga-rine
oleo-resin
ol-fac-tion
ol-fac-tive
ol-fac-tory
oli-gar-chic
oli-gar-chy
oli-gopo-lis-tic
oli-gop-oly
ol-ive
olym-piad
Olym-pic
om-buds-man
om-elette
or om-elet
omen
omi-nous
omis-si-ble
omis-sion
omit
omit-ted
omit-ting
om-ni-bus
om-nifi-cent
om-nipo-tence
om-nipo-tent
om-nivo-rous
on—again, off—again *(adj.)*
once
one
cf. won
one-night stand *(n.)*
oner-ous
one-self
one—sided *(adj.)*
one—way *(adj.)*
on-go-ing
on-ion
on-ion-skin
on—line *(adj.)*
on-looker
only
on-set
on-shore
on-side
on-slaught
on-stage
on—the—job *(adj.)*
on—the—scene *(adj.)*
onto
onus
on-ward
ool-o-gist
ool-ogy
ooze
opaci-ties
opac-ity
opal
opaque
op cit
open
open—circuit *(adj.)*
open—ended *(adj.)*
opener
open-handed
open house *(n.)*
open—minded *(adj.)*
open—mouthed *(adj.)*
op-era
op-era-ble
op-era-bly
op-era-goer *(n.)*
op-er-and
op-er-ant
op-er-ate
op-er-atic
op-era-tion
op-era-tional
op-era-tive
op-era-tor
op-er-etta
ophid-ian
ophi-ol-ogy
ophi-opha-gous
oph-thal-mic
oph-thal-molo-gist
oph-thal-mol-ogy
opi-ate
opine
opin-ion
opin-ion-ated
opium
opos-sum
op-po-nent
op-por-tune
op-por-tun-ism
op-por-tun-ist
op-por-tun-is-tic
op-por-tu-ni-ties
op-por-tu-nity
op-pos-able
op-pose
op-po-site
op-po-si-tion
op-press
op-pres-sion
op-pres-sive
op-pres-sor
op-pro-brium
op-pugn
op-ta-tive
op-tic
op-ti-cal
op-ti-cian
op-ti-mism
op-ti-mist
op-ti-mis-tic
or op-ti-mis-ti-cal
op-ti-mi-za-tion
op-ti-mize
op-ti-mum
op-tion
op-tional
op-tome-trist
op-tome-try
opt out *(v.)*
opu-lence
opu-lent
opus
opera
or opuses *(n. pl.)*
or
cf. oar

cf. ore
or-a-cle
cf. au-ri-cle
orac-u-lar
oral
cf. au-ral
or-ange
or-ang-ish
or-angy
or or-angey
orate
ora-tion
ora-tor
ora-tor-i-cal
ora-tory
orb
or-bit
or-bital
or-biter
or-chard
or-ches-tra
or-ches-tral
or-ches-trate
or-ches-tra-tion
or-chid
or-dain
or-deal
or-der
or-derly
or-di-nal
or-di-nance
cf. ord-nance
or-di-nary
or-di-nate
or-di-na-tion
ord-nance
cf. or-di-nance
ore
cf. or
cf. oar
oreg-ano
or-gan
or-gandy
or or-gan-die
organ—grinder *(n.)*
or-ganic
or-gan-ism
or-gan-ist
or-ga-ni-za-tion
or-ga-ni-za-tional
or-gan-ize
or-ga-nizer
or-gi-as-tic
or-gies
orgy
ori-ent
ori-en-tal
ori-en-tate
ori-en-ta-tion
ori-fice
ori-gin
origi-nal
origi-nal-ity
origi-nate
origi-na-tion
origi-na-tive
origi-na-tor
or-na-ment
or-na-men-tal
or-na-men-ta-tion
or-nate
or-nery
or-nithic
or-ni-tholo-gist
or-ni-thol-ogy
oro-graphic
orog-ra-phy
or-phan
or-phan-age
or-phrey
orth-odon-tics
orth-odon-tist
or-tho-dox
or-tho-doxy
or-tho-epist
or-tho-epy
or-tho-graphic
or or-tho-graphi-cal
or-tho-pae-dic
or or-tho-pe-dic
or-tho-pae-dist
os-cil-late
os-cil-la-tion
os-cil-la-tor
os-cil-la-tory
os-cu-late
os-cu-la-tion
os-cu-la-tory
os-matic
os-mo-sis
os-motic
os-si-fi-ca-tion
os-si-fied
os-sify
os-ten-si-ble
os-ten-si-bly
os-ten-ta-tion
os-ten-ta-tious
os-te-olo-gist
os-te-ol-ogy
os-teo-my-eli-tis
os-tra-cism
os-tra-cize
os-trich
other
oth-er-wise
oto-lar-yn-golo-gist
oto-lar-yn-gol-ogy
ot-ter
ot-to-man
ought
cf. aught
ounce
our
cf. hour
our-self
our-selves
oust
ouster
out
out—and—out *(adj.)*
out-bid
out-board
out-break
out-burst
out-cast
out-class
out-come
out-crop
out-cry
out-dated

out-dis-tance
outdo
out-door
out-doors-man
out-doorsy
out-draw
outer
out-er-coat
out-er-most
outer space *(n.)*
out-fit
out-go-ing
out-growth
out-land-ish
out-law
out-lay
out-let
out-line
out-moded
out-num-ber
out—of—bounds *(adj.) (adv.)*
out—of—date *(adj.)*
out—of—doors *(n. pl.)*
out—of—the—way *(adj.)*
out-pa-tient
out-post
out-put
out-rage
out-ra-geous
out-right
out-side
out-spo-ken
out-ward
or **out-wards**
out-wit
out-wore
out-worn
oval
ovary
ova-tion
oven
over
over-abun-dance
over-achiever
over-act
over-ac-tive
over-all
over-bear-ing
over-bid
over-blown
over-board
over-bur-den
over-ca-pac-ity
over-cast
over-charge
over-coat
over-come
overdo
cf. **over-due**
over-drawn
over-due
cf. **overdo**
over-eat
over-em-pha-size
over-ex-pose
over-flow
over-grow
over-hang
over-head
over-in-dulge
over-kill
over-lap
over-lay
over-load
over-look
over-night
over-re-act
over-rule
over-seas
over-sight
over—the—counter *(adj.)*
over-throw
over-time
over-ture
over-turn
over-view
over-weight
over-whelm
over-wrought
ovu-late
ovum
ova *(n. pl.)*
owed
cf. **ode**
owl
own
ox
oxen *(n. pl.)*
ox-ford
oxi-da-tion
ox-ide
oxi-diz-able
oxi-dize
oxi-dizer
oxy-gen
oxy-gen-ate
oys-ter
ozone
ozo-no-sphere

P

pace
pace-maker
pacer
pace-set-ter
pachy-derm
pach-ys-an-dra
pa-cific
paci-fi-ca-tion
pa-cifi-cism
pa-cifi-ca-tor
paci-fier
paci-fism
paci-fist
pac-ify
pack
pack-able
pack-age
pack-board
packed
cf. **pact**
packer
packet
pack-horse
pack-ing-house
pact
cf. **packed**

pad
pad-ded
pad-dle
pad-lock
pa-dre
pa-gan-ism
page
pag-eant
pag-eantry
page boy
pagi-nate
pagi-na-tion
pail
cf. **pale**
pail-ful
pain
cf. **pane**
pains-tak-ing
paint
painter
pair
cf. **pare**
cf. **pear**
pal-ace
pal-at-able
pal-ate
cf. **pal-let**
cf. **pal-ette**
pa-la-tial
pa-la-ver
pale
cf. **pail**
Pa-leo-lithic
pa-le-on-to-lo-gist
pa-le-on-tol-ogy
Pa-leo-zoic
pal-ette
cf. **pal-ate**
cf. **pal-let**
pali-sade
pal-la-dium
pal-let
cf. **pal-ate**
cf. **pal-ette**
pal-lid
pal-lor
palm
palm-ist
palm-istry
pal-pa-bil-ity
pal-pa-ble
pal-pa-bly
pal-pate
pal-pi-tate
pal-pi-ta-tion
palsy
pal-try
pam-per
pam-phlet
pam-phle-teer
pan
pana-cea
pana-cean
pan-ama
pan-cake
pan-chro-matic
pan-creas
panda
cf. **pan-der**
pan-de-mo-nium
pan-der
cf. **panda**
Pan-do-ra's box *(n.)*
pane
cf. **pain**
panel
pan-el-ist
pang
pan-han-dle
Pan-hel-lenic
panic
pan-icked
pan-orama
pansy
pant
pan-ta-loon
pan-the-ism
pan-theon
pan-ther
pan-to-mime
pan-to-mimic
pan-to-mim-ist
pan-try
pant-suit
panty hose
pan-zer
pap
pa-pacy
pa-pal
pa-paya
pa-per
pa-per-back
pa-per-boy
pa-per-hanger
pa-per-weight
pa-per-work
papier—mâché
pa-pilla
pa-pist
pa-poose
pa-prika
Pap smear *(n.)*
pa-py-rus
par
para-ble
pa-rab-ola
para-bolic
para-bo-loid
para-chute
para-chut-ist
pa-rade
para-dise
para-dox
para-doxi-cal
par-af-fin
para-gene-sis
para-gon
para-graph
para-keet
par-al-de-hyde
par-al-lel
par-al-lel-epi-ped
par-al-lel-ism
par-al-lel-o-gram
pa-ralo-gism
pa-raly-sis
para-lytic
para-lyze
para-medic
para-medi-cal
pa-rame-ter

para-met-ric
or **para-met-ri-cal**
pa-rame-ter-ize
para-mili-tary
para-mount
para-noia
para-noid
para-pet
para-pher-na-lia
para-phrase
para-phras-tic
para-ple-gia
para-pro-fes-sional
para-psy-cholo-gist
para-psy-chol-ogy
par-a-site
para-sitic
or **para-sit-i-cal**
para-sit-ism
para-sol
para-trooper
par-boil
par-cel
par-cel post
parch
par-don
par-don-able
pare
cf. **pair**
cf. **pear**
pare-go-ric
par-ent
pa-ren-tal
par-ent-age
par-en-the-sis
par-en-thetic
or **par-en-thet-i-cal**
pa-ren-the-size
par-ent-hood
pa-re-sis
par ex-cel-lence *(adj.)*
par-fait
pari—mu-tuel *(n.)*
par-ish
pa-rish-io-ner
par-ity
park
parka
Par-kin-son's Law
park-land
park-way
par-lay
cf. **par-ley**
par-ley
cf. **par-lay**
par-lia-ment
par-lia-men-tar-ian
par-lia-men-tary
par-lour
pa-ro-chial
pa-ro-chi-al-ism
paro-dist
par-ody
pa-role
pa-rolee
par-quet
par-ri-cide
par-rot
parry
par-si-mo-ni-ous
par-si-mony
pars-ley
pars-nip
par-son
par-son-age
part
par-take
Par-the-non
par-tial
par-tici-pant
par-tici-pate
par-tici-pa-tion
par-tici-pa-tive
par-tici-pa-tor
par-tici-pa-tory
par-ti-cip-ial
par-ti-ci-ple
par-ti-cle
par-ticu-lar
par-ticu-lar-ize
par-ti-san
par-tite
par-ti-tion
par-ti-tion-ist
part-ner
part-ner-ship
par-tridge
part—time *(adj.)*
par-tu-ri-tion
par value
pass
pass-able
pass-ably
pas-sage
pas-sage-way
pass-book
passé
passed
cf. **past**
pas-sen-ger
pass-erby
pass—fail *(n.)*
pas-si-ble
pas-sion
pas-sion-ate
pas-sive
pas-siv-ism
pass-key
pass out *(n.)*
Pass-over *(n.)*
pass-port
past
cf. **passed**
paste
paste-board
pas-tel
pas-teur-iza-tion
pas-teur-ize
pas-time
pas-tor
pas-to-ral
pas-to-rate
pastry
pas-tur-age
pas-ture
pat
patch
patch-board
patch cord
patch test
patch-work

pate
pâté
pâté de foie gras
pa-tent
pa-ter-nal
pa-ter-nal-ism
pa-ter-nal-is-tic
pa-ter-nity
path
pa-thetic
pa-theti-cal
path-o-logi-cal
pa-tholo-gist
pa-thology
path-way
pa-tience
cf. **pa-tients**
pa-tina
pa-tio
pa-tri-arch
pa-tri-ar-chal
pa-tri-cian
pat-ri-cide
pat-ri-lin-eal
pa-triot
pa-tri-otic
pa-tri-o-tism
pa-trol
pa-tron
pa-tron-age
pa-tron-ize
pat-ter
pat-tern
pau-city
paunch
pau-per
pause
cf. **paws**
pave
pa-vil-ion
pawl
pawn
pawn-bro-ker
pawn-shop
paws
cf. **pause**
pay-able
pay—as—you—go *(adj.)*
pay-cheque
pay-day
payee
pay-load
pay-roll
pea
peace
cf. **piece**
peace-able
peace-ably
peace corps *(n.)*
peace-time
pea-cock
peak
cf. **peek**
cf. **pique**
peal
cf. **peel**
pea-nut
pearl
cf. **purl**
peas-ant
peat
peb-ble
pe-can
peck
pe-cu-liar
pe-cu-liar-ity
pe-cu-ni-ary
peda-gogic
peda-gogi-cal
peda-gogue
or **peda-gog**
peda-gogy
pedal
cf. **ped-dle**
ped-ant
ped-dle
cf. **pedal**
ped-dler
or **ped-lar**
ped-es-tal
pe-des-trian
pe-di-at-ric
pe-di-a-tri-cian
pedi-gree
pe-dom-e-ter
peek
cf. **peak**
cf. **pique**
peek-a-boo
peel
cf. **peal**
peep
peer
cf. **pier**
peer-age
peeve
pee-vish
peg
peg-board
peli-can
pel-let
pell—mell *(adv.)*
pelt
pel-vic
pel-vis
pen
pe-nal
pe-nal-ize
pen-alty
pen-ance
pen-chant
pen-cil
cf. **pen-sile**
pen-dant
pen-du-lous
pen-du-lum
pene-trate
pene-tra-tion
peni-cil-lin
pen-in-sula
peni-tence
peni-tent
peni-ten-tial
peni-ten-tiary
pen-knife
pen-light
pen-man-ship
pen-nant
penny
penny ar-cade *(n.)*
pen-ny-weight

pe-nolo-gist
pe-nol-ogy
pen pal *(n.)*
pen-sile
cf. **pen-cil**
pen-sion
pen-sioner
pen-sive
pen-ta-gon
pen-tath-lon
Pen-te-cost
Pen-te-cos-tal
pent-house
pe-nult
pen-ul-ti-mate
pe-nu-ri-ous
pen-ury
peon
pe-on-age
peo-ple
pep-per-mint
pep-pery
pep talk *(n.)*
pep-tic
per-am-bu-late
per-am-bu-la-tion
per-am-bu-la-tor
per-cale
per cap-ita
per-ceiv-able
per-ceiv-ably
per-ceive
per-cent
per-cent-age
per-cen-tile
per cen-tum
per-cept
per-cep-ti-bil-ity
per-cep-ti-ble
per-cep-tion
per-cep-tive
per-cep-tual
perch
per-chance
per-co-late
per-co-la-tor
per-cus-sion
per diem
per-di-tion
pe-remp-tory
pe-ren-nial
per-fect
per-fec-tion
per-fec-tion-ist
per-fidi-ous
per-fidy
per-fo-rate
per-fo-ra-tion
per-force
per-form
per-for-mance
per-former
per-fume
per-func-tory
per-fuse
per-fu-sion
per-haps
pe-rime-ter
pe-riod
pe-ri-odic
pe-ri-odi-cal
peri-odon-tics
peri-pa-tetic
pe-riph-eral
pe-riph-ery
peri-scope
per-ish
per-ish-able
peri-win-kle
per-jure
per-jurer
per-jury
perky
per-ma-frost
per-ma-nence
per-ma-nency
per-ma-nent
per-me-able
per-me-ate
per-mis-si-bil-ity
per-mis-sible
per-mis-si-bly
per-mis-sion
per-mis-sive
per-mit
per-mu-ta-tion
per-ni-cious
per-ox-ide
per-pen-dicu-lar
per-pe-trate
per-pe-tra-tion
per-pe-tra-tor
per-pet-ual
per-petu-ate
per-pe-tu-ity
per-plex
per-plex-ity
per-qui-site
per se
per-se-cute
cf. **prose-cute**
per-se-cu-tion
per-se-ver-ance
per-se-vere
per-si-flage
per-sist
per-sis-tence
per-sis-tent
per-son
per-sona
per-son-able
per-sonal
cf. **per-son-nel**
per-son-al-ity
per-son-al-iza-tion
per-son-al-ize
per-sona non grata
per-soni-fi-ca-tion
per-son-ify
per-son-nel
cf. **per-sonal**
per-spec-tive
cf. **pro-spec-tive**
per-spicu-ous
per-spi-ra-tion
per-spire
per-suade
per-sua-sion
per-sua-sive
pert
per-tain

per-ti-na-cious
per-ti-nent
per-turb
pe-ruse
per-vade
per-va-sion
per-verse
per-ver-sion
per-vert
pes-si-mism
pes-si-mis-tic
pes-ter
pes-ti-cide
pes-ti-lence
pes-tle
cf. **pis-til**
cf. **pis-tol**
pet
petal
petit
pe-ti-tion
pet-rify
pet-ro-chemi-cal
pet-rol
pe-tro-leum
pet-ti-ness
petty
petu-lance
petu-lant
pe-tu-nia
pew
pew-ter
pha-lanx
phan-tasm
phan-tom
pha-raoh
phari-see
phar-ma-ceu-ti-cal
phar-ma-cist
phar-ma-col-ogy
phar-ma-co-poeia
phar-macy
phase
cf. **faze**
phe-no-bar-bi-tal
phe-nome-nal
phi-lan-der
phi-lan-derer
phil-an-thropic
phi-lan-thro-pist
phi-lan-thropy
phi-late-list
phil-har-monic
Phil-lip-pi-ans
phi-lis-tine
philo-den-dron
phi-lolo-gist
phi-lol-ogy
phi-loso-pher
philo-sophic
phi-loso-phize
phi-loso-phizer
phi-loso-phy
phle-bi-tis
phlegm
phleg-matic
phlox
pho-bia
Phoe-ni-cian
pho-netic
pho-nics
pho-no-graph
pho-nog-ra-phy
pho-nolo-gist
pho-nol-ogy
phony
phos-gene
phos-phate
phos-pho-resce
phos-pho-res-cence
phos-pho-res-cent
phos-pho-rus
pho-to-bi-ol-ogy
pho-to-cath-ode
pho-to-cell
pho-to-chemi-cal
pho-to-chem-is-try
pho-to-com-po-si-tion
pho-to-copy
pho-to-elec-tric
pho-to-en-grave
pho-to-flash
pho-to-ge-nic
pho-to-ge-ol-ogy
pho-to-graph
pho-to-graphic
pho-tog-ra-phy
pho-to-gra-vure
pho-to-jour-nal-ism
pho-to—off-set
pho-to-sen-si-ti-za-tion
pho-to-sphere
pho-to-stat *(v.)*
pho-to-static
pho-to-syn-the-sis
pho-to-tube
pho-to-type-set-ting
pho-to-ty-pog-ra-phy
phrasal
phrase
phrase-olo-gist
phrase-ol-ogy
phre-nolo-gist
phre-nol-ogy
physic
cf. **phy-sique**
phys-i-cal
phy-si-cian
physi-cist
physi-co-chemi-cal
phys-ics
physi-og-nomy
physi-og-ra-phy
physi-o-logi-cal
physi-olo-gist
physi-ol-ogy
phys-io-thera-pist
phy-sique
cf. **physic**
pi
cf. **pie**
pia-nis-simo
pia-nist
pi-ano
pi-as-ter
or **pi-as-tre**
pi-azza
pica
cf. **piker**
pica-dor
pica-yune

pic-ca-lilli
pic-colo
pick
pick-axe
pick-erel
picket
picket line
pickle
pick-pocket
pic-nic
pi-co-sec-ond
pic-to-gram
pic-to-graph
pic-tog-ra-phy
pic-to-rial
pic-to-ri-al-ize
pic-ture
pic-tur-esque
picture tube
picture window
picture writing
pic-tur-ize
pid-dle
pie
cf. **pi**
piece
cf. **peace**
piece-meal
pie chart
pie-crust
pied-mont
pie in the sky
pier
cf. **peer**
pierce
pi-etism
pi-etis-tic
pi-ety
pif-fle
pig
pig-boat
pi-geon
pi-geon-hole
pigeon—toed
pig-gish
pig-gy-back
pig-headed
pig in a poke
pig iron
pig latin
pig-let
pig-men-ta-tion
pig-pen
pig-skin
pig-sty
pike
piker
cf. **pica**
pi-las-ter
pile
pile driver*(n.)*
pileup
pil-fer
pil-fer-age
pil-grim
pil-grim-age
pill
pil-lage
pil-lar
pill-box
pil-lory
pil-low
pil-low-case
pi-lot
pi-lot-house
pilot light *(n.)*
pil-sner
or **pil-sener**
pi-mento
pim-ple
pin
pin-afore
pi-ñata
or **pi-nata**
pin-ball ma-chine
pince—nez
pin-cer
pinch
pinch—hit *(v.)*
pinch hitter *(n.)*
pin curl *(n.)*
pin-cush-ion
pine
pine-ap-ple
pine-cone
ping
pin-hole
pin-ion
pink
pin money *(n.)*
pin-na-cle
pi-nochle
pin-point
pin-prick
pins and needles *(n. pl.)*
pin-set-ter
pin-spot-ter
pin-stripe
pint
pin-tle
pinto
pint—size
or **pint—sized**
pinup
pin-wheel
pio-neer
pi-ous
pip
pipe
pipe cleaner
pipe dream
pipe fit-ter
pipe-line
pipe or-gan
piper
pipe wrench
pip-pin
pip—squeak
pi-quancy
pi-quant
pique
cf. **peak**
cf. **peek**
pi-racy
pi-ra-nha
pi-rate
pi-rat-i-cal
pir-ou-ette
pis-ta-chio
pis-til
cf. **pes-tle**

cf. **pis-tol**
pis-tol
cf. **pes-tle**
cf. **pis-til**
pis-ton
piston ring *(n.)*
piston rod *(n.)*
pit
pit—a—pat *(n.)*
pitch
pitch—black *(adj.)*
pitch—dark *(adj.)*
pitcher
pitch-fork
pitch pipe
pite-ous
pit-fall
pithy
piti-able
piti-ably
piti-ful
piti-less
pit-tance
pit-ter—pat-ter *(n.)*
pi-tu-itary
pit viper *(n.)*
pity
pivot
piv-otal
pixie
or **pixy**
pizza
piz-zazz
pla-ca-bil-ity
pla-ca-ble
pla-ca-bly
plac-ard
pla-cate
pla-ca-tion
pla-ca-tive
pla-ca-tory
place
place-holder
place-kick
place mat *(n.)*
pla-centa
pla-cen-tae
or **pla-centas**
placid
pla-gia-rism
pla-gia-rist
pla-gia-ris-tic
pla-gia-rize
pla-gia-rizer
pla-giary
plague
plaid
plain
cf. **plane**
plain-tiff
plain-tive
plait
cf. **plate**
plan
plane
cf. **plain**
plane-load
planet
plan-etar-ium
plan-etary
plan-etoid
plan-etolo-gist
plan-etol-ogy
plank
plank-ton
planned
plan-ning
plant
plan-tain
plan-ta-tion
planter
plaque
plasma
plas-ter
plas-ter-board
plas-ter-cast *(n.)*
plas-ter of paris
plas-ter-work
plas-tic
plas-tic-ity
plas-ti-cize
plate
cf. **plait**
pla-teau
pla-teaus *(n. pl.)*
or **pla-teaux**
plate-ful
plate-glass
plat-form
plati-num
plati-tude
plati-tu-di-nal
plati-tu-di-nar-ian
plati-tu-di-nize
plati-tu-di-nous
pla-tonic
pla-toon
plat-ter
plau-dit
plau-si-bil-ity
plau-si-ble
plau-si-bly
play
play-back
play-boy
play—by—play *(adj.)*
player
play-ground
play-house
play-land
play-mate
play-pen
play-room
play-suit
play-wright
plaza
plea
plead
pleas-ant
please
plea-sur-able
plea-sur-ably
plea-sure
pleat
ple-be-ian
plebi-scite
pledge
ple-nipo-tent
pleni-po-ten-tiary
pleni-tude
plen-ti-ful

plenty
pleth-ora
pleu-risy
Plexi-glas
plexus
pli-abil-ity
pli-able
pli-ably
pli-ancy
pli-ant
pli-cate
pli-ca-tion
pli-ers
plight
plink
plod
plop
plopped
plot
plough
plough-share
ploy
pluck
pluck-ier
plucki-est
plug
plugged
plum
cf. **plumb**
plum-age
plumber
plun-der
plun-der-able
plun-der-age
plun-der-ous
plunge
plunger
plunk
plu-ral
plu-ral-ism
plu-ral-ist
plu-ral-is-tic
plu-ral-ity
plu-ral-ize
plus
plush
plush-ier
plushi-est
plu-toc-racy
plu-to-crat
plu-ton
plu-tonic
plu-to-nium
ply
ply-wood
pneu-matic
pneu-mo-nia
pneu-monic
pneu-mo-tho-rax
poach
poacher
pocket
pock-et-book
pock-et-knife
pocket—size
or **pocket—sized**
pock-mark
pod
po-dia-trist
po-dia-try
po-dium
po-etic
po-eti-cal
po-eti-cism
poet laureate
po-etry
pogo stick
po-grom
poi
poi-gnancy
poi-gnant
poin-ci-ana
poin-set-tia
point
point—blank
poise
poi-son
poi-son-ous
poison—pen *(adj.)*
poke
po-ker
poky
or **pokey**
po-lar
Po-laris
po-lar-ity
po-lar-iz-abil-ity
po-lar-iz-able
po-lar-iza-tion
po-lar-ize
Po-lar-oid
pole
cf. **poll**
po-lemic
po-lemi-cize
po-le-mist
pole—vault *(v.)*
pole-ward
po-lice
po-lice-man
po-lice-woman
poli-cies
pol-icy
pol-icy-holder
poli-cy-mak-ing
po-lio
po-lio-my-eli-tis
po-lio-vi-rus
pol-ish
po-lit-buro
po-lite
poli-tic
po-lit-i-cal
poli-ti-cian
po-liti-ci-za-tion
po-liti-cize
po-lit-ico
po-liti-cos *(n. pl.)*
or **po-liti-coes**
polka
polka dot
poll
cf. **pole**
pol-len
pol-lin-ate
pol-li-na-tion
pol-li-wog
or **pol-ly-wog**
poll-ster
pol-lut-ant
pol-lute

pol-lu-tion
polo
po-lo-naise
poly-chrome
poly-clinic
poly-es-ter
poly-es-trous
poly-eth-yl-ene
poly-gamic
po-lyga-mous
po-lyga-mist
po-lyg-amy
poly-gon
poly-graph
poly-mer
Poly-ne-sian
poly-nu-clear
poly-pro-pyl-ene
poly-sty-rene
poly-syl-labic
poly-syl-la-ble
poly-tech-nic
poly-the-ism
poly-the-is-tic
poly-un-sat-u-rated
poly-ure-thane
po-made
pome-gran-ate
pom-mel
po-mol-ogy
pomp
pom-pa-dour
pom-pos-ity
pomp-ous
pon-cho
pon-der
pon-der-able
pon-der-ous
pon-tiff
pon-tifi-cal
pon-tifi-cate
pon-tifi-ca-tion
pon-toon
pony
po-ny-tail
poo-dle
pooh—pooh
pool
poor box
poor-house
poor—mouth *(v.)*
pop
pop art *(n.)*
pop-corn
pope
pop-lar
cf. **popu-lar**
popped
pop-ping
poppy
pop-py-cock
popu-lace *(n.)*
popu-lar
cf. **pop-lar**
popu-lar-ity
popu-lar-ize
popu-late
popu-lous *(adj.)*
por-ce-lain
porch
por-cu-pine
pore
cf. **pour**
por-nog-ra-pher
por-no-graphic
por-nog-ra-phy
po-ros-ity
po-rous
por-poise
por-ridge
por-ringer
port
por-ta-bil-ity
por-ta-ble
por-ta-bly
por-tage
por-tal
por-tend *(v.)*
por-tent *(n.)*
por-ten-tous
por-ter
port-fo-lio
port-hole
por-tico
por-tion
por-trait
por-trai-ture
por-tray
por-trayal
por-trayer
pose
po-si-tion
posi-tive
posi-tiv-ism
posse
pos-sess
pos-ses-sion
pos-ses-sive
pos-si-bili-ties
pos-si-bil-ity
pos-si-ble
pos-si-bly
post
post-age
postal
postal card
post-card
poster
pos-te-rior
pos-ter-ity
post-grad-u-ate
post-hu-mous
post-hyp-notic
post-mark
post-mor-tem
post-na-sal
post-na-tal
post-nup-tial
post office
post-op-era-tive
post-pone
post-script
pos-tu-lant
pos-tu-late
pos-tu-la-tor
pos-ture
post-war
pot
po-ta-ble
po-tage
pot-ash

po-tas-sic
po-tas-sium
po-tato
po-tent
po-ten-tate
po-ten-tial
po-ten-ti-al-ity
pot-head
pot-hole
po-tion
pot-luck
pot-pourri
pot roast *(n.)*
pot-shot
pot-ted
pot-ter
pot-tery
pouch
poul-try
pounce
pound
pour
cf. pore
pout
pov-erty
pow-der
power
pow-er-boat
pow-er-house
power play *(n.)*
pow-wow
pox
pox *(n. pl.)*
or poxes
prac-ti-ca-bil-ity
prac-ti-ca-ble
prac-tice *(n.)*
prac-tice—teach *(v.)*
prac-ti-cum
prac-tise *(v.)*
prac-ti-tio-ner
prag-matic
prag-mat-i-cism
prag-mat-i-cist
prag-ma-tism
prag-ma-tist
prai-rie
praise
praise-wor-thy
pram
prance
prank
prank-ster
pray
cf. prey
prayer
prayer book *(n.)*
pray-ing man-tis *(n.)*
preach
pre-am-ble
pre-ar-range
pre-atomic
Pre-cam-brian
pre-cari-ous
pre-cast
pre-cau-tion
pre-cau-tion-ary
pre-cede
cf. pro-ceed
pre-ce-dence
prece-dent
pre-cept
pre-cep-tive
pre-cep-tor
pre-ces-sion
cf. pro-ces-sion
pre—Christian *(adj.)*
pre-cious
preci-pice
pre-cipi-tate
pre-cipi-ta-tion
pre-cipi-ta-tive
pre-cipi-tous
pré-cis
pre-cise
pre-ci-sion
pre-clude
pre-co-cious
pre-con-ceive
pre-con-cep-tion
preda-tor
preda-to-rial
preda-tory
pre-de-cease
pre-de-ces-sor
pre-des-ti-na-tion
pre-des-tine
pre-de-ter-mine
pre-dic-a-ment
predi-cate
predi-ca-tion
predi-ca-tory
pre-dict
pre-dict-able
pre-dict-ably
pre-dic-tion
pre-dic-tive
pre-di-lec-tion
pre-dis-pose
pre-domi-nance
pre-domi-nant
pre-domi-nate
pre-emer-gence
pre-emi-nence
pre-emi-nent
pre-empt
preen
pre-fab
pre-fab-ri-cate
pref-ace
pre-fer
pref-er-able
pref-er-ably
pref-er-ence
pref-er-en-tial
pre-ferred
pre-fer-ring
pre-flight
preg-nancy
preg-nant
pre-heat
pre-his-toric
pre-judge
preju-dice
preju-di-cial
preju-di-cious
prel-ate
pre-limi-nary
pre-lude
pre-mari-tal
pre-ma-ture

pre-medi-cal
pre-medi-tate
pre-medi-ta-tion
pre-mier
cf. pre-miere
prem-ise
pre-mium
pre-mo-ni-tion
pre-na-tal
pre-oc-cu-pa-tion
pre-oc-cu-pied
pre-or-dain
prepa-ra-tion
pre-pa-ra-tory
pre-pare
pre-pared-ness
pre-pay
pre-pon-der-ance
prepo-si-tion
cf. propo-si-tion
pre-pos-ter-ous
pre—reg-is-tra-tion
pre-req-ui-site
pre-roga-tive
pres-age
Pres-by-te-rian
pres-by-tery
pre-school
pre-scribe
cf. pro-scribe
pre-scrip-tion
pre-scrip-tive
pres-ence
cf. pres-ents
pre-sent *(v.)*
pre-sent-able
pre-sen-ta-tion
pre-sen-ti-ment
pres-er-va-tion-ist
pre-ser-va-tive
pre-serve
pres-er-va-tion
pre-set
pre-shrunk
pre-side
presi-dency
presi-dent

pre-si-dio
pre-soak
press
pres-sure
pres-sur-iza-tion
pres-sur-ize
pres-ti-digi-ta-tion
pres-ti-digi-ta-tor
pres-tige
pres-ti-gious
pre-sum-able
pre-sum-ably
pre-sume
pre-sump-tion
pre-sump-tive
pre-sump-tu-ous
pre-sup-pose
pre-tend
pre-tender
pre-tence
or pre-tense
pre-ten-sion
pre-ten-tious
pre-test
pre-text
pretty
pre-vail
preva-lence
preva-lent
pre-vari-cate
pre-vari-ca-tion
pre-vari-ca-tor
pre-vent
pre-vent-able
or pre-vent-ible
pre-ven-tion
pre-ven-tive
pre-ver-bal
pre-view
pre-vi-ous
prey
cf. pray
price
prickly
pride
priest
priest-hood

prig
prig-gish
prim
prima donna
prima fa-cie
pri-mal
pri-mar-ily
pri-mary
pri-mate
prime
primer
cf. prim-mer
pri-me-val
primi-tive
primp
prince
prin-cess
prin-ci-pal
cf. prin-ci-ple
prin-ci-pal-ity
prin-ci-ple
cf. prin-cip-al
print
print-able
printer
print-out
prior
pri-or-ess
pri-or-ity
prism
pris-matic
prison
prissy
pris-tine
pri-vacy
pri-vate
pri-va-teer
pri-va-tion
privi-lege
prize
prize-fight
prize-win-ner
prob-abi-lis-tic
prob-abil-ity
prob-able
prob-ably
pro-bate

pro-ba-tion
pro-ba-tional
pro-ba-tion-ary
pro-ba-tioner
probe
prob-lem
prob-lem-atic
or prob-lem-ati-cal
pro-bos-cis
pro-ce-dural
pro-ce-dure
pro-ceed
cf. pre-cede
pro-cess
pro-cess-ible
or pro-cess-able
pro-ces-sion
cf. pre-ces-sion
pro-ces-sional
pro-ces-sor
pro-claim
proc-la-ma-tion
pro-cliv-ity
pro-cras-ti-nate
pro-cras-ti-na-tion
pro-cras-ti-na-tor
pro-cre-ate
pro-cre-ation
proc-tor
pro-cure
prod
prodi-gal
pro-di-gious
prod-igy
pro-duce
pro-duc-ible
pro-duce
pro-ducer
prod-uct
pro-duc-tion
pro-duc-tive
pro-duc-tiv-ity
pro-fane
pro-fan-ity
pro-fess
pro-fes-sion
pro-fes-sional
pro-fes-sion-al-ism
pro-fes-sion-al-iza-tion
pro-fes-sion-al-ize
pro-fes-sor
pro-fes-so-rial
pro-fes-so-riat
or pro-fes-so-ri-ate
pro-fes-sor-ship
prof-fer
pro-fi-ciency
pro-fi-cient
pro-file
profit
cf. prophet
prof-it-able
profi-teer
pro-flu-ent
pro forma
profound
pro-fun-dity
pro-fuse
pro-fu-sion
pro-gen-i-tor
prog-eny
prog-no-sis
prog-nos-tic
pro-nos-ti-cate
prog-nos-ti-ca-tion
pro-gram
or pro-gramme
pro-gram-matic
pro-grammed
pro-gram-mer
prog-ress *(n.)*
pro-gress *(v.)*
pro-gres-sion
pro-gres-sional
pro-gres-sion-ist
pro-gres-sive
pro-hibit
pro-hi-bi-tion
pro-hi-bi-tion-ist
pro-hibi-tive
pro-ject
cf. proj-ect
pro-ject-able
pro-jec-tile
pro-jec-tion
pro-le-tar-ian
pro-le-tari-an-iza-tion
pro-le-tari-an-ize
pro-le-tar-iat
pro-lif-er-ate
pro-lif-era-tion
pro-lif-er-ous
pro-lific
pro-locu-tor
pro-logue
or pro-log
pro-long
prome-nade
promi-nence
promi-nent
pro-mis-cu-ity
pro-mis-cu-ous
prom-ise
prom-isor
or prom-iser
prom-is-sory
prom-on-tory
pro-mot-able
pro-mote
pro-moter
pro-mo-tion
pro-mo-tional
prompt
pro-mul-gate
pro-nate
prone
prong
pro-noun
pro-nounce
pro-nounce-able
pro-nun-cia-tion
proof
proof-read
prop
pro-pa-ganda
pro-pa-gan-dism
pro-pa-gan-dist
pro-pa-gan-dis-tic
pro-pa-gan-dize
propa-gate
propa-ga-tor

propa-ga-tion
pro-pane
pro-pel
pro-pel-lant
or **pro-pel-lent**
pro-pelled
pro-pel-ler
or **pro-pel-lor**
pro-pen-sity
proper
prop-erty
proph-ecy
cf. **proph-esy**
prophet
cf. **profit**
pro-phetic
pro-phy-lac-tic
pro-pin-quity
pro-pi-tious
prop-jet engine *(n.)*
pro-po-nent
pro-por-tion
pro-por-tional
pro-por-tion-ate
pro-posal
pro-pose
propo-si-tion
cf. **prepo-si-tion**
pro-pound
propped
pro-pri-etar-ies
pro-pri-etary
pro-pri-etor
pro-pri-etor-ship
pro-pri-ety
pro-pul-sion
pro-pul-sive
pro-pyl-ene
pro rata
pro-rate
pro-saic
pro-sa-ist
pro-scribe
cf. **pre-scribe**
pro-scriber
pro-scrip-tion
prose-cute
cf. **per-se-cute**
prose-cu-tion
prose-cu-tor
prose-lyte
prose-ly-tism
prose-ly-tize
pro-semi-nar
pros-pect
pros-pec-tive
cf. **per-spec-tive**
pros-pec-tor
pro-spec-tus
pros-per
pros-per-ity
pros-per-ous
pros-tate
pros-thetic
prosth-odon-tics
pros-ti-tute
pros-ti-tu-tion
pros-trate
pros-tra-tion
pro-tago-nist
pro-tect
pro-tec-tion
pro-tec-tor
pro-tec-tor-ate
pro-tégé
pro-té-gée
pro-tein
pro tem
pro tem-pore
Pro-tero-zoic
pro-test
pro-tester
or **pro-tes-tor**
prot-es-tant
pro-tes-ta-tion
pro-to-col
pro-to-lithic
pro-ton
pro-to-plasm
pro-to-type
pro-to-zoan
pro-tract
pro-trac-tile
pro-trac-tion
pro-trac-tor
pro-trude
pro-tru-sion
pro-tu-ber-ance
proud
prov-able
prove
prov-erb
pro-ver-bial
Prov-erbs
pro-vide
provi-dence
provi-dent
provi-den-tial
pro-vider
prov-ince
pro-vin-cial
pro-vin-cial-ism
pro-vi-sion
pro-vi-sional
pro-viso
provo-ca-tion
pro-voca-tive
pro-voke
pro-vost
prow
prow-ess
prowl
proxi-mate
prox-im-ity
prox-ies
proxy
prude
pru-dence
pru-dent
pru-den-tial
prud-ish
prune
pru-ri-ence
pru-ri-ent
pry
psalm
psalm-book
p's and q's *(n. pl.)*
pseudo
pseud-onym

pseud-onym-ity
pshaw
psi
pso-ria-sis
psyche
psy-che-delic
psy-chia-try
psy-chi-at-ric
psy-chia-trist
psy-chic
psy-cho
psy-cho-analy-sis
psy-cho-ana-lyze
psy-cho-drama
psy-cho-dy-nam-ics
psy-cho-gene-sis
psy-cho-logi-cal
psy-cholo-gize
psy-chol-ogy
psy-cho-met-ric
psy-cho-neu-ro-sis
psy-cho-path
psy-cho-pathic
psy-cho-pa-thol-ogy
psy-chopa-thy
psy-cho-sex-ual
psy-cho-sis
psy-cho-so-matic
psy-cho-thera-peu-tic
psy-cho-ther-apy
ptar-mi-gan
pto-maine
pub
pu-berty
pu-bes-cence
pu-bes-cent
pub-lic
pub-li-ca-tion
pub-li-cist
pub-lic-ity
pub-li-cize
public—spirited *(adj.)*
pub-lish
pud-ding
pud-dle
pudgy
pueblo
pu-er-ile
puff
pu-gi-lism
pu-gi-list
pug-na-cious
puis-sance
pul-chri-tude
pull
pul-let
pul-ley
pull-over
pul-mo-nary
pul-mo-tor
pulp
pul-pit
pul-sate
pul-sa-tion
pulse
pul-ver-ize
pum-ice
pum-mel
pump
pum-per-nickel
pun
punch
punch-ball
punch bowl
punch card *(n.)*
or punched card
punc-tili-ous
punc-tual
punc-tu-al-ity
punc-tu-ate
punc-tu-a-tion
punc-ture
pun-dit
pun-gent
pun-ish
pu-ni-tive
punk
pun-ster
punt
pupa
pu-pae *(n. pl.)*
pu-pil
pup-pet
pup-pe-teer
pup-petry
puppy
pur-chase
pure
pure-blood
pure-bred
purer
pur-est
pur-ga-tory
purge
pu-ri-fi-ca-tion
pu-rify
pur-ism
pur-ist
pu-ri-tan
pu-ri-tani-cal
pu-rity
purl
cf. pearl
pur-loin
pur-ple
pur-plish
pur-port
pur-pose
purr
purse
purser
pur-su-ant
pur-sue
pur-suit
pur-vey
pur-veyor
pur-view
pus
push
push-cart
pusher
push-over
pu-sil-lani-mous
put
pu-tre-fac-tion
pu-trefy
pu-trid
putt
put-ter
putty
puz-zle

Pyg-ma-lion
pygmy
py-ja-mas
py-lon
py-or-rhea
pyra-mid
py-ra-mi-dal
pyre
py-rene
Py-rex
py-rite
py-ro-chem-i-cal
py-ro-genic
py-ro-ma-nia
py-ro-ma-niac
py-ro-tech-nic
Pyth-ias
py-thon

Q

quack
quack-ery
quad-ran-gle
quad-rant
qua-dra-tic
qua-drille
quad-ru-ped
qua-dru-ple
qua-dru-pli-cate
quag-mire
quail
quaint
quake
Quak-er-ism
quali-fi-able
quali-fi-ca-tion
quali-fied
quali-fier
quali-fy
quali-ta-tive
qual-ity
qualm
quan-da-ries
quan-dary
quan-ti-fi-ca-tion
quan-ti-fier
quan-tify
quan-ti-tate
quan-ti-ta-tive
quan-tity
quar-an-tin-able
quar-an-tine
quar-rel
quar-rel-some
quarry
quar-ter
quar-ter-deck
quar-ter-horse *(n.)*
quar-ter-mas-ter
quar-tet
or **quar-tette**
quar-tile
quartz
cf. **quarts**
quash
quasi
qua-ver
queasy
queen
queer
quell
quench
query
quest
ques-tion
ques-tion-able
ques-tion-naire
queue
cf. **cue**
quib-ble
quick
quicken
quick—freeze *(v.)*
quid-nunc
quid pro quo
qui-es-cence
qui-es-cent
quiet
qui-etude
quill
quilt
quince
qui-nine
quin-tes-sence
quin-tet
or **quin-tette**
quin-tu-ple
quin-tu-plet
quin-tu-pli-cate
quip
quire
cf. **choir**
quirk
quis-ling
quit
quit-claim
quite
quit-ter
quiver
qui-xote
quix-otic
quiz
quiz-mas-ter
quiz show *(n.)*
quizzed
quiz-zi-cal
quoit
Quon-set
quota
quot-able
quo-ta-tion
quote
quo-tient

R

rab-bet
cf. **rab-bit**
rabbi
rab-bin-ate
rab-binic
rab-bit
cf. **rab-bet**
rab-bit ears *(n.)*
rab-bit punch
rab-ble
rabble—rouser
ra-bid
rabies
rac-coon

race
race-course
race-horse
ra-ceme
racer
race riot
ra-cial
ra-cial-ism
rac-ism
rack
cf. wrack
racket
or rac-quet
racke-teer
ra-con-teur
racy
ra-dar
ra-dar-scope
ra-dial
ra-di-ance
ra-di-ant
ra-di-ate
ra-dia-tion
ra-dia-tor
radi-cal
radi-cal-ism
radi-cal-ize
radi-cle
ra-dio
ra-dio-ac-tivity
ra-dio-broad-cast
ra-dio-gram
ra-dio-iso-tope
ra-di-ol-o-gist
ra-di-ol-ogy
ra-dio-man
ra-di-ome-ter
ra-dio-phone
ra-dio-ther-a-pist
ra-dio-ther-apy
radio wave
ra-dius
raf-fle
raft
raf-ter
rag
raga-muf-fin
rage
rag-ged
ra-gout
rag-tag
rag-time
rag-weed
rah—rah *(adj.)*
raid
raider
rail
rail-road
rain
cf. reign
cf. rein
rain-bow
rain cheque
rain-coat
raise
cf. raze
rai-sin
rai-son d'être
raja
or ra-jah
rake
rak-ish
rally
ram
ram-ble
ram-bunc-tious
rami-fi-ca-tion
ram-ify
rammed
ram-ming
ramp
ram-page
ram-pant
ram-part
ram-rod
ram-shackle
ran
ranch
rancher
ranch house
ran-cid
ran-cor
ran-dom
random—access *(adj.)*
ran-dom-iza-tion
rang
range
ranger
rangy
rani
or ra-nee
rank
rank and file
ran-kle
ran-sack
ran-som
rant
rap
cf. wrap
ra-pa-cious
rape
rapid
ra-pier
rap-ine
rapped
rap-per
rap-port
rapt
cf. wrapped
rap-ture
rare
rar-efied
or rari-fied
rar-ity
ras-cal
ras-cal-ity
rash
rasp
rasp-berry
rat
ratchet
rate
rater
rather
raths-kel-ler
rat-ify
ra-tio
ra-tion
ra-tio-nal
ra-tio-nale
ra-tio-nal-ism

ra-tio-nal-ity
ra-tio-nal-ize
rat-tan
rat-tle
rat-tler
rat-tle-snake
rat-trap
ratty
rau-cous
raun-chy
rav-age
rave
ravel
ra-ven
rav-en-ous
ra-vine
ravi-oli
rav-ish
raw
raw deal
raw-hide
raw score
ray
rayon
raze
cf. **raise**
ra-zor
raz-zle—daz-zle *(n.)*
razz-ma-tazz
reach
reach-able
re-act
re-ac-tion
re-ac-tion-ary
re-ac-ti-vate
re-ac-tor
read
cf. **reed**
read-able
reader
readily
read-out *(n.)*
ready
ready—made *(adj.) (n.)*
ready—to—wear *(adj.)*
real
cf. **reel**
re-align
re-al-ism
re-al-ity
re-al-iza-tion
re-al-ize
re-ally
realm
real time *(n.)*
re-alty
ream
reap
rear
re-arm
re-ar-ma-ment
rea-son
rea-son-able
re-as-sur-ance
re-as-sure
re-bate
rebel
re-bel-lion
re-bel-lious
re-birth
re-bound
re-buff
re-build
re-buke
re-but
re-but-tal
re-cal-ci-trance
re-cal-ci-trant
re-call
re-cant
re-cap
re-ca-pitu-late
re-cap-ture
re-cede
re-ceipt
re-ceiv-able
re-ceive
re-ceiver
re-cent
re-cep-ta-cle
re-cep-tion
re-cep-tion-ist
re-cep-tive
re-cess
re-ces-sion
re-ces-sional
re-charge
re-cidi-vism
re-cidi-vist
rec-ipe
re-cipi-ent
re-cip-ro-cal
re-cip-ro-cate
re-cip-ro-ca-tive
reci-proc-ity
re-cital
reci-ta-tion
re-cite
reck-less
reckon
re-claim
rec-la-ma-tion
re-cline
re-cluse
re-clu-sion
rec-og-ni-tion
re-cog-ni-zance
rec-og-nize
rec-og-niz-able
re-coil
rec-ol-lect
rec-ol-lec-tion
rec-om-mend
rec-om-men-da-tion
re-com-mit
rec-om-pense
rec-on-cil-able
rec-on-cile
rec-on-cili-ation
re-con-dite
re-con-nais-sance
re-con-noi-tre
re-con-sider
re-con-sti-tute
re-con-struct
re-con-struc-tion
re-cord
re-count
re-coup
re-course
re-cover

re-cov-ery
re-cre-ation
rec-re-ation
re-crimi-nate
re-cruit
rect-an-gle
rect-an-gu-lar
rec-ti-fi-able
rec-ti-fier
rec-tify
rec-ti-tude
rec-tor
rec-tory
re-cu-per-ate
re-cu-pera-tion
re-cu-pera-tive
re-cur
re-cur-rent
re-cy-cla-ble
re-cy-cle
re-dact
re-deco-rate
re-deem
re-deem-able
re-deemer
re-demp-tion
re-dis-trict
red—letter *(adj.)*
re-doubt
re-dress
re-duce
re-duc-tion
re-dun-dancy
re-dun-dant
reed
cf. read
re-edu-cate
re-edu-ca-tive
reef
reel
cf. real
re-elect
reel—to—reel *(adj.)*
re-en-act
re-en-ter
re-en-try
re-fer
ref-er-ee
ref-er-ence
ref-er-en-dum
re-fer-ral
re-ferred
re-fine
re-fin-ery
re-fin-ish
re-flect
re-flec-tion
re-flec-tive
re-flec-tor
re-flex
re-for-est
re-for-es-ta-tion
re-form
ref-or-ma-tion
re-for-ma-tory
re-former
re-frac-tion
re-frac-tive
re-frac-tor
re-frain
re-fresh
re-frig-er-ant
re-frig-er-ate
re-frig-era-tor
re-fuel
ref-uge
refu-gee
re-fund
re-fur-bish
re-fusal
re-fuse
re-fute
re-fut-able
re-fut-ably
re-gain
re-gal
re-gale
re-ga-lia
re-gard
re-gatta
re-gency
re-gen-er-acy
re-gen-er-ate
re-gen-era-tion
re-gen-era-tive
re-gen-era-tor
re-gent
regi-cide
re-gime
or ré-gime
regi-ment
regi-men-ta-tion
re-gion
re-gional
re-gion-al-ism
re-gion-al-ize
reg-is-ter
reg-is-tra-ble
reg-is-trant
reg-is-trar
reg-is-tra-tion
reg-is-try
re-gress
re-gres-sion
re-gret
re-gret-ta-ble
re-gret-ta-bly
re-group
regu-lar
regu-lar-ity
regu-lar-ize
regu-late
regu-la-tion
regu-la-tive
regu-la-tor
regu-la-tory
re-gur-gi-tate
re-gur-gi-ta-tion
re-ha-bili-tate
re-ha-bili-ta-tion
re-ha-bili-ta-tor
re-hash
re-hearsal
re-hearse
re-house
reichs-mark
reign
cf. rain
cf. rein
re-im-burs-able
re-im-burse

rein
cf. **rain**
cf. **reign**
rein-deer
re-in-force
re-in-state
re-is-sue
re-it-er-ate
re-it-era-tion
re-ject
re-jecter
or **re-jec-tor**
re-jec-tion
re-joice
re-join
re-ju-ve-nate
re-kin-dle
re-lapse
re-late
re-la-tion
re-la-tion-ship
rela-tive
rela-tiv-ism
rela-tiv-ity
re-lax
re-lax-ant
re-laxa-tion
re-lay
re-lease
rele-gate
rele-ga-tion
re-lent
rele-vance
rele-vant
re-li-abil-ity
re-li-able
re-li-ably
re-li-ance
relic
re-lief
re-lieve
re-li-gion
re-li-gious
re-lin-quish
rel-ish
re-lo-cate
re-luc-tance
re-luc-tant
rely
re-main
re-main-der
re-mand
re-mark
re-mark-able
re-me-dial
rem-edy
re-mem-ber
re-mem-brance
re-mind
remi-nisce
remi-nis-cence
remi-nis-cent
re-mise
re-miss
re-mis-si-ble
re-mis-sion
re-mit
re-mit-tance
re-mit-ted
re-mit-ting
rem-nant
re-model
re-mon-strate
re-morse
re-mote
re-mov-able
re-moval
re-move
re-mu-ner-ate
re-mu-nera-tion
re-mu-nera-tive
ren-ais-sance
rend
ren-der
ren-dez-vous
ren-di-tion
rene-gade
re-nege
re-new
re-new-able
re-newal
re-nounce
reno-vate
re-nown
rent
rent—a—car *(n.)*
rental
re-num-ber
re-nun-cia-tion
re-open
re-or-ga-ni-za-tion
re-or-ga-nize
re-pair
repa-ra-ble
repa-ra-tion
rep-ar-tee
re-past
re-pa-tri-ate
re-pa-tria-tion
re-pay
re-peal
re-peal-able
re-peat
re-pel
re-pelled
re-pel-lent
or **re-pel-lant**
re-pel-ling
re-pent
re-pen-tance
re-pen-tant
re-per-cus-sion
rep-er-toire
rep-er-tory
repe-ti-tion
repe-ti-tious
re-pet-i-tive
re-place
re-play
re-plen-ish
rep-lica
re-pli-cate
rep-li-ca-tion
re-ply
re-port
re-port-able
re-porter
re-pose
re-posi-tory
re-pos-sess
rep-re-hen-si-ble

rep-re-sent
rep-re-sent-able
rep-re-sen-ta-tion
rep-re-sen-ta-tive
re-press
re-pres-sion
re-prieve
rep-ri-mand
re-pri-sal
re-proach
rep-ro-bate
re-pro-duce
re-pro-duc-tion
re-prove
rep-tile
rep-til-ian
re-pub-lic
re-pub-li-can
re-pu-di-ate
re-pu-dia-tion
re-pugn
re-pug-nance
re-pug-nant
re-pulse
re-pul-sion
re-pul-sive
repu-ta-ble
repu-ta-tion
re-pute
re-quest
re-quiem
re-quire
req-ui-site
req-ui-si-tion
re-quital
re-quite
re-sal-able
re-sale
re-scind
res-cue
re-search
re-search-able
re-sem-blance
re-sem-ble
re-sent
res-er-va-tion
re-serve
re-serv-ist
res-er-voir
re-set
re-set-table
re-set-ting
re-shape
re-shuf-fle
re-side
resi-dence
resi-den-cies
resi-dency
resi-dent
resi-den-tial
re-sid-ual
resi-due
re-sign
res-ig-na-tion
re-sil-ience
re-sil-iency
re-sil-ient
resin
res-in-ous
re-sist
re-sis-tance
re-sis-tant
re-sister
re-sist-ible
or **re-sist-able**
re-sis-tor
re-sole
re-solu-ble
reso-lute
reso-lu-tion
re-solv-able
re-solve
reso-nance
reso-nant
reso-nate
reso-na-tor
re-sorp-tion
re-sort
re-sound
re-source
re-spect
re-spect-abil-ity
re-spect-able
re-spect-ably
re-spec-tive
re-spi-ra-ble
res-pi-ra-tion
re-spi-ra-tory
res-pi-ra-tor
re-spite
re-splen-dence
re-splen-dent
re-spond
re-spon-dent
re-sponse
re-spon-si-bil-ity
re-spon-si-ble
re-spon-si-bly
re-spon-sive
rest
cf. **wrest**
res-tau-rant
res-tau-ra-teur
rest home *(n.)*
res-ti-tute
res-ti-tu-tion
res-tive
re-stor-able
res-to-ra-tion
re-stor-ative
re-strain
re-straint
re-strict
re-stric-tion
re-stric-tive
re-struc-ture
re-sult
re-sume
cf. **ré-sumé**
re-sump-tion
re-sur-face
re-sur-gence
re-sur-gent
res-ur-rect
res-ur-rec-tion
re-sus-ci-tate
re-sus-ci-ta-tion
re-sus-ci-ta-tive
re-sus-ci-ta-tor
re-tail
re-tain

re-tainer
re-tali-ate
re-tali-ation
re-tal-ia-tory
re-tard
re-tar-dant
re-tar-da-tion
retch
cf. **wretch**
re-ten-tion
re-ten-tive
re-test
re-think
reti-cence
reti-cent
ret-ina
reti-nue
re-tire
re-tiree
re-tort
re-tract
re-tract-able
re-trac-tion
re-trac-tor
re-tread
ret-ri-bu-tion
re-trieval
ret-ro-ac-tive
ret-ro-grade
ret-ro-gres-sion
retro—rocket *(n.)*
ret-ro-spect
ret-ro-spec-tion
ret-ro-spec-tive
ret-sina
re-turn
re-turn-able
re-union
re-unite
re-us-able
re-vamp
re-veal
rev-eille
revel
reve-la-tion
re-ve-la-tory
re-venge
reve-nue
re-ver-ber-ant
re-ver-ber-ate
re-ver-bera-tion
re-ver-bera-tive
re-vere
rev-er-ence
rev-er-rend
rev-er-ent
re-ver-sal
re-verse
re-vers-ible
re-vers-ibly
re-ver-sion
re-vert
re-vet
re-view
cf. **re-vue**
re-viewer
re-vile
re-vise
re-vi-sion
re-vi-tal-iza-tion
re-vi-tal-ize
re-vival
re-vive
re-vo-ca-ble
re-vo-ca-tion
re-voke
re-volt
revo-lu-tion
revo-lu-tion-ary
revo-lu-tion-ize
re-volve
re-vue
cf. **re-view**
re-vulsed
re-vul-sion
re-ward
rhap-sodic
rhap-so-dize
rhap-sody
rheto-ric
rhe-tori-cal
rheu-matic
rheu-ma-tism
rheu-ma-toid
Rh factor *(n.)*
rhine-stone
rhi-noc-eros
rhi-noc-er-oses *(n. pl.)*
or **rhi-noc-eros**
or **rhi-noc-eri**
Rh—negative *(adj.)*
rho-do-den-dron
Rh—positive *(adj.)*
rhu-barb
rhyme
rhythm
rhyth-mic
rib
rib-ald
ribbed
rib-bon
ri-bo-fla-vin
rice
rich
rick-ety
rick-shaw
or **rick-sha**
rico-chet
rid
ridded
rid-den
rid-dle
ride
ridge
ridi-cule
ri-dicu-lous
riff
riff-raff
ri-fle
ri-flery
ri-fling
rift
rig
riga-ma-role
rigged
rig-ging
right
cf. **rite**
cf. **write**
righ-teous
right—of—way

rigid
ri-gid-ity
rig-our
rigor mor-tis
rig-or-ous
rim
rimmed
rind
ring
cf. **wring**
rink
rinse
riot
ri-ot-ous
rip cord *(n.)*
ripe
ripen
rip off *(v.)*
rip—off *(n.)*
ri-poste
ripped
rip-ple
rise
risk
ris-qué
rite
cf. **right**
cf. **write**
rit-ual
ritu-al-ism
ritu-al-is-tic
ritu-al-ize
ri-val
ri-valry
river
riv-er-bed
rivet
ri-vi-era
rivu-let
roach
road
cf. **rode**
road-abil-ity
road-bed
road hog *(n.)*
road-ster
road test
roam
roar
roast
roaster
rob
robbed
rob-bery
rob-bing
robe
ro-bot
ro-bust
rock
rock—bottom *(adj.)*
rocket
rock-etry
rocket ship
rod
rode
cf. **road**
ro-dent
ro-deo
roe
cf. **row**
roent-gen
rogue
role
cf. **roll**
roller derby *(n.)*
roly—poly *(adj.)*
ro-mance
ro-man-tic
ro-man-ti-cism
ro-man-ti-cize
rondo
roof
rookie
room
roomer
cf. **ru-mour**
room-mate
roost
rooster
root
cf. **route**
rope
Ror-schach test *(n.)*
ro-sary
rose
ro-sette
Rosh Ha-sha-nah
ros-ter
rosy
rot
ro-tary
ro-tate
ro-ta-tion
ro-ta-tor
rote
cf. **wrote**
ro-tis-serie
ro-to-gra-vure
ro-tor
rot-ten
ro-tund
ro-tunda
roué
rouge
rough
cf. **ruff**
rough-age
rough—and—ready *(adj.)*
rough-neck
rou-lette
round
rouse
roust
rout
route
cf. **root**
rou-tine
rou-tin-ize
rover
row
cf. **roe**
row-boat
rowdy
royal
roy-alty
rub
rubbed
rub-ber
rub-bish
rub-ble
rub-down

ru-bella
ru-be-ola
ruby
rud-der
ruddy
rude
ru-di-ment
ru-di-men-tary
rue
ruff
cf. **rough**
ruf-fle
rug
rug-ged
ruin
ru-in-ate
ru-in-ation
ru-in-ous
rule
ruler
rumba
rum-ble
ru-mi-nant
ru-mi-nate
rum-mage
ru-mour
cf. **roomer**
rump
rum-ple
run
rung
cf. **wrung**
run-ner
run-ning
run—of—the—mill *(adj.*
ru-pee
ru-ral
ruse
rust
rus-tle
rusty
rut
rye
cf. **wry**

S

Sab-bath
sab-bat-i-cal
sa-bre
or **sa-ber**
sa-ble
sabo-tage
sabo-teur
sac
cf. **sack**
sac-cha-rin
cf. **sac-cha-rine**
sack
cf. **sac**
sac-ra-ment
sac-ra-men-tal
sa-cred
sac-ri-fice
sac-ri-fi-cial
sac-ri-lege
sac-ro-sanct
sad
sad-der
sad-dle
sa-dism
sa-dist
sa-dis-tic
sa-fari
safe
safe-guard
safety
safety belt
sag
saga
sa-ga-cious
sa-gac-ity
sage
sagged
Sag-it-tar-ius
sail
cf. **sale**
sailor
saint
sake
sake
or **saki**

sale-able
or **sal-able**
salad
sa-lami
sal-ary
sale
cf. **sail**
sales check *(n.)*
sales-clerk
sales-room
sales slip
sales tax
sa-li-ent
sa-line
sa-li-ni-za-tion
sa-li-nize
sa-liva
sali-vary
sali-vate
sal-low
salmon
sal-mo-nella
sa-lon
cf. **sa-loon**
salt
salt-cel-lar
sa-lu-bri-ous
salu-tary
salu-ta-tion
sa-lute
sal-vage
cf. **sel-vage**
or **sel-vedge**
sal-va-tion
salve
salvo
Sa-mari-tan
same
samo-var
sam-ple
sam-pler
samu-rai
sana-to-rium
sanc-ti-fi-ca-tion
sanc-tify
sanc-ti-mo-nious
sanc-tion

sanc-tity
sanc-tu-ary
sand
san-dal
sand-bag
sand-pa-per
sand-wich
sane
cf. seine
sang
san-gui-nary
san-guine
san-guin-eous
sani-tary
sani-ta-tion
san-ity
sank
sap
sa-pi-ens
sap-phire
sar-casm
sa-cas-tic
sar-coma
sar-copha-gous
cf. sar-copha-gus
sar-dine
sar-donic
sari
sa-rong
sar-sa-pa-rilla
sash
sassy
Sa-tan
sa-tanic
satchel
sate
sat-el-lite
sa-tia-ble
sa-tiate
satin
sat-ire
sa-tiri-cal
sati-rist
sat-is-fac-tion
sat-is-fac-to-rily
sat-is-fac-tory
sat-isfy

satu-rate
satu-ra-tion
satyr
sauce
sau-cer
sauer-kraut
sauna
saun-ter
sau-sage
sauté
sau-téed
sau-terne
sav-age
sav-agery
sa-vanna
or sa-van-nah
sav-iour
or sav-ior
sa-vour
or savor
saw
saxo-phone
say
say—so *(n.)*
scab
scab-bard
scaf-fold
scald
scale
scal-lion
scal-lop
scalp
scal-pel
scamp
scan
scan-dal
scan-dal-ize
scan-dal-ous
scanned
scan-ner
scant
scape-goat
scap-ula
cf. scapu-lar
scar
scarab
scarce

scar-city
scare-crow
scarf
scar-ify
scar-let
scarred
scarves *(n. pl.)*
scary
scathe
scat-ter
scat-ter-brain
scat-ter rug
scav-en-ger
sce-nario
sce-nar-ist
scene
scen-ery
sce-nic
scent
cf. cent
cf. sent
sched-ule
Sche-hera-zade
sche-matic
scheme
schism
schis-matic
schiz-oid
schizo-phre-nia
scholar
scho-las-tic
scho-las-ti-cism
school
school age *(n.)*
school board *(n.)*
school-book
school bus
school dis-trict *(n.)*
school-house
school-teacher
school-work
schooner
schot-tische
sci-at-ica
sci-ence
sci-en-tific
sci-en-tist

scimi-tar
scin-tilla
scin-til-late
scin-til-la-tor
scin-til-la-tion
scion
scis-sors
scle-ro-sis
scoff
scoff-law
scold
scone
scoop
scope
scorch
score-board
score-keeper
scorn
Scor-pio
scor-pion
scoun-drel
scour
scourge
scout
scout-mas-ter
scow
scowl
scram-ble
scrap
scrap-book
scrape
scratch
scrawl
scraw-nier
scraw-ni-est
scrawny
scream
screech
screen
screen-play
screen test *(n.)*
screw
screw-driver
screw-worm
scrib-ble
scribe
scrim-mage
scrimp
scrim-shaw
scrip
cf. **script**
Scrip-ture
script-writer
scroll
scrounge
scrub
scrubby
scruff
scrunch
scru-ple
scru-pu-lous
scru-ta-ble
scru-ti-nize
scru-tiny
scuba
scuff
scuf-fle
scull
cf. **skull**
scul-lery
sculp-tor
sculp-tress
sculp-ture
sculp-tur-esque
scum
scur-ried
scur-ril-ity
scur-ri-lous
scurry
scurvy
scut-tle
scut-tle-butt
scythe
sea
cf. **see**
sea-coast
sea-farer
sea horse
seal
seam
cf. **seem**
seam-stress
seamy
sé-ance
sea-plane
sea power
sear
cf. **seer**
search
search-light
search war-rant
sea shell
sea-shore
sea-sick
sea-son
sea-sonal
sea-son-ing
seat
sea-weed
sea-wor-thy
se-cede
se-ces-sion
se-ces-sion-ist
se-clude
se-clu-sion
sec-ond
sec-ond-arily
sec-ond-ary
second—rate *(adj.)*
se-cre-cies
se-crecy
se-cret
sec-re-tar-iat
secretaries—general *(n.pl.)*
sec-re-tary
secretary—general
se-crete
se-cre-tion
se-cre-tive
sect
sec-tar-ian
sec-tion
sec-tional
sec-tor
secu-lar
secu-lar-ism
secu-lar-ize
se-cure
se-cu-rity
se-dan

se-date
se-da-tion
seda-tive
sed-en-tary
sedi-ment
sedi-men-tary
sedi-men-ta-tion
se-di-tion
se-di-tious
se-duce
se-duc-tion
se-duc-tive
sedu-lous
see
cf. **sea**
seed
cf. **cede**
seek
seem
cf. **seam**
seep
seep-age
seer
cf. **sear**
seer-sucker
see-saw
seethe
seg-ment
seg-re-gate
seg-re-ga-tion
seg-re-ga-tion-ist
seine
cf. **sane**
seis-mic
seis-mo-graph
seize
cf. **sees**
sei-zure
sel-dom
se-lect
se-lec-tion
se-lec-tive
se-lec-tor
self
self—addressed *(adj.)*
self—assured *(adj.)*
self—centred *(adj.)*
self—complacent *(adj.)*
self—composed *(adj.)*
self—conceit *(n.)*
self—confidence *(n.)*
self—conscious *(adj.)*
self—contained *(adj.)*
self—defence *(n.)*
self—denial *(n.)*
self—destruct *(v.)*
self—discipline *(n.)*
self—educated *(adj.)*
self—employed *(adj.)*
self—esteem *(n.)*
self—evident *(adj.)*
self—immolation *(n.)*
self—imposed *(adj.)*
self—incrimination *(n.)*
self—indulgence *(n.)*
self-ish
self—made *(adj.)*
self—mastery *(n.)*
self—pity *(n.)*
self—poised *(adj.)*
self—possessed *(adj.)*
self—preservation *(n.)*
self—regulating *(adj.)*
self—reliance *(n.)*
self—respect *(n.)*
self—righteous *(adj.)*
self—sacrifice *(n.)*
self—satisfaction *(n.)*
self—sufficient *(adj.)*
self—support *(n.)*
self—taught *(adj.)*
sell
cf. **cell**
seller
cf. **cel-lar**
sell—out *(n.)*
sell out *(v.)*
selt-zer
sel-vage
or **sel-vedge**
cf. **sal-vage**
se-man-tic
or **se-man-ti-cal**
se-man-ti-cist
sema-phore
sem-blance
se-mes-ter
se-mes-ter hour *(n.)*
se-mes-tral
se-mes-trial
semi
semi-an-nual
semi-arid
semi-au-to-matic
semi-cir-cle
semi-clas-si-cal
semi-co-lon
semi-con-scious
semi-dark-ness
semi-des-ert
semi-di-ur-nal
semi-for-mal
semi-nal
semi-nar
semi-nar-ian
semi-nar-ies
semi-nary
Semi-nole
semi-pre-cious
semi-pri-vate
semi-pro-fes-sional
semi-re-tired
Sem-ite
semi-ter-res-trial
Se-mitic
Sem-itism
semi-trailer
semi-tropi-cal
sen-ate
sena-tor
sena-to-rial
send
send—off *(n.)*
se-nile
se-nil-ity
sen-ior
sen-ior-ity
se-ñor
se-ñora
se-ño-rita
sen-sa-tion

sen-sa-tional
sen-sa-tion-al-ism
sen-sa-tion-al-ist
sense
sen-si-bil-ity
sen-si-ble
sen-si-bly
sen-si-tive
sen-si-tiv-i-ties
sen-si-tiv-ity
sen-si-ti-za-tion
sen-si-tize
sen-sory
sen-sual
sen-su-al-ism
sen-su-al-ist
sen-su-al-is-tic
sen-su-al-ize
sen-su-ous
sent
cf. **cent**
cf. **scent**
sen-tence
sen-ten-tious
sen-tient
sen-ti-ment
sen-ti-men-tal
sen-ti-men-tal-ism
sen-ti-men-tal-ist
sen-ti-men-tal-ity
sen-ti-men-tal-ize
sen-ti-nel
sen-try
sen-try box
sepa-ra-bil-ity
sepa-ra-ble
sepa-ra-bly
sepa-rate
sepa-ra-tion
sepa-ra-tion-ist
sepa-ra-tism
sepa-ra-tist
sepa-ra-tor
se-pia
sep-sis
sep-ten-nial
sep-tet
sep-tic
sep-ti-ci-dal
sep-ul-chre
or **sep-ul-cher**
se-quence
se-quen-tial
se-ques-ter
se-ques-trate
se-ques-tra-tion
se-ques-trum
se-quin
se-raglio
ser-aph
sera-phim
sere-nade
se-rene
serf
cf. **surf**
serge
cf. **surge**
ser-geant
se-rial
cf. **ce-real**
se-ri-al-ist
se-ri-al-iza-tion
se-ri-al-ize
se-ri-ate
se-ries
se-ri-ous
ser-mon
ser-mon-ize
se-rol-ogy
ser-pent
ser-pen-tine
ser-rated
ser-ra-tion
se-rum
serve
serv-ice
serv-ice-abil-ity
serv-ice-able
serv-ice-ably
service charge
service station
ser-vile
ser-vi-tude
ses-ame
ses-qui-cen-te-nary
ses-qui-cen-ten-nial
ses-sion
cf. **ces-sion**
ses-tet
set
se-ta-ceous
set—aside *(n.)*
set-back *(n.)*
set back *(v.)*
set—in *(adj.)*
set-off *(n.)*
set off *(v.)*
set-screw
set-ter
set-ting
set-tler
set-up *(n.)*
set up *(v.)*
seven
sev-en-fold
seven seas *(n. pl.)*
sev-en-teen
sev-en-teenth
sev-enth
sev-en-ti-eth
sev-enty
sever
sev-er-abil-ity
sev-er-able
sev-eral
sev-er-al-fold
sev-er-ance
se-vere
se-ver-ity
sew
cf. **so**
cf. **sow**
sew-age
sewer
sew-er-age
sex
sexa-ge-nar-ian
sexa-gesi-mal
sex-ism
sex-ol-ogy
sex-tant

sex-tet
sex-til-lion
sex-ton
sex-tu-ple
sex-tu-pli-cate
sex-ual
sex-ual-ity
sexy
Shab-bat
shab-bier
shab-bi-est
shabby
shade
shadow
shad-ow-box *(v.)*
shadow box *(n.)*
shady
shaft
shag
shagged
shag-gier
shag-gi-est
shaggy
shak-able
or shake-able
shake
shake-down *(n.)*
shake-down *(v.)*
shaken
shaker
Shake-spear-ean
or Shake-spear-ian
shake—up *(n.)*
shake up *(v.)*
shako
shaky
shale
shall
shal-lop
shal-low
sha-lom
sham
sha-man
sham-ble
shammy
sham-poo
sham-rock

shang-hai
Shangri—la
shank
shanty
shape-able
or shap-able
shape
shapen
shard
share
share-crop-per
share-holder
shark
shark-skin
sharp
sharpen
shat-ter
shat-ter-proof
shave
shaver
shave-tail
shawl
shay
she
sheaf
shear
cf. sheer
sheath
cf. sheathe
sheath knife *(n.)*
she-bang
shed
sheen
sheep
sheep-herder
sheep-ish
sheep-skin
sheer
cf. shear
sheet
sheik
or sheikh
sheik-dom
or sheikh-dom
shelf *(n.)*
shelf-life
shel-lac

shell-fire
shel-ter
shelve
she-nani-gan
shep-herd
shep-herd-ess
sher-bet
sher-iff
sher-lock
sherry
shib-bo-leth
shield
shift
shift-ier
shifti-est
shil-le-lagh
or shil-la-lah
shilly—shally
shim-mer
shin
shin-dig
shine
shin-gle
Shinto
Shin-to-ism
Shin-to-ist
shiny
ship
ship-board
ship-builder
ship-per
ship-shape
ship-wreck
ship-yard
shirk
shirt
shirt—sleeve
shirt—sleeved
shirt-tail
shish ke-bab
shiva-ree
shiver
shoal
shock
shock-proof
shock ther-apy
shock wave

shoddy
shoe
shoe-horn
shoe-lace
shoe-string
sho-far
sho-froth *(n. pl.)*
sho-gun
shone
cf. **shown**
shoo—in *(n.)*
shook
shook—up *(adj.)*
shoot
cf. **chute**
shop
or **shoppe**
shop-keeper
shop-lift
shop-per
shop-talk
shore
shore leave *(n.)*
shorn
short
short-age
short-change
short—circuit *(v.)*
short cir-cuit *(n.)*
short-com-ing
short-cut
shorten
short-hand
short—sighted
shot
shot-gun
should
shoul-der
shoul-der bag *(n.)*
shoul-der strap *(n.)*
shove
shovel
show
show-boat
show-case
show-down
shower
shower bath
shown
cf. **shone**
show—off *(n.)*
show off *(v.)*
show-piece
show-place
show-room
shrap-nel
shred
shred-ded
shrewd
shriek
shrill
shrimp
shrine
shrink
shrink-age
shrivel
shroud
shrub
shrub-bery
shuck
shud-der
shuf-fle
shuf-fle-board
shunt
shush
shut
shut—down *(n.)*
shut down *(v.)*
shut—in *(adj.) (n.)*
shut in *(v.)*
shut-ter
shut-ter-bug
shut-tle
shy
shy-ster
Sia-mese
sibi-lant
sibi-late
sibi-la-tion
sib-ling
sick
sick and tired *(adj.)*
sick bay
sick-bed
sick call
sicken
sicker
sick-ish
sickle
sick leave
sick pay
sick-room
sic pas-sim
side
side-arm
side ef-fect
side-kick
side-light
side-line
side show
side-swipe
side-walk
si-dle
siege
si-erra
sieve
sift
sigh
sight
cf. **cite**
cf. **site**
sight-seeing *(adj.)*
sigma
sign
cf. **sine**
sig-nal
sig-nalled
or **sig-naled**
sig-na-ture
sign-board
sig-ni-fi-able
sig-nifi-cance
sig-nifi-cancy
sig-nifi-cant
sig-ni-fi-ca-tion
sig-nify
sign-post
Sikh
si-lage
si-lence
si-lent

sil-hou-ette
sil-ica
silica gel
sili-cate
si-li-ceous
or **si-li-cious**
sili-con
sili-cone
sili-co-sis
silk
silken
silk—screen *(v.)*
silk screen *(n.)*
silk-worm
sill
sil-lier
sil-li-est
silly
silo
silt
sil-ver
sil-ver—plate *(v.)*
sil-ver plate *(n.)*
sil-ver-smith
sil-ver spoon *(n.)*
sil-ver-ware
sim-ian
simi-lar
simi-lar-ity
sim-ile
sim-mer
si-mo-nize
sim-pa-tico
sim-per
sim-ple
sim-pler
sim-plest
sim-ple-ton
sim-plic-ity
sim-pli-fi-ca-tion
sim-plify
sim-plis-tic
sim-ply
simu-late
simu-la-tion
simu-la-tor
si-mul-cast
si-mul-ta-ne-ity
si-mul-ta-ne-ous
sin
since
sin-cere
sin-cer-ity
sine
cf. **sign**
si-ne-cure
sine qua non
sinew
sin-ful
singe
sin-gle
sin-gle-ton
single—track *(adj.)*
sin-gu-lar
sin-gu-lar-ity
sin-is-ter
sink
sink-age
sink-hole
sinned
si-nol-ogy
sinu-ous
si-nus
si-nus-itis
si-nu-soid
si-phon
sire
si-ren
sir-loin
sisal
sissy
sis-ter
sis-ter-hood
sister—in—law
sisters—in—law *(n. pl.)*
si-tar
sit—down *(n.)*
site
cf. **sight**
cf. **cite**
sit—in *(n.)*
sit in *(v.)*
sit-ter
situ-ate
situ-ation
situ-ational
sit—up *(n.)*
sit up *(v.)*
sitz bath *(n.)*
sitz-mark
six-fold
six—pack *(n.)*
six-teen
sixth
six-ti-eth
siz-able
or **size-able**
size
siz-zle
skat
skate
ske-dad-dle
skeet
skein
skele-tal
skel-ter
skep-tic
skep-ti-cal
skep-ti-cism
sketch
skewer
ski
ski-able
ski-bob
ski-boot
skid
ski-doo
skiff
ski jump
ski lift
skill
skil-let
skim
ski mask
skimmed
skim-mer
skim milk
skim-ming
skimp
skin
skin—dive *(v.)*

skin-flint
skinned
skin-nier
skin-ni-est
skinny
skin—tight *(adj.)*
skip
ski pole
skipped
skip-per
skir-mish
skirt
ski run
skit
ski tow
skit-tish
ski-wear
skul-dug-gery
skulk
skull
cf. **scull**
skull-cap
skunk
sky
sky-borne
sky-cap
sky-jacker
sky-lark
sky-line
sky-rocket
sky-scraper
slab
slack
slacken
slacker
slag
sla-lom
slam
slam—bang *(adj.)*
slammed
slam-ming
slan-der
slang
slant
slap
slapped
slap-ping
slap-stick
slash
slat
slate
slat-tern
slaugh-ter
slaugh-ter-house
slaugh-ter-ous
slave
slav-ery
slay
cf. **sleigh**
sleazy
sled
sled dog
sledge
sledge-ham-mer
sleek
sleep
sleeper
sleep-ier
sleepi-est
sleepy
sleeve
sleigh
cf. **slay**
sleight
cf. **slight**
slen-der
slen-der-ize
slept
sleuth
slew
slick
slide
slide rule *(n.)*
slight
cf. **sleight**
slim
slime
slim-mer
slim-mest
slimsy
or **slimpsy**
sling
sling-shot
slink
slip
slip-cover
slip-page
slipped
slip-per
slip-pery
slit
slither
sliver
slob
slo-gan
slope
sloppy
slouch
slough
sloven
slow
sludge
slug
slug-fest
slugged
slug-gish
sluice
slum
slum-ber
slump
slunk
slur
slush
sly
small
small-pox
smart
smart al-eck *(n.)*
smash
smear
smell
smile
smirch
smite
smock
smog
smoke
smooch
smooth
smor-gas-bord
smother

smoul-der
smudge
smug
smug-gle
smut
snack
snack bar
snag
snail
snake
snake-skin
snap
snap-pier
snap-pi-est
snappy
snare
snarl
snatch
sneak
sneaker
sneer
sneeze
snide
sniff
snif-fle
snip
snipe
snitch
snob
snook
snoopy
snooze
snore
snout
snow
snow-ball
snow-bank
snow—blind *(adj.)*
or snow—blinded
snow-bound *(adj.)*
snow-drift
snow-fall
snow fence
snow-flake
snow-mo-bile
snow-plough
snow-suit

snow—white *(adj.)*
snub
snubbed
snuff
snug
snug-gle
so
cf. sew
cf. sow
soak
soap
soap-box
soar
cf. sore
sob
sobbed
so-ber
so-bri-ety
soc-cer
so-cia-bil-ity
so-cia-ble
so-cia-bly
so-cial
so-cial-ism
so-cial-ist
so-cial-is-tic
so-cial-ite
so-cial-ize
so-ci-etal
so-ci-ety
so-cio-eco-nomic
so-cio-logi-cal
so-ci-olo-gist
so-ci-ol-ogy
sock
socket
soda
so-dal-ity
sod-bust-er
sod-den
so-dium
sofa
soft
soft-ball
soft—boiled *(adj.)*
soft—cover *(adj.)*
soft drink *(n).*

soften
soft-ware
soggy
soil
soil-age
soil bank *(n.)*
soi-ree
or soi-rée
so-journ
so-lace
so-lar
so-lar-ium
so-lar-iza-tion
so-lar-ize
solar plexus *(n.)*
sol-der
sol-dier
sole
cf. soul
sol-emn
so-lem-nify
so-lem-nity
sol-em-nize
so-le-noid
so-licit
so-lici-ta-tion
so-lici-tor
so-lici-tous
so-lici-tude
solid
soli-dar-ity
so-lid-ify
so-lid-ity
solid—state *(adj.)*
so-lilo-quy
soli-taire
soli-tary
soli-tude
sol-mi-za-tion
solo
so-lo-ist
so-lon
sol-stice
solu-bil-ity
solu-bi-lize
solu-ble
so-lu-tion

solv-able
solve
sol-vency
sol-vent
som-bre
or som-ber
som-brero
some
cf. sum
son
cf. sun
sore
cf. soar
so-ror-ity
sor-row
sorry
sort
sor-tie
souf-flé
soul
cf. sole
soul food *(n.)*
sound
soup
soup du jour
sour
source
sour-dough
south
south-east
south-east-ern
south-ern
South-erner
south pole *(n.)*
south-wester
south-west-ern
sou-ve-nir
sov-er-eign
sov-er-eignty
so-viet
sow
cf. sew
cf. so
soy-bean
spa
space
space-craft
space-flight
space heater *(n.)*
space-ship
space suit *(n.)*
spa-cious
cf. spe-cious
spade
spa-ghetti
span
span-iel
span-ner
spare
spare-ribs
spark
spar-kle
spark plug *(n.)*
spar-row
sparse
spasm
spas-modic
spas-modi-cal
spas-tic
spas-tic-ity
spat
spat-ter
spat-ula
spawn
speak
speak-er-phone
spear
spear-head
spe-cial
spe-cial-ism
spe-cial-ist
spe-ci-al-ity
spe-cial-ize
spe-cialty
spe-cie
cf. spe-cies
spe-cific
speci-fi-ca-tion
speci-fic-ity
spec-ify
spe-cious
cf. spa-cious
speck
spec-ta-cle
spec-tacu-lar
spec-ta-tor
spec-tre
or spec-ter
spec-tral
spec-tro-graph
spec-trum
specu-late
specu-la-tor
specu-la-tion
specu-la-tive
speech
speed
speed-boat
speed-ome-ter
speed-trap *(n.)*
speed-way
spell
spell-bound
spe-lunker
spe-lunk-ing
spend
spend-thrift
spent
sperm
sper-ma-to-zoan
sperm oil
sperm whale
spew
spheral
sphere
spheri-cal
spher-oid
sphinx
sphinxes
or sphin-ges *(n. pl.)*
spice
spic-ier
spici-est
spicy
spigot
spike
spill
spin
spin-ach
spin-dle
spine

spin-ster
spinned
spin-ning
spi-ral
spire
spirit
spir-it-ism
spiri-tual
spiri-tu-al-ism
spiri-tu-al-ist
spit
spite
splash
splash-board
splash-down
splat-ter
splen-dent
splen-did
splen-dif-er-ous
splen-dour
splice
split
split—level *(adj.)*
splurge
spoil
spoil-age
spoke
spo-ken
spokes-man
spokes-woman
sponge
sponge cake
spongy
spon-sor
spon-ta-ne-ous
spoof
spool
spo-radic
spore
sport
sport-fish-ing
sports car
sports-cast
sports-wear
sports-writer
sporty
spot
spot—check *(v.)*
spot-light
spot-ter
spouse
spout
sprain
sprawl
spray
spray gun *(n.)*
spread
spread-able
spreader
spree
sprig
sprightly
spring
spring-time
springy
sprin-kle
sprite
sprocket
sprout
spruce
spry
spun
spur
spurge
spu-ri-ous
spurn
spur—of—the—moment *(adj.)*
spurred
spurt
sput-nik
sput-ter
spu-tum
spy
squab
squab-ble
squad
squad-ron
squalid
squall
squa-lor
squan-der
square
squash
squat
squat-ter
squaw
squawk
squeak
squea-mish
squee-gee
squeeze
squelch
squid
squint
squire
squirm
squir-rel
squirt
stab
stabbed
sta-bil-ity
sta-bil-ize
sta-bi-lizer
sta-ble
stac-cato
stack
sta-dium
staff
stag
stage
stage-coach
stage-struck
stag-ger
stag-nant
stag-nate
staid
cf. stayed
stain
stair
cf. stare
stair-way
stake
cf. steak
stake-out
sta-lac-tite
sta-lag-mite
stale
stale-mate
Sta-lin-ism
stalk

stall
stal-lion
stal-wart
stam-ina
stam-mer
stam-pede
stance
stan-chion
stan-dard
stan-dard-iza-tion
stan-dard-ize
standby
stand—in *(n.)*
stand-ing room
stand-off *(adj.) (n.)*
stand off *(v.)*
stanza
stare
cf. **stair**
star-fish
star-gazer
stark
star-let
star-light
star-ling
starry
starry—eyed *(adj.)*
start
starter
star-tle
star-va-tion
starve
stash
state
state-hood
state-house
state-room
static
sta-tion
sta-tion-ary
cf. **sta-tion-ery**
station wagon
stat-ism
sta-tis-tic
sta-tis-ti-cal
stat-is-ti-cian
statu-ary
statue
cf. **stat-ure**
cf. **stat-ute**
statu-esque
sta-tus
sta-tus quo
stat-ute
cf. **statue**
cf. **stat-ure**
statu-tory
staunch
stay
stayed
or **staid**
cf. **staid**
stead-fast
stead-ier
steadi-est
steady
steak
cf. **stake**
steal
cf. **steel**
stealth
steam
steam-boat
steam iron *(n.)*
steam-ship
steed
steel
cf. **steal**
steel-yard
steep
stee-ple
steer-age
stein
stel-lar
stem
stemmed
stem-ware
stench
sten-cil
steno-graph
ste-nog-ra-pher
ste-nog-ra-phy
ste-no-sis
steno-type
step
cf. **steppe**
step-brother
step—by—step *(adj.)*
step-lad-der
steppe
cf. **step**
step-son
ste-reo
ste-reo-scope
ste-reo-scopic
ste-reo-type
ster-ile
ster-il-iza-tion
ster-il-ize
ster-ling
stern
ster-num
stetho-scope
stet-son
ste-ve-dore
stew
stew-ard
stew-ard-ess
sticks
cf. **Styx**
sti-fle
stigma
stig-ma-tism
stig-ma-tize
stile
cf. **style**
still
still-born
still life *(n.)*
stilt
stimu-lant
stimu-late
stimu-lus
sting
sting-ray
stingy
stint
sti-pend
stipu-late
stipu-la-tion
stir

stirred
stir-rup
stitch
stock
stock-ade
stock-broker
stock-car
cf. stock car
stock mar-ket
stock-pile
stock-room
stock-yard
stoic
sto-icism
stoke
stom-ach
stom-ach-ache
stone
stooge
stool
stoop
stop
stop-light
stop-page
stopped
stop-per
stop-watch
store
sto-ried
stork
storm
stout
stout-hearted
stove
stove-pipe
stow
stow-age
strad-dle
Stradi-var-ius
strafe
strag-gle
straight
cf. strait
straight-edge
straighten
straight face
strain
strait
cf. straight
strand
strange
stranger
stran-gle
stran-gu-late
strap
stra-te-gic
stra-te-gi-cal
stra-te-gies
strat-egy
strati-fi-ca-tion
strat-ify
strato-sphere
stra-tus
straw
straw-berry
streak
stream
street
street-car
street-light
strength
strengthen
strenu-ous
strep-to-ba-cil-lus
strep-to-coc-cal
strep-to-coc-cus
strep-to-my-cin
stress
stretch
stretch-able
stretcher
stretcher bearer *(n.)*
strew
stricken
strict
stric-ture
stride
stri-dency
stri-dent
strife
strike
strike-out *(n.)*
strike out *(v.)*
strike-over
string
strin-gent
strip
strip chart *(n.)*
strip—cropping *(n.)*
stripe
strip mine *(n.)*
strip—mine *(v.)*
strive
strode
stroke
stroll
strong
strong-box
struck
struc-tural
struc-ture
stru-del
strug-gle
strum
strummed
strum-ming
strut
strych-nine
stub
stubbed
stub-ble
stub-born
stubby
stucco
stud
stu-dent
stu-dio
stu-di-ous
study
stuff
stuff-ier
stuffy
stul-ti-fi-ca-tion
stul-ti-fied
stum-ble
stump
stun
stun-ning
stunt
stu-pe-fac-tion
stu-pe-fied

stu-pefy
stu-pen-dous
stu-pid
stu-pid-ity
stu-por
stur-dier
stur-di-est
sturdy
stur-geon
stut-ter
stut-terer
sty
style
cf. **stile**
style-book
styl-ish
styl-ist
sty-lus
sty-mie
sty-rene
Sty-ro-foam
Styx
cf. **sticks**
su-able
suave
sub-con-scious
sub-con-trac-tor
sub-cul-ture
sub-dea-con
sub-di-vid-able
sub-di-vide
sub-di-vi-sion
sub-due
sub-hu-man
sub-ject
sub-jec-tion
sub-jec-tive
sub-jec-tiv-ism
sub-ju-ga-tion
sub-ju-gate
sub-junc-tion
sub-junc-tive
sub-king-dom
sub-let
sub-li-ma-tion
sub-li-mate
sub-lime
sub-limi-nal
sub-lim-ity
sub-ma-chine gun
sub-mar-ginal
sub-ma-rine
sub-merge
sub-mer-gence
sub-merg-ible
sub-merse
sub-mers-ible
sub-mer-sion
sub-mi-cro-scopic
sub-mis-sion
sub-mis-sive
sub-mit
sub-mit-ted
sub-mit-ting
sub-nor-mal
sub-nor-mal-ity
sub-or-bital
sub-or-di-nate
sub-pilot
sub-poena
sub-po-lar
sub-ro-ga-tion
sub-ro-gate
sub-rosa *(adj.)*
sub-rosa *(adv.)*
sub-sat-el-lite
sub-scribe
sub-script
sub-scrip-tion
sub-sec-tion
sub-se-quent
sub-ser-vi-ence
sub-side
sub-sid-iary
sub-si-di-za-tion
sub-si-dize
sub-si-dies
sub-sidy
sub-sist
sub-sis-tence
sub-soil
sub-space
sub-spe-cies
sub-stance
sub-stan-dard
sub-stan-tial
sub-stan-ti-ate
sub-stan-tia-tion
sub-stan-tive
sub-sta-tion
sub-sti-tute
sub-sti-tu-tion
sub-strato-sphere
sub-stra-tum
sub-sur-face
sub-sys-tem
sub-ter-fuge
sub-ter-ra-nean
sub-ti-tle
sub-tle
sub-tler
sub-to-tal
sub-tract
sub-trac-tion
sub-trac-tive
sub-tra-hend
sub-tropi-cal
sub-urb
sub-ur-ban
sub-ur-ban-ite
sub-ur-ban-iza-tion
sub-ur-ban-ize
sub-ur-bia
sub-ven-tion
sub-ver-sion
sub-vert
sub-way
suc-ce-dent
suc-ceed
suc-cess
suc-ces-sion
suc-ces-sive
suc-ces-sor
suc-cinct
suc-cour
cf. **sucker**
suc-co-tash
suc-cu-lence
suc-cu-lent
suc-cumb
such

suck
sucker
cf. **suc-cour**
suckle
su-crose
suc-tion
sud-den
sudsy
sue
suede
or **suède**
suet
suf-fer
suf-fer-able
suf-fer-ably
suf-fer-ance
suf-fice
suf-fi-ciency
suf-fi-cient
suf-fix
suf-fo-cate
suf-fo-ca-tion
suf-frage
suf-frag-ette
suf-frag-ist
suf-fuse
suf-fu-sive
sugar
sug-ar-cane
sug-ary
sug-gest
sug-gest-ible
sug-ges-tion
sug-ges-tive
sui-cidal
sui-cide
suit
suit-abil-ity
suit-able
suit-ably
suit-case
suite
cf. **sweet**
sui ge-neris
suitor
su-ki-yaki
Suk-koth

sulfa
sul-fa-dia-zine
sulk
sul-len
sul-phur
or **sul-fur**
sul-tan
sul-try
sum
cf. **some**
su-mac
or **su-mach**
summa cum laude
(adv.) (adj.)
sum-ma-ri-za-tion
sum-ma-rize
sum-ma-ries
sum-marily
sum-mary
sum-ma-tion
sum-mer
summer stock
sum-mer-time
sum-mery
sum-mit
sum-mon
sump
sump pump *(n.)*
sump-tu-ous
sun
cf. **son**
sun-baked
sun-bath
sun-burn
sun-dae
cf. **Sun-day**
sun-dial
sun-dries
sun-dry
sunk
sunken
sun-lamp
sun-light
sunny
sun-rise
sun-roof
sun-set

sun-shine
sun-stroke
sun-suit
sun-tan
sup
su-per
su-per-an-nu-ate
su-per-an-nua-tion
su-perb
su-per-charge
su-per-cil-ious
su-per-ego
su-per-fi-cial
su-per-fi-ci-al-ity
su-per-flu-ous
su-per-high-way
su-per-im-pose
su-per-in-ten-dence
su-per-in-ten-dency
su-per-in-ten-dent
su-pe-rior
su-pe-ri-or-ity
su-per-jet
su-per-la-tive
su-per-mar-ket
su-per-natu-ral
su-per-natu-ral-ism
su-per-pa-triot
su-per-power
su-per-scribe
su-per-script
su-per-scrip-tion
su-per-sede
su-per-sen-si-tive
su-per-sonic
su-per-star
su-per-sti-tion
su-per-stra-tum
su-per-struc-ture
su-per-tanker
su-per-vise
su-per-vi-sion
su-per-vi-sor
su-pi-na-tion
su-pi-na-tor
su-pine
sup-per

sup-plant
sup-ple
sup-ple-men-tal
sup-ple-men-tary
sup-pli-cate
sup-pli-ca-tion
sup-pli-ca-tory
sup-plied
sup-ply
sup-port
sup-port-able
sup-port-ive
sup-pose
sup-po-si-tion
sup-posi-tory
sup-press
sup-pres-sant
sup-pres-sion
sup-pres-sive
sup-pres-sor
su-pra-na-tional
su-prema-cist
su-prem-acy
su-preme
sur-charge
sure
surety
surf
cf. **serf**
sur-face
surface—to—air missile
surf-board
sur-feit
surge
cf. **serge**
sur-geon
sur-gery
sur-gi-cal
surly
sur-mise
sur-mount
sur-name
sur-pass
sur-plice
cf. **sur-plus**
sur-prise
sur-real
sur-re-al-ism
sur-re-al-ist
sur-re-al-is-tic
sur-ren-der
sur-rep-ti-tious
sur-ro-gate
sur-ro-ga-tion
sur-round
sur-tax
sur-veil-lance
sur-vey
sur-veyor
sur-vival
sur-vive
sus-cep-ti-bil-ity
sus-cep-ti-ble
sus-cep-tive
sus-pect
sus-pend
sus-pender
sus-pense
sus-pen-sion
sus-pi-cion
sus-pi-cious
sus-tain
sus-tain-able
sus-te-nance
su-ture
svelte
swab
swab-ber
swag-ger
swain
swal-low
swamp
swamp-land
swan
swan dive *(n.)*
swank
swan song *(n.)*
swarm
swash-buckle
swas-ti-ka
swat
swath
sway
swear
sweat
sweep
sweep—second
sweet
cf. **suite**
sweet-heart
swell
swept
swerve
swift
swim
swim-suit
swin-dle
swine
swing
swing shift *(n.)*
swipe
swirl
switch
swivel
swoon
swoop
sword
syca-more
syco-phant
syl-labic
syl-labi-cate
syl-labi-ca-tion
syl-labi-fi-ca-tion
syl-lab-ify
syl-la-ble
syl-lo-gism
syl-lo-gis-tic
sym-bol
cf. **cym-bal**
sym-bolic
sym-bol-ism
sym-bol-ize
sym-met-ri-cal
or **sym-met-ric**
sym-me-try
sym-pa-thetic
sym-pa-thize
sym-pa-thy
sym-phonic
sym-pho-ni-ous

sym-pho-nist
sym-phony
sym-po-sium
symp-tom
symp-tom-atic
syn-a-gogue
syn-chro-mesh
syn-chro-nism
syn-chro-nis-tic
syn-chro-ni-za-tion
syn-chro-nize
syn-chro-nous
syn-co-pate
syn-co-pa-tion
syn-di-cate
syn-di-ca-tion
syn-drome
syn-er-gism
syn-er-gist
syn-er-gis-tic
syn-e-sis
syn-ge-neic
synod
syn-onym
syn-ony-mous
syn-on-ymy
syn-op-sis
syn-op-tic
syn-tax
syn-the-sis
syn-the-size
syn-thetic
or **syn-thet-i-cal**
syphi-lis
syphi-litic
sy-ringe
syrup
system
sys-tem-atic
sys-tem-atize
sys-tem-iza-tion
sys-tem-ize
systems analysis
systems analyst

T

tab
tabbed
tab-er-na-cle
ta-ble
tab-leau
tab-leaux *(n. pl.)*
or **tab-leaus**
ta-ble-cloth
ta-ble d'hôte
table—hop *(v.)*
ta-ble-spoon
tab-let
ta-ble-top
tab-loid
ta-boo
or **tabu**
tabu-lar
tabu-late
tabu-la-tion
tach
ta-chis-to-scope
ta-chome-ter
tachy-car-dia
ta-chyme-ter
taci-turn
tack
tackle
taco
taco-nite
tact
tac-tics
tac-ti-cal
tac-ti-cian
tac-tile
tad-pole
taf-feta
taffy
tag
tag-board
tagged
tag-ging
tail
cf. **tale**
tail-gate
tail-light
tai-lor
tailor—made *(adj.) (n.)*
tail pipe *(n.)*
tail-spin
taint
take
take-down *(adj.) (n.)*
take down *(v.)*
taken
talc
tal-cum powder *(n.)*
tale
cf. **tail**
tal-ent
talent scout
talent show
tales-man
cf. **tal-is-man**
talk
talk-athon
talk-ative
talk show *(n.)*
tall
tal-low
tally
tal-lyho
Tal-mud
talon
ta-male
tam-bou-rine
tame
tam—o'—shanter
tamp
tam-per
tan
tan-dem
tang
tan-gent
tan-ger-ine
tan-gi-ble
tan-gle
tango
tank
tan-kard
tanker
tanned
tan-nery

tan-nic
tan-ning
tan-ta-lize
tan-ta-mount
tan-trum
Tao
Tao-ism
tap
tap dance *(n.)*
tap—dance *(v.)*
tape
tape deck *(n.)*
tape mea-sure
tape player
ta-per
cf. **ta-pir**
tape—record *(v.)*
tape re-corder *(n.)*
tap-es-tried
tap-es-try
tapi-oca
ta-pir
cf. **ta-per**
tap-root
tar
ta-ran-tula
tar-dily
tardy
tare
cf. **tear**
tar-get
tar-iff
tar-nish
tarp
tar paper *(n.)*
tar-pon
tart
tar-tan
tar-tar
task
task force
task-mas-ter
task-mis-tress
tas-sel
tas-selled
or **tas-seled**
taste
taste bud
tast-ier
tasti-est
tasty
tat-ter
tat-ter-sall
tat-tle
tat-tle-tale
tat-too
taught
cf. **taut**
taunt
Tau-rus
taut
cf. **taught**
tav-ern
taw-dry
tawny
tax
tax-able
taxa-tion
tax—exempt *(adj.)*
taxi
tax-ied
taxi-ing
or **taxy-ing**
taxi-der-mist
taxi-dermy
taxi stand
tax-payer
tax-shelter
tax stamp
T—bar lift
T—bone
tea
cf. **tee**
tea bag
tea ball
tea cake
tea cart
teach
teach-able
teacher
teach—in *(n.)*
teach-ing ma-chine *(n.)*
tea-cup
teak
tea-ket-tle
team
cf. **teem**
team-mate
team-ster
team-work
tea-pot
tear
cf. **tare**
tear-drop
tear-jerker
tea-room
tear-sheet
tease
tea service
tea-spoon
tech-ne-tronic
tech-ni-cal
tech-ni-cali-ties
tech-ni-cal-ity
tech-ni-cian
tech-nique
tech-noc-racy
tech-no-crat
tech-no-logi-cal
tech-nolo-gist
tech-nol-ogy
te-dious
te-dium
tee
cf. **tea**
teem
cf. **team**
teen
teen-age
teen-ager
tee-pee
tee shirt
tee-ter
tee-ter-board
teeth
teethe
tee-to-tal-ler
or **tee-to-taler**
Tef-lon
tele-cam-era
tele-cast

tele-com-mu-ni-ca-tion
tele-gram
tele-graph
tele-graphic
te-leg-ra-phy
tele-ki-ne-sis
tele-me-ter
tele-pathic
te-lepa-thy
tele-phone
te-le-pho-nist
te-le-phony
tele-photo
tele-pho-tog-ra-phy
tele-play
tele-printer
tele-scope
tele-scopic
tele-thon
Tele-type
tele-type-writer
tele-typ-ist
tele-view
tele-vise
tele-vi-sion
tele-vi-sor
telex
tell
teller
tell-tale
tem-er-ar-ious
te-mer-ity
tem-per
tem-pera
tem-pera-ment
tem-pera-men-tal
tem-per-ance
tem-per-ate
tem-pera-ture
tem-pest
tem-pes-tu-ous
tem-plate
or tem-plet
tem-ple
tempo
tem-po-ral
tem-po-rar-ily
tem-po-rary
tem-po-rize
tempt
tempter
temp-tress
tem-pura
ten
tena-ble
te-na-cious
te-nac-ity
ten-ancy
ten-ant
tend
ten-den-cies
ten-dency
ten-den-tious
or ten-den-cious
ten-der
tender
ten-der-foot
ten-der-hearted
ten-der-ize
ten-der-izer
ten-der-loin
ten-don
tene-brous
tene-ment
te-net
ten-fold
ten-nis
tenon
tenor
cf. ten-ure
ten-pin
tense
cf. tents
ten-sile
ten-sion
ten-sity
ten-sor
tent
ten-ta-cle
ten-tacu-lar
ten-ta-tive
tents
cf. tense
te-nu-ity
ten-ure
cf. tenor
tepid
te-quila
ter-cen-ten-nial
teri-yaki
ter-ma-gant
ter-mi-na-ble
ter-mi-nal
ter-mi-nate
ter-mi-na-tion
ter-mi-na-tor
ter-mi-nol-ogy
ter-mi-nus
ter-mite
term paper
tern
cf. turn
ter-nary
terp-si-cho-rean
ter-race
ter-ra—cotta
terra firma
ter-rain
ter-ra-pin
ter-razzo
ter-res-trial
ter-ri-ble
ter-ri-bly
ter-rier
ter-rific
ter-ri-fied
ter-rify
ter-ri-to-rial
ter-ri-to-ri-al-ism
ter-ri-to-ri-al-ize
ter-ri-tory
ter-ror
ter-ror-ism
ter-ror-ist
ter-ror-ize
terse
ter-tian
ter-tiary
test
tes-ta-ceous
tes-tacy

tes-ta-ment
tes-ta-men-tary
tes-tate
tes-ta-tor
test ban
test case
test—drive *(v.)*
test—fire *(v.)*
test—fly *(v.)*
tes-ti-fier
tes-ti-fy
tes-ti-mo-nial
tes-ti-mony
tes-tos-ter-one
test pattern
test pilot
test—tube *(adj.)*
test tube *(n.)*
teta-nus
tête-à-tête *(adj.) (adv.) (n.)*
tether
tet-ra-chlo-ride
tet-ra-hy-drate
tet-ra-pod
te-trar-chy
text
text-book
tex-tile
tex-tual
tex-ture
Thai
Thai-land
thal-a-mus
tha-lid-o-mide
than
cf. **then**
thank
thanker
thanks-giv-ing
that
thatch
thaw
the-atre
or **the-ater**
the-atre-goer
theatre—in—the—round *(n.)*
the-at-ri-cal
the-at-rics
theft
their
cf. **there**
cf. **they're**
the-ism
the-ist
the-is-ti-cal
them
the-matic
theme
them-selves
then
cf. **than**
thence
thence-for-ward
the-oc-racy
theo-crat
theo-lo-gian
theo-logi-cal
the-olo-gize
the-ol-ogy
the-ono-mous
theo-rem
theo-ret-i-cal
theo-rist
theo-rize
theo-ries
the-ory
the-oso-phy
thera-peu-tic
thera-pist
ther-apy
there
cf. **their**
cf. **they're**
there-abouts
or **there-about**
there-af-ter
thereat
thereby
there-for
cf. **there-fore**
therein
there-upon
ther-mal
ther-mo-dy-nam-ics
ther-mo-elec-tric
ther-mog-ra-phy
ther-mome-ter
ther-mo-nu-clear
ther-mo-plas-tic
ther-mos
ther-mo-sphere
ther-mo-stat
the-sau-rus
the-sauri *(n. pl.)*
or **the-sau-ruses**
the-sis
thes-pian
they
they're
cf. **their**
cf. **there**
thia-mine
thia-zide
thia-zine
thick
thick-headed *(adj.)*
thicken
thicket
thief
thieves *(n. pl.)*
thigh
thim-ble
thin
thing
think
think-able
think tank
thin-ner
third
thirst
thirst-ily
thir-teen
thirty
this
this-tle
thither
thong
tho-racic
tho-rax
thorn

thor-ough
thor-ough-bred
thor-ough-fare
thor-ough-go-ing
thou
though
thought
thou-sand
thrall
thrash
thread
thread-bare
threat
threaten
three
three-fold
three—ring circus
three-some
thresh
thresher
thresh-old
threw
cf. **through**
thrice
thrift
thrift shop
thrill
thril-ler
thrive
throat
throb
throbbed
throe
cf. **throw**
throm-bo-sis
throne
cf. **thrown**
throng
throt-tle
through
cf. **threw**
through-out
through-put
through street
throw
cf. **throe**
throw-away *(n.) (adj.)*
throw away *(v.)*
thrown
cf. **throne**
thrush
thrust
thru-way
thud
thug
thumb
thumb-nail
thumb-print
thumb-tack
thump
thun-der
thun-der-bolt
thun-der-clap
thun-der-cloud
thun-der-head
thun-der-ous
thun-der-shower
thun-der-storm
thus
thwart
thyme
thy-mus
thy-roid
ti-ara
tibia
tic
cf. **tick**
ticker tape *(n.)*
ticket
tickle
tick-lish
tidal
tidal wave
tid-bit
tide
cf. **tied**
tide-land
tide-wa-ter
tidy
tie
tied
cf. **tide**
tier
ti-ger
tight
tighten
tile
till
till-age
til-ler
tilt
tim-ber
cf. **tim-bre**
time
time-keeper
time—lapse *(adj.)*
time lock *(n.)*
timer
time—saver *(n.)*
time—sharing *(n.)*
time-ta-ble
timo-rous
tin
tin can *(n.)*
tinc-ture
tin-der
tine
tin-foil
tinge
tinge-ing
or **ting-ing**
tin-gle
tin-ker
tin-kle
tin-sel
tint
tip
tipped
tip-ping
tip-toe
ti-rade
tire
tis-sue
ti-tan
ti-tantic
ti-tan-ism
ti-ta-nium
tithe
tit-il-late
tit-il-la-tion
ti-tle

ti-tle-holder
title page
titu-lar
to
cf. too
cf. two
toad
toad-stool
toast
toaster
toast-mas-ter
to-bacco
to-bog-gan
toc-sin
cf. toxin
to-day
tod-dle
tod-dler
toe
cf. tow
toe-hold
toe-nail
toga
to-gether
tog-gle
toil
toi-let
toi-letry
to-ken
to-ken-ism
tol-er-abil-ity
tol-er-able
tol-er-ably
tol-er-ance
tol-er-ant
tol-er-ate
tol-era-tion
tol-era-tor
toll
toll-booth
toll bridge
toll call
toll-gate
toma-hawk
to-mato
tomb
tom-boy
tomb-stone
tome
to-mor-row
tom—tom
tonal
tone
tong
tongue
tonic
ton-nage
ton-sil
ton-sil-lec-tomy
ton-sil-li-tis
ton-so-rial
too
cf. to
cf. two
tool
tool-box
tooth
tooth-paste
top
to-paz
topic
topi-cal
to-pog-ra-pher
to-po-graphic
to-po-graphi-cal
to-pog-ra-phy
to-po-logi-cal
to-pol-ogy
top-onymic
to-pon-ymy
top-ping
top-ple
top-side
topsy—turvy
To-rah
to-re-ador
to-rero
tor-ment
tor-men-tor
or tor-menter
tor-nado
tor-pedo
torque
tor-rent
tor-ren-tial
tor-rid
tor-sion
tor-sion bar *(n.)*
torso
tort
tor-ti-lla
tor-toise
tor-tu-ous
tor-ture
tor-tur-ous
toss
to-tal
to-tal-ism
to-tali-tar-ian
to-tali-tar-ian-ism
to-tal-ity
to-tal-ize
tote
to-tem
tot-ter
touch
touch-able
touch-down *(n.)*
touch down *(v.)*
touché
tough
toughen
tou-pee
tour
tour-ism
tour-ist
tour-na-ment
tour-ni-quet
tou-sle
tout
tow
cf. toe
to-ward
or to-wards
towel
tower
town
town house
town-ship
tow rope
tow truck

toxic
toxi-cant
toxi-co-log-i-cal
toxi-col-ogy
toxin
cf. **toc-sin**
toy
trace
trace-able
tracer
tra-chea
tra-che-itis
tra-cheo-bron-chial
tra-che-ot-omy
track
tract
trac-ta-ble
trac-tion
trac-tor
trade
trade-mark
trading stamp
tra-di-tion
tra-di-tional
tra-di-tion-al-ism
tra-di-tion-al-ist
tra-duce
traf-fic
traf-fic-able
trag-edy
tragic
or **tragi-cal**
trail
trailer
trailer park
train
trainee
traipse
trait
trai-tor
trai-tor-ous
tra-ject
tra-jec-tion
tra-jec-tory
tram
tramp
tram-po-line
tran-quil
tran-quil-lity
or **tran-quil-ity**
tran-quil-lize
or **tran-quil-ize**
tran-quil-lizer
or **tran-quil-izer**
trans-act
trans-ac-tion
trans-at-lantic
trans-re-ceiver
tran-scend
tran-scen-dence
tran-scen-dency
tran-scen-dent
tran-scen-den-tal
tran-scen-den-tal-ism
trans-con-ti-nen-tal
tran-scribe
tran-scriber
tran-script
tran-scrip-tion
trans-duce
trans-duc-tion
tran-sept
trans-fer
trans-fer-abil-ity
trans-fer-able
trans-feral
trans-fer-ence
transferred
trans-figu-ra-tion
trans-fig-ure
trans-fix
trans-form
trans-for-ma-tion
trans-former
trans-fuse
trans-fus-ible
or **trans-fus-able**
trans-fu-sion
trans-gress
trans-gres-sion
trans-gres-sor
tran-sience
tran-sient
tran-sis-tor
tran-sis-tor-ize
tran-sit
tran-si-tion
tran-si-tive
tran-si-tiv-ity
tran-si-tory
trans-late
trans-la-tion
trans-la-tive
trans-lu-cence
trans-lu-cent
trans-mi-gra-tion
trans-mis-si-ble
trans-mis-sion
trans-mit
trans-mit-tance
trans-mit-ter
trans-mu-ta-tion
trans-oce-anic
tran-som
tran-sonic
or **trans-sonic**
trans-par-ence
trans-par-ency
trans-par-ent
tran-spire
trans-plant
trans-port
trans-port-able
trans-por-ta-tion
trans-pose
trans-pos-able
trans-po-si-tion
trans-sex-ual
trans-ship
tran-sub-stan-ti-ate
trans-verse
trans-ves-tism
trans-ves-tite
trap
trap-door
tra-peze
trape-zoid
trape-zoi-dal
trapped
trap-ping
trash

trauma
trau-matic
trau-ma-tism
trau-ma-tize
tra-vail
travel
trav-elled
or **trav-eled**
trav-el-ogue
or **trav-elog**
tra-verse
trav-es-ties
trav-esty
trawl
tray
cf. **trey**
treach-er-ous
treach-ery
trea-cle
tread
trea-dle
tread-mill
trea-son
trea-son-able
trea-son-ous
trea-sur-able
trea-sure
trea-surer
trea-sury
treat
treat-able
trea-tise
treaty
tre-ble
tree
tree-top
trek
trekked
trel-lis
trem-ble
tre-men-dous
tremor
tremu-lous
trench
tren-chancy
tren-chant
trend
tre-pan
tre-phine
trepi-da-tion
tres-pass
tress
trey
cf. **tray**
triad
tri-alogue
tri-an-gle
tri-an-gu-lar
tri-an-gu-late
tri-an-gu-la-tion
tri-ar-chy
tribal
trib-al-ism
tribe
tribu-late
tribu-la-tion
tri-bu-nal
tri-bune
tribu-tary
trib-ute
tri-ceps
trichi-no-sis
tri-choto-mous
trick
trick-ery
trickle
trick-ster
tri-cus-pid
tri-dent
tried
tri-en-nial
tri-fle
tri-fo-cal
tri-fo-lio-late
tri-fur-cate
trig-ger
trigo-no-met-ric
trigo-nome-try
tri-lat-eral
tri-lin-gual
trill
tril-ogy
trim
tri-mes-ter
trim-mer
tri-monthly
trin-ity
trin-ket
trin-ocu-lar
tri-no-mial
trio
trip
tri-par-tite
tri-par-ti-tion
tri-ple
trip-let
trip-li-cate
tri-plic-ity
tri-pod
trite
tri-umph
tri-um-phant
tri-um-vi-rate
trivia
triv-ial
trivi-al-ity
troika
troll
trol-ley
trom-bone
tromp
troop
cf. **troupe**
troop-ship
tro-phy
tropic
tropi-cal
tro-po-sphere
trot
Trots-ky-ism
trot-ter
trou-ba-dour
trou-ble
trough
trounce
troupe
cf. **troop**
trou-ser
trous-seau
trout
trowel

tru-ancy
tru-ant
truce
truck
truck-load
tru-cu-lent
trudge
true
tru-ism
truly
trump
trum-pet
trum-peter
trun-cate
trun-cheon
trun-dle
trunk
truss
trust
trustee
trustee-ship
trusti-ness
trust-wor-thy
truth
try-out
tryst
tsetse
T—shirt *(n.)*
T square *(n.)*
tuba
tube
tu-ber
tu-ber-cu-lar
tu-ber-cu-lin
tu-ber-cu-loid
tu-ber-cu-lo-sis
tu-ber-cu-lous
tu-ber-ous
tu-bu-lar
tuck
tuft
tug
tug-boat
tu-ition
tu-lip
tum-ble
tu-me-fac-tion

tu-mes-cent
tu-mour
tu-mour-ous
tu-mult
tu-mul-tu-ous
tuna
tun-dra
tune
tung-sten
tu-nic
tun-nel
tur-ban
tur-bine
turbo
tur-bo-fan
tur-bo-jet
tur-bo-prop
turbo—propeller engine
turboprop—jet engine
turbo-ram-jet engine
tur-bu-lence
tur-bu-lent
turf
tur-gid
tur-key
tur-meric
tur-moil
turn
cf. tern
turn-about
turn-around
turn-coat
tur-nip
turn-over *(n.)*
turn over *(v.)*
turn-pike
turn-stile
turn-ta-ble
turn-up *(n.) (adj.)*
turn up *(v.)*
tur-pen-tine
tur-pi-tude
tur-quoise
tur-ret
tur-tle
tusk
tus-sle

tu-te-lage
tu-te-lary
tu-tor
tu-tor-age
tu-to-rial
tu-tor-ship
tux-edo
twad-dle
twang
tweak
twee-zer
twelfth
twelve
twid-dle
twig
twi-light
twill
twin
twine
twinge
twin-kle
twin—size *(adj.)*
twin-ning
twirl
twist
twitch
twit-ter
twixt
two
cf. to
cf. too
two—by—four *(n.)*
two-some
tym-panic
type
type-case
type-face
type-script
type-set-ter
type-write
type-writer
ty-phoid
ty-phus
typi-cal
typi-fied
typ-ify
typ-ist

typo
ty-pog-ra-pher
ty-po-graphic
ty-po-graphi-cal
ty-pog-ra-phy
ty-po-logi-cal
ty-ran-ni-cal
ty-ran-ni-cide
tyr-an-nize
ty-ran-no-saur
tyr-anny
ty-rant
tzar

U

ubiq-ui-tous
ubiq-uity
ud-der
ugh
ug-lier
ug-li-est
ug-li-ness
ugly
uh—huh
uku-lele
ul-cer
ul-cer-ate
ul-cer-ous
ulna
ul-te-rior
ul-ti-macy
ul-tima ra-tio
ul-ti-mate
ul-ti-ma-tum
ul-tra
ul-tra-con-ser-va-tive
ul-tra-fiche
ul-tra-high
ul-tra-mi-cro-scopic
ul-tra-mod-ern
ul-tra-sonic
ul-tra-so-phis-ti-cated
ul-tra-vi-o-let
Ulys-ses
um-bili-cal
um-bi-li-cus
um-brage
um-brella
um-pire
ump-teen
un-abated
un-abridged
un-ac-cept-able
un-ac-com-mo-dated
un-ac-com-pa-nied
un-ac-cus-tomed
un-adorned
un-adul-ter-ated
un-af-fected
un-alien-able
un-al-ter-able
una-nim-ity
unani-mous
un-an-swer-able
un-an-tici-pated
un-ap-peal-able
un-ap-peas-able
un-ap-pe-tiz-ing
un-ap-proach-able
un-armed
un-ashamed
un-as-sail-able
un-as-sisted
un-as-suage-able
un-at-tached
un-at-trac-tive
un-avail-able
un-avoid-able
un-aware
un-bal-anced
un-bear-able
un-beat-able
un-be-com-ing
un-be-known
un-be-liev-able
un-be-liever
un-bend
un-bi-assed
un-born
un-bound
un-bri-dle
un-bro-ken
un-buckle
un-budge-able
un-bur-den
un-but-toned
uncalled—for *(adj.)*
un-cere-mo-ni-ous
un-cer-tain
un-cer-tainty
un-chal-lenge-able
un-change-able
un-char-ac-ter-is-tic
un-chari-ta-ble
un-charted
un-chaste
un-chiv-al-rous
un-chris-tian
un-civi-lized
un-clas-si-fied
un-cle
un-clean
un-clench
un-climb-able
un-cloak
un-clut-ter
un-com-fort-able
un-com-mit-ted
un-com-mon
un-com-mu-ni-ca-ble
un-com-mu-ni-ca-tive
un-com-plain-ing
un-com-pli-cated
un-com-pli-men-tary
un-con-ceiv-able
un-con-cerned
un-con-di-tional
un-con-for-mity
un-con-ge-nial
un-con-scio-na-ble
un-con-scious
un-con-soli-dated
un-con-sti-tu-tional
un-con-trol-la-ble
un-con-ven-tional
un-cou-ple
un-couth

un-cover
unc-tion
unc-tu-ous
un-curl
un-de-bat-able
un-de-ni-able
un-der
un-der-achiever
un-der-act
un-der-coat
un-der-de-vel-oped
un-der-dog
un-der-edu-cated
un-der-em-pha-size
un-der-em-ployed
un-der-es-ti-mate
un-der-ex-pose
un-der-gradu-ate
un-der-growth
un-der-hand
un-der-in-sured
un-der-lie
un-der-mine
un-der-neath
un-der-nour-ished
un-der-paid
un-der-pass
un-der-pin-ning
un-der-play
un-der-privi-leged
un-der-pro-duc-tive
un-der-score
un-der-sell
un-der-signed
un-der-sized
un-der-stand
un-der-stand-able
un-der-state
un-der-stood
un-der-strength
un-der-take
under—the—counter *(adj.)*
un-der-way *(adj.)*
un-der way *(adv.)*
un-de-sir-able
un-dis-guised

undo
cf. un-due
un-dressed
un-due
cf. undo
un-du-late
un-duly
un-earned
un-earthly
un-eas-ily
un-em-ployed
un-en-cum-bered
un-en-dur-able
un-en-thu-si-as-tic
un-equal
un-equivo-cably
un-even
un-ex-cep-tional
un-ex-ploited
un-faith-ful
un-fa-mil-iar
un-fash-ion-able
un-fas-ten
un-fath-om-able
un-fa-vour-able
un-fin-ished
un-fit-ting
un-flinch-ing
un-fold
un-for-get-ta-ble
un-for-giv-ing
un-for-tu-nate
un-gainly
un-gram-mati-cal
un-grate-ful
un-gu-late
un-hap-pily
un-healthy
unheard—of *(adj.)*
un-hinge
un-holy
uni-corn
uni-cy-cle
uni-fi-ca-tion
uni-fo-lio-late
uni-form
uni-for-mity

unify
uni-lat-eral
uni-lin-ear
uni-lin-gual
un-imag-in-able
un-im-peach-able
un-in-hib-ited
un-in-tel-li-gi-ble
un-in-ten-tional
union
union-ism
union-iza-tion
union shop *(n.)*
uni-po-lar
unique
uni-sex
uni-son
unit
uni-tar-ian
uni-tary
unite
unity
uni-ver-sal
uni-ver-sal-ity
uni-verse
uni-ver-si-ties
uni-ver-sity
univo-cal
un-kempt
un-let-tered
un-like-li-hood
un-lim-ited
un-listed
un-load
un-loosen
un-mask
un-men-tion-able
un-mis-tak-able
un-miti-gated
un-natu-ral
un-nec-es-sar-ily
un-ob-tru-sive
un-oc-cu-pied
un-of-fi-cial
un-or-ga-nized
un-or-tho-dox
un-pal-at-able

un-prece-dented
un-pre-dict-able
un-pre-ten-tious
un-prin-ci-pled
un-print-able
un-prof-it-able
un-quali-fied
un-ques-tion-able
un-quote
un-real
cf. un-reel
un-re-al-is-tic
un-rea-son-able
un-reel
cf. un-real
un-re-strained
un-ri-valled
or un-ri-valed
un-ruf-fled
un-satu-rated
un-sci-en-tific
un-scru-pu-lous
un-sea-son-able
un-set-tled
un-sheathe
un-sightly
un-so-cia-ble
un-so-phis-ti-cated
un-speak-able
un-sta-ble
un-stop-pa-ble
un-struc-tured
un-suc-cess-ful
un-sym-met-ri-cal
un-ti-dily
un-til
un-touch-able
un-tu-tored
un-usual
un-wary
un-wa-ver-ing
un-wor-thi-ness
un-wor-thy
up
up-braid
up-bring-ing
up-heaval
up-hill
up-hol-ster
up-per
up-per-most
up-right
up-roar
up-set
up—to—the—minute
(adj.)
up-ward
or up-wards
ura-nium
ur-ban
cf. ur-bane
ur-ban-ism
ur-ban-ity
ur-ban-iza-tion
ur-ban-ize
ur-ban re-newal *(n.)*
ure-mia
ure-thra
urge
ur-gency
ur-gent
uri-naly-sis
uri-nary
urine
urn
cf. earn
urolo-gist
urol-ogy
us-able
or use-able
us-age
use
usher
usual
usu-ri-ous
usurp
usury
uten-sil
uter-ine
uter-us
utili-tar-ian
util-ity
uti-li-za-tion
uti-lize
ut-most
uto-pia
uto-pi-an-ism
ut-ter
ut-ter-ance
uxo-ri-ous

V

va-cancy
va-cant
va-cate
va-ca-tion
va-ca-tioner
va-ca-tion-land
vac-ci-nate
vac-ci-na-tion
vac-cine
vac-il-late
vac-il-la-tion
va-cu-ity
vacu-ous
vac-uum
vac-uums *(n. pl.)*
or vacua
vacuum—packed *(adj.)*
vaga-bond
va-gary
va-grancy
va-grant
vague
vain
cf. vane
cf. vein
va-lance
cf. va-lence
vale
cf. veil
vale-dic-to-rian
vale-dic-tory
va-lence
cf. va-lance
val-en-tine
va-let
Val-halla
val-iant

valid
vali-date
vali-da-tion
va-lid-ity
va-lise
val-ley
valour
valu-able
valu-ate
valu-ation
value
valve
vamp
vam-pire
van
van-dal
van-dal-ism
van-dal-ize
vane
cf. **vain**
cf. **vein**
van-guard
va-nilla
van-ish
van-ity
van-quish
van-tage
va-pour
va-por-ize
va-por-ous
vari-able
vari-ance
vari-ant
vari-ation
vari-cose
var-ie-gate
va-ri-et-ies
va-ri-ety
vari-ous
var-mint
var-nish
var-sity
vary
cf. **very**
vas-cu-lar
vase
vas-sal
vast
vaude-ville
vault
vaunt
veal
vec-tor
veer
vege-ta-ble
vege-tate
vege-ta-tion
ve-he-mence
ve-he-ment
ve-hi-cle
veil
cf. **vale**
vein
cf. **vain**
cf. **vane**
veld
or **veldt**
vel-lum
ve-loci-ties
ve-loc-ity
vel-vet
vel-ve-teen
vel-vety
ve-nal
cf. **ve-nial**
vend
vendee
vendor
or **vender**
ven-detta
vend-ible
or **vend-able**
ve-neer
ven-er-able
ven-er-ate
ven-era-tion
ve-ne-tian blind
ven-geance
ve-nial
cf. **ve-nal**
ve-nire
veni-son
venom
ven-om-ous
vent
ven-ti-late
ven-ti-la-tion
ven-tri-cle
ven-tricu-lar
ven-trilo-quism
ven-trilo-quist
ven-ture
ven-turer
ven-ture-some
ven-tur-ous
venue
ve-ra-cious
cf. **vo-ra-cious**
ve-randa
verb
ver-bal
ver-ba-tim
ver-biage
ver-bose
ver-bo-ten
ver-dant
ver-dict
verge
ver-gence
veri-fi-able
veri-fi-ca-tion
veri-fied
ver-ify
ver-ily
veri-simi-lar
veri-ta-ble
veri-ta-bly
ver-micu-lite
ver-min
ver-min-ous
ver-mouth
ver-nacu-lar
ver-nacu-lar-ism
ver-nal
ver-sa-tile
ver-sa-til-ity
verse
ver-sion
ver-sus
ver-te-bra

ver-tex
cf. **vor-tex**
ver-ti-cal
ver-ti-cil-late
ver-tigo
very
cf. **vary**
vesi-cant
ves-pers
ves-pi-ary
ves-pid
ves-sel
vest
ves-tal
ves-ti-bule
ves-tige
vest-ment
ves-try
vetch
vet-eran
vet-eri-nar-ian
vet-eri-nary
veto
vetoes *(n. pl.)*
vex
vexed
cf. **vext**
vexa-tion
vexa-tious
via
vi-able
via-duct
vial
cf. **vile**
cf. **viol**
vibes
vi-brant
vi-bra-phone
vi-brate
vi-bra-tion
vi-bra-tor
vi-bra-tory
vicar
vi-cari-ous
vice
cf. **vise**
vice—chancellor
vice—consul
vice—presidency
vice—president
vice-roy
vice squad
vi-chys-soise
Vi-chy water
vi-cin-ity
vi-cious
vi-cis-si-tude
vi-cis-si-tu-di-nous
vic-tim
vic-tim-ize
vic-tor
Vic-to-rian
vic-to-ri-ous
vic-tory
vict-ual-ler
vi-cuña
video
vid-eo-phone
vid-eo-tape
Viet-nam-ese
view
vigil
vigi-lance
vigi-lant
vigi-lante
vi-gnette
vigour
vile
cf. **vial**
cf. **viol**
vili-fi-ca-tion
vil-ify
villa
vil-lage
vil-lain
vil-lain-ous
vim
vin-ci-ble
vin-di-cate
vin-di-ca-tion
vin-di-ca-tory
vin-dic-tive
vine
vin-egar
vine-yard
vin-tage
vi-nyl
vint-ner
viol
cf. **vial**
cf. **vile**
vi-ola
vio-la-bil-ity
vio-la-ble
vio-la-bly
vio-late
vio-la-tion
vio-lent
vio-let
vio-lin
vi-per
vi-per-ous
vi-rago
vi-ral
vir-gin
vir-ginal
vir-gin-ity
Virgo
vir-gule
vir-ile
vi-ril-ity
vi-rol-ogy
vir-tual
vir-tu-al-ity
vir-tue
vir-tu-os-ity
vir-tu-oso
vir-tu-ous
viru-lent
vi-rus
visa
vis-age
vis—à—vis
vis-ceral
vis-cid
vis-cose
vis-cos-ity
vis-count
vis-cous
vise
cf. **vice**

vise-like
Vishnu
visi-bil-ity
vis-ible
vis-ibly
vi-sion
vi-sion-ary
visit
visi-ta-tion
visi-tor
vi-sor
vista
vis-ual
visual aid *(n.)*
vi-su-al-iza-tion
vi-su-al-ize
vita
vi-tal
vi-tal-ity
vi-tal-ize
vi-ta-min
vi-ti-cul-ture
vit-riol
vi-tu-per-ate
vi-tu-pera-tion
vi-tu-pera-tive
vi-va-cious
vi-vac-ity
viva voce
vivid
vivi-fi-ca-tion
viv-ify
vivi-sec-tion
vixen
vo-cabu-lary
vo-cal
vo-cal-ist
vo-cal-ize
vo-ca-tion
vo-ca-tional
vo-ca-tion-al-ism
vo-cif-er-ous
vodka
vogue
voice
voice-over
voice-print
void
void-able
void-ance
vola-tile
vol-ca-nic
vol-cano
vo-li-tion
voli-tive
vol-ley
volt
volt-age
vol-ta-me-ter
volt-me-ter
volu-ble
vol-ume
vo-lu-mi-nous
vol-un-tarily
vol-un-tary
vol-un-teer
vo-lup-tu-ary
vo-lup-tu-ous
vomit
voo-doo
voo-doo-ism
vo-ra-cious
cf. ve-ra-cious
vo-rac-ity
vor-tex
cf. ver-tex
vote
vouch
voucher
vouch-safe
vow
vowel
vox po-puli
voy-age
voya-geur
vul-ca-ni-za-tion
vul-ca-nize
vul-gar
vul-gar-ism
vul-gar-ity
vul-gar-ize
vul-ner-abil-ity
vul-ner-able
vul-ture
vul-tur-ous

W

wacky
wad
wad-ding
wade
cf. weighed
wa-fer
waf-fle
waft
wag
wage
wa-ger
wagon
waif
wail
cf. whale
waist
cf. waste
waist-line
wait
cf. weight
waiter
wait-ress
waive
cf. wave
waiver
cf. waver
wake
waken
walk
walkie—talkie
wal-let
wall-flower
wal-lop
wall-pa-per
wall plug
wal-nut
wal-rus
waltz
wam-pum
wan-der
wan-der-lust
wane

wan-gle
want
wan-ton
war
war-ble
war-bler
war crime
ward
war-den
ward-robe
ware
cf. wear
cf. where
ware-house
war-fare
war hawk
warm
war-mon-ger
warmth
warm—up *(n.)*
warm up *(v.)*
warn
warp
war-path
war-rant
war-ran-tee
war-ran-tor
or war-ranter
war-rior
war-ship
wart
wary
war zone
wash
wash-able
wash and wear *(adj.)*
washer
wash-room
wasp
waste
cf. waist
waste-bas-ket
waste-land
waster
wast-rel
watch
watch-band
watch-dog
watch-word
wa-ter
wa-ter-colour
wa-ter-cress
wa-ter-fall
wa-ter-line
wa-ter-log
wa-ter-mark
wa-ter-proof
water—repellent *(adj.)*
water ski *(n.)*
water—ski *(v.)*
watt
watt-age
wave
cf. waive
wave-length
wa-ver
cf. waiver
wavy
wax
waxen
way
cf. weigh
ways and means *(n. pl.)*
way-side
way-ward
we
cf. wee
weak
cf. week
weaken
weak—kneed *(adj.)*
wealth
weapon
wear
cf. ware
cf. where
wear and tear *(n.)*
wea-ri-some
weary
wea-sel
weather
cf. whether
weath-er-fore-caster
weather strip *(n.)*
weather vane
weather—wise *(adj.)*
weave
cf. we've
web
web-bing
wed
wed-ding
wedge
wed-lock
wee
cf. we
weed
week
cf. weak
week-day
weep
wee-vil
weigh
cf. way
weighed
cf. wade
weight
cf. wait
weird
wel-come
weld
welder
wel-fare
welt
wel-ter-weight
wept
were-wolf
west
west-ern
West-erner
west-ward
wet
cf. whet
wet suit *(n.)*
we've
cf. weave
whack
whale
cf. wail
whale-boat
wham

wharf
what-ever
what-not
what-so-ever
wheat
whee-dle
wheel
wheel-bar-row
wheel-chair
wheeze
whelp
when
whence
where
cf. ware
cf. wear
where-abouts
whereas
whereby
where-fore
where-upon
where-withal
whet
cf. wet
whether
cf. weather
which
whiff
while
cf. wile
whim
whim-per
whim-si-cal
whine
cf. wine
whinny
whip
whip-lash
whir
or whirr
whirl
whirl-pool
whisk
whis-ker
whisky
or whis-key
whis-per
whis-pery
whist
whis-tle
whit
cf. wit
white
whiten
whither
cf. wither
whit-tle
whiz
or whizz
whiz-zer
who-ever
whole
cf. hole
whole-sale
whole-some
wholly
whom-ever
whom-so-ever
whoop
whoop—de—do
or whoop—de—doo
whop-per
whose
why
wick
wicked
wicket
wick-iup
wide
wide—screen *(adj.)*
wid-get
widow
wid-ow-hood
width
wield
wife
wig
wig-gle
wig-wag
wig-wam
wild
wil-der-ness
wild-life
wile
cf. while
will
will—o'—the—wisp *(n.)*
wil-low
wilt
wily
wince
wind
wind-age
wind-bag
wind-blown
wind chill
wind-fall
wind-lass
wind-mill
win-dow
win-dow box
wind-shield
wind-storm
wine
cf. whine
wine-glass
win-ery
wing
wink
win-ner
win-ning
win-now
win-some
win-ter
win-ter-ize
win-ter-green
win-ter-time
win-try
wipe
wiper
wire
wire—puller *(n.)*
wire-tap
wis-dom
wise
wish
wish-bone
wishy—washy *(adj.)*
wisp

wit
cf. whit
witch
witch-craft
witch hunt *(n.)*
with
with-draw
with-drawal
with-drawn
wither
cf. whither
with-hold
within
with-out
with-stand
wit-ness
wit-ness box
witty
wives
wiz-ard
wiz-ardry
wizen
wob-ble
woe
woe-be-gone
wolf
wolf-ish
woman
wom-an-hood
wom-an-power
womb
won
cf. one
won-der
won-der-land
won-drous
wont
cf. won't
woo
wood
cf. would
wood-chop-per
wood-craft
wooden
wood-land
wood pulp
wood-shed
wood-wind
wood-work
wool
wool-len
or woolen
woozy
word
word-age
word-book
word—for—word *(adj.)*
word—of—mouth *(adj.)*
wore
work
work-able
worka-day
work-bench
work-book
work-day
worker
work farm *(n.)*
work-horse
work-load *(n.)*
work-shop
world
worm
wor-ri-ment
worry
worse
wor-ship
worst
worth
worth-while
worth-ier
worthi-est
wor-thy
would
cf. wood
wound
wrack
cf. rack
wran-gle
wrap
cf. rap
wrap-around
wrapped
cf. rapt
wrap-per
wrath
wreath
cf. wreathe
wreck
wreck-age
wrecker
wrench
wrest
cf. rest
wres-tle
wretch
cf. retch
wrig-gle
wring
cf. ring
wrin-kle
wrist
wrist-band
wrist-lock
wrist-watch
writ
write
cf. right
cf. rite
writer
writhe
wrong
wrong-doer
wrote
cf. rote
wrought
wry
cf. rye

X

xeno-phile
xeno-phobe
xeno-pho-bia
xe-rog-ra-phy
xe-rox *(v.)*
X—ray
X—ray therapy
X—ray tube
xy-log-ra-phy

xy-lopha-gous
xy-lo-phone
xy-lo-phon-ist

Y

yacht
yak
yam
Yan-kee
yap
yard
yard-age
yard-stick
yaw
yawl
yawn
yea
year
year-book
year-ling
year-long
yearly
yearn
year—round *(adj.)*
yeast
yell
yel-low
yelp
yen
yes
yes-ter-day
yes-ter-year
yet
yew
cf. **ewe**
cf. **you**
Yid-dish
yield
yip
yo-del
yoga
yogi
yo-gurt
or **yo-ghurt**
yoke
cf. **yolk**
yo-kel
yolk
cf. **yoke**
Yom Kip-pur
yon-der
yoo—hoo *(interj.)*
yore
cf. **your**
cf. **you're**
you
cf. **ewe**
cf. **yew**
you'd
you'll
cf. **Yule**
young
young-ster
your
cf. **yore**
cf. **you're**
your-self
your-selves
youth
yowl
yo—yo *(n.)*
Yule
cf. **you'll**
Yule log *(n.)*
Yule-tide

Z

zag
zany
zap
zeal
zealot
ze-bra
Zen
ze-nith
zephyr
zep-pe-lin
zero
zest
Zeus
zig-zag
zil-lion
zin-nia
Zion
Zi-on-ism
Zi-on-ist
zip
zip-per
zir-con
zither
zo-diac
zo-dia-cal
zom-bie
zonal
zone
zoo
zoo-logi-cal
zo-olo-gist
zo-ol-ogy
zoom
zoom lens *(n.)*
zuc-chini
zwie-back

Index